Department Stores and the
Black Freedom Movement

**The John Hope Franklin Series in
African American History and Culture**

Waldo E. Martin Jr. and Patricia Sullivan, *editors*

Department Stores and the Black Freedom Movement

Workers, Consumers, and Civil Rights from the 1930s to the 1980s

· ·

TRACI PARKER

The University of North Carolina Press Chapel Hill

This book was published with the generous assistance of the University of Massachusetts.

© 2019 The University of North Carolina Press
All rights reserved
Set in Charis and Lato by Westchester Publishing Services
Manufactured in the United States of America

The University of North Carolina Press has been a member of the Green Press Initiative since 2003.

Library of Congress Cataloging-in-Publication Data
Names: Parker, Traci, author.
Title: Department stores and the black freedom movement : workers, consumers, and civil rights from the 1930s to the 1980s / Traci Parker.
Other titles: John Hope Franklin series in African American history and culture.
Description: Chapel Hill : University of North Carolina Press, [2019] | Series: The John Hope Franklin series in African American history and culture | Includes bibliographical references and index.
Identifiers: LCCN 2018031171| ISBN 9781469648668 (cloth : alk. paper) | ISBN 9781469648675 (pbk : alk. paper) | ISBN 9781469648682 (ebook)
Subjects: LCSH: African Americans—Civil rights—History—20th century. | Department stores—United States—History—20th century. | African American white collar workers—History—20th century. | African American consumers—Political activity—History—20th century. | Middle class African Americans—History—20th century.
Classification: LCC E185.61 .P254 2019 | DDC 323.1196/0730904—dc23
LC record available at https://lccn.loc.gov/2018031171

Cover illustration: *Ondria Tanner and Her Grandmother Window-shopping, Mobile, Alabama, 1956* (photograph by Gordon Parks, courtesy of and copyright The Gordon Parks Foundation).

An earlier version of chapter five was previously published in a different form as "Southern Retail Campaigns and the Struggle for Black Economic Freedom in the 1950s and 1960s," in *Race and Retail: Consumption across the Color Line,* eds. Mia Bay and Ann Fabian (New Brunswick, NJ: Rutgers University Press, 2015), 77–98. Portions of the epilogue previously appeared in "Shopping while Black," in *The SAGE Encyclopedia of Economics and Society,* eds. Frederick F. Wherry and Juliet B. Schor (Thousand Oaks, CA: SAGE Publications, 2015), 1473–75. Used with permission.

To my parents, Ronald and Jacqueline,
and my grandmothers, Edith and Armstella

Contents

Figures

Acknowledgments

Completing this very personal endeavor has required the assistance and support of many people. Since this project's infancy, Thomas C. Holt, Adam Green, and Amy Stanley have taken precious time from their own work to provide thoughtful feedback, support, and advice. I am most indebted to Tom, who has read every draft of this project. His guidance and support have been invaluable. His questions, comments, and occasional personal stories have enabled me to see the full scope and significance of this project, while his advice on writing has sharpened my argument and strengthened my narrative. Adam Green has provided insightful comments on black consumption and the civil rights movement. I also had the pleasure of serving as his teaching assistant. I remain inspired and encouraged by his dedication and approach to teaching and his students. Amy Stanley has taught me a great deal. I first began asking questions about African American labor and consumption in department stores while taking her class Market, Culture, and Society. I also must thank Leora Auslander, Julie Saville, Matthew Briones, Michael Dawson, Tracye Matthews, Cyndee Breshock, David Goodwine, and Sonja Rusnak—all of whom have greatly contributed to my intellectual and professional development during my time as a graduate student and postdoctoral scholar at the University of Chicago.

I am pleased to have received support from the University of Massachusetts Amherst. I received financial assistance from and feedback on my research at the Humanities and Fine Arts College, the Interdisciplinary Students Institute, the W. E. B. Du Bois Library Faculty Fellowship and Seminar, the Massachusetts Society of Professors, and the Politics of Resistance / 20th Century Imperialism Working Group at the Five Colleges Women's Research Center. My colleagues in the W. E. B. Du Bois Department of Afro-American Studies—John Bracey, James Smethurst, Britt Rusert, Stephanie Shonekan, Dania Francis, Yemisi Jimoh, Toussaint Losier, Amilcar Shabazz, Agustin Lao-Montes, and Steve Tracy—have been supportive of this project and its completion. I also am indebted to Joye Bowman, John Higginson, and Barbara Krauthamer in the Department of History, all of whom are amazing mentors and friends; Tricia Loveland of the Du Bois Department, whose contributions to the department and my work are too numerous to count; and Kiara Hill and Cécile Yézou, my graduate research assistants, who made the timely completion of the sixth and final chapter possible.

Time and funds to research African American experiences in twentieth-century department stores have been precious commodities. I received assistance from the Andrew W. Mellon Foundation, the National Endowment for the Humanities, the Woodrow Wilson Foundation, the New England Regional Fellowship Consortium, the University of Chicago's Department of History and the Center for the Study of Race, Politics, and Culture, the Hagley Museum and Library, and the Virginia Historical Society. I owe many thanks to the archivists and librarians at the American Friends Service Committee Archives; Chicago History Museum; Chicago Public Library; Connecticut Historical Society; Hagley Museum and Library; Historical Society of Washington, D.C.; the Jewish Museum of Maryland; the Library of Congress; Macy's Corporate Archives; Maryland Historical Society; National Archives and Record Administration in College Park, Maryland; the Sears, Roebuck, and Company Archives; Tamiment Library and Robert F. Wagner Labor Archives; the University of Illinois at Chicago Special Collections; the Wilson Library at the University of North Carolina; U.S. National Park Service; Valentine Richmond History Center; Virginia Historical Society; and the Special Collections at the Virginia Commonwealth University Library. I also thank Richard L. Jones III, who shared the personal papers of his father, Richard Jones, and helped me better understand South Center Department Store; and James Scanlan, Karen Baker, Alice Kessler-Harris, and Rosalind Rosenberg, who shared their experiences in and understanding of the Sears discrimination cases.

I am appreciative of the opportunities I have had to present my work, share arguments and analysis, and benefit from questions asked and comments shared at DePaul University; Massachusetts Historical Society / Schlesinger Seminar at Harvard University's Radcliffe Institute for Advanced Study; the Newberry Library Seminar on Women and Gender; the Centre for the History of Retailing and Distribution at the University of Wolverhampton, UK; the Center of Race and Ethnicity at Rutgers University; the University of Chicago's Social History and Race Center workshops; the Virginia Historical Society; and other workshops and conferences. I received insightful feedback from Mia Bay and Ann Fabian as I prepared to publish a portion of my book in *Race and Retail: Consumption across the Color Line*.

I am also extremely grateful to Jacqueline Goldsby and the Mapping the Stack (MTS) Project, funded by the Andrew Mellon Foundation, Commonwealth Edison, and the University of Chicago's Center for the Study of Race, Politics, and Culture and the Division of Humanities. As an MTS team member, I learned the art of archival processing and became a better researcher, as well as made lasting friendships with my MTS colleagues and the staff at the Vivian G. Harsh Research Collection—Michael, Bob, Beverly, Lucinda, Denise, and Cynthia. Michael Flug has been particularly supportive of my research, providing feedback, advice, and personal stories that have pushed my thinking and analysis in ways I never imagined.

The folks at the University of North Carolina Press have been incredible. To my editor Chuck Grench and readers Victoria Wolcott, Ruth Feldstein, and Patricia Sullivan, thank you for your feedback and counsel.

My family and friends helped make this arduous process a little less stressful and a lot more enjoyable. The words "thank you" simply do not express how much I appreciate each of you. My parents, Ronald and Jacqueline Parker, remained so incredibly positive throughout this process, never doubting my abilities for one moment. This project would have never been conceived had they not dragged my sister Lauren and me to *all* nearby department stores for *every* weekend and holiday sale. Never would I have imagined thanking them for that experience. My unpaid editor and incredible sister Lauren Parker read every chapter and every draft of my project, identified the most minute errors, and with brute honesty informed me of sections or writing that confused and even bored her. She always took the time to help even in the midst of her hectic work, graduate school schedules, and now growing family. My grandmothers, Edith Parker and Armstella Dorsey, told me all of their stories and, like my parents, trained me in the art of shopping. In many ways, this book is the story of their lives.

I shared many laughs and tears with my dearest friends Marcia Walker and Deidre Ferron. They provided countless words of encouragement when I was exhausted, frustrated, and sure I had no more words left to write. Tanyka Sam, Yveline Alexis, Danielle Parker, Crystal Coates, Kafi Moragne-Patterson, Alrita Lewis, and Patrick Kelly—all deserve recognition for their support. And finally, to my love and best friend, Evan Lewis, who has intellectually and emotionally sustained me throughout this process.

Introduction

· ·

Just about every weekend in the late 1980s and 1990s, my parents shuttled my younger sister and me from our home in Baltimore City to one of Maryland's suburban shopping malls for an all-day excursion. Our tour guide of sorts was my mother. No matter what shopping center we visited—Golden Ring Mall, White Marsh Mall, or Eastpoint Mall—we parked by the entrance of Hecht Company and began our jaunt in the store's shoe department. For what felt like hours, my mother browsed and tried on shoes, while my father wandered over to the men's department and partook in his own shopping ritual (which, to be honest, remains a bit of a mystery because my sister and I tended to stay within eyeshot of my mother). Effectively, my sister and I were left to our own devices: we pranced the selling floor in oversized display shoes, played make-believe with store mannequins, or found a quiet place to camp out and read books we had brought from home. Occasionally, my sister and I bickered over a pair of shoes we both wanted to try on; but our spats ended as quickly as they began with one stern look from my mother—a look that unmistakably said, "Don't make me come over there." Here, amid the display of women's shoes, the two of us constructed a playground or nursery of sorts—amenities that had disappeared from department stores nearly twenty years earlier.

After my mother finished shopping for shoes, and despite our silent wishes to head to the toy department or leave the mall altogether, she led us to women's handbags, sportswear, housewares, and then the children's department. Even if she found what she was looking for at Hecht's, she would always "take a quick look at what they've got" in Woodward & Lothrop, Macy's, and Lord & Taylor. Of course, nothing about her "taking a quick look" was quick. In those stores, my mother followed her same shopping pattern—shoes, handbags, clothes, housewares, and then more clothes. She visited each store with the same exuberance as she had in Hecht's, while the rest of us grew increasingly impatient, bored, restless, and tired. Frequently she crossed paths with family members and friends and proceeded to stand in the aisles gossiping and exchanging information about her purchases or lack thereof, which were usually attributed to poor store inventory or sales. Our birthdays were the only times we deviated from my mother's shopping pattern. Rather than head directly to Hecht's shoe department, we would have a "fancy" lunch at Woodies—one of the few department store restaurants that remained in northern Maryland—and then begin my mother's ritual.[1]

For several years in the late 1980s, my mother worked as a part-time saleswoman at Hecht's, selling handbags. The hours permitted her to continue working as a part-time bank teller as well and to care for two young children. But department store sales work lacked the prestige and status that had accompanied this work in the early to mid-twentieth-century. No longer were sales workers versed in the art of selling and tasked with "dressing customers from head to toe." Instead, since the proliferation of self-service retailing after World War II, sales workers often had very little to do until the customer was ready to make a purchase; they were mere cashiers, for all intents and purposes. Further, as my mother quickly learned, few saleswomen made a career out of department store work anymore. For most women, as for her, this work was a temporary stop on the way to something better. So, when she was offered a full-time position at the bank—a position that offered the potential for advancement—she gladly accepted.[2]

As my sister and I grew older, we continued to join our parents on their department store visits—much to our chagrin. But while they perused traditional retail emporiums, my sister and I met up with friends in the mall food court and then wandered in and out of specialty stores that sold clothing, books, and trinkets. We did not have the same relationship with department stores as our parents or grandparents, who also spent their weekends hunting for bargains on nonessentials that marked their middle-class aspirations and standard of living. Instead, we pined for outfits and accessories that resembled those of young celebs and were sold in specialty stores such as the Gap, the Limited, and Abercrombie and Fitch, which played current music loudly and employed teenagers (some of whom were my friends).

In our view, department stores were not "cool." They were not trendy, fashion-forward sites of leisure, nor did they confer the type of image and status teenagers and budding adults sought in the final decades of the twentieth century. Arguably, many still hold this opinion. Department stores have become less relevant to adult shoppers, and therefore less profitable, especially since the advent and proliferation of online shopping. They have been on a downward trajectory, with their decline leading some to believe that these institutions and the retail industry generally are in the midst of a "retail apocalypse." In 2017, Macy's closed nearly 70 stores, J.C. Penney closed 138 locations, and more than 350 Sears and Kmart stores shuttered. The bloodletting, however, continues. In early 2018, J.C. Penney announced plans to close 8 stores before the year's end, which translates into approximately 480 job cuts.[3] Macy's planned to close 11 stores by the end of the first quarter of the fiscal year. Sears was scheduled to close 39 stores and 64 Kmart locations by early April. Bon-Ton Stores, the corporate parent of Carson's, Boston Store, and other department store chains, revealed plans to close 47 of its 260 stores and is on the fast track to bankruptcy, according to news reports.[4] (Department stores are not the only retailers suffering, as more than 5,000 traditional retailers closed due to poor sales and increased competition from Amazon and other online retailers in 2017; their fate speaks volumes about the future of American retailing, citizenship and identity, and capitalism.)

I tell my story here because, in essence, it is the story of this book. Department stores were epicenters, or as one historian called them, "palaces," of American consumption and modernity in the twentieth century.[5] For the better part of this period, these establishments were lavishly designed buildings of tremendous size that treated customers, particularly female customers, for whom department stores were built, to various luxuries and services.[6] They arguably informed the lives of all Americans. They were places of consumption, leisure, and work, as well as sites for self-fashioning, self-expression, and human satisfaction.[7] They enthroned consumption as the route to democracy and citizenship and invited everyone—regardless of race, gender, age, class, and country of origin—to enter, browse, and purchase often superfluous material goods. But even as department stores celebrated democracy, they were, in fact, Jim Crow institutions designed to satisfy the needs and desires of middle-class whites, albeit with an ambiguous color line. African Americans, therefore, were initially hired only in menial positions, though a few eventually moved up to white-collar jobs in sales and in the office. Meanwhile, African American customers were welcome to shop, but were provided uneven, unequal service and found their movements and participation in the usual shopping "experience" severely constrained. They were routinely refused service at lunch counters, restaurants, and beauty shops. They were forbidden use of dressing rooms and restrooms, were prohibited from trying on and returning clothes, and could be arbitrarily refused entrance or service at any moment.

In many ways, then, department stores resembled hotels, amusement parks, swimming pools, and other coveted leisure and commercial sites to which African Americans were denied access and equal treatment in the twentieth century. Hotels excluded blacks from their premises, flouting the law of hospitality and the Civil Rights Act of 1875, forcing travelers of color to journey miles—sometimes hundreds of miles—out of the way to secure admittance to safe lodging.[8] Amusement parks, dance halls, theaters, and movie houses, along with bowling alleys, pool halls, and parks, were spaces where the social classes and genders mixed, but racial segregation was rigorously maintained.[9] Swimming pools, however, were different. Initially, they were "austere public baths" that reinforced class and gender divisions yet allowed racial integration. In the 1920s, as the economy prospered, European immigration declined, black migration increased, and a sexual revolution thrived, municipal pools became "leisure resorts, where practically everyone in the community except black Americans swam together."[10]

The African American struggle for equality in public accommodations, thus, has been largely conceived as an effort to control and gain equal access to public spaces. Increasingly, however, scholars now recognize that this struggle was never completely separated from black Americans' efforts to dismantle voting, school, housing, and employment discrimination. Both Victoria Wolcott and Jeff Wiltse, for example, argue that contestations over segregated amusement parks and swimming pools reflected the changing demographics of urban and suburban neighborhoods (the movement of African Americans into localities that had previously been inhabited by whites) and the new residents' desire—or rather right—to partake in the recreation facilities in areas where they lived.[11] Wolcott also notes that "demands for access to recreation and other public accommodations . . . [were] not unrelated to labor activism, as black and white workers experienced the limits of brotherhood in their leisure time."[12]

Such connections—and more—were glaringly apparent in department stores. As places of both employment and consumption, department stores promoted a racialized democracy even as they inadvertently exposed the blatant contradictions of a Jim Crow society espousing democratic ideals. Consequently, these stores became optimal sites for black resistance to discrimination at work and at leisure. Thus, African Americans organized the department store movement, a potpourri of campaigns that varied across time and space in leadership, size, tactics, and organization. This movement aimed to secure for blacks, like my mother and myself, the right to freely experience all that this industry and American consumer culture offered. It promised to not only dismantle Jim Crow but also facilitate the growth of a modern black middle class and advance black economic freedom and well-being.

Movement leaders understood that Jim Crow was particularly vulnerable in department stores, especially at a historical juncture when ordinary Americans' realization of true democracy had become intricately tied to their identity as consumers. They leveraged their collective labor and buying power, employed various protest strategies, including persuasion, boycotts, and picket lines, and obeyed the canons of bourgeois respectability to fully integrate their demands for equal treatment as both workers and consumers. Although some of the earliest documented cases of black activism in the department store industry date back to the First Great Migration,[13] the department store movement was an outgrowth of the "Don't Buy Where You Can't Work" movement and began in the late 1930s. Building on the goals, tactics, organization, and momentum of the "Don't Buy" movement, it fixated exclusively on department stores both in and outside black neighborhoods. During the Second World War, the department store movement broadened its reach to recruit the power of store workers and labor unions. In the postwar era, the movement held behind-the-scenes meetings with store officials, executed successful lunch counter sit-ins and selective patronage programs in the 1950s and 1960s, and challenged the reconsolidation of race discrimination in the courts in the 1970s. The movement effectively ended in 1981, with the unsuccessful conclusion of the Sears, Roebuck, and Co. affirmative action cases and in the context of the radical transformation of consumption practices and labor relations.

As African Americans integrated sales and clerical work and dismantled the barriers to their full participation in consumer culture, a modern black consciousness took shape that was both raced and classed; indeed, the department store was arguably a key site for the inception of a modern black middle class. "Modern" here refers to class identity produced by consumer capitalism, rather than a worker's status in industrial capitalism. During the first half of the twentieth century, class status in black communities was defined as much by relationships with American consumer culture as by occupation: consumption patterns connoted respectability and aspirations as well as relative well-being, while white-collar occupations placed individuals on a social escalator to greater prestige and wealth and enabled them to observe middle-class consumption habits. Thus, working in sales and offices and consuming material accoutrements and services in department stores, rather than in dry goods and discount stores or from mail-order houses, marked African Americans as respectable, refined, and deserving of respect, dignity, and full citizenship.

The Department Store Movement and the
Labor-Oriented Civil Rights Movement

The five-decade department store movement was contemporaneous with both the black labor movement of the 1930s and 1940s and the civil rights movement of the 1950s and 1960s. Therefore, it provides a privileged perspective on these two movements and their interrelationships. The modern labor movement, historians Robert Korstad and Nelson Lichtenstein argue, began as African Americans became increasingly urban, industrial, and proletarian and were encouraged to unionize by New Deal labor policies, higher wages, increased industrial employment, and a more radical white union movement.[14] This movement advocated on behalf of black workers, challenging "the public and the private, the stigmatic and the material harms of Jim Crow" in the North and South. It emphasized the right to work and economic security (including higher wages, equal pay for equal work, access to seniority and promotion to skilled position, elimination of "involuntary servitude" and work indignities, and union representation).[15]

The labor-oriented phase of the black freedom movement ended or was, as Korstad and Lichtenstein claimed, "lost" in the anticommunist and antilabor climate of the early Cold War era. African American activists subsequently eschewed a "broad-based critique of racial capitalism" and focused primarily on ending public discrimination and segregation and the psychological stigma of state-enforced racial classifications.[16] In short, blacks concentrated on securing "public rights" in the marketplace. Occasionally, however, African Americans addressed labor and material inequalities in the form of the 1963 March on Washington for Jobs and Freedom, the War on Poverty, the inclusion of Title VII in the Civil Rights Act of 1964, and the efficacy of black caucuses within labor unions well into the 1970s. But, for many scholars, these efforts were peripheral to the black freedom movement's primary goals. Lichtenstein argued in 2010 that these initiatives "[recast] . . . the civil rights impulse so far away from its New Deal and laborite roots" that they "could not re-create the employment, labor, and civil rights agenda as it had been formulated in the late 1930s."[17] Similarly, historians James McGregor and James Stewart conclude, "if one looks at deeds not words, and to the deployment of movement resources, it is clear that economic rights were slighted—until it was probably too late to make a real difference."[18]

This book, however, does not entirely share these opinions. It accepts that the labor-oriented civil rights movement slowed in the early Cold War era but holds that African Americans remained committed to labor *and* economic rights. Spotlighting the department store movement, this book reinterprets the civil rights movement to illuminate its centrality in opening the economic mainstream to African Americans. The department store movement was powerful in the 1930s and 1940s, benefiting from a pro-labor political climate, wartime labor shortages, retail unions' antidiscrimination campaigns, and the Supreme Court's ruling in *New Negro Alliance v. Sanitary Grocery Co.* in 1938. It reached its height in the two decades after the Second World War, however: Steady economic growth transformed African Americans' relations to the economy and consumer society; civil rights and labor groups organized grassroots campaigns; and African American lawyers produced major Supreme Court rulings that became the foundation of the midcentury movement and its gains.[19]

The department store movement also benefited from the efforts of the National Association for the Advancement of Colored People (NAACP) to redress labor unions' racially exclusive membership policies in the 1940s, establish fair bargaining contracts in the 1950s, and emphasize a constitutional right to equal access to job training programs in the 1960s. Its efforts—though they focused primarily on industrial and manufacturing jobs—often resulted in legal suits that were brought before administrative agencies, presidential committees, and state and federal courts.[20]

Labor's potential for advancing racial and economic equality may have narrowed, or rather weakened, in the postwar era; but, as it did, the potential of black consumer power intensified. Because of this, and as American consumer culture reached unprecedented heights and profitability, the NAACP, the National Urban League (NUL), Congress of Racial Equality (CORE), and the American Friends Service Committee (AFSC) leveraged labor *in tandem* with consumption to realize black economic emancipation and full citizenship.

The civil rights movement, thus, was a battle waged for and by black workers *and consumers*. Their alliance razed the vestiges of Jim Crow not only in department stores but also in the building trades, manufacturing, and professional employment, among others. Take, for example, the southern lunch counter sit-ins of the 1950s and 1960s, which this book examines in chapter 5. On their face, or at least how they were portrayed in the media, sit-ins used black purchasing power to desegregate public accommoda-tions. But, as they did in the Montgomery Bus Boycott, activists also nego-tiated the dismantling of race discrimination in the workplace behind the scenes, away from the prying eyes of the public. Their resolve to institute racial egalitarianism in the retail industry not only opened white-collar work and broadened the labor movement but also helped safeguard the inclusion of Titles II and VII in the Civil Rights Act of 1964. Title II prohib-its discrimination based on race, color, religion, or national origin in pub-lic accommodations; Title VII forbids discrimination on the basis of race and sex in hiring and promotion and provided for the creation of the Equal Employment Opportunity Commission (EEOC) to enforce the law. Fair employment, thus, had never disappeared from the civil rights agenda; instead, it was realized alongside the desegregation of consumption and ur-ban spaces and without the attention granted to dramatic televised sit-in demonstrations.

Once the EEOC was established, African American workers took little time to file complaints with the agency to "[force] public officials to act." They "were themselves setting national policy. They established an agenda for affected employers and for government watchdogs by explaining what they believed discrimination was, and spelling out what constituted fair-ness," historian Nancy McLean argues.[21] Title VII emboldened African American retail workers, especially those employed by Sears, Roebuck, and Co., to confront race and gender discrimination. The EEOC eventu-ally filed lawsuits against the retailer, thereby becoming a new leader in the department store movement. But what appeared to be the beginning of a new phase of the department store movement instead marked its end. Despite the commission's good intentions and hard work, its efforts were crippled by economic and political transformations: department stores had relocated to shopping malls in suburban areas, far from the reach of urban black populations and on private property where protest was prohib-ited (this process started in the immediate postwar era and escalated with the racial upheavals and urban decline in the late 1960s); merchants re-sumed their discriminatory practices in their new environments, hoping to reclaim their white middle-class clientele; increased competition from discount retailers, such as Wal-Mart and Kmart, degraded the skill of sell-ing and the pleasure of shopping; and an economic depression and the na-tion's turn to the right weakened the power of labor. The EEOC and Sears cases, thus, did little to improve the black economic condition and effec-tively ended the department store movement.

The Department Store and the Rise of a
Modern Black Middle Class

While it had its fair share of setbacks and disappointments, the five-decade department store movement nonetheless helped dismantle racialized patterns of labor and consumption and, in the process, facilitated the emergence of a modern black middle class. The department store has historically been a key agent in the formation of the white middle class and promised to do the same for African Americans in the twentieth century. The white middle class emerged in the three decades before the Civil War, as the market revolution fueled the proletarianization of master artisans, skilled craft workers, and small capitalists, and the ascendance of nonmanual work in sales, clerical, and managerial occupations. The ranks of the white middle class swelled, just as department stores ushered in a new world of retailing in the mid- to late nineteenth century.[22] Its members—a high percentage of whom were white native- and foreign-born women[23]—performed mental rather than physical labor in stores and offices, holding out hope that, with industriousness and loyalty, they would be promoted to manager, become an entrepreneur, or secure a husband and economic security; they consumed respectable—a word synonymous with middle class—material goods and leisure activities, such as bicycle excursions and hiking and picnicking in local parks;[24] they were "train[e]d and disciplin[ed] to erase the signs of working-class origins and to apply a veneer of middle-class or elite culture";[25] they borrowed prestige from their employer and customers, as well as from the firm itself; and they derived their power from the direct supervision of other workers.[26]

The department store not only facilitated the growth of professional and white-collar workers; it served this new population. The store "played a crucial role in determining the essentials of middle-class life and aspirations."[27] It shifted the way Americans saw material goods. It enticed consumers with environments of luxury, desire, exoticism, service ideology, and easy credit and convinced them that what had been occasional luxuries were in fact everyday necessities for a middle-class standard of living and sharing in American democracy.[28]

The spectrum of African American class and internal relations, however, was incongruent with white class boundaries and characteristics, although from the late nineteenth to the mid-twentieth century, both were redefined in terms of consumption rather than the means of production. The decades after the Second World War marked fundamental transformations in African

Americans' relation to the economy and consumer society and facilitated the emergence of a sizable black middle class. A demand for black labor in the urban industries and the mechanization of farms, which displaced and released black agricultural workers from the sharecropping system, encouraged millions of African Americans to migrate to cities.[29] Here, in their new urban environments, blacks took advantage of expanding educational opportunities, the dramatic postwar growth of industrial and white-collar employment, and the relaxation of racial employment barriers. These gains permitted an appreciable number of African Americans to move out of low-skill and low-wage work into skilled and white-collar jobs.[30] In 1940, only 6 percent of African Americans held white-collar jobs. This number nearly doubled to 13 percent, "with the greatest part of the gain being in sales and clerical jobs," in 1960; by 1970, the proportion of blacks in white-collar occupations increased to 24 percent.[31]

Black urbanization and occupational advances accelerated the "fashioning [of] institutional, entrepreneurial, market-driven, and national forms of black culture" and collectively shaped an unprecedented black consumer consciousness in the postwar era. Most notably, the founding and development of *Ebony* magazine presented upwardly mobile African Americans with the tools and "grammar for their postmigration existence, one matching new realities of urban challenge, societal complexity, and material change." *Ebony* did not sell out blacks, argues the historian Adam Green; instead, it "sold the race new identities, a process that encouraged imagination of a black national community and made new notions of collective interest and politics plausible."[32]

But all of this should not suggest that the department store was inconsequential to the formation of the modern black middle class. In fact, the contradictions of the department store (and consumer capitalism generally) provided African Americans with "an available and legitimate recourse for challenging race discrimination" in the marketplace and acquiring the material base needed to climb the socioeconomic ladder.[33] Leveraging their work consciousness (which flourished as a result of New Deal politics) and new consumer consciousness, black activists built worker-consumer alliances to pressure merchants to adopt fair employment and customer service practices. The result was the making of a sizable contingent of sales and clerical workers of color who now had the freedom and economic means to consume material accoutrements and services in department stores that marked them as middle-class citizens.

Rethinking the Role of the Black Middle Class in the Civil Rights Movement

Several scholars have recognized that these structural and demographic transformations in the postwar era fueled challenges to previous constraints on African Americans' rights as both workers and consumers. It is not surprising, then, that this new black middle class and those aspiring to ideal middle-class status would profoundly shape the course of the civil rights movement during the first postwar decade. In contrast with scholars who interpret this development as somehow a distraction from earlier freedom struggles, however, one might well see it as the natural outcome of these broader developments and in many ways a fulfillment of the labor-oriented initiatives that preceded it and were concurrent with it.

It is evident that, along with occupation and respectability, consumption emerged as an essential component of black class formation in the twentieth century in two major ways. First, consumption was the basis for black political activism. Department store protests were contemporaneous with, if not largely preceding, better-known consumer protests around Jim Crow transportation. Despite its efforts to enforce white supremacy and reduce cross-racial contact, modern transportation, like department stores, was one of the early spaces that exposed the racial contradictions and fluidity of consumption and, thus, became a training ground for black consumer protest in the twentieth century. In the shared space of railroads and streetcars, where the races were separated by a simple rope or car, African Americans, particularly those of a growing southern middle class, covertly and overtly crossed the color line. Others filed suits against southern transportation, and, although a few won, the landmark case of *Plessy v. Ferguson* (1896) effectively legitimized state segregation laws.[34]

Still, many continued to launch frontal attacks against segregation and discrimination in the consumer sphere.[35] Focusing on southern buses in the late 1930s and early 1940s, the historian Robin D. G. Kelley argues, "Unlike in the workplace where [black] workers entered as disempowered producers dependent on wages for survival and beholden, ostensibly at least, to their superiors, working people enter public transportation as consumers—and with a sense of consumer entitlement."[36] Acts of resistance, from making noise and using profanity to playful pranks to verbal and physical fights, were daily occurrences. They provided blacks with the means to demand "more space for themselves . . . receive equitable treatment . . . be personally treated with respect and dignity . . . be heard and possibly understood . . . get to work on time, and above all . . . exercise power over institutions that controlled them or on which they were dependent."[37] By the 1950s and 1960s, as Lizabeth Cohen argues, "mass consumption [had] begot a mass civil rights movement" that not only negated the *Plessy* decision but also forced white business owners, advertisers, and consumers to recognize and value African Americans in the consumer sphere and reduced the economic and psychological effects of racism.[38]

Second, consumption was in itself a means of escape and liberation. Many African Americans found that buying material goods and being served on equal terms with whites released them from some of the traditional trappings of race and the constraints of subordinated class status.[39] Conspicuous consumption was a major avenue through which African Americans transcended race, rejected their "subservient worker" identity, "assert[ed] their independence," and "demand[ed] respect."[40] It functioned as "a substitute for complete integration into the general American society," while it simultaneously "allow[ed] individuals to gain social stability and inner satisfaction, despite conditions in the Black Ghetto and their rejection by white America."[41]

The world of department stores was arguably one of the most effective sites for providing African Americans with opportunities to simultaneously engage consumption as sites for resistance and liberation. The department store, thus, reveals aspects of the black middle class that might enhance our understanding of the politics of the black freedom movement in the twentieth century, not least of which is why its targets were so often sites of consumption. Unlike dry good and discount stores and mail-order houses, department stores immersed visitors in splendor, beauty, and wealth and afforded them with "the luxurious feeling of affluence, of being 'somebody,' or having [their] wishes catered to."[42] They were places to be seen and to become worthy of being seen. On picket lines and at lunch counters, African Americans paraded their respectability and leveraged their labor and purchasing powers in the public theater of the department store to forcefully dismantle race discrimination and claim, express, and be treated, or rather served, as modern middle-class citizens.

Once protests ended (or rather were curtailed by the relocation of department stores to suburban shopping malls) and as the retail industry was transformed by increased competition from discount retailers in the late 1960s and early 1970s, African Americans, especially those in or aspiring to be in the middle class, placed greater emphasis on the ostentatious display of clothing and other material goods. Wearable merchandise, in particular, marked blacks' department store patronage and generated and affirmed their respectability, refinement, and wealth in and outside the store. Clothing "was bought as much for achieving prestige and a particular image as for utilitarian purposes, hence the popularity of brand names and prestige stores such as Saks Fifth Avenue and Bloomingdale's." Further, because middle-class blacks typically earned less than their white counterparts, members of this stratum found clothes and jewelry easier to access when compared with other consumables that were often used to communicate status, such as housing (especially in the suburbs), educational opportunities, public services, and neighborhood amenities.[43]

· · · · · ·

The story of African Americans' relationship with employment and consumption, then, complicates the evolving narrative and analysis of the civil rights movement of the 1950s and 1960s. A locus of black successes and failures, protest and class development, the department store reveals aspects of the mid-twentieth-century evolution of the black middle class that might enhance our understanding of the politics of the larger black freedom movement during that period. This book seeks to tell that story. It begins by exploring the racial and class dimensions of early American department stores and shows why these retail institutions became prime locations for protesting and claiming civil rights. In chapters 2 and 3, the book then examines the rise of the department store movement in the urban North and Midwest and the exceptionality of the retail unions governing Macy's Herald Square in New York City and South Center Department Store in Chicago in advancing black labor and civil rights. Chapter 4 considers the department store movement and the birth of a modern black middle-class consciousness in the 1930s and 1940s. The movement in the southern cities is the subject of chapter 5, which explores black worker-consumer alliances in sit-in demonstrations and their utility in helping black southerners claim middle-class citizenship during the civil rights movement. The book concludes with an examination of the Sears affirmative action cases. These cases exposed the industry's ongoing transformations, ones that revolutionized, or rather diminished, the status of retail work and the former "palaces" of consumption, which facilitated the reconsolidation of racial discrimination.

Department Stores and the Black Freedom Movement embraces the long civil rights movement approach to the extent that it acknowledges the earlier struggles that shaped the civil rights movement and, in the process, broadens our understanding of the midcentury movement beyond the confines of the American South and its ostensible integrationist agenda. This approach recognizes that, alongside integration, black economic power and self-determination were priorities of the black freedom struggle not only during the Great Depression and Second World War but also during the civil rights movement and the struggles that followed. The movement never demoted economic issues; instead, it embraced different approaches, all of which mobilized an unprecedented number of people, black and white, to attend to economic issues—of labor and consumption—in workplaces, public accommodations, and the home sphere. What *Department Stores and the Black Freedom Movement* does, then, is reorient the long civil rights movement paradigm so as to bring attention to those consistent economic dimensions and their effects on the civil rights revolution in the North and South, from the 1930s through the 1960s and beyond.

1 Race and Class Identities in Early American Department Stores

. . . .

It, the 1927 silent film based on Elinor Glyn's popularization of the terms "it" and "it girl," tells the story of Betty Lou Spence, a department store salesgirl, and her "romantic pursuit" of the store's new owner, Cyrus Waltham. The plot centers on a predictable "class-crossed romance"; yet the film, itself, provides visual, albeit fictionalized, evidence of department store culture in the early twentieth century. *It* opens with a series of simple, illustrative shots of the fictional department store Waltham's, which closely resembles Macy's Herald Square in New York City. The "establishing shot" focuses on "a sign, on top of a massive brick building, that reads: 'Waltham's, World's Largest Store.'" "The camera pans down to a view of [a] bustling street," with customers hurriedly entering and exiting the store, and then tracks inside Waltham's to reveal an even busier, glitzy palace of consumption.[1] On the floor are white middle-class male and female customers dressed in their finest clothes. Some are wandering the aisles, surveying and desiring not simply the store's dazzling goods but also the luxurious lifestyle promised to those who purchase this merchandise. Other customers are purchasing these coveted goods from white working-class saleswomen, who are plainly dressed compared with their middle-class customers. Saleswomen stand behind glass counters assisting swarms of patrons, selling and arranging merchandise, and gossiping with their coworkers about their new, handsome boss. Concurrently, male managers pace the floor observing, and occasionally sexually appraising, the saleswomen.[2]

At the time of *It*'s release, the department store was a popular haven of luxury and amenity for white middle-class women and the uncontested leading American retailer for nearly forty years—making it a logical choice to set a Cinderella tale. Much of its success lay in store merchants' and commercial impresarios' transformation of dry goods stores into palaces of consumption.[3] Architects of this new system of retailing—men such as Alexander T. Stewart, Rowland H. Macy, John Wanamaker, and Marshall Field—established institutions that epitomized urban affluence and appealed to middle-class women, many of whom controlled their family's disposable income and handled the consumption needs of their household. Retailers erected stores of unprecedented size and opulence and confronted customers with both an astounding array of high-quality, stylish merchandise and lavish services that enticed customers to buy much more than the essentials (figures 1 and 2). They mastered the art of creating and satisfying consumers' personal desires and indoctrinating them with the belief that an urban bourgeois lifestyle could be realized and flaunted through shopping. By the 1910s and 1920s, the department store thus had become an arbiter of middle-class life and aspirations as well as an instrument of social mobility and maintenance.

Although eager to attract the lucrative trade of the middle and upper classes, the department store welcomed all visitors. Stores operated under the principle of free entry and browsing—the right to look around the store without the obligation to buy. This principle helped usher in a new conception of American democracy that was intricately tied to the practices of consumption that the department store fostered. According to the historian William Leach, this democracy had two sides. First, it stressed the diffusion of comfort and prosperity as the centerpiece of the American experience and identity. And second, it championed the democratization of desire, "or, more precisely, equal rights to desire the same goods and to enter the same world of comfort and luxury."[4] Under this market notion of democracy, white people from different classes—workers and consumers, native-born and immigrant, proletarians and the bourgeoisie—met, mingled, shared similar experiences, and, in the process, forged a common sense of racial and class identity. A woman from the humblest of backgrounds could browse the aisles alongside a woman from high society. Of course, these women were not greeted with the same customer service nor were their purchases equally valued, but they had equal opportunity to look and desire, if not buy, the goods on offer.

Not everyone, however, could look around and access the store equally. Even as the democracy of the department store was open to the broad participation of whites, it conformed to and endorsed notions of racial order and purity. The store, as illustrated in the opening scenes of *It*, was a "fairyland of whiteness," where white consumers were peddled the good life by a genteel and ambitious, exclusively white selling staff.[5] Managers feared that any noticeable presence of African Americans or any perception of racial equality would upset the dream world designed for the white middle class and those whites aspiring to join it. But rather than brand themselves as "white only" and deny blacks access, like other public accommodations

FIGURE 1 *Macy's, New York, N.Y.*, 1908. Detroit Publishing Company Photograph Collection, Library of Congress Prints and Photographs Division, LC-DIG-det-4a22989.

and workplaces of this era, many stores received African Americans under the principle of free entry and browsing but then constrained their movement and participation in this space. Stores hired them only as maintenance and stockroom workers, elevator operators, porters, and maids—all invisible from the salesroom floor—but barred them from white-collar staff positions in sales, clerical, and management. Black customers were welcome to spend their money on material goods in many stores but were frequently ignored and underserved. They were refused service at eateries and beauty shops, prohibited from trying on and returning clothes, and denied credit. Some stores, especially those in border and southern cities, forbade black patronage entirely or often on a whim, while others confined them to bargain basements. This racial order remained intact until challenged by department store campaigns that began in the late 1930s and

FIGURE 2
*Tiffany Mosaic Dome,
Marshall Field & Co.'s
Retail Store* postcard
(Chicago, Illinois).
V. O. Hammon
Collection, Newberry
Library, Chicago,
VO1343.

TIFFANY MOSAIC DOME, MARSHALL FIELD & CO.'S
RETAIL STORE, CHICAGO

No. 1343.   V. O. Hammon Pub. Co., Chicago

continued through the late twentieth century. Before those campaigns, the racialized democracy of the department store shaped the ways that race and class were imagined and employed to create both worker and consumer identities, making the department store an epitome of racial discrimination and thus an ideal site to challenge racial discrimination.

Shopping and working in these cathedrals of consumption afforded white people at all social levels opportunities to enact an ostensibly common racial and class identity—consuming and displaying white middle-class accoutrements and behaviors—in order to diminish differences and create or affirm an elevated social position. At the same time and in contrast with many other public spaces in America, the department store's wavering color line made that space racially ambiguous, contradictory, and thus vulnerable. In many ways it made blacks equal to whites as consumers, offering them occasions to browse through and dream of purchasing luxurious commodities, to be waited on by white sales workers, and even to secure employment considered a step above domestic and factory work. They met and engaged whites, not as their servants but as putatively equal shoppers. All of this, African Americans insisted by the start of World War II, was key to achieving and demonstrating social mobility and equality.

Fashioning a White Middle-Class Identity

Early department stores were constructed largely with white middle-class women and their needs and fantasies in mind. In these grand emporiums, women engaged a world of possibilities where their dreams and desires could be at once imagined and fulfilled and they could defy the constraints of their everyday reality. With the purchase of an elegant dress and complementary shoes, hat, and jewelry, a woman could temporarily escape her woes, such as a neglectful spouse, unappreciative children, or the humdrum activities of her daily life. In one afternoon, with store clerks anticipating and attending to her every wish, she could transcend her reality and shed any existing feelings of worthlessness, disappointment, and boredom. Happiness, comfort, prosperity, class mobility, social superiority, attractiveness, and sexual appeal could be hers, if only for a few moments. The working-class woman also could find some relief from her daily struggles in the department store. She could escape the drudgeries of wage slavery by wandering store aisles, looking, desiring, fantasizing, and finding solace in what could be hers someday.

To ensure that such an experience awaited these customers, store architects modeled the space "along two complementary lines: the home and the downtown club" and, in the process, created a new public sphere for white women. As a home, the store treated "the customer . . . not just as a potential spender, but also as a guest, catered to and coddled." With this intent, some stores, in an attempt to sell furniture, constructed model rooms. In 1908, Wanamaker's New York on Broadway and 9th Streets opened to the public a twenty-two-room private home called "The House Palatial." Located inside the store, this house modeled the decorated styles and furniture "of a family of taste and wealth, the best of its type that can be seen on Fifth Avenue or Hyde Park, London, and costing, with its furnishing and art works, over $250,000."[6] Such displays encouraged women to not only see the department store as a second home but also impelled them to believe that they "could 'buy a virtuous home,' to see her moral universe as [a] purchasable commodity."[7]

As a downtown club, the store provided an impressive range of accommodations and services "to ease the rigors of consumption for females much as men's clubs eased the burdens of paid employment for men" and to prolong women's time in the store.[8] During the first three decades of the twentieth century, the services and amenities offered by department stores proliferated exponentially. A 1929 nationwide survey of ninety-one stores conducted by the *Journal of Retailing* "revealed that over half offered the following services: public telephones, parcel checkrooms, lost and found services, shopping assistance, free delivery, waiting rooms, gift suggestion departments, mail-order departments, telephone order departments, accommodation bureaus, barber shops, restaurants, post offices, hospitals, radio departments, bus service, and shoe-shining stands. Over a fifth provided nurseries for shoppers' children, and a few offered Saturday afternoon children's theaters. One or more stores offered forty-eight other services."[9] These were, then, truly emporiums of consumption.

For many middle- and upper-class women, the emphasis on amenities and luxury in the store suggested that these grand emporiums were more than new public spaces for women. These institutions and their employees were their servants—servants most could not have otherwise afforded—upon whom women shoppers could act as and exert the power of a mistress. Thus, stores fostered a sense of entitlement and superiority among many of these women, which was an ironic contradiction to the democratization of consumption the stores otherwise touted. These women asserted that they "ought to be treated as individuals with special interests and with desires for comfort and pleasure" and were likely "induced . . . to believe that they ought to be served, not to serve others."[10] Shoppers "sometimes became imperious, pressing minor or fabricated complaints, taking for granted and abusing privileges, which stores considered favors."[11] Others rudely treated the store's staff as second- or third-class citizens and expected them to fulfill the most arbitrary of demands. For example, according to one trade journal, some women who were known for carrying their poodles while they shopped "put [a] store [through] the expense of delivering a single spool of thread."[12]

Although department stores were tailored to appeal to white women of privileged strata, they also convinced working-class and immigrant women that occasional store purchases, particularly at sales prices, or shopping in bargain, lower-priced departments, could confer a bourgeois life.[13] Many, however, preferred to shop in chain stores or ethnic neighborhood shops owned by kin or friends. Here, unlike in large downtown department stores, working-class customers were catered to and respected.[14]

Equally as important as the accommodations and services offered to customers were the sales staff who served them. Managers worked to match their selling staff to their desired clientele. They assumed, rightly or wrongly, that customers wished "to be served by Americans."[15] Here, "American" refers to race and class as well as country of origin. White, native-born, middle-class women were most desired as salesclerks, but few had been willing to stand behind a counter before the economic crisis of the late 1920s and 1930s.[16] Managers were unable to secure women with this combination of personal attributes, however, so whiteness became the most important requirement, trumping class and country of origin. Managers hired white working-class women, native and foreign-born, and then tried to transform them into "genteel but deferential workers, advisors as well as servants of the customers." They skillfully assessed their backgrounds and transformation to determine where workers would be assigned. Generally, older and native-born women were appointed to higher-priced departments that required the touch of women with manners, while younger and immigrant women—those believed to be appropriate for bargain shoppers—were assigned to cheaper-priced departments.[17]

Regional characteristics, specifically the presence of industry and demographic composition, also influenced the hiring process. From 1890 to 1939, in more industrialized areas, such as Rhode Island, New Jersey, Ohio, Illinois, Massachusetts, and Maryland, native-born women overwhelmingly worked in stores, while foreign-born women labored in factories and mills. In early twentieth-century Baltimore, native-born American women worked in all of the city's thirty-four stores, and in twenty-two they were the majority. Conversely, in less industrialized areas, such as Florida and Montana, women in stores were slightly more likely to be foreign-born than working women as a whole.[18]

Among foreign-born workers, merchants favored certain groups. They always preferred those from the British Isles, Scandinavia, and Germany— all groups that already had been assimilated into the white population— and increasingly accepted Russian immigrants in the 1920s. For example, in 1909, "girls of German extraction" dominated the sales force in five out of thirty-four Baltimore stores. Eastern and southern Europeans, with the exception of Jews, were not well represented on the selling floor before

World War II. This was in part due to the Immigration Act of 1924, a discriminatory policy that restricted their entry into America, and a widespread belief that these Europeans were "unfit," of "inferior stock," and racially different.[19]

Jews also were subjected to discrimination. Elizabeth Butler found in 1909 that eight Baltimore stores refused to hire Jewish women; and Elizabeth Stern reported in her 1926 autobiography that all Chicago stores, both those owned by Jews and those owned by non-Jews, maintain informal quotas for Jews. Generally, however, Jews were well received in the department store industry. Indeed, Jewish immigrants owned and operated several landmark American department stores, including Abraham & Straus, Neiman Marcus, I. Magnin, Gimbels, Hochschild-Kohn, Hecht's, Bloomingdale's, Filene's and Bergdorf Goodman, and Rich's. Scattered throughout the country, these stores offered Jews employment that promised upward mobility and a work environment "that was, at the very least, fair to Jews, if not outright welcoming." John Sondheim, former vice president of and onetime employee at Baltimore's Hochschild-Kohn, commented: "I would assume that Jewish employees at these stores had more opportunity to rise than they would at a non-Jewish place of employment. The owners and their families were not about to stop anyone from moving up because they were Jewish." At Julius Gutman department store, another Jewish-owned store in Baltimore, Jewish employees always held many posts in upper management and merchandising. Similarly, in 1916, Filene's in New York City employed approximately 250 Jews, roughly 10 percent of its entire staff. Nearly fifteen years later, Filene's and other New York City department stores reported that half of their workers were Jewish.[20]

In Jewish-owned department stores, Jews found a community where they could express "their multi-faceted identity, including their Jewishness."[21] Employee newsletters celebrated Jewish traditions and served as vehicles for Jewish expression, while management recognized High Holidays and their importance in creating a productive work atmosphere for their employees. A former Hochschild-Kohn employee recollected "great warmth in people on a personal level. On the afternoon before High Holiday, management would be walking around wishing people a happy holiday, a happy new year, and a good fast." Hochschild-Kohn, like other Jewish department stores in Baltimore, never closed for the Jewish holidays but maintained "a very relaxed attitude about Jews staying home" on these occasions.[22]

For white sales workers, regardless of nativity or religious affiliation, the racial exclusivity of department stores helped temper the many challenges that arose from selling, including the long hours, low wages, unpaid overtime, Christmastime rush, and the abuse to which they were subjected by customers and management. It permitted them an opportunity to forge an identity that was grounded in race, citizenship, class, and labor. For native-born white saleswomen, the department store produced a sense of superiority over immigrants and reinforced their self-identification as white Americans; and for foreign-born store employees, work in the store office and on the sales floor encouraged them to Americanize their identities, accept mainstream middle-class norms of behavior, and emphasize class over ethnicity.

Frances Donovan, a sociologist who worked in two New York City department stores as a participant observer in the 1920s, noted that saleswomen of all "racial types . . . meet together in the shops as Americans."[23] Managers regulated dress and behavior to erase signs of working-class and/or immigrant origins, apply a veneer of bourgeois culture, and encourage friendly worker-customer relations to increase sales. Some managers required that women dress in uniforms, such as all black, or in "business-like styles and neutral shades."[24] Others instituted welfare work and training programs that provided education not only in salesmanship and merchandise but also in personal hygiene, etiquette, and grammar. In a few cases, managers insisted that saleswomen memorize "a few French words and names of chic Parisian streets."[25] As a result of these efforts, saleswomen presented "an astonishing similarity of appearance. In their manners they conform to certain established conventions of saleswomanly [sic] behavior; outwardly they are Americans. But if you trace them back into their homes you find a vast difference in culture status, and customs and traditions utterly foreign to the established American standards."[26] Their lives often resembled those of their immigrant and/or blue-collar parents. Many resided in working-class neighborhoods, attended "booze parties," and "tolerated unconventional sexual practices such as premarital heterosexual intercourse, prostitution, and homosexuality."[27]

Efforts to refine saleswomen's identity were met in two distinct ways. For some, training and discipline underscored their subordinate position because they encouraged her to adopt a middle-class veneer but did not provide any of its rights and privileges. In fact, these efforts often bred resentment toward and strife with her employer and middle- and upper-class customers. Others, however, embraced the elevated status, glamour, fulfillment, and hope of financial security (which was often met through marriage to a rich man, as exemplified in *It*) that accompanied the white-collar work of sales and the racial exclusivity of the department store to reaffirm or create a white racial identity. These white women entered the department store above women of color and—in many, but certainly not all, cases—above men of color. Accordingly, the position of saleswomen—though it placed white working-class women "below" most white male workers in the store and their white middle- and upper-class female customers—situated them above the store's African American personnel. Segregation in the department store likely allowed white saleswomen, similar to white women mill workers in Atlanta in 1897, "to protect their position in the social hierarchy" despite the challenges that arose from selling their labor and working long hours for low wages.[28]

Whiteness was invested with concrete, material meaning. For many working-class salespeople, their labor in the store afforded them the opportunity to purchase the occasional high-quality, stylish ready-made clothing consumed by their middle-class white clientele and provided them with the funds to reside in "more desirable" and "fashionable" neighborhoods and engage in leisure activities typically consumed by those they served. As a way of emulating the wealthy, salesmen and saleswomen participated in bicycling and social clubs and attended operas and "legitimate" theater performances when discounted tickets were available. These workers "not only . . . dreamed of moving up the occupational ladder, but also liked spending leisure time with those a rung above. . . . By attending these venues and thus associating with individuals above them in the social hierarchy, office and sales workers posed as full-fledged members of the middle class."[29] All of this supplied workers with pleasure and comfort as well as a sense that they could narrow the gap between themselves and their wealthier customers. It also enhanced their stature in their own eyes and in those of their peers. In other words, they too could participate in the democracy of goods and the democracy of desire, as described by historians Roland Marchand and William Leach, and achieve—if only for a few brief moments—the freedom, self-expression, happiness, and salvation they associated with the white middle-class experience.

Among workers' leisure activities were minstrel shows and "comedic" racist narratives.[30] Participating in and attending these activities, as examined by scholars David Roediger, Michael Rogin, and Eric Lott, had long been an integral component of ethnic assimilation and working-class formation. They afforded workers occasions to hide and disprove images of the unfit and inferior immigrant and the boorish, uneducated working-class American; to forge a common sense of whiteness; and to perform and assume the behaviors, manners, and lifestyle of the white middle class. Even if this lifestyle was never achieved, minstrelsy and more broadly adopting a racialized view of the world, whereby whites were superior and blacks were inferior, provided workers with the illusion that they could be like their white middle-class customers.[31]

Minstrel shows pervaded American department store culture as well. These racist forms of entertainment were consumed in stores located in the North, South, and Midwest; in Jewish- and non-Jewish-owned stores; and in establishments that welcomed black trade as well as those that prohibited African American consumers entirely. In 1900, Gimbels in Philadelphia featured a float of "pickaninnies" in its Christmas parade; New York City's Abraham & Straus held a similar celebration in 1926. At the 1940 anniversary of Baltimore's Hochschild-Kohn, the sales staff performed a minstrel show ostensibly set on a veranda of an old southern plantation. The show was peppered with lively renditions of the cakewalk and slave spirituals. Photographs of the anniversary show were proudly featured in the store's employee newsletter. In 1950, Hochschild-Kohn, which served numerous local blacks, presented a float with two blackface minstrel characters at Baltimore's Thanksgiving "toyland parade." Minstrelsy eventually lost its lure in northern department stores in the 1950s, as blacks intensified their protests of these racist portrayals. However, in border and southern cities, racist performances continued to be prized as a legitimate form of entertainment and community building until the late 1960s.[32]

Salespeople also derived a common identity as whites from racist tales presented in the employee newsletter. The Strawbridge and Clothier's employee-produced magazine, *Store Chat*, is a treasure trove of information on the work and leisure lives of clerical and sales employees in twentieth-century Philadelphia. For example, a story of racist humor ran in a 1911 edition of this publication. In this "racist parable, a black wife calls a doctor about her sick husband. According to the wife, the husband has fallen ill for no apparent reason after he spent what is billed as a 'typical day' in the park. The typical day for this stock character involves overeating, heavy drinking, tumbling off two amusement park rides, and getting into a razor fight. The wife cannot understand what is wrong with her husband and urges the doctor to visit."[33] The story's introduction propounds that it "is really one of the most characteristic tales of the colored race ever printed. It is more than that; however, it actually points a moral of importance to all of us."[34]

The tale printed in *Store Chat* "depicts dissipation as 'characteristic' of African Americans"—a trait that rendered the man, and blacks generally, unemployable and an abject provider. To top it all off, his wife is too ignorant to grasp the situation.[35] Racist narratives afforded salespeople opportunities to affirm their distance from so-called black characteristics such as laziness, drunkenness, and stupidity that made African Americans unfit for sales and clerical work and simultaneously validated salespeople's superior positions in the department store in particular and in society in general. These performances and race more generally provided the basis for white employee solidarity and stressed that African Americans did not belong in this field of work; and for immigrant employees, the race performances facilitated their assimilation into mainstream society by minimizing the differences between themselves and their native-born white coworkers.

African American Store Personnel

Department stores' contradictory treatment of black consumers and workers created two distinct yet intricately interwoven worlds—one white, the other black—separate and unequal. Before World War II, the world of black employees was largely defined by relative invisibility and their menial status in the stores' labor force. As anti-immigrant prejudices waned, white immigrants were privileged to hold sales and clerical jobs alongside the native-born, while blacks were relegated to low-wage, low-profile staff positions away from the selling floor. While the world slept, black men toiled as porters and janitors in warehouses located miles away from the primary downtown store, or in stockrooms and receiving and packing areas away from customers' eyes. Most black women performed duties similar to those of their counterparts in domestic service, working as maids, cooks, matrons, and seamstresses. Some were employed in more-public jobs as elevator operators and restaurant wait staff. William Atkinson, an African American elevator operator and later a leader of Local 1-S in the 1940s, remembered that at Macy's blacks worked "in the Food Department as cooks, the Receiving Department, and the Elevator Department."[36] And even these jobs were insecure, especially during times of economic downturn. The racial division of department store labor had major consequences for African Americans: it rendered them not only subordinate to white fellow employees but virtually invisible to the store's consuming public, on the one hand; while, on the other hand, it afforded at least some of them opportunities for advancement. Thus, after many years of service a few blacks were promoted to white-collar positions in the black domain of the store, even as the racial division of labor and the limited opportunities for black advancement inadvertently fostered a black work culture and identity.

Between 1890 and 1939, despite being denied access to white-collar positions and merely tolerated as shoppers, African Americans were generally welcomed as maintenance and service workers. These employees of color made up a formidable population in American department stores, generally constituting between 4 and 20 percent of a store's employee population during a period when most other blacks were relegated to agricultural and domestic labor. The exact number of black workers, however, is difficult to determine. Department stores were not recognized as a distinct type of general merchandise store in the United States Census until 1930, and even then the data were not broken down by race.[37] Consequently, one must rely on available store employment records to ascertain black representation in the industry. Those records indicate that black service workers made up 4–11 percent of workforces in northern department stores, and 10–20 percent in southern stores. In 1915, Wanamaker's New York location employed more than 250 African Americans to run the store's elevators, work in its restaurant's kitchen, and play in the store band. One large store employed 125 women of color in its mail-order department in 1922, tasked with packing goods.[38] In 1943, Macy's of New York maintained a workforce of 10,000 people, 400 of whom were African American and none were members of the sales staff. This figure varied throughout the year, however. For instance, during the Christmas season, Macy's "may be employing 16,000 . . . [of whom] 600 or more colored."[39] Klein's Department Store in New York had a smaller staff, employing 1,000 people in 1944, of whom 30–40 were African Americans working as matrons and elevator operators in the store's bargain basement.[40] Southern department stores appeared to have maintained larger black workforces, reflecting perhaps the continued concentration of the black population in that region. Richmond's Miller & Rhoads employed 1,410 workers in 1935. Of these workers, approximately 155 were African American. In all Richmond department stores, blacks made up roughly one-fifth of store employees through the 1960s.[41]

Maintenance and service work in department stores was not much different from other domestic and industrial occupations available to African

Americans during this period. It was grueling and messy, routine and repetitive. It involved, as described by J. G. Guyer, supervisor of the porters at Miller & Rhoads, an "endless chain of mops, buckets, brooms, dust cloths, painters, etc. toiling daily from the cellar to the roof." On a daily basis, African Americans were tasked with shoveling ten to twelve tons of coal into boilers, lifting anything and everything from cash registers to elevators, collecting and carting away garbage, cleaning bathrooms, running the passenger elevators, and pressing and storing clothes.[42] However, unlike most jobs open to blacks, this "dirty" work required higher levels of academic and work training. In 1923, Mary Louise Williams answered the following newspaper advertisement: "Wanted: a young colored girl, high school graduate preferred. Apply Dey's Department Store." She dressed with "care expecting to find at least a saleslady opening." However, upon meeting with the manager of this Syracuse store, Williams learned that the store "desired a bootblack in the ladies' rest room." The manager denied Williams the position and eventually hired a high school graduate who had trained two years as a teacher. Williams ended her story posing the question: "Is it not a pity that a colored girl must be educated to qualify as bootblack?"[43]

The racial division of labor translated into the physical separation of black employees from white workers and customers. Before World War II, most, if not all, department stores maintained segregated entrances, bathrooms, lunchrooms, and/or social events and activities. Workers at Miller & Rhoads joined either the Employee Association or the Colored Employee Association depending on their race. Macy's of New York segregated news by race in the employee newsletter, allocating one small column on the last page to black employee news and gossip. Black employees at Wanamaker's New York and Philadelphia formed their own employee associations in 1911 and 1912, respectively. These associations sponsored choirs, bands, dances, picnics, and athletic teams. Most northern department stores ended these separate accommodations during and after World War II. Southern stores, however, continued them through the 1960s. In 1959, Thalhimers held segregated winter banquets: the white banquet was held in the elegant Virginia Room of the Hotel John Marshall, which was "beautifully arranged for the affair and the tables were softly candle-lit," and the black banquet, held the following evening, was at Ike's Shrimp House.[44]

Segregation, coupled with African Americans' position in and the racial dynamics of the store, rendered them virtually invisible. White workers paid little attention to their black coworkers. Scholar Jerome Bjelopera found that, throughout the workday, saleswomen at Philadelphia's Strawbridge and Clothier used public elevators as social spaces, or rather informal employee lounges, where they met to relax and gossip away from the watchful, disapproving gaze of their bosses. "But their sense of freedom," he concluded, "also suggests that the black elevator operators who silently observed them were either invisible or of no consequence to them."[45]

When they did pay attention to African Americans, white employees often viewed them unfavorably. Again, Bjelopera revealed, "In 1909, a white employee at Strawbridge and Clothier claimed that the burden of responsibilities he faced on the job and at home was the chief distinction between himself and African Americans working in the store. Black workers, he thought, could be happy-go-lucky because their ostensibly simple lives provided them with no real worries. The white employee believed that black workers in the store abided by the mantra 'don't worry, smile.'"[46] Such statements ignored store policy that all employees, white and black, were required to demonstrate courtesy to customers, and indicate that courtesy was to be practiced differently based on race. White workers were expected to signal courtesy through their conversations with customers, and black staff were to signal courtesy through their appearance and silence. African Americans were expected to be smiling and attentive to their uniforms, hair, and even their fingernails, because "your hands are under customer observation as you open and close your car doors." Whenever black divisions received new uniforms, store newsletters would publish their photo; one photo appeared with the comment "They really look nice and deserve to be proud of their appearance."[47]

In many ways, blacks were expected to play the role of the happy Sambo and doting Mammy, and if they broke character—or more accurately, challenged the racial order—trouble quickly ensued. For example, in 1907, a female patron at Macy's characterized black elevator operators as "nigger[s] in a little authority." In her complaint letter to store management, she wrote: "Yesterday one was disrespectful to me. Besides I heard of the Negroes on the main floor vilely insult one of the shop girls. It made me almost faint. Such things may be overlooked in a white man, but they become almost a tragedy from a Negro." She further requested that the store follow the example of Altman's and Lord & Taylor and employ only white elevator men. In response to her letter, management replied that the offending elevator operator would be "summarily dismissed." But Macy's refused to fire all of its black elevator operators. Management justified this decision on the basis of racial benevolence, stating: "We wish that we could say that our white employees never gave cause for such criticism. We have found that our colored elevator boys are as polite as any other employes, and to dispense with all the colored elevator boys because one has been delinquent would scarcely be fair to the race. There are so few employments open for the colored people in mercantile establishments, we would consider it cruel to deprive them of this only one in our establishment where they monopolize the situations, and therefore the only place where we can employ them."[48]

African American employees had to show deference to both their white colleagues and the customer—and both often had unreasonable and conflicting demands. In 1940, a note of "appreciation" for Thalhimers colored staff that was included in the employee newsletter speaks to this phenomenon: "'Pete, take this to the warehouse at once'—'Bessie, not so much ice in my Coca Cola'—'Jackson, don't any of these elevators go DOWN?' We couldn't possibly get along without you and wish to record as many of your activities each month as possible because you are a part of us." At Miller & Rhoads in 1943, Fannie Johnson, a maid, was "sent out to buy ice cream for some white salespeople. Upon returning to the store, she unexpectedly encountered one of the store's top executives and was forced to quickly stuff the forbidden treats under her apron (ruining both the apron and her uniform in the process) to keep them from the eye of her employer. White customers and even just random white people on the street felt that black department store employees in uniform were at their beck and call as well. When a Richmond woman lost her watch, she flagged down a Thalhimers delivery truck and 'asked the boys if they would mind driving two or three blocks and [look] for it.'" They both courteously agreed, found the watch, and returned it to the customer.[49]

As African Americans were rendered separate, virtually invisible, and inferior, they also were described and sometimes treated as if they were part of "one big, happy family." At Thalhimers and Miller & Rhoads, "when African Americans were out sick or were mourning the death of a family member, white employees joined African American staff in sending gifts, cards, and flowers. During the World War II era, in particular, the newsletters dispensed with the segregation of the news and featured black servicemen's letters (many of which were written to their former white employers) alongside [letters from] whites." Overall, then, the "message that emerge[s] is that white employees were all part of an idealistic family, whereas African

Americans occupied a precarious status in the genealogy, requiring their deference and acceptance of white supremacy."[50]

In spite of these drawbacks, department store work offered several advantages over domestic or factory work. Specifically, it provided blacks with steady employment with fairly consistent hours and work expectations, and good benefits (paid vacations, in-store health care, and inexpensive access to insurance by joining the employee association). And for a select few, the department store presented them with opportunities for advancement and promotion. Frank Jackson was promoted twice during his tenure at Abraham & Straus in New York. First, he was elevated to superintendent of the colored employees. He "handled this position so well that Mr. Abraham (founder of the firm) remembered him in his will. He left a trust fund for him and also stated that as long as Jackson lived he should have a position with the department store." In 1928, Jackson was promoted once again, this time to the position of executive assistant.[51]

At Thalhimers, John Harper, who began as a porter in 1892, ran the shipping and receiving department, worked as an elevator operator, and managed and repaired the store's cash registers. In addition to these duties, Harper was responsible for hiring all African American employees (a responsibility that further captures the degree to which blacks and whites operated in two separate worlds even within the same store) during his first forty-seven years. His "range of responsibilities earned him a weekly salary of $25 in 1919, a high salary for an African American man at a time when the national average weekly wage for all workers, white included, was $23.10."[52] However, in 1939, as the number of African American employees increased, Thalhimers took the authority of hiring away from Harper and placed it in the hands of a white woman in the personnel department. Harper was transferred to the wrapping department—"in charge of wrapping all packages that could not be wrapped elsewhere in the store"—and remained in this "tedious" position until retiring in August 1945.[53]

For black women, department store work was a step up from domestic service. Young black women were able to find shorter hours, higher wages, protection from sexual harassment and violence, and a degree of autonomy in stores, and as a result had begun to "abandoned [sic] domestic work completely."[54] At the turn of the twentieth century, domestics "labored from sunup to sundown six to seven days a week" and earned anywhere from four to twelve dollars a month, with the average falling between four and eight dollars a month.[55] As menial store workers, women earned from seven to fifteen dollars a week. Men earned on average fifteen dollars a week, with some making as much as twenty-two dollars a week. Management also rewarded hardworking women with promotions and monetary raises. At Thalhimers, Hazel Harris and Grace Bradley moved from maids to elevator girls; Carrie McLaughlin, employed with the company for fifteen years, took time out of a vacation in Philadelphia to visit a ticket machine distributor and eventually became supervisor of the black women operating ticket-making machines in the warehouse; and in 1942, Florence White was promoted to supervisor of a marking table in the receiving and marking department (in this position, White and four helpers were responsible for the checking and marking of all incoming merchandise for the main floor men's furnishings, camera shop, art needlework, fifth-floor draperies, and the smoke shop).[56]

Promotions and opportunities for advancement, however, were few and modest. They usually involved graduating from one form of menial work to another or supervising only other blacks. With this realization, and an understanding that even after multiple decades of hard work most black workers remained maids, porters, or kitchen staff, some black employees strategically used department store work as a stepping-stone. In October 1943, Mary Johnson started at Thalhimers in the maintenance department. After approximately two years, Johnson was promoted from maid to hospital attendant. In this position, Johnson realized "that some professional training would help her to be more of assistance in cases of emergency" and decided to "take a nine months' course in practical nursing at the Maggie Walker High School . . . during her off-duty hours." This program involved the completion of two hundred training hours at the Community Hospital. After she earned her nursing certificate, Mary became "a full-fledged practical nurse." Similarly, while working in the engine room at Thalhimers, Bishop Gordon earned a bachelor of arts degree in history in 1952 from the Virginia Union University, after which he entered graduate school at Union. Soon thereafter, Gordon left Thalhimers and went into the insurance business.[57] Another beneficiary of department store work was elevator operator and future union leader William Atkinson. While working at Macy's, Atkinson attended St. John's with the hopes of becoming a lawyer. Unfortunately, after the superintendent of elevators changed Atkinson's schedule, he was unable to finish his last year of college.[58]

The racial exclusivity of the department store allowed white workers to maintain the illusion that they were part of a homogenous and privileged family. But coincidentally, it did the same for its black employees, although the boundaries of their family were different. According to scholar Beth Kreydatus, in the space of the department store, where hundreds of blacks were employed and segregated from their white counterparts, African Americans nurtured a "cohesive, even familial, work culture" and established "supportive networks" of current and former workers. In southern department stores, they often referred family and friends for open positions; "dozens of surnames" are found in the company records. Black store employees also regularly shared family and community news, including births, deaths, and marriages (many of which wedded one black employee to another), in the "colored" section of store newsletters.[59]

This sense of community, likely coupled with the employee benefits, influenced many African Americans who left for military service or another position to stay in touch and return to the store months and even years later. Macy's *Sparks*, the store's employee newsletter, often printed letters from former employees serving in World War II. Sergeant Jackson H. Miller, a former elevator operator, wrote: "Although I do hear from many of the men that I had the pleasure of working with in the Elevator Dept., it is good to read about what is happening in other departments of the Store. . . . The last record of me in your business file showed I was Private, but that had changed and for the past couple of months the title has been Sergeant."[60] Powell Williams and Robert Scott, both deliverymen at Thalhimers, returned to their old jobs after serving in the war. Williams had been stationed in Texas, while Scott spent eleven months in Africa and fifteen months in Italy as platoon sergeant in a Quartermaster Trucking Company.[61] Typically, and in contrast with many industrial jobs, these men almost always returned to the same position they held before leaving, despite gaining valuable experiences that might have proved useful in white-collar positions.

· · · · · ·

It is undeniable that race segregation and discrimination circumscribed thousands of African Americans to the least prestigious, lowest-paying jobs in department stores. However, not all blacks worked behind the scenes. From 1890 to 1918, a period that roughly marks when the department store became the leading American retailer and the height of the First Great Migration, a select few were hired as sales and clerical workers and given the opportunity to taste the urban bourgeois lifestyle being sold and celebrated in these grand emporiums. Most employers preferred not to broadcast these hires. Therefore, virtually no evidence exists that provides any deep insight into the hiring process and work experiences of African American white-collar workers in department stores during this period. Scholars Lorenzo J. Greene and Carter G. Woodson suggest that, as early as 1900, stores sometimes hired a token number of African American sales workers in an effort to appease and retain their black customers, who had been pressuring retailers to modify their hiring practices, or as a strategy to increase black patronage. For example, in response to black pressure, white businesses employed black clerks in Lexington, Kentucky, in 1900: "Graves, Coy and Company set the example by employing Sam L. Tolley, who held this position a number of years; the Kaufman Clothing Company was next, having in their charge Noah Woolridge."[62]

Other African Americans, many of whom were of lighter complexion, high school or college graduates, and exemplars of respectability, applied and aggressively persuaded the personnel manager to hire them. In 1901, Mattie Johnson (figure 3) sought an interview with the manager of Siegel, Cooper & Co. in Chicago. As was the case at virtually all American department stores in the early twentieth century, Siegel, Cooper & Co. abided by a strict racial policy, whereby sales workers were white and African Americans were relegated to menial behind-the-scenes occupations. Nevertheless, Johnson—with a firm belief in her abilities, an aspiration to improve her station, and the fortitude to challenge existing norms—applied for a sales position and successfully persuaded the manager to meet with her for five minutes. At the expiration of the five minutes, she was hurried out of the meeting. Johnson returned to the store within a few days and once again "earnestly pushed her claim." Impressed by her persistence, the manager gave Johnson a six-week trial in the Hazel Pure Food Department. After the trial period, she was fired "but again resumed her attacks upon the manager. When heartily discouraged she wrote him a polite note stating that she would annoy him no longer. He immediately sent for her and installed her in her old position." Soon thereafter Johnson took charge of this department.[63]

Johnson's hire was widely reported by the black press and noted in lectures and publications as evidence of black progress. Reports insisted that she was "looked upon by her employers as one of the most competent women in the store" and that she had "many friends among the patrons of the establishment."[64] Johnson symbolized racial progress and raised African Americans' hopes that other department stores would soon follow suit. These reports also celebrated Johnson's hard work and persistence and implied that the manager was swayed by her performance to retain Johnson as a saleswoman. However, no existing records indicate that Siegel, Cooper &

FIGURE 3 Mattie Johnson, ca. 1890–1915. Library of Congress Prints and Photographs Division, LC-USZ62-40474.

Co. was convinced enough by Johnson's superior performance to subsequently employ other African Americans in similar positions.

In some cases, humanitarian sentiments drove the hiring of blacks. At Sears, Roebuck, and Company, Julius Rosenwald, president and CEO, was a pioneer in advancing the black condition. Rosenwald adhered to the "self-help" philosophy of his personal friend Booker T. Washington and to Andrew Carnegie's philosophy of civic stewardship. He supported black causes convinced that black advancement could be achieved through rugged individualism.[65] While he never succeeded in convincing Sears's board of directors to adopt this perspective, he oversaw the hiring of a few African Americans in nontraditional positions. In the early 1900s, a young Claude Barnett (the future founder of the Negro Associated Press) met Rosenwald while working as a houseboy for Richard Warren Sears, cofounder of Sears, Roebuck, and Company. Barnett recalled, "Mr. Sears, while generous, was no philanthropist. My contact with Julius Rosenwald came about through the Rosenwald fund except for one memorable incident. After I stopped working in the

Sears home he told me to go downtown to the store and get a job. I was employed in the grocery department packaging and shipping sugar. . . . So far as I knew I was the only colored employee who was not a janitor."[66] Barnett remained employed at Sears until he entered Tuskegee University in September 1904.

The token appointment of African Americans to higher-paying, higher-status jobs in early department stores appears to have done little to dismantle Jim Crow practices in the retail industry, however. The work environment for these employees remained fraught with racism and discrimination. Like their nonselling and racially passing counterparts, black sales workers were often seen but not acknowledged, tolerated but not accepted, and subjected to racist and derogatory comments. To cope, black sales workers likely established close and supportive relationships with other African American workers; or perhaps they kept to themselves, fearing that they might draw additional attention to their race and color or that nonselling blacks would ostracize them. To make matters worse, black workers' tenure on the selling floor remained insecure. They were often overlooked for promotions and replaced if a manager found a "more qualified" white worker. Of course, in truth, whiteness was the only qualification needed to win a black salesclerk's position.

The mass migration of African Americans to urban centers profoundly altered relationships between blacks and whites and changed the basic economic and social structure of urban black communities in both the North and the South. The increased numbers of blacks threatened the established racial order, and whites in northern cities such as Chicago, New York, and Philadelphia responded by hardening the color line not only in employment but also in housing and politics.[67] Almost immediately, stores steadfastly observed their "no black salesclerk" or more broadly "no blacks in position of responsibility" policy. In southern department stores, as the number of African American employees increased, African American supervisors were demoted and found their positions handed to white employees. At Thalhimers in 1939, as previously discussed, John Harper was relieved of his supervisory duties of hiring and training the store's black employees; those duties were given to a white woman in the personnel department.[68] The majority of black store workers remained in subordinate positions, therefore, until mass civil rights agitation in the post–World War II era.

Of course, there were exceptions to this rule. During World War I, and likely because of Rosenwald's influence and most certainly out of need, Sears, Roebuck, and Company hired black women migrants as labelers and stampers in its mail-order house. As soon as the war ended and business leveled off, however, Sears immediately terminated those workers. Not long thereafter, in 1919, Sears hired 1,200 black women as office workers at the behest of the Chicago Urban League—an organization with which Rosenwald was closely affiliated. These workers were paid ten to fourteen dollars per week. But, once again, their time at Sears was temporary, as the Depression forced the retailer to close some of its facilities.[69]

As major department stores ceased hiring blacks in skilled positions, African Americans pursuing this work applied to black-owned stores and white-owned stores trying to capitalize on black migration, or engaged in "passing." Black-owned department stores offered a small, yet significant, number of African Americans work as sales and office workers. These stores were embodiments of black self-help and "buy black" philosophies and movements. They aimed to create white-collar positions for African Americans, provide African American consumers with quality, affordable merchandise and first-class customer service, and advance black economic development and independence. In 1905, with the support of the Independent Order of St. Luke, Maggie Lena Walker founded the Saint Luke Emporium in Richmond, Virginia (figure 4), to expand black women's employment opportunities. The Emporium employed fifteen African American saleswomen, which constituted a significant percentage of black women in white-collar and skilled occupations in this southern city. Here, black women "worked in healthier, less stressful environments" free from racism and were better paid than domestic servants, factory workers, and even professionals. In fact, they often earned two and even three times more money than black professional women. For example, one teacher received eighteen dollars a month and a nine-month salary, while black female clerks in the office of the Independent Order of Saint Luke earned fifty dollars per month.[70]

Other black-owned department stores existed in New York City, Buffalo, Philadelphia, Detroit, and even Muskogee, Oklahoma.[71] In Chicago, the Sandy W. Trice & Company Department Store employed four African American clerks, a stenographer, and a bookkeeper. According to a *New York Age* article, "The clerks act as if they had been in the business all their lives, and the daily receipts indicate that they know how to sell goods."[72] The Metropolitan Department Store of Baltimore employed twenty-five persons: "Manager, Assistant Manager, Fore-Lady, Bookkeeper, Milliner, Superintendent of Grocery Department, 4 sales ladies, two grocery clerks, one driver, one porter, eight solicitors, or agents (outside), two bundle wrappers, one collector."[73] And in Wilmington, North Carolina, another black-owned department store

FIGURE 4 St. Luke Emporium, dry goods department, ca. 1905.
Independent Order of St. Luke Collection, The Valentine, Richmond History Center.

was celebrated for "feeding, clothing, and housing one hundred (100) members of our race daily . . . [and for] provid[ing] employment for the educated ones of the race so as to give them employment to practice what they learn."[74]

Although not black owned, the South Center Department Store in Chicago's Black Belt employed African Americans in all areas and departments of the store. South Center opened in 1928, hoping to capitalize on the city's massive black population growth by hiring and catering to whites and blacks. It was "the nation's first department store to integrate its personnel and advance the position of African Americans in executive positions in retail and marketing." South Center "hired blacks to whites at a ratio of 16 to 1 among its 220 non-maintenance and service staff." By 1936, the store had 230 employees, 70 percent of whom were African American.[75] According to the *Pittsburgh Courier*, South Center had "no 'colored' or 'white' jobs. When it comes to filling a job whether it is in the meat division or in the bookkeeping department, we place the person in there whom we think is best qualified for that job. One time we had a colored girl as cashier in a certain department and at another time we had a white girl. Who will be the next one to occupy that position we do not know. It will be determined solely on the basis of merit, efficiency and willingness to work."[76] This policy extended to the store's managerial and executive positions. In 1928, South Center hired Richard Lee "Dick" Jones as the store's general superintendent, making him the only African American to fill such a position in a large department store, and, in 1939, appointed Jones to the South Center board of directors.[77]

In addition to creating sales and managerial positions for African Americans, black-owned department stores offered members of the African American community opportunities to learn the fundamental principles and policies of business needed to advance the individual and the race. A. I. Hart and Company in Harlem provided "young men and women of the race . . . mercantile training" that they would not receive otherwise.[78] Similarly the South Center Department Store offered classes in salesmanship and merchandising to its employees and the public. These classes sought "to help supply the growing need for trained clerks. . . . Instruction is to be both in theory and practice. After theories of salesmanship have been discussed, the pupils are to be allowed the opportunity to test out the theories in the store's practical laboratory behind the counters." Representatives of manufacturers instructed students on "the facts about the quality and source of the merchandise they handle."[79] Students received training in customer service. They were instructed to abide by certain rules: "(1) Serve every customer as you would want to be served, (2) Study to know your store—its character, its clientele, its methods, (3) Study to know your customers—their station in life, their means, their interests, and (4) Study to know other stores like yours—their offerings, their inducements and their methods."[80]

This education equipped African Americans with the skills—including appearance, personality, speech, and salesmanship—needed to successfully secure white-collar work in the retail industry. Graduates of the South Center training school, for example, were frequently hired at the South Center Department Store and neighboring retailers. According to Jones, "A colored man who was at the head of our shoe department is now connected with a colored shoe store, the Metropolitan, across the street. His assistant is now head and the man beneath that chief is now in training for that position. . . . There is Hill, who used to be head of our men's department, who is now assistant manager of the Food Mart across the street."[81] Jones also reported that "one of our men is now an important merchandise executive in the May's Department Store; another is in the buying division of Marshall Field's." These hires contradicted May's and Field's discriminatory hiring policies. They suggest either that token hires persisted, albeit even more secretively than before, as none of the major black papers reported this news or that these companies were unaware that their merchandise executive and buyer were African American.

· · · · · ·

Secrecy was often involved in black hiring, however. Throughout the early twentieth century, racial passing was a reality for an untold number of black women, in particular, those seeking employment other than domestic help. These women were "so nearly white that they [could] be mistaken for white girls, in which case they [were] able to secure very good positions and keep them as long as their color is not known."[82] According to William A. Crossland, in St. Louis department stores there may have been more black saleswomen than either employers or students of the labor force were aware. Specifically, he notes that a "majority of the colored female clerks are employed in department stores. This fact, however, is not known to the employer. There are a few Negro women of very light color, who are working in the finest stores in the city."[83]

Given the secrecy of passing, it is nearly impossible to calculate how many women attained nonmaintenance store work in this manner. Nevertheless, passing offered many black women the opportunity to secure higher-status, higher-paying positions in the department store. But passing came at significant costs. Scholar Cheryl Harris affectionately recalled her grandmother, an African American woman, who passed for white working as an office clerk in a Chicago department store in the 1930s. Day after day, her grandmother "made herself invisible, then visible again, for a price too inconsequential to do more than barely sustain her family." She came to know her coworkers, learning their most intimate secrets, but they never knew her. Harris's grandmother "occupied a different place . . . where white supremacy and economic domination meet." This place was entirely unknown to her white coworkers: "They remained oblivious to the worlds within worlds that existed just beyond the edge of their awareness and yet were present in their very midst."[84] Living this double life proved too much to bear and eventually resulted in Harris's grandmother leaving the store.

Many "passing" women worked in constant fear of being exposed and terminated. One African American woman hired as Christmas help at Marshall Field's "was scared to death that someone—some colored person—

would see her and recognize her." While working in the costume jewelry section, she avoided serving African American customers by turning her back and ignoring them even when they "made a point of trying to speak to her." Finally she became such a "nervous wreck" that she quit. Others, however, seemed to handle passing in the department store with a bit more ease. Another woman working in the handkerchief department at Field's had little fear of interacting with black customers. She recalled: "People were coming in all the time that I knew; but I always spoke to them and would wait on them if they came to my counter. So I got along all right. Lots of people who sensed that I was going to speak to them would just nod and move away quickly. They weren't resentful. I really needed the money; but it wasn't a life-and-death matter, so I couldn't think of not speaking to someone that I knew."[85]

Whether they were passing or a token hire, African American sales and office workers were plagued by insecurities. They could be discharged on a whim, to make room for a white employee, for committing a minor infraction, or because their "true" identity had been revealed. Nevertheless, for a significant, albeit small, number of blacks who thrived in these positions of responsibility, sales and clerical work augmented their participation in American consumer culture as shoppers (à la Fordism), and facilitated their ascent into a modern black middle class.

African American Consumers

During the segregation era, all public institutions worked to keep whites and blacks separate. "For most whites," one scholar noted, "blacks represented sources of unspecified physical and moral pollution."[86] However, the department store, which was unique in that all were welcome, brought these groups together. Anxieties and fears, nonetheless, abound that black and white bodies might touch in the exchange of clothes they tried on or use the same forks and plates at the store lunch counters. Consequently, department stores not only prohibited African American employment except as porters, maids, and elevator operators; they also restricted African American consumers' movement and participation in this sphere. Restrictions, or rather racial boundaries, which varied depending on the store and/or region, in the North as well as the South, ensured that the department store remained a whites-only amusement and that blacks remained in a place of second-class citizenship.

Prohibitions aimed at keeping black and white bodies separate were sometimes justified as measures to prevent blacks from contaminating whites with their "Negro health problems." African Americans were refused service at lunch counters and restaurants, and at barber and beauty shops. They were forbidden from trying on clothes, especially hats, gloves, and intimate apparel, and from returning items after purchase. When Josiah Henry, a prominent African American attorney, entered Stewart's Department Store in Baltimore in 1928 to order a dress for his mother, the salesclerk informed him that there were no available facilities for his mother to try on the garment until the building was remodeled. Henry scanned the selling floor for the dressing area and noticed that white patrons were using the dressing rooms. Becoming quickly aware of the situation, he announced that he would put off his purchase until the appropriate facilities were available.[87] Many others, however, coped with these restrictions, regarding them as inconveniences, and tried to ignore the insult. Bill Lee recalled shopping with his grandmother: "There were four of us, two boys, two girls. The boys would be first. It was kind of easy for the boys. My grandmother just put a shirt up in front of us. But with two girls it was a little more difficult. You couldn't try anything on in most of the stores. Sure it made you angry. But what could you do? It's just the way it was."[88]

Stores rarely extended African Americans the same customer service they did to whites. Some stores marked black credit accounts with a star in the store ledger to distinguish them from those of whites (an early form of racial profiling), while others denied blacks credit entirely.[89] Black consumers complained they were never addressed with terms of respect, such as "mister," "mistress," or "miss." Instead, they endured being called "boy," "girl," "uncle," "auntie," and even "nigger," and, by extension, were treated as such. For example, when James Underhill and his wife went shopping in a large department store, "they were met by a white salesman who beckoned to them . . . and began the rattling of his heels and toes in the style of tap-dancing." As the salesman showed Underhill the pianos, he continued tap dancing and added "the whistling and humming of jazz notes." Underhill and his wife became disturbed by the salesman's preconceived ideas of African Americans and performance and expressed as much to the store manager. The manager immediately called for the salesman, told him that his services were no longer required, and apologized to Underhill on the salesman's behalf. He told Underhill: "I am sorry for what has happened, but I will see that you get the best services; I will see that you are treated white." To the astonishment of the manager, Underhill responded that he simply wanted to be "treated as a man."[90]

African Americans were never served first in stores when white customers were present, were forced to wait patiently to be spoken to by white clerks rather than dare to address them first, and could be ignored and denied service entirely. In August 1919, the *Chicago Whip* reported an incident where Viola Penn was ignored while trying to make a purchase in the dress goods department of Marshall Field and Company. "The matter," the paper wrote, was taken up "with the management of the store to find out why out people cannot spend the coin of the realm in their establishment. The proper city and state authorities have also been appealed to. Miss Penn, personally, intends to bring suit against the firm."[91] In Baltimore, Stewart's was known for accepting African American trade in some of its departments, but refused it in others. In 1929, a reporter for the *Afro-American* was sent to investigate complaints that Stewart's discriminated against black female shoppers. In the linen and furniture departments, the reporter was attended to quickly and efficiently. However, in the lingerie department, the reporter experienced tremendous difficulty securing the attention of a salesgirl: "No matter at what section of the counter the reporter went, the sales girls immediately moved in another direction and became extremely busy." Determined to be waited on and make a purchase, the reporter took up station next to a white customer. Within a few minutes, "a salesgirl approached and offered to wait on the white customer." Graciously, the white customer declined her assistance, replying that she was already being helped. The reporter, seeing that the salesgirl was available to assist customers, asked to see the nightgowns, to which the salesgirl replied "I'm busy" as she walked away. In a final attempt to be served, the reporter approached the floorwalker for help getting a salesgirl's assistance. The floorwalker informed the reporter that he would not be able to help as "we expect to be busy all the afternoon."[92]

Service, however, was only one of the ways that department stores reinforced race hierarchies. Several stores engaged in activities such as staging minstrel shows that celebrated the romanticized racial roles of the antebellum South. Most major retailers also peddled racially derogatory merchandise, particularly toys, that, like minstrelsy and advertisements for pancake mix, soap, and other domestic products of this era, stereotyped and commodified black bodies and buttressed white supremacy. In 1921 and 1922, respectively, Sears sold the "Famous Alabama Coon Jigger" toy and the "Colored Minstrel Boys, Oh, What Music" toy. The "Alabama" toy was described as "a realistic dancing negro who goes through the movements of a lively jig. Very amusing and fascinating." The "Minstrel Boys" toy portrayed "two coons with exaggerated head and foot movement of real darkies." In 1924, the Sears catalog introduced the "Aunt Jemima Doll with Ma-Ma Voice." The catalog described the doll as dressed in a "costume of floral pattern cotton material with a large white apron and color; also red bandanna and Aunt Jemima label." The sale of racially offensive products continued well into the 1930s. One of these products was the "Chicken Snatcher"—a figure of a "scared looking negro" that danced with "a chicken dangling in his hand and a dog hanging on the seat of his pants."[93]

Providing inequitable service and selling offensive goods may well have been rooted in fears that consumption would enable African Americans to transcend their station by purchasing their way into a seeming equality with whites. Through consumption, African Americans could reject racist stereotypes and their subservient position in society, reinvent themselves as middle class, and challenge social boundaries. There is evidence that the department store, in particular, could inadvertently assist in this process. In the early twentieth century, as a result of migration, urbanization, and war, more African Americans secured better jobs and, in turn, had expendable income. This, along with the extension of credit, such as charge accounts and installment credit, increased the number of individuals that could access the new consumer market and maximized store profits. With credit, even the working class could purchase goods on time—small, regular payments made weekly, biweekly, or monthly. Just about anything could be purchased on credit—clothing, rugs, clocks, bedding, dishes, kitchenware, sewing machines, and furniture. For some black consumers, the ability to purchase goods that they otherwise would not be able to afford provided them with feelings of pleasure, affluence, and importance. These expectations of department store consumption mirrored those held by whites but had a special valence for a historically demeaned and degraded people.

But with credit came credit default. During this period, credit defaults began to characterize the buying habits of both white and black consumers. (Charge accounts, however, were not fully extended to African Americans until the credit equality campaigns of the 1960s and 1970s.) Consumers often found themselves victims of usurious interest rates and debt that threatened any efforts to better their class position or achieve financial independence. The ease with which consumers could purchase goods on time "naturally minimized [sic] the importance of the price."[94] Many consumers were unable to make payments and were subsequently harassed by collection agencies. For example:

> A Negro woman was employed as [a] cook in the home of a doctor. She agreed to pay $39.75 for a coat and then failed to keep her contract. A collector for the "instalment credit" store telephoned to the doctor concerning the failure of his cook to pay her bill. The doctor, angered by the tone of the voice of the collector, told him that his cook didn't have to pay for the coat, because the price they had forced her to agree to pay was entirely too high. The collector then threatened to telephone the doctor every fifteen minutes until the coat was paid for. After his telephone had jingled almost constantly for two or three days, the doctor, in his desperation, paid for the coat.[95]

While in this instance the consumer was bailed out by her employer, others were not so lucky. Many were frightened or compelled by collection experts to make some sort of monthly payment, often forgoing paying for daily essentials, had their purchases repossessed by the store, or faced criminal charges.[96]

Nonetheless, many whites feared that the department store might offer African Americans the means to undermine white supremacy. Women of different races could meet in the street wearing the same hat or dress, while men might meet driving the same vehicle.[97] A saleswoman working in a New York City department store recounted the following story:

> You know there are a lot of rich Negroes in this town and they are adopting the customs of whites and sometimes they go them one better. One day the wife of a rich colored lawyer came in to order some paper napkins to use at picnics at her country place and she asked me to have her monogram engraved on them. I had never had any monogrammed paper napkins ordered before but I thought it a good idea so when—I'll call her Mrs. Reginald Whitford of Park Avenue—came in to get some paper napkins for her yacht, I suggested the monogram to her. "What a splendid idea!" she said right away, delighted, and ordered a couple of thousand. I had a good laugh all to myself after she went out. I wondered what she'd say if she knew that she was imitating colored society.[98]

One could only imagine Mrs. Whitford's horror if she ever learned of this story. Such stories alarmed white shoppers, often leading them to demand harsher racial codes as a result. Meanwhile, stores, fearing that white customers would not patronize a fully integrated store, restricted blacks' access to their space. In the 1920s and 1930s, as African Americans migrated en masse to urban centers and pursued higher standards of living, a group of white women successfully pressured Baltimore stores to discourage African American trade. Walter Sondheim, manager of Hochschild-Kohn, reasoned that "we lose some of our best white trade, especially in the shoe, hat, and dress departments, and we have taken this step as a business proposition and decided that it would be best from this standpoint, not to encourage colored customers."[99] Such policies, which stores continually insisted were in response to the demands of their desired clientele, remained in effect well into the 1960s.

As stores responded to pressure from racist white customers, African Americans complained that salesclerks were "acting funny." Stores that initially desired black patronage were now singing a different tune. Hutzler Brothers originally permitted upper-class African Americans to charge their purchases. By 1915, however, it determined that it was undesirable to do so and began the process of "getting rid of those accounts which are at present used by their colored patrons." In 1925 black customers experienced difficulty being served at Hochschild-Kohn. One patron took some photographic film to be developed and was told that they were not handling the film of "colored people." Another customer, who wanted to match a bit of lace, was told it was not in stock, although the customer could see it herself on the shelf. Hochschild-Kohn management explained that the store "had just developed to the place where it was more profitable to dispense with their colored trade. They have been raising the standard of their products and catering to a more prestigious clientele."[100]

Many retailers hardened the physical racial boundaries in their facilities. One Baltimore department store opposed holding a Christmas carnival because the presence of large crowds of black shoppers would hurt business.[101] Others banished African American shoppers to the much less glamorous bargain basement, which sold merchandise that some patrons regarded as "gaudy and in bad taste." Often the merchandise was poorly made and of inferior materials. For example, "low-grade woods were often stained to resemble mahogany and walnut, silver content was sometimes less than claimed, and fabrics were given names such as 'linon' that could mislead the unwary or semiliterate."[102] In 1916 Marshall Field's in Chicago ordered that African Americans be treated with "'indifference' whenever they made their appearance as prospective buyers on the main floor or above and were to be directed to the basement by all sales-persons as the most likely place where they could find the articles they desired to purchase." It furthered ordered that salesclerks show black patrons "'inattention' and treat them in a manner indicative of the fact that their trade was not desired."[103] By relegating African Americans to the basement, stores were able to maintain the racial order and segregate their customers in the same manner as their workers. These basements also ensured that African Americans could not consume in the same way or purchase the same goods as whites of the same class. Such discriminatory policies ultimately guaranteed that white customers would continue to patronize stores and white supremacy would continue to reign.

Some stores went so far as to exclude African Americans entirely from the white selling space. Hecht Company, based in the Baltimore-Washington area, designated certain stores for blacks to shop. Before the 1940s, the Hecht's on Baltimore and Pine Streets was the only Hecht's store at which African Americans were permitted to shop. In what were deemed "white-only" department stores in Baltimore, African Americans could make purchases only on behalf of their white employer. At Hochschild-Kohn, blacks were permitted to shop only when they were in their domestic uniform; they could shop for their master and mistress but not for themselves.[104] At other Baltimore stores, all African Americans were forbidden from entering the store. Instead, they had to provide a list of items to a store employee at the entrance. The store employee would retrieve the items and bring them to the black customer at the door. This was often the process when a black maid shopped for the white family for whom she worked.[105]

In an effort to avoid degrading treatment and merchandise, many African Americans patronized black-owned department stores and purchased goods from mail-order companies. Black-owned department stores welcomed African Americans; they did not simply tolerate them like the majority of their white counterparts. In these stores, African Americans could purchase from vast stocks of high-grade, reasonably priced merchandise and receive courteous, fair customer service. The Saint Luke Emporium offered a "complete line of up-to-date stock direct from the New York market," while the Sandy W. Trice & Company Department Store carried "a complete line of ladies' and gents' furnishings, hats, caps, shoes, underwear, ribbons, laces, notions and dry goods."[106] They also likely sold "colored dolls," "colored" books, and other products that promoted black pride and consciousness among black children.[107] The A. I. Hart & Company comprised more than thirty departments, each of which was artistically and attractively arranged. It also maintained a luncheonette—an amenity African Americans were forbidden to patronize in white-owned stores. The luncheonette provided customers with a space to take a break from hours of strenuous shopping and grab a hot meal, a light lunch, a cold drink, or some ice cream.[108]

Black-owned department stores catered to their clientele and attempted, within their limited budgets, to create an air of luxury comparable to that of their white counterparts. But in reality, the success of these establishments lay in their treatment of black customers. They extended simple decency to these customers—something white-owned stores insisted was reserved only for whites. In these black-owned enterprises, African Americans were addressed by their appropriate titles, permitted to try on and return clothes, and extended credit. They were not required to wait until all of the white customers had been served before a salesclerk approached them. Rather, they were served in the order in which they arrived at the counter. And, graciously and patiently, salesclerks showed customers articles that they desired and suggested others that they believed would appeal to customers.

For all of this, black-owned department stores experienced several years of success. However, their success was short-lived. Stiff opposition and competition from white merchants, the lack of capital black businessmen had at their disposal, and blacks' habit of spending their paycheck in white stores proved detrimental to these establishments. For example, when the Saint Luke Emporium opened, efforts were made to cripple the business. A white Retail Dealers' Association was formed for the purpose of hindering the store's operations. It warned wholesale merchants in Richmond and as far away as New York City not to sell to the Emporium at the risk of losing the business of the city's white merchants. It also charged that the Emporium was underselling Richmond's white merchants. Perhaps the Emporium would have weathered this storm if local blacks had not been "so wedded to those who oppress him." The Emporium aimed to expand economic opportunities in the African American community. Yet black people continued to patronize stores that disrespected them and "increasingly hired white women as salesclerks and secretaries, while blacks were without employment and the black community as a whole was losing resources, skills, and finances."[109] The Emporium eventually closed its doors in 1912.

A. I. Hart & Company met the same fate. Harlem's African Americans, like their southern brethren, likely favored the selection and prestige that accompanied shopping at Macy's and Abraham and Strauss. Such that, in 1923, after seven years in business, the store stood on the verge of "pass[ing] out [of] our hands, unless it receives a larger share of our patronage." The *New York Amsterdam News* pleaded with its readers to "go there TODAY and buy something you need now or which you will need in the future." Fervently, it argued that "the success of this store will reflect credit upon every Colored person in this community, and upon the entire Race, and for this reason it should not be permitted to fail or to pass into other hands."[110] Similarly, A. I. Hart, the store's president, appealed to blacks' sense of racial advancement and community and asked them to see their individual success as being intricately intertwined with that of the community: "We need more Negro stores. We can't have them unless we create them. After creation we can't keep them unless we maintain them. To succeed we must do what other races have done, and are doing, giving preference to their own, first, last, and all the time."[111] Unfortunately, these pleas fell on deaf ears. The store fell into bankruptcy and closed in 1924.[112]

Black consumers, however, share only part of the blame for the failure of these businesses. The historian Lizabeth Cohen argues that "the causes of black business failure lay much deeper, in the insurmountable economic barriers that kept black entrepreneurs from competing viably." Black businessmen often lacked the capital needed to compete with chain department stores. Often these men secured loans from black-owned banks. But these banks were unable to provide the larger loans and resources that white-owned banks could extend to their patrons. With limited capital, black-owned department stores were unable to offer customers the credit that a chain department store typically gave its clientele, to expand and maintain a large and diverse stock of goods and keep prices low, or simply to remain competitive with other stores. All of this likely drove African American customers to shop elsewhere.[113]

Shopping through the mail presented African Americans with another way to evade the tensions, fears, and humiliations of visiting a white-owned store. Shopping in catalogs and ordering goods from Chicago mail-order houses like Montgomery Ward and Sears, Roebuck, and Company allowed African Americans to consume without white knowledge and control. For African Americans residing in the rural South, this was particularly important. Often these individuals lived a great distance from a department store and were usually paid in scrip, redeemable only at plantation stores. So, although few southern African Americans had the means to buy much from the catalogs, when they did save enough cash to make a purchase, mail-order catalogs allowed black agricultural workers to avoid the debts and indignities of racist plantation stores.[114]

Catalogs opened another world to these consumers, whereby they could experience the fun, romance, and extensive selection of goods that characterized shopping in urban palaces of consumption. A photograph taken by Marion Post Wolcott illustrates the power of the mail-order catalog: on Good Hope Plantation, located in the Mississippi Delta, in 1939, three children sit in a relatively well-decorated and furnished room in what appears to be a shack. Two of these children, a boy and a girl, study a catalog. I can only imagine that these children—much as I remember doing as a child when the Sears and J.C. Penney Christmas catalogs came in the mail—entered a fantasy. They could imagine themselves playing with dolls equipped with a pulley system, an electric train set, or a View-Master, or fantasize about wearing a new, stylish outfit. Perhaps these catalogs instilled the dream and motivation to escape the agricultural regime that limited their parents' lives.[115]

For many, shopping in black-owned stores and from mail-order catalogs provided them with viable, cost-effective alternatives to being subjected to discriminatory treatment in white-owned department stores. But these alternatives did not hold the same meaning, nor did they foster the same feelings that accompanied shopping in these palaces of consumption. Consequently, many blacks pursued more extreme—and even clandestine— means to engage the world of luxury, happiness, and possibilities promised to department store shoppers. Some fabricated cover stories that they were shopping on behalf of the white family for whom they worked in hopes of getting better service. Others passed as white to shop. Passing was considered justifiable when done for the "thrill of it all"—to shop, to sleep, or to eat meals at racially exclusive establishments—and without any intention of permanently forsaking the race. In this capacity, passing was often "looked upon as having fun at the white folks' expense," as a way of flouting absurd and unjust laws, and as a means of exercising choice (a freedom that, if black, was limited as a result of race discrimination and segregation).[116]

Jessie Redmon Fauset's novel *Plum Bun: A Novel without a Moral* (1928), and other Harlem Renaissance novels, honestly depicts the realities of passing in the consumer sphere. Mattie Murray, the mother of the black female protagonist, "employed her colour very much as she practised certain winning usages of smile and voice to obtain indulgences which meant much to her and which took nothing from anyone else." Murray's passing is attributed to her passion for consumption: She "loved pretty clothes, she liked shops devoted to the service of women; she enjoyed being even on the fringe of a fashionable gathering. A satisfaction that was almost ecstatic seized her when she drank tea in the midst of the modishly gowned women in a stylish tea-room. . . . She had no desire to be of these people, but she liked to look on; it amused and thrilled and kept alive some unquenchable instinct for life which thrived within her."[117]

Others viewed passing as a means of rejecting or simply seeking relief from the feelings of inferiority and suffocation that accompanied racism and sexism; it was considered a way of performing and holding, albeit momentarily, middle-class citizenship. For black women, in particular, passing offered respite from both the labors and drudgery of domestic and work spheres. White-only stores and restaurants were alluring because they functioned as stages where black women could perform and display their adherence to white bourgeois standards of beauty, femininity, gentility, respectability, and conspicuous consumption. John Jacob Oliver, great grandson of *Afro-American* founder John J. Murphy, recalled that his mother and sisters frequently passed to try on clothes in Baltimore department stores.[118] Similarly, Irene Redfield in Nella Larsen's *Passing* (1929) identifies as black and occasionally passes as white for "the sake of convenience, restaurants, theatre tickets," and other forms of amusement.[119] In one scene, Irene visits the white-only restaurant in the Drayton Hotel to find relief from the summer heat after a long day of shopping. Occurrences such as these compelled several stores to hire watchers to spot African Americans trying to pass and violate stores' strict racial boundaries and to ensure that these boundaries were upheld.

Affluent blacks, such as *Afro-American* publisher Carl Murphy, traveled great distances to shop at establishments that provided decent customer service. Murphy refused to patronize Baltimore department stores and endure the humiliations of their discriminatory policies. Instead, he and his family regularly traveled north to Philadelphia to shop at Strawbridge & Clothier, which did not subject its patrons of color to the humiliations of the final sale rule.[120] Philadelphia stores, including Wanamaker's and Strawbridge's, courted African American shoppers; they frequently took out advertisements in black newspapers and programs produced by middle-class black organizations.[121] Lit Brothers hired employees of all backgrounds and appealed to a more urban clientele. Other northern stores, such as the Simpson-Crawford department store in New York City, permitted their black clientele to try on clothes but directed them to do so at the back of the store.[122]

At one southern establishment, the proprietor made it a point to personally greet his customers—both black and white—by name as they entered the store. The proprietor insisted that his courtesy toward and respect for African Americans attributed to his establishment's popularity among blacks. Some southern merchants welcomed African Americans as customers because they considered them easier to handle than whites. According to these men, blacks entered the store knowing precisely what they wanted, rarely complained, and seldom made returns. But this should not imply that African Americans always left the store as satisfied customers. Black customers, aware of "their place," likely feared the consequences of protesting poor service or returning merchandise. Supporting this point are the comments of a shoe department manager in a southern department store. He stated: "I'd rather have Negro than white customers, they are so much easier satisfied. But if one of them ever gets fresh with me, I'll crack him over the head with a chair." Another southern establishment, while not openly courting African American customers, was more than willing to take their money and certainly did not want to lose their business. Such that when this store installed a drinking fountain and placed above it a sign that read "For White Patrons Only," it lost so many black patrons that the sign was quietly removed.[123]

In department stores, African American shoppers, like their white working-class counterparts, learned the limitations and potentials of the consumer sphere. They discovered that, on the most basic level, consumption offered material, physical, and psychological satisfaction and comfort. Simply put, it provided African Americans with a taste of the good life. Additionally, despite being mistreated and underserved in the retail industry, black consumers learned that their dollars were valued and powerful. Their dollars could undermine, and potentially dismantle, the racist structures on which American consumer culture and democracy were built and thrived. All together, consumption, department stores, and black purchasing power, which were just in their infancy in the first three decades of the twentieth century (compared to the civil rights era and thereafter), presented blacks with opportunities to imagine what could be. And what could be, they decided, was racial equality and economic advancement, which they sought to pursue.

· · · · · ·

The movie *It* ends in quintessential romantic-comedy fashion: Betty Lou and Cyrus Waltham passionately kiss on a yacht, signaling their reconciliation after a conflict that derived from a misunderstanding, of course, and Betty Lou's transition from working-class saleswoman to the future wife of a wealthy business owner. Given the romantic ending, the film is aptly set in a department store. For the better part of the twentieth century, department stores were major sites of not only work but also consumption, an activity that celebrated romantic desire, fantasy, and the acquisition of goods and services that shaped (or transformed) modern identity. And as subsequent chapters will show, they became sites of protest and contested identities as a result. These stores presented white workers, like the female protagonist in *It*, with opportunities to reinvent themselves and construct identities rooted in whiteness, citizenship, class, and gender. They were spaces where white customers, particularly those of the middle and upper classes, had their every wish anticipated and fulfilled, their race and class positions reaffirmed, and their troubles momentarily escaped. In these spaces, consumers attained some degree of power and freedom, though often fleeting.

African American workers and consumers, too, experienced the transformative effects of department stores. On the one hand, stores obeyed Jim Crow tenets and restricted the movement and participation of African Americans, deeming them virtually invisible and reaffirming their second-class citizenship. On the other hand, retailers encouraged black participation in the democracy of goods and, in the process, empowered African Americans to undermine white supremacy and imagine a middle-class life. Here, in this ambiguous and contradictory space, black collective action in the consumer sphere blossomed and subsequently facilitated the rise and shaped the direction of the department store movement specifically and the civil rights movement more broadly. These linked movements, as the next chapters will show, leveraged the growing black labor and consumer power and spotlighted the gross contradictions between the visions of democratic plenty for all and the reality of racial discrimination and segregation not only in these stores but across the nation. So, perhaps, it is no wonder that a department store seamstress named Rosa Parks initiated the Montgomery Bus Boycott in another notable site of consumption where blacks and whites met and shared a democratic vision, across a deep racial divide.

2 Before Montgomery

Organizing the Department Store Movement

· ·

Just as African Americans had gained a virtual monopoly on department store service operations and labor, which, despite being back-breaking, menial, and dirty, held the potential for upward mobility, the Great Depression weakened their hold on this niche in store functions. The Depression was a crisis of consumption, in the sense that falling consumer demand drove it. Thousands of black men and women found that their jobs in department stores as well as in other industries had, as the activist-educator Nannie Helen Burroughs lamented, "gone to machines, gone to white people, or gone out of style" as a result.[1] Black store workers were dismissed en masse or had their hours and wages severely reduced when storeowners endeavored to expand the number and kinds of jobs available to whites and to reduce operating costs by eliminating stock handling and maintenance jobs. One large department store in Chicago, for example, fired most of the black help employed in its laundry department, with the justification that it "wished to experiment with white help in the department." In 1931, a store in Toledo replaced its black elevator operators and stock girls with white women "because they [could] serve as clerks in an emergency"; and Richmond retailers fired their black drivers when they "discontinued their delivery service and entered into contracts with express companies to handle their packages." Likewise, in 1934, Miller & Rhoads department store discharged "forty-five colored girls . . . to make room for white girls who come out of high school with nothing to do." And when not being displaced, black workers were hired to replace higher-paid whites working in semiskilled or unskilled jobs. For example, in early 1930s Newark and Pittsburgh, black elevator operators supplanted whites, but at lower wages.[2]

The number of African Americans dismissed from department stores was less than those discharged from domestic and industrial jobs, but their dismissal was no less significant. For African American store workers, termination begot the loss of social status as well as financial instability, eliminated any prospect for upward mobility, and diminished black communities formed at work. Consequently, these assaults on black store workers rippled through the African American community. Blacks working in department stores, many believed, was a sign of progress, reflected positively on the race as a whole, and increased the circulation of black dollars in black neighborhoods and institutions. Others believed that the loss of these jobs meant that they themselves would never escape drudgework and gain "cleaner" employment befitting their education and skill, even if only to a small degree. This was particularly important considering that African Americans now residing in the North and West were becoming more educated. While black children in the South were forcibly discouraged from attending school and instead pressured to work in the fields until the crops were harvested, in the North and West they were encouraged to attend school regularly and for the entire academic year. Moreover, the Great Migration attracted the better educated, including southern teachers and college students.[3] Although some of these migrants stayed only during summer months, many permanently relocated.

It is not surprising, then, that the firing of black store workers was met with anger and frustration in the larger community. These sentiments intensified as the Depression continued to hamper employment prospects for African Americans and white merchants ossified their refusal to hire blacks for white-collar positions. With their rapid migration out of the rural South and expanding presence in the urban marketplace during the first half of the twentieth century, African American communities turned their frustration into action, adroitly leveraging their growing consumer power to advance their socioeconomic condition. (The "Negro Market" and black purchasing power had grown to unprecedented levels with the Great Migration of southern blacks to compact communities in northern cities.) But instead of fighting to regain their menial jobs, they organized mass consumer campaigns—the "Don't Buy Where You Can't Work" movement and later the department store movement—that leveraged black purchasing power to secure better jobs in sales and office work. The "Don't Buy" movement built on an earlier tradition of black consumer boycotts, such as those waged against Jim Crow streetcars in the South in the late nineteenth and early twentieth centuries.[4] The movement encouraged African Americans to withhold their dollars from white businesses in urban black neighborhoods, including but not limited to retail establishments, that discriminated against workers of color. It also urged blacks to spend their dollars at black-owned businesses, whose success was expected to translate into new avenues for black employment and a separate black economy.

The department store movement of the 1940s and 1950s was an outgrowth of this Depression-era campaign, and it would be shaped by New Deal and wartime programs in turn. While it built on the tactics, goals, and momentum of its predecessor, the later movement targeted department stores exclusively. These stores were now not only symbols of American democracy and prosperity but also inherently public spaces where all the races, genders, and classes might confront each other daily, and consequently where conflict and its eventual resolution would be most visible. This movement employed confrontational protest tactics such as picketing and boycotts as well as quiet meetings with and the exertion of subtle pressure on retailers to combat employment and consumer discrimination and demonstrate how this public sphere, despite being an ostensibly democratizing space for white people of different classes and backgrounds, was blatantly undemocratic for blacks.

Historians have overwhelmingly argued that the black middle class drove the goals and agenda of the "Don't Buy" movement, and similar conclusions might be made about the department store movement, since middle-class blacks were its most conspicuous and outspoken leaders. August Meier and Elliot Rudwick have insisted that because of this leadership, "Don't Buy" movements were "imbued with a petit bourgeois black business philosophy" and "devoted their efforts to securing [white-collar] jobs for blacks in white-owned firms, yet ideologically they often placed equal or even primary emphasis on creating 'bigger and better Negro business.'"[5] Similarly, the department store movement aimed to place trained and educated African Americans in sales and clerical positions, both to prove that whites and blacks could work side by side without conflict and to provide an emerging new black bourgeoisie with jobs and material goods that conferred status and prestige to the individual and the entire community.

The class character of these movements, however, was far more complicated than it might appear on the surface. While the cleavage between the working and middle classes lessened during the Depression, the "jobs sought were in reality thoroughly working-class, service-sector positions," but they could be secured only by African Americans who were exemplars of middle-class respectability. Furthermore, while it is true that some "Don't Buy" leaders focused on black-owned businesses, most participants in this movement, as well as those in the department store movement, "saw the campaign as an attack on racism in the labor market and on the indignities that black customers, many of them working class, suffered at the hands of white clerks."[6] As such, both the "Don't Buy" movement and its department store successor appealed to and mobilized the leadership and participation of African Americans from all classes and backgrounds, in support of the goal of dismantling the racial and economic barriers that circumscribed *all* black lives, albeit to varying degrees, and uplifting members of the race and the race itself. These movements were primarily initiated by and for African Americans who aspired to "get ahead" and "live respectable"—characteristics that have historically been attributed to those of or seeking to be middle class but also shared by members of the working class.[7] The "Don't Buy" movement, even more than the department store movement, thus, helped solidify middle-class blacks' class position and facilitated working-class and poor blacks' ascent.

The "Don't Buy Where You Can't Work" Movement

As early as 1919, African Americans responded to the loss of occupational gains won during the First World War with small, targeted consumer boycotts. But it was the Great Depression that aggravated black unemployment and inspired an even more intense and widespread black consumer activism, which came to be known as the "Don't Buy Where You Can't Work" movement. The movement grew out of African Americans' long-standing grievance that white merchants in segregated black neighborhoods monopolized black retail trade but hired African Americans only to perform menial labor. Many retailers insisted that neither white customers nor white salespeople would accept black sales and office workers, while others insisted that African Americans were not qualified to perform white-collar work in any case. Some activists sought to disavow these misconceptions, but overall, as the writer Richard Durham noted, the "aim was not to obtain a proportionate political representation, nor to break down social barriers; it was a much simpler one—to secure the right for Negroes to work in the community in which they lived."[8] Simply put, the "Don't Buy" movement aimed to nurture black economic independence and stability.

The movement had its first expression in Chicago in the spring of 1929, when Bishop Conshankin, later known as Sufi Abdul Hamid by Harlem consumer activists, crafted a new protest strategy to challenge employment discrimination in Bronzeville—one that was economic, visual, and confrontational. According to one scholar, while this black enclave was reputed to have more black-owned businesses than any other place in the country, white merchants in the area "monopolized over 90 percent of black retail trade, yet with rare exception failed to employ black workers in their establishment outside an occasional janitor or porter." Conshankin's strategy combined the traditional consumer boycott with picketing and sit-ins to draw attention to this injustice, build group morale, and yield quick results. It stopped customers from shopping by making crossing a picket line or sit-in a public display of race betrayal, while damaging the stores' sales revenue and image.[9]

Within two months, Conshankin's movement opened up over three hundred jobs to black Chicagoans and attracted the attention of the racially militant newspaper the *Chicago Whip*. Although the *Whip* was impressed by Conshankin's protest strategy, it was unwilling to work with the leader, because his "unconventional dress, unorthodox religion, abrasive tongue, and roughhouse style of picketing (which included an occasional brick through a store window)"—the antithesis of black respectability—"was not to the liking of the [paper's] young middle class leaders." Moreover, his "growing popularity with the grassroots unemployed represented a threat to the *Whip*['s] . . . ambition to become the new [spokesman] for black Chicago."[10]

So, in the summer of 1929, the newspaper, adopting Bishop's approach, organized a community-wide coalition of over two hundred civic, social, fraternal, and religious associations and successfully waged campaigns with the slogan "Don't Buy Where You Can't Work." The *Whip*, according to editor Joseph D. Bibb, believed that "an impoverished people could get little out of politics unless the finances of [the] race could underwrite political campaigns in their districts." It thus conceived of the "Don't Buy" movement as a means of "get[ting] more money in our districts" and ending the "mean, vicious cycle that left us in an anomalous condition."[11]

Between 1929 and 1931,[12] the *Whip*'s "Don't Buy" campaign secured thousands of new, mostly white-collar and skilled jobs at five-and-dime stores, department stores, grocery stores, movie houses, restaurants, coal yards, dairy companies, and public works.[13] Notable victories were made at Woolworth's (which hired twenty-one African American girls and women at its 51st Street location in October 1930; within one year, 25 percent of all female employees at Woolworth's on the South Side were black), Walgreens, and Sears.[14] News of this movement's success captured the attention of black America, and before long, the movement spread to cities where black southern migrants had settled, creating significant centers of consumer power, including Cleveland, Detroit, New York, Washington, D.C., Baltimore, Los Angeles, St. Louis, Oakland, and even the southern cities of Richmond and Newport News, Virginia.[15] All of these job campaigns, although sporadic in nature and ideologically diverse, were nonetheless linked in their rec- ognition of the importance of the public sphere and the marketplace in advancing the black economic condition.[16]

By the early 1930s, the "Don't Buy" movement was aided further by the New Deal—a series of programs implemented by President Franklin D. Roo- sevelt's administration that sought to resuscitate the economy by vindicat- ing the rights of labor and legitimating labor organizing by way of the National Industrial Recovery Act in 1933 and the National Labor Relations Act in 1935. These acts effectively made consumption a political project by encouraging and empowering American consumers to spend. Informed by Keynesian economics, the New Deal sought to remedy the economic downturn by injecting money back into the economy. The "government . . . play[ed] a major role in fueling aggregate demand—through such strate- gies as job programs, public works, [and] progressive tax policies—and thereby raise[d] the level of production and employment," according to historian Lizabeth Cohen. "The Keynesian revolution," she concludes, made "consumers . . . [responsible] for high productivity and full employ- ment, whereas a decade earlier that role had uncontestedly belonged to producers."[17]

The "Don't Buy" movement has been credited with integrating white- collar work in department stores in black communities. And it certainly did. But these neighborhood stores were neither distinct nor special, as they often resembled five-and-dime stores rather than the grand emporiums that marked downtown retail scenes. They fit the classification of department store only in the broadest sense, maintaining a variety of departments where they sold apparel and accessories for the entire family, home furnishings, appliances, and even groceries. Because they catered to African Americans of all classes, and not just middle- and upper-class whites, the neighborhood stores often lacked the grandness and glamour that characterized their downtown counterparts. They were simply among the many white-owned retail establishments that profited from black dollars while refusing to hire black clerks.

Nevertheless, in the economic crisis of the 1930s, department stores became ideal sites of protests. Stores in virtually all locations struggled to get customers to spend money, while trying to "[uphold] their image of bastions of luxury." They tried numerous tactics to counter declining sales and profits: they increased expenditure on advertising and promotional schemes, modernized and expanded facilities, standardized operations and cut payrolls, lowered prices, and "stud[ied] their markets and [made] preliminary adaptions to suburbanization and the automobile." Additionally, historian Vicki Howard theorizes, "it must have seemed even more imperative to satisfy those willing and able to spend money and maintain customer loyalty. This could mean taking a large step to overturn structural inequality through reform of hiring practices, or it could be as minor as changing personal behavior."[18]

One of the "Don't Buy" movement's most publicized department store initiatives involved Kaufman's Department Store in Washington, D.C. In December 1933, after a successful boycott that forced the white-owned Hamburger Grill to rehire three black workers who had been replaced by whites, the New Negro Alliance (NNA) had set its sights on Kaufman's at 1316 7th Street N.W. The NNA was a newly formed organization of "young, college-educated blacks dissatisfied with the listless performance of established civil rights groups during the Depression."[19] During the Christmas shopping season, the organization picketed the storefront for nine hours each day, reducing trade by one-third. Seeking to halt the demonstration, store owner Harry Kaufman secured a temporary injunction on December 20 that prohibited the NNA's picketing. However, no sooner than the court order was issued than the white Young People's Socialist League (YPSL) and the League for Industrial Democracy (LID) replaced the NNA protesters, carrying signs that read "Negroes do not buy where you cannot work" and "Jobs, Jobs, Jobs." Kaufman immediately returned to court and had the injunction amended to restrain the NNA from "conspiring with, aiding or abetting" the YPSL and LID.[20]

In early January 1934, Kaufman sought a permanent injunction. Standing before the U.S. District Court for Washington, D.C., he tapped into white fears about integration and charged that the NNA insisted that he dismiss "many" of his white employees and hire "alliance-chosen" black workers. The NNA, he further testified, also demanded that the department store "place behind its sales counter colored and white employees working side by side, without regard to the natural and inevitable result of such a situation." But as the historian Paul Moreno notes, Kaufman "exaggerated" the scope of the NNA's demands. The NNA only wanted the retailer to "return in employment to the black community what it took in revenue," which it understood would challenge segregation and produce an integrated workforce. However, the organization never demanded "a specific percentage or quota for black employment"; in fact, it deliberately tried to "[avoid] the contentious tactic of 50 or 100 percent demands and the displacement of incumbent white workers."[21]

While Kaufman appealed to the court on the basis of a threat to the existing racial order, the NNA tackled the injunction from a different angle: it argued that its campaign and tactics were legal and legitimate. NNA attorneys Belford V. Lawson, Thelma D. Ackiss, and William Henry Hastie contended that race discrimination was an assault on organized labor and therefore the Kaufman demonstration was inherently a "labor dispute" as defined and protected under the Norris-LaGuardia Anti-Injunction Act of 1932. The Norris-LaGuardia Act broadly defined a "labor dispute" as "any controversy concerning terms or conditions of employment . . . regardless of whether or not the disputants stand in the proximate relation of employer and employee."[22] To this, Kaufman's attorney cited legal cases settled before the passage of the Norris-LaGuardia Act and argued that employer-employee relationships did not exist between the NNA and the retailer.[23] In the end, the court sided with Kaufman and issued a permanent injunction in early January 1934. The NNA asked the District of Columbia Court of Appeals to review the decision but it declined.[24]

Over the next few years, the NNA continued to picket stores and had some success. But race discrimination continued at Kaufman's until the U.S. Supreme Court's 1938 *New Negro Alliance v. Sanitary Grocery Company* decision. That verdict expanded the legal definition of "labor dispute" to include conflicts involving race and color discrimination in employment. It not only endorsed but also reinvigorated black consumer protests in American cities.[25] Almost immediately thereafter, many white retailers became more willing to compromise with civil rights activists rather than be subjected to disruptive boycotts and picket lines. Kaufman's Department Store hired two African American clerks but, to the dismay of the NNA, required that they also perform the menial tasks of "[relieving] the elevator operator and pressing articles for the window display." As a result, the organization renewed its pressure in an effort to end such employment discrimination. Subsequently, in 1939, Kaufman's promised to hire an African American man as a shipping clerk. Other stores on 7th Street, including Leventhal's and Oxenburg's department stores, also began using black clerks in 1938 and 1939. By 1940, according to the NNA, every store located within this business district employed at least one African American clerk.[26]

But who were these black pioneers who integrated the District's sales forces? Existing historical employment records do not reveal their identities, but the composition of the city's black population provides some insight. Washington's African American community was highly educated and accomplished: in 1930 it included 273 ecclesiastics, 95 college professors, 303 teachers, 191 physicians, 98 lawyers, and 173 trained nurses. Other evidence suggests the likelihood that some of these individuals were unable to pursue the professional work for which they were trained because of discriminatory hiring practices, while others were the offspring of these black professionals and desired white-collar work that matched their and their family's education and position.[27]

An examination of the alliance membership also suggests that those hired as salesmen and saleswomen were college bound or college educated. The NNA invited all Washingtonians of color, regardless of class and color distinction, to participate, but it was, in essence, an organization of upper- and middle-class African Americans. Some of its early members included attorneys Belford Lawson, William H. Hastie (a future federal judge), Charles Houston (who led early desegregation efforts that led to the *Brown v. Board of Education* decision), and Robert Weaver (a future federal cabinet secretary for housing and urban development); Howard University faculty members Jesse W. Lewis and Howard Naylor Fitzhugh; and local businessmen Eugene Davidson and R. Grayson McGuire Jr. Other supporters came from the black church, the African American–owned newspaper *Washington Tribune*, prominent black Washingtonians and national leaders, local homemakers, black fraternities and sororities, and small community groups. Another notable backer was the D.C. branch of the National Association for the Advancement of Colored People (NAACP), although it refused to sanction picketing or actively cooperate.[28]

Not all black Washingtonians supported the NNA or the D.C. "Don't Buy" movement, however. During the NNA's early years, Howard University professors Ralph Bunche and Abram L. Harris chastised the organization "for a narrow 'radicalism' and a failure to understand that the race's economic salvation lay in an alliance with white labor"; they demanded its immediate dissolution. The organization responded by modifying its ideology: it denied that its primary interest was to create a black capitalist class, abandoned its ideas of creating a separate black economy, and embraced instead the goal of integrating African Americans into the economy. The NNA also set out to cultivate working alliances with local unions and white socialist groups.[29]

The alliance also sometimes had difficulty obtaining the support of rank-and-file members of Washington's black community. Harold Lewis, a professor at Howard University, once recounted that while collecting petition signatures against a downtown department store he encountered an African

American woman who refused to back the movement. Her reasons were not ideological but rather practical and self-serving. "No, indeed," she exclaimed, "I'm not going to sign any petition. They are the only ones that sell the type of shoe I wear."[30] This woman's refusal to participate likely reflected the opinion of others. Perhaps this woman viewed the campaign as being of no personal benefit. Maybe she was of the lower class and recognized that she would not be hired as a sales or clerical worker at any of the retail establishments along 7th Street. Or possibly she was of the middle class and, like some Howard University faculty members, believed that the D.C., "Don't Buy" movement would alienate white Americans already supporting black advancement. In any event, she, among others, was not willing to prioritize this struggle over the immediate gratification received from the purchase of a wanted or needed item.

While the NNA's Kaufman Department Store campaign helped legalize the "Don't Buy" movement and its tactics, the 1934 Blumstein's Department Store boycott in Harlem is arguably the most notable "Don't Buy" department store protest. The first incarnation of the "Don't Buy" movement in Harlem ended as quickly as it began. In 1932, Sufi Abdul Hamid, formerly Bishop Conshankin, journeyed to New York after the disintegration of his Chicago movement, having started a similar one in Baltimore, Maryland, and organizing the black nationalist Negro Industrial and Clerical Alliance. The alliance was a diverse group "made up of unemployed high school and college youths, relief recipients, some hustlers, and people who did not have anything else to do," all of whom were committed to ending job discrimination in Harlem.[31] One of the alliance's first targets was F. W. Woolworth Company on 125th Street, a campaign that soon proved unsuccessful. According to August Meier and Elliot Rudwick, the Woolworth boycott was "generally ignored by the New York black weeklies and enjoy[ed] little support" and "disintegrated after four months when the police discouraged further demonstrations by arresting Hamid and fourteen followers."[32]

In 1934, the Harlem movement resurfaced and waged a successful campaign against Blumstein's Department Store at 230 West 125th Street, the largest department store in Harlem. The reemergence of Harlem's "Don't Buy" movement was not spontaneous; rather, it was the culmination of years of black resistance. During the 1920s, the *Amsterdam News*, the New York Urban League (NYUL), the NAACP, and the Harlem branch of the State Employment Service fought to increase the number of local jobs available to African Americans through quiet negotiations. This approach was not enough to persuade merchants, however. In 1931, the Harlem Housewives League, a black bourgeois organization that claimed a membership of over 1,000 women, visited with white merchants and requested that they hire African Americans proportionate to black patronage. In Harlem, whites owned 83 percent of the 1,200 stores, 59 percent of which employed only whites, and 24 percent of which employed blacks but only in menial positions.[33] Blumstein's eventually hired an African American doorman and elevator operator—although it is unclear whether it was the direct result of the Housewives' demands. Nevertheless, the Housewives League expressed its gratitude to the owner "for this recognition of the purchasing power of Negroes."[34]

These early initiatives were often unconcerned with the specific position or level of responsibility assigned to black workers. They were simply concerned with securing as many jobs for blacks as possible. The Housewives League's gratitude that Blumstein's hired black menial workers is just one example of this disposition. In the autumn of 1932, the Wanamaker Department Store in Philadelphia also hired black elevator operators to the applause of the *Philadelphia Tribune*, the local black newspaper and future leader in the city's "Don't Buy" movement: "Ordinarily, it is not a subject for a holiday when Negroes, or anybody else for that matter are employed as elevator operators; but in these times when as small a financial matter as three dollars a week often stands between wolf and starvation and some man's family, any kind of job is worthy of notice." Further, the paper noted, "when most white firms seem prone to disregard entirely the Negro trade they enjoy and dismiss Negroes without any logical reason, it is indeed refreshing to notice that at Wanamaker's the old traditions of the founder are in full swing."[35]

African Americans' demand for and acceptance of low-level retail work reveals their willingness to embrace any work, even the most menial, to meet their family's needs, their recognition of employment discrimination, and their belief that they lacked the resources or power to wage a successful battle for more prestigious jobs during the economic depression. It also suggests, however, that operating elevators or manning doors was not all bad. These positions were similar to that of Pullman Porters (African American men hired to work as porters on the sleeping cars for the Pullman Rail Car Company). They provided a steady income, were clean jobs (meaning that they did not involve manual labor), and could offer the trappings of middle-class respectability.

But Harlem's black elite, in particular, remained unsatisfied, as they were eager to secure status jobs in sales for themselves and their children. So, in February 1934, the newly formed Harlem Women's Association, a group of middle- and upper-class black women, set out to "determine in dollars and cents the amount of patronage given white stores on West 125th Street by Negroes" and to persuade store owners to hire African Americans.[36] With the assistance of Reverend John H. Johnson of the Saint Martin's Episcopal Church, the association subsequently formed the Citizens' League for Fair Play (CLFP).[37] The CLFP was a broad-based coalition of eighteen churches and forty-four of Harlem's political, social, religious, and business groups. These groups included the *New York Age*, the Unity Democratic Club, the Fusion-Republican Club, the Cosmopolitan Social and Tennis Club, Young West Indian Congress, Premier Literary Circle, and the New York Chapter of the Universal Negro Improvement Association (UNIA). Individual members included Fred Moore, editor of the *New York Age*; Ira Kemp, president of the African Patriotic League; Arthur Reid, a Garveyite from Barbados; Arthur A. Schomberg, curator of the New York Public Library's Negro Division; Reverend William Lloyd Imes of St. James Presbyterian Church; Attorney William Pickens, son of an NAACP executive; Florence Richardson, representing Harlem actors; and Bessy Bearden, a prominent social chronicler of Harlem's elite.[38] Hamid and his alliance never joined the CLFP. Their antiwhite slogans, black separatist ideology, and abrasive tactics had once again alienated those who wanted a "respectable" jobs campaign; as a result, Hamid and his alliance worked in tandem with but separate from the CLFP.

The CLFP was an organization with a range of individuals and groups that held differing political views; for example, some held nationalist political beliefs, while others advocated for integration. While these differences threatened conflict, everyone involved agreed that black employment was the primary goal and decided that Blumstein's Department Store should be their first target. In June 1934, the CLFP approached store owner Louis Blumstein and asked him to hire African American sales clerks. They presented him with receipts totaling $5,000, likely the result of the Harlem Women's Association survey, to remind him of the volume of black patronage, hoping to "convince [him] . . . to cooperate with the community in [the] crisis of depression and employ some of the jobless educated Negroes." He replied that he was already cooperating, as he had employed African Americans in menial positions and often made charitable contributions to the National Urban League (NUL). When activists pressed, however, Blumstein promised to consider hiring African Americans as sales clerks in the fall—the season when sales positions typically became available—but added that he currently had no need for any salesmen or saleswomen.[39]

Displeased, the CLFP adopted Hamid's approach and began picketing and boycotting Blumstein's. "Between 400 and 1,500 [Harlemites] attended any given weekly CLFP meeting, and the 'honor roll' of picketers included 58 men and 83 women who marched regularly," carrying "Don't Buy Where You Can't Work" signs and handing out leaflets that beseeched "all self-respecting people of Harlem" to support the campaign and take their business elsewhere.[40] Generally, picketers were respectful, peaceful, and orderly—the embodiment of a "respectable" job campaign. But some also embraced Hamid's more aggressive and intimidating tactics. One picketer recalled: "Half a dozen of us would watch for coloured shoppers coming out [of] Blumstein's, trail them to the corner, [taking and] destroying their purchases, and slap them around a little to teach them national pride. I suppose it was a bit gangsterism, but we lived in a gangster age." Other disreputable tactics included shouting derogatory remarks, dragging patrons out of the store by their hair, and photographing black shoppers coming out of Blumstein's and publishing their betrayal on the front page of the *New York Age*.[41]

By June, nearby retailers H. C. F. Koch Department Store and F. W. Woolworth and Company hired "some sixty" and thirty-five black sales workers, respectively, after witnessing the direction of the Harlem "Don't Buy" movement and fearing that they would be targeted next.[42] A couple of months later, in early August, Blumstein's finally capitulated and agreed to "take on fifteen" African Americans as clerks "between now and August 15th and twenty more in September."[43] Extant records suggest that the majority of these new hires were black women—which is not surprising given that department stores were woman-centric sites, that women played prominent roles in job boycotts, and that movement leaders envisioned young black women to be "the solution to the problem of employment discrimination."[44] Lizabeth Cohen notes, "Black female consumer activists of the 1930s [were] neither more black nor more female in their loyalties; they blended both. Feminist hopes for securing good salesclerk jobs for women and demonstrating female political solidarity were inseparable from the effort to improve working and living conditions for the race through 'direct spending.'"[45] Securing employment as a department store clerk, however, was sometimes complicated. On the one hand, it was exponentially

Negro Staff at Blumstein's

THE NEGRO MEMBERS of the sales staff at Blumstein's Department Store on 125th street, who are said to be making a fine record there, are shown above. They are front (left to right) Maxine Stackhouse, Gladys Coombs, Thelma Haylock, Mae Griffin, Mamin Morin, Virginia Pettiford, Vivian Hawkins, Cleonia Williams, Mae Santee. Back row, William Adams, Clarence Dudley, Kenneth Broadhurst, Zealand Green, Matthew Epps, Sadie Reed, Nora Stevenson, Carrie Warley, Robert Braddicks, Lucy Thomas, Muriel Miller, Margaret Johnson, Norris Williams, and (extreme rear) John Johnson.

FIGURE 5 "Negro Staff at Blumstein's," *New York Amsterdam News* (1922–1938), September 15, 1934.

better than "dirty" and low-paying domestic work (during the Depression, domestic servants earned anywhere from fifty cents a day to three dollars per week)[46] and more acceptable and reflective of an individual's intellectual abilities and skills. On the other hand, as one historian noted, clerking "was [not] entirely edifying or interesting"; instead, it was often "tedious and monotonous."[47]

Only a certain class and type of black woman was placed in these jobs, however. As writer and poet Claude McKay observed, "The girl breaking into [this work] may be a Harlem debutante. She is sure to belong to a professional family that looks askance at organized labor."[48] In other words, only the "best" women—those deemed to be exemplars of black respectability by movement leaders—were chosen to integrate department stores and represent and advance the race. These women were of the middle and upper classes, high school or college graduates, and active in the black freedom struggle but not involved in disruptive protest activities. (All of this is particularly striking given that white saleswomen typically hailed from the working class and held at most a high school diploma.)

The "best" hires also were those who conformed to European standards of beauty. In the autumn of 1934, a photograph of Blumstein's new sales workers—all of whom appeared to be white—was published in several black newspapers (figure 5). The *Baltimore Afro-American* commented, "Only a few girls can be distinguished as being colored. They are called 'pinks' and what a stir they have created! Not even the beautiful brown-skinned girls were included in the set-up."[49] The alliance's black nationalists—specifically Kemp, Reid, and Henry Veal—forcefully protested. They argued that darker-skinned black women had "actually done the picket work and made the openings," but only lighter-complexioned women reaped the benefits.[50] Kemp and Reid also accused Fred Moore of the *New York Age* of being the "ringleader of a group aiming at the exclusion of dark skinned Negro girls from employment opportunities in the shopping area of West 125th Street" and surmised that Moore and several other Leaguers handpicked the women hired by the department store. Moore and the CLFP vehemently disputed these charges, and even accused Kemp and Reid of discriminating against light-skinned and mulatto women.[51] But it turns out that Kemp and Reid may have been correct. More than thirty years after the Blumstein protest, in 1966, alliance leader Reverend Johnson confessed "that some members unofficially may have given Blumstein a list of names, but only as individuals, not as League members."[52]

Intraracial color discrimination underscores the role of class in the "Don't Buy" movements. Historically, skin color was a marker of economic and social status in the African American community.[53] Before the First Great Migration, the black class structure was largely divided into two groups: the old bourgeois and the working class. The old bourgeois was a small, educated class of professionals and businessmen tied to white patronage, often of white ancestry, and patrons of a lifestyle that imitated the tastes and values of upper- and middle-class whites. The black working class, however, comprised a broad array of laborers in agriculture and domestic and personal service, along with a small group of industrial workers. As African American southerners relocated en masse to the urban, industrial North in the early twentieth century, the black class structure was transformed. Although still based on achievement and respectability, black class status now depended much less on kinship or other contact with whites and was increasingly defined by the reinforcement and strengthening of racial boundaries formed by Jim Crow. Black class structure now consisted of a new bourgeois elite of small business owners and professionals of all complexions who earned their living catering to burgeoning, segregated black communities, followed by an extremely small stratum of artisans, public service employees, better-paid domestic and personal service employees such as headwaiters and porters, and a working class of common laborers and domestic and service workers.[54]

By the 1934 "Don't Buy" campaign, the black bourgeois in Harlem was more diverse but remained largely governed by its forefathers. The long-standing members of this privileged class were concerned that they and their offspring were often unable to secure employment appropriate to their high levels of education, ancestry, and class—coincidentally, all qualifications needed to secure white-collar work. This problem reached new proportions as the ranks of the black bourgeois grew between 1910 and 1930. But, as one scholar of black Philadelphia has argued, black newcomers from the rural South—from small entrepreneurs, especially those who earned their living by engaging the "underworld" to manual laborers—often lacked the education and respectability needed to compete for positions of responsibility in an urban economy and, even worse, in a depressed economy.[55]

These color and class dynamics certainly do not excuse the CLFP's color prejudice, but they explain the favoring of light-skinned and elite blacks for retail jobs by protest leaders drawn largely from that class. Further, because of this preferential treatment, an incalculable number of dark-skinned and middle- and working-class African Americans were relegated to perform the unskilled retail work abandoned by their light-skinned bourgeois counterparts. The Harlem "Don't Buy" movement, thus, facilitated the socio-economic ascension of educated and respectable New York blacks.

Color and class issues, as well as power struggles for control over the jobs campaign, eventually split the CLFP. The decisive blow was the New York Supreme Court's ruling in *A. S. Beck Shoe Corp v. Johnson* (1934) that the picketing was illegal, since it was "solely a racial dispute, born of the understandable desire on the part of some of the Negroes in this community that the stores in the neighborhood where they spend their money should employ a percentage of Negro help."[56] Not long thereafter, in early 1935, this incarnation of the Harlem "Don't Buy" movement effectively ended.

Worse yet, without the tactic of picketing and the disintegration of the CLFP, some of the movement's most hard-won triumphs disappeared. Blumstein's kept the first fifteen black women on staff but never hired the promised twenty in the fall of 1934. Koch's Department Store, which claimed sixty black sales workers in June 1934, employed only fifty-seven African Americans as salesclerks, stock clerks, porters, and elevator operators in August. Other 125th Street stores that had agreed to hire blacks reneged. And by early 1935, half of all African Americans who had won clerical jobs the previous year had been laid off.[57]

The collapse of the movement, coupled with mounting anger and frustrations about racial discrimination in the marketplace, came to a head in March 1935 when a sixteen-year-old black Puerto Rican boy was caught shoplifting a cheap penknife from S. H. Kress Five and Dime store on 125th Street. Rumor spread that the child was brutally beaten and killed, sparking a full-scale riot where approximately 10,000 people looted white-owned businesses on 125th Street, while sparing black-owned stores and white-owned stores that employed African Americans.[58]

Despite this brief detour from organized consumer activism, civil rights and labor organizations continued to push for jobs over the next three years, albeit acting separately. Black nationalist groups like the Harlem Labor Union and the Negro Industrial Clerical Alliance "turned the drive for black jobs increasingly into an explicitly anti-white campaign, often targeting particular white ethnic groups." The NYUL and the NAACP focused on litigation, letter writing, and quiet pressure to win jobs, while the Communist Party encouraged black and white working-class unity by demanding the hiring of blacks (without the firing of whites) at large chain stores and public utilities "rather than small family stores where racial antagonism might intensify and undermine class unity." These groups, however, won only small victories.[59]

The Harlem "Don't Buy" movement fully resurged in 1938 when the *New Negro Alliance* court ruling legalized the use of picketing to protest employment discrimination and Adam Clayton Powell Jr. and William Imes formed the broad-based Greater New York Coordinating Committee. The committee involved over 200 organizations and 170,000 members—over three times the number of the CLFP—and embraced the goals and tactics of nationalist and integrationist job efforts. The committee was similar to the CLFP in two particular ways: first, the committee was made up of educated and skilled members of the black middle class who provided much of its energy, strength, and political motivation and sought to open work commensurate with their qualifications and status; and second, the committee's movement was a mass movement of domestics, laborers, and service workers. Because of its broad approach and participation, the Greater New York Coordinating Committee succeeded in expanding work opportunities for African Americans in white-owned stores and New York public utilities, without displacing whites or undermining labor unions. Some of its victories included the placement of black nonmenial workers at A&P, Consolidated Edison, New York Telephone Company, the World's Fair Corporation, and every large store on 125th Street.[60]

As Harlem's "Don't Buy" movement regained its momentum, the Brooklyn movement was one year into its own rebirth. During the Christmas season of 1938, the Brooklyn YWCA, under the leadership of Anna Arnold Hedgeman, sent black female college students to apply for sales clerkships at borough department stores, hoping to persuade store officials to hire one or more blacks in positions traditionally reserved for whites. But officials refused. She then invited the young women to recount their experiences to the predominantly white Race Relations Committee of the Federation of Protest Churches in New York City. Standing "so poised" before the crowd, the women expressed their disappointment and frustration that, despite their preparation and qualifications, managers wanted to hire them only as maids. As the women spoke, the audience wept. "When they had finished their accounts of their visits," Hedgeman recalled, "there wasn't a dry eye in the room." The Race Relations Committee subsequently joined the Brooklyn campaign and sent a mixed-race delegation of churchwomen to lobby store management. When these visits did not produce the desired results, the churchwomen elected to employ their consumer power. The women, many of whom held large charge accounts, withheld their patronage from local stores and penned on their monthly bills: "We expect to see Negro clerks among the other clerks in our stores. As Christians we must patronize those stores which respect all human beings." The Brooklyn YWCA also received the support of the local Urban League and the NAACP. As a result, Abraham and Strauss, A.I. Namm and Sons, and Loeser's & Company, among others, hired black saleswomen.[61]

The Brooklyn movement may not have garnered as much attention, either contemporarily or scholarly, as other economic campaigns of the 1930s. Nevertheless, this movement is noteworthy for (1) its strong attention to department stores and (2) that it foreshadows the next direction of African American worker and consumer protests in its targets, timing (the holiday shopping season repeatedly proved to be a ripe time to pressure stores), gender dimensions, and in its ability to forge biracial alliances and leverage the powers of multiple civil rights and labor organizations to open the job market to African Americans.

The Second World War and the Emergence of the Department Store Movement

The "Don't Buy" movement succeeded in creating thousands of white-collar and skilled jobs for African Americans in businesses located in urban black neighborhoods, but its results were limited nonetheless because those businesses were unable to accommodate everyone in need of work, while the movement's ebbs and flows restricted its far-reaching potential. Consequently, the "Don't Buy" movement failed to substantially change the nature and character of America's labor force; the country remained largely segregated, and thousands of blacks remained un- or underemployed. In 1940, approximately 60 percent of African American women remained confined in domestic service, and an estimated 38 percent of African American men were employed as craft and kindred workers, operatives, and nonfarm laborers. A mere 6 percent of black workers labored in white-collar jobs, 2 percent of whom were in sales, clerical, and kindred positions.[62]

The department store movement, however, improved the situation, doubling the percentage of African Americans in white-collar occupations and almost quadrupling those in sales and clerical work by 1960.[63] The movement matured during the Second World War, as the global conflict created the conditions needed to expand African American job opportunities and integrate workplaces.[64] First, the federal government "moved consumption into the civil realm" and assumed a stronger role in regulating private transactions between consumers and retailers via price stabilization and consumer protection.[65] However, as blacks "enthusiastically" supported price and rent controls and rationing, "blatant inequit[ies] in the implementation and enforcement of OPA [Office of Price Administration] regulations" and persisting segregation and discrimination in the marketplace "left African Americans frustrated at the denial of their rightful protection and participation, as American citizens," and simultaneously provided firmer grounds on which to demand first-class citizenship.[66]

Second, the NUL, the NAACP, and other civil rights organizations became more mindful of the needs of working-class blacks, as a result of "criticism and competition from black radicals" and the burgeoning power of the Congress of Industrial Organizations and affiliated labor unions in the 1930s and 1940s, mobilization for World War II, and the growing and formidable presence of working blacks in their ranks.[67] They launched merit-hiring campaigns that built on the successes and limitations of the "Don't Buy" movement and capitalized on the country's need for all labor to support the war and on African Americans' increasing political and economic strength. Merit-hiring campaigns sought to place respectable blacks in visible and skilled jobs and divest whites of their racial prejudices using consumer activism, negotiation, and protest. The NAACP also challenged discrimination in employment and unions in the courts; the majority of these cases concerned the boilermakers and railroad unions, and other complaints involving defense industries. Discrimination in the retail industry, however, was almost entirely fought via merit-hiring campaigns.[68]

Third, the expansion of industry and production, and the simultaneous loss of white workers due to the wartime draft, produced a need for black workers in the federal government, factories, stores, and other enterprises. And finally, biracial civil rights advocacy, especially that of A. Philip Randolph, whose efforts led to the issuance of Executive Order 8802 and the formation of the Fair Employment Practices Commission (FEPC) in 1941, spotlighted racist conditions and provided the legal and cultural basis for nondiscrimination in the workforce.

In this milieu, the NUL and the NAACP fixed their attention on downtown department stores, not simply those located in black enclaves that had been targeted by the "Don't Buy" movement. Downtown department stores, they understood, "were central to the social and economic life of cities and towns" and thus were ideal places to display the "best" members of the race to a large audience of whites on a daily basis.[69] Activists also believed that the nation's most recent troubles, specifically the war, impacted department stores in ways that primed them to accept African Americans in positions of responsibility. Department stores underwent numerous changes to weather the economic and wartime crises of the 1930s and 1940s. They cut back and consolidated services, extended credit to more shoppers to improve sales, eliminated tearooms and opened less expensive, more profitable lunch counters—the sites of future civil rights activism—and successfully lobbied the federal government to make the fourth Thursday of November the official observance of Thanksgiving, thereby extending the Christmas shopping season by one week.

After the war broke out, department store workforces changed in size, in composition, and with regard to their responsibilities. Retailers, many of whom had laid off workers to survive the Depression, experienced an exodus of white workers: white male workers were drafted into the armed forces, while white female workers abandoned their department store jobs for higher-paying skilled jobs in the defense industries. This labor drain compelled retailers to embrace self-service retailing (a model that was on the fringes during the 1930s), whereby customers wandered unassisted through store aisles and open displays to identify desired merchandise with little or no assistance from salespeople. Mass production and the standardization of merchandise, along with innovations in advertising and marketing, complemented this new method of retailing and educated customers on goods sold in department stores, making skilled and knowledgeable sales workers increasingly superfluous. Selling, thus, became less of an art or skill and came to resemble the more mundane and mechanized work of cashiering.[70]

Wartime personnel shortages, coupled with a desire to show wartime patriotism and the Double V campaign (an African American initiative that spotlighted the contradictions between American domestic and foreign policies on the issues of democracy and political freedoms), compelled store managements to reexamine the racialized organization of their labor forces. As a result, some retailers promoted African Americans to now de-skilled but still visible positions: Thalhimers in Richmond upgraded Mary Johnson from maid to hospital attendant and Hazel Harris and Grace Bradley from maids to elevator operators, while African Americans prevailed in elevator operating and tearoom waitressing by 1944; in Philadelphia, Wanamaker's began employing black women as stock clerks, wrappers, and cashiers— positions that placed them on the selling floor and in contact with customers; and, in Harlem, Blumstein's set a precedent when it hired Miriam Andrews as its window trimmer in 1944, becoming what many believed was "the only Negro window trimmer working in a big store in the country."[71]

Major department stores in New York, Boston, and Hartford went further and promoted African Americans to sales and clerical occupations. At G. Fox Company in Hartford, store president Beatrice Fox Auerbach was committed to employee advancement and believed in-store training programs and promotions from within would help meet this end. Her philosophy, however, was not exclusive to white workers. So, in 1942, G. Fox began employing black executives and sales workers. Three years later, as black employment expanded, the store hired Anaretha Shaw to manage its personnel of color, although Shaw resigned after just two years to tend to her family.[72] Sarah Murphy, a former Women's Army Corps member and graduate of New York University's personnel administration program, then assumed the position. In addition to her personnel duties, and after excelling in her retail sales training, Murphy was assigned to the lingerie department. Her assignment to this department was particularly important, as it was "a heavy sales department" that typically excluded African Americans. Traditionally, whites objected to African Americans, whom they regarded as unclean and diseased, handling their intimate clothing. Shaw and Murphy, however, were not anomalies: a black woman who started as an inspector wrapper in the children's clothing department in 1942 was promoted to head of stock in this department after several years of strong performance.[73]

The adoption of merit hiring at G. Fox Company occurred without protest or much agitation.[74] The same, however, cannot be said of most American department stores. The Philadelphia Youth Council confronted race discrimination at Oppenheim and Collins's department store in 1941.[75] In New York City in 1942, the NUL, the United Retail, Wholesale, and Department Store Employees' Union (URWDSEU), and other civil rights and labor organizations pressured Macy's, Gimbels, Bloomingdales, and other Manhattan department stores to hire black sales and office workers.[76] Their campaign was most influential at Macy's Herald Square—where, by July 1946, it employed twenty-five African American saleswomen, fifty black clerical workers, and an African American personnel executive.[77] (It also is likely that the campaign found success here because the Jewish American Straus family owned Macy's, and, with the rise of Nazism, Jews publicly condemned bigotry and committed themselves to working with blacks and other allies to end discrimination.) The black press celebrated this accomplishment and paid special attention to the hiring of Lemuel L. Foster as the assistant to the director of executive placement and review. The press (and Foster himself) heavily credited Foster's achievements, not civil rights activism, for his appointment, hoping that other stores and businesses would take notice, overcome their fear of and resistance to integration, and follow suit. Foster was qualified, if not overqualified, for his new position. Born in Meridian, Mississippi, Foster was a Fisk University alumnus with over twenty years of relevant work experience: he sold insurance at Lincoln Reserve Life Insurance Company, directed the New York branch of Victory Life's Insurance Company, worked as race relations director of the Works Progress Administration in New York, and later served as the race relations officer in the Industrial Personnel Division of Army Service Forces. His credentials certainly made him a "quality" and "better class of applicant," but his appointment would not have been possible without protest and agitation.[78]

In Boston, as a result of civil rights activism and encouraging reports of black sales and office workers in other northern stores, Gilchrist Department Store and Jordan Marsh Company adopted merit hiring during the 1944 Christmas season.[79] After many appeals from the local Urban League and the Massachusetts's Governor's Committee for Racial and Religious Understanding, Gilchrist hired ten African American saleswomen, and an undetermined number of black saleswomen were hired at Jordan Marsh. However, by the end of the Christmas shopping season, only three African American workers remained at Gilchrist. In the 1940s, the Boston Urban League resumed its activism against the store and pressured management to hire more black workers and continue its employment of "approximately ten or slightly better" African American salesclerks at all times. After the war, an American Friends Service Committee (AFSC) investigator reported: "Negro salespeople are widely distributed. One (Mrs. Ellie) is in the shoe department in charge of the slipper section; another is in charge of the basement glove counter; two others are in the book section; another (Miss Clarke) is in hosiery, and is considered 'excellent'; another (Mrs. Frances Roberts) is in the umbrella department; and still another (Miss Jones) is in the silverware department on the first floor and was upgraded from a basement job." The investigator also observed African Americans employed as assistant buyers and working in Gilchrist's storeroom and in a branch of the U.S. Post Office.[80]

Typically, activists relied on a combination of persuasion and protest to sway retailers to hire black sales and office workers, much like they had in "Don't Buy" efforts. In 1944, for example, the Women's Division of the Chicago Urban League (CUL) and the Congress of Racial Equality (CORE) polled nearly 2,000 white customers at ten major department stores in the Loop, Chicago's central business district, about their receptiveness to African American saleswomen. Sixty-nine percent of those interviewed, these organizations learned, were open to the idea. As a result, the CUL and CORE organized an interracial campaign with the support of the Hyde Park Cooperative Society, the Chicago Round Table of Christians and Jews, the YWCA, Friendship House, the Chicago Council on Racial and Religious Discrimination, the American Jewish Congress, the Chicago Branch of the National Association of College Women, and others. This campaign arranged meetings with local retailers, recruited and trained "well-qualified girls" to apply for openings, and initiated a "widespread educational campaign [that] includ[ed] petitions from shoppers and leaflets with favorable comments from the buying public."[81]

The Chicago campaign achieved its first major success that same year when CUL field representative Ora Higgins called M. J. Spiegel to solicit funds for the league. During their conversation, Spiegel shared that his company "had only one Negro on the payroll and he felt this was wrong, in view of Chicago's growing Negro population . . . the question of hiring Negroes [had] been discussed and discarded because many of the supervisors lacked the confidence in the abilities of Negro workers and were also fearful of reaction on part of white employees."[82] In spite of this, however, Spiegel was determined to launch a fair employment program as soon as possible and, subsequently, invited Higgins, who was completing her master's degree in personnel administration at Northwestern University, to come work for the mail-order company. She agreed and became the company's first African American personnel director.[83]

Within one year, Spiegel's removed the question "What race?" from its job applications and inaugurated a merit hiring program. Working alongside Spiegel and Leslie Clark, the retailer's personnel manager, Higgins coordinated Spiegel's integration project. She "interviewed hundreds of job-seekers and virtually hand-picked her first small team of qualified Negro workers." Spiegel's merit hiring program "resulted in successfully integrated employment on all levels. . . . Within three more years, Spiegel was completely integrated"—years ahead of the city's department stores. As a result of this success, and while still working as Spiegel's personnel director, Higgins was appointed personnel advisor for department store training classes conducted by the Board of Education and served as a consultant for similar programs in various retail institutions in downtown Chicago for several decades.[84] Because of Higgins's success at Spiegel's, most African Americans seeking employment—the majority of whom were women—through the CUL's Industrial Department were fed into the mail-order and mail service industries in the late 1940s and 1950s.[85]

More often than not the black press applauded the achievements of civil rights groups. In early 1943, Roy Wilkins of the New York Amsterdam Star-News wrote, "Too much sweat and pleading and swearing" was involved "to get them a chance to work." But, he warned, "it is up to the workers to hold them." Specifically, Wilkins hoped that "the girls who have been hired by New York department stores" would expertly serve their customers and take greater pride in their work than black lunch counter waitresses and busboys in downtown department store eateries, who, he claimed, socialized much more than they perform their job duties. He feared that their poor job performance "is . . . making it impossible for other Negroes to get similar jobs or to hold on to them after the war is over."[86]

Thankfully, the subpar performances of a few did not hinder future progress. Instead, it was widely reported that African American executives and sales workers were generally well received. G. Fox personnel director Maurice Berins maintained that, beyond some initial resentment, African American employees at his store were accepted on the basis of individual merit. "In only a few instances," Berins continued, "have we had employees tell us that they will not work beside a Negro. In such instances[,] we talk to these employees about fairness and democracy in action, and if this does not work, we simply re-state our employment policy and do not retreat from it." White customers, too, favorably received black salesclerks, so much so that "in one or two instances customers [had] expressed preference for being served by Negro sales people."[87] At Gilchrist, its first black salesclerks were purposely assigned to departments where they had little contact with white clerks. This arrangement, one African American sales worker in the umbrella department insisted, "diminished the chance of friction." Soon, however, black and white saleswomen became "so friendly that they could later work together without difficulty." Gilchrist's customers also mostly welcomed the employment of African American salesclerks. They expressed their pleasure with and appreciation of the store's employment of blacks in positions of responsibility in letters and in-person communications; others—albeit just a "few"—openly criticized and disapproved of integration.[88]

Wartime letters, surveys, and white customers' patronage corroborate these accounts. In 1943, an African American woman visiting New York City from Washington, D.C., wrote to the *New York Amsterdam News* and disclosed that she "was agreeably surprised" to see a black saleswoman at Macy's. "While she was feeling a pleasant glow," however, she overheard another woman (presumably of the white race) "from farther south . . . strenuously" sharing her objections to one of the white saleswomen. To this, the saleswoman "let her biased customer know that they were not only glad to have the Negro girls there but that their work was just as good as any."[89] In May 1944, the Brooklyn Urban League conducted one of the earliest surveys on the topic and reported that officials at six of twelve department stores surveyed were "satisfied" with their black sales hires and willing to hire more when openings arose.[90] One year later, the *Afro-American* reported that hoards of whites visited and were being served by African Americans in Harlem's shopping district without any problems.[91]

• • • • • •

While the main objective of the early department store movement was the implementation of fair employment in urban northern cities specifically, it also challenged the segregation of public accommodations and consumer discrimination, although to a smaller or simply less notable degree. World War II revived the economy overall, but also exerted price and wage controls, which had the effect of restraining private, household consumption. It taught Americans on the home front that the best way to support the war was as defense workers and as "responsible consumers" who obeyed OPA and rationing regulations and purchased war bonds. However, "as African Americans embarked on proving themselves loyal Americans" by heeding the aforementioned, "they consistently met discrimination as consumers. In a wartime atmosphere where the idea of a good consumer and a good citizen increasingly were intertwined, that unfair treatment in the marketplace took on new political significance."[92] The war reminded African Americans that, despite their best efforts, their country continued to treat them as second-class citizens. "The change in the Negro's mentality came about so rapidly that few people, even Negroes, realized its extent. . . . Most fundamentally, it was expressed in the Negro's refusal to accept segregation without complaint," St. Clair Drake and Horace Cayton observed. "But underneath all this," they concluded, "was the Negro's determination to become a full citizen. . . . He began to make demands, not for concessions, not for small gains, but for *equality.*"[93]

This realization inspired several protests—mostly small—on behalf of black consumers in retail establishments, theaters, restaurants, and hotels and on modes of public transportation throughout the nation. In 1940, Eloise Townsend filed suit against Spurgeon's Dry Goods Store in Lincoln, Illinois, when it prohibited her from trying on hats. Three years later—the same year that Pauli Murray and her fellow Howard University students staged sit-ins at a United Cigar Store and the Little Palace Cafeteria in Washington, D.C. (the former of which is believed to be the "first sit-in of the twentieth century civil rights movement"[94])—an all-white jury ruled that the department store violated the Illinois Civil Rights Act and awarded Townsend twenty-five dollars.[95] In 1941, the Consolidated Housewives League initiated an "all-out" campaign against 125th Street retailers that propagated "second-rate goods" while showing "lack of co-operation" and "insincerity in Negro employment." It demanded that black Harlemites patronize the merchants who advertise in the *Amsterdam Star-News* and even encouraged their "meetings by sending samples for distribution." It asked that African Americans withhold their patronage from retailers who overcharged, used "pullers-in" and "pressure selling," practiced "indefinite pricing," substituted goods, and refused courtesy.[96] In Chicago, CORE organized substantial efforts to desegregate White City Roller Rink, Jack Spratt's Coffee House, and Stoner's Restaurant. In St. Louis, African American women, with the occasional support of their white counterparts, protested lunch counter discrimination at Stix, Baer and Fuller, Famous-Barr Co., and Scruggs, Vandervoort and Barney from late 1943 to 1945. In the fall of 1944, these three stores offered to allow blacks to eat at Jim Crow basement lunch counters, hoping that this overture would pacify protesters. The women unanimously rejected the offer. Negotiations continued into 1945, until Scruggs agreed to open its lunch counter to African Americans (although it refused to integrate its upstairs dining room). Stix and Famous-Barr, however, did not integrate their eateries until pressured by the local CORE chapter in the 1950s.[97]

Other activists engaged store and government officials in "quiet, gentlemanly, intelligent conferences and correspondences," shying away from protests (which were often characterized as unpatriotic in time of war).[98] They leveraged the country's democratic mission abroad to compel its application and installation on the home front. Notably, in February 1943, a committee of Baltimore civil rights leaders met with J. W. Mehling, secretary of the Retail Merchants Association, and presented him with "a program of action" to "remove the unwritten policy of discrimination" in local department stores. They assured Mehling that "there will be no public discussion of this campaign at present." At the meeting's end, Mehling agreed to share their recommendations with the association. Nothing seemed to have come from this endeavor, however.[99]

When lobbying failed, activists often grew more forthright. Sometimes, they accused—subtly and blatantly—department store owners, many of whom were Jewish, of practicing a form of Nazi racism when retailers resisted integration. African Americans expected Jewish merchants to know better and do better than whites, believing that Jews had a responsibility to assist the black freedom movement given the similarities between American racism and German Nazism.[100] At other times, activists pursued large-scale, direct-action programs to induce retailers to abandon their segregationist policies. One of these programs, and arguably the most effective wartime consumer effort, was the *Baltimore Afro-American*'s 1945 "orchid and onions" campaign. Previously, Baltimore's "Don't Buy" movement had tried to dismantle all forms of discrimination in department stores. However, it was more successful on the jobs' front. By 1940, one contemporary observed, Baltimore remained the "only large city in the country, north or south, which completely bars Negroes from its downtown department stores . . . announcing that they were only 'following the pattern of the South' (but Negroes can buy in the stores of Atlanta, Mobile,

New Orleans, Raleigh, Birmingham, Memphis, Houston, Dallas, and Jackson, Miss., to name a few).["101]

The "orchid and onions" campaign picked up where the "Don't Buy" movement left off. As described by the *Afro-American*, it involved "reporters canvassing downtown stores to determine their policy toward blacks. Those who were nondiscriminatory and said so to *Afro* reporters were listed as 'orchids' on the newspaper's front page. Those who were not were listed as 'onions.'"[102] In January, the paper reported, out of 28 downtown apparel stores, "17 give equal and similar service to colored customers, while 11 have discriminatory policies." Montgomery Ward, Sears Roebuck, Brager-Eisenberg, and Hecht Brothers were among the department stores touted as "orchids." Conversely, Stewart and Company, Hutzler Brothers, the May Company, Hochschild-Kohn, Julius Gutman, and O'Neill's discouraged or refused to serve African American patrons and/or maintained policies that permitted blacks to shop but prohibited them from trying on clothes and prevented them from returning or exchanging purchases by marking their receipts "sales final" or "final sale."[103] The May Company, in particular, refused to wait on African American customers "in the various store departments, but are referred to the 'personal service' department on the fifth floor. Here, the woman in charge finds out what purchase the customer wants, goes down to the respective department and obtains it for the customer."[104] In February, after one month of surveying, the *Afro* reported that the total number of orchid stores had risen to forty-four. Several department stores remained "onions," however, and kept this title until the resumption of public protests, most notably the sit-in demonstrations staged by Morgan State College students, in the postwar years.[105]

Not all expressions of black consumer protest and outrage, however, were so composed and organized; in fact, several pointedly sought violent and destructive revenge. In the Detroit Race Riot of 1943, African Americans looted and destroyed white-owned stores that exploited black customers in retaliation for white opposition to their entry into Sojourner Truth Houses (the city's first public housing project) and to the integration of the Packard Motor Company assembly line, and for other incidents of racial violence and discrimination. One month later, rumors that a white policeman had killed a black soldier in the Braddock Hotel sparked an upheaval in Harlem along 125th Street. Men and women, the young and the old, the poor and the affluent—all of whom were frustrated and angered by not only the reported killing but also the history of racial oppression and violence—raided exploitative white-owned stores, passing over black businesses. Insurgents made off with armfuls of merchandise that they believed "had been unfairly denied to them."[106] Malcolm X (then Malcolm Little) recalled walking down Nicholas Street when he "saw all of these Negroes hollering and running north from 125th Street. Some of them were loaded down with armfuls of stuff. . . . Negroes were smashing store windows, and taking everything they could grab and carry—furniture, jewelry, clothes, whisky." Other accounts reveal that Blumstein's Department Store, once a target of the "Don't Buy" movement, was ravaged. Rioters took everything and ceremoniously paraded the streets in pilfered suits, dresses, hats, and shoes.[107] Wartime riots not only ended race discrimination in the marketplace but also created an awareness and discourse that would benefit the black freedom struggle in the postwar era.

• • • • • •

It is hardly an accident that the department store movement originated in the 1930s and 1940s; claiming to be and being a full-fledged American— the heart of this movement—came to be deeply associated with consumer capitalism by the 1950s. The political and economic conditions of the Depression and the Second World War placed greater emphasis on the role of consumption in defining American citizenship and supporting and rebuilding the nation, and facilitated the development and early success of the department store movement. The movement was in its infancy during the war, and its gains often resembled tokenism, were quite tenuous, and most directly benefited middle-class blacks. But, as other civil rights organizations and labor unions joined the effort, an explosion of more substantial employment and consumer protests transpired. These protests continued to leverage black purchasing and labor power, industrial expansion, and increased biracial advocacy to improve African Americans' position in labor and consumer markets. They may have been beholden to liberal attitudes and managerial initiatives, but they owed their strength and effectiveness to black protest to forcefully end racial discrimination and segregation in employment and consumption in northern and western cities. Years later, southern ones would follow.

3 To All Store and Office Workers ... Negro and White!

Unionism and Antidiscrimination in the Department Store Industry

● ●

In the 1930s and 1940s, the National Association for the Advancement of Colored People (NAACP) and the National Urban League (NUL) allied with the Congress of Industrial Organizations (CIO) in an attempt to strengthen their commitment to addressing the problems of black workers, who now constituted a large and powerful delegation within their ranks. Compared with the NAACP and the NUL, which were practiced in legal and social work approaches, the CIO was better "prepared to act effectively in the workplaces and working-class neighborhoods where black Americans fought their most decisive struggles."[1] This union movement was influenced by the Communist Party's racial ideological standard that formal equality should prevail in workplaces and unions, as well as "in courts and at the ballot box . . . and in the realm of social life: the neighborhoods, schools, summer camps, dance halls, and marriage beds."[2] The CIO openly recruited and organized African American workers—whose numbers reached nearly a half million by the end of the Second World War—as a result. However, the CIO's racial practices often diverged from the Communist Party's ideology. The movement fought for "nondiscrimination, fair employment, political enfranchisement, higher pay, and equal pay." But integration was not a priority. According to one historian, "integration and desegregation might well be products of this struggle, but they were secondary to the main objective." (Further, integration "emerged as a key element on the labor-liberal agenda" in the 1960s; by then, "it represented an actual devaluation of this laborite perspective.")[3]

The coming together of civil rights and labor activists, however, did ensure that integration and other troubles beleaguering working blacks were addressed. Together, these activists facilitated the emergence and proliferation of what the historian Robert Korstad calls "civil rights unionism," a "national movement" that simultaneously engaged the struggle for workplace rights and civil rights.[4] This unionism was prominent in manufacturing industries, but it struggled to gain a strong foothold in retail establishments. Historically, the retail industry lacked a large-scale labor union movement that afforded African American workers a political and social space to advance their employment and civil rights. Most of the prevailing unions generally ignored racial discrimination and focused on improving the working conditions of those already employed, and thus prioritized the concerns of whites over blacks and oftentimes reinforcing the existing racial regime in the process. Others denounced racial inequality but did little, if anything at all, to challenge it. Because of this, civil rights organizations such as the Urban League, Future Outlook League in Cleveland, and the Housewives League in Detroit not only built powerful campaigns to pressure merchants into hiring African Americans for white-collar positions but also functioned as "proto-trade unions" that took up the workplace concerns of workers of color.[5]

However, in several New York and Chicago stores, civil rights unionism thrived. Here, the United Retail Employees of America (later renamed the United Retail Wholesale and Department Store Employees Union [URWDSEU] and then the Retail Wholesale Department Store Union) and the United Service Employees Union (USEU) of the CIO, respectively, operated in a manner that resembled the Brotherhood of Sleeping Car Porters and the Packinghouse Workers Organizing Committee, as they were integral players in efforts to dismantle racial segregation and discrimination in department stores from the 1930s through the 1950s. New York and Chicago retail unions successfully linked worker and consumer rights and improved African Americans' social and economic conditions, even propelling some of them into the middle class. Also, in acting as both labor and civil rights organizations, New York and Chicago locals expanded views of fair employment in this industry beyond bread-and-butter issues and promoted equal economic opportunity. They made tremendous strides toward increasing the number of black hires so that one day their in-store presence might be proportionate to their citywide presence; eliminating traditional and new barriers that restricted African American employment and promotion, such as job testing and lowering wages for sales and clerical positions below those of menial work to discourage blacks from seeking white-collar work; instituting equal pay for equal work; and creating safe work and community spaces free from racism for both workers and consumers. In short, these unions point to the nature and direction of the black freedom struggle, albeit without the presence of strong unionism.

New York City Department Store Unions

In late 1934, as "Don't Buy" picketers confronted Harlem retailers, workers at S. Klein's and Ohrbach's department stores in Union Square (in Manhattan) waged strikes demanding pay raises, a forty-hour workweek, and an end to discrimination against union members. Poor working conditions had long characterized these establishments: "Many workers found the store environment cramped, loud, and unsanitary."[6] To make matters worse, management provided low wages and painstakingly supervised everything from the "appearance of nails, neatness of clothing, [and] general good taste shown by grooming" to worker-consumer interactions.[7] They used race, ethnicity, and gender to assign workers to specific work and department assignments—a strategy that tended to hinder broad worker camaraderie and unionization. But compared with factory work, department store work was preferable in many ways: it was recognized as a legitimate profession, involved little physical exertion and danger, and offered consistent, although comparably lower, wages, a shorter workday, and status.

However, as the Great Depression threatened to bankrupt stores, managers sharply reduced wages, increased work hours, and began experimenting with self-service retailing in an attempt to bolster business. Ohrbach's employees objected to having to work six days a week. At Klein's, one saleswoman complained that "girls . . . receiving ten dollars per week" were "discharged in favor of the new group who were getting only eight. . . . Also that the girls hired after my group are getting seven and seven fifty." Further, she detailed that saleswomen were required to work a fifty-seven-hour workweek, "from nine-thirty in the morning until seven in the evening, including Saturday."[8]

Despite their dissatisfaction with these new working conditions, employees were constrained by the economic catastrophe that was destabilizing the American economy. Without the option of quitting and securing a better job and encouraged by the National Industrial Recovery Act (NIRA), a federal provision that protected collective bargaining, disgruntled workers at Klein's and Ohrbach's chose unionization as the solution for their grievances. They solicited the assistance of the Office Workers Union (OWU), an affiliate of the communist-led Trade Union Unity League (TUUL), in 1934. The TUUL encouraged "a more democratic, activist, and participatory unionism," one that functioned from the bottom up as opposed to the bureaucratic or top-down approach adopted by the American Federation of Labor (AFL).[9]

It was also an approach that engaged women and African American workers. In its mission statement, the organization explicitly recognized that "women workers play an important role in American industry. . . . [They] are subjected to the fierce speed-up of capitalist rationalization, and are super-exploited." It condemned "trade union leaders [who] have typically failed to make a fight for the women workers, barring them from the unions and discriminating against them in industry" and pledged to fight for their rights. With regard to African Americans, the TUUL founded the Negro Bureau. Under the direction of prominent black communist James W. Ford, the bureau sought to unite black and white workers in a struggle to secure "full racial, political, and social equality and the right of national self-determination for Negroes. It makes relentless war against lynching, Jim Crowism, and discrimination of all kinds against Negroes. It roots out the race prejudice of chauvinism of white workers against Negroes." Additionally, it "organizes Negroes into the new industrial unions with the white workers on the basis of the fullest equality . . . [and] connects up the fight of the Negro workers in this country with the world-wide struggle of the Negro race."[10]

The OWU, however, had a narrower mission. Organized by the TUUL, the OWU sought to organize department store and office workers primarily, and thus its membership and leadership largely consisted of women. When the OWU agreed to support Klein's and Ohrbach's employees, Clarina Michelson, one of its two full-time organizers, was appointed the organizer of department store workers, a position she held for five years. Unlike the working-class women employed at and patronizing these two department stores, Michelson was a proud communist and a Massachusetts native from an upper-class family who had never held a job. She was also the recording secretary for the League of the Struggle for Negro Rights, a communist group active in New York's "Don't Buy" movement. Through her involvement with these organizations, Michelson recognized the needs of under-represented workers and likely encouraged interracialism in the department store movement. Presumably, she believed that a broad-based coalition of African Americans, whites, men, and women would be most effective in forcing management to surrender to workers' demands for higher wages, a forty-hour workweek, paid overtime, the elimination of speedups, and union recognition.

With OWU and Michelson at the helm, Ohrbach's workers went on strike in the winter of 1934. Not long thereafter, in December, Klein's workers joined the picket line when store managers fired all union employees. Both retailers had avowed support for the NIRA earlier that year, but when Klein's employees joined the OWU, management openly defied the NIRA, revealing that it was in fact strongly antiunion, and terminated all employees affiliated with the union. Store owner Samuel Klein denied holding any bias against union members. In an interview with *Newsweek* in December 1934, he insisted that "store business always falls off at Christmas time. . . . About Dec. 1 each year I have to lay off a few employees. This year we let only 87 go, against 300 last year and 250 in 1932. Then the other day I got a 'summons' from the [National Recovery Administration]," the agency tasked with ensuring that employers followed the NIRA codes.[11] Klein refused to admit that nearly all of the workers he discharged were OWU members.

The strike was modest—only 200 of the 2,600 employees at Klein's and Ohrbach's participated. Yet despite its size, movement leaders established a broad-based coalition and skillfully negotiated the space of both the store and Union Square to pressure management to concede. Store employees identified as "white-collar workers." According to the historian Daniel Opler, in distinguishing themselves as "white-collar workers," not department store or working-class workers, Klein's and Ohrbach's employees drew the support of other white-collar workers, including office workers, actors, chemists, doctors, and writers. This approach enabled these store workers to cross class lines that divided workers and create an alliance based on labor.[12]

The strikers' broad-based coalition not only crossed lines of class, ethnicity, and religion, as examined in existing historical scholarship; it also built camaraderie among workers divided by race. In the workspace of the department store, African Americans had been invisible to their white coworkers. Every day white employees rode passenger elevators serviced by African Americans, consumed foods prepared by blacks in the employee cafeteria, and sold merchandise on selling floors cleaned by colored workers, but they never developed relationships with or simply acknowledged their coworkers. At Ohrbach's, African American workers recalled:

We were ordered around by almost anyone in the store. In one instance, an operator was almost fired because he told one executive that he was ordered by his starter not to take more than one rack at a time on the elevator when girls were going up to lunch, and that he would not take more than one rack up.

Another instance: One operator who was once a starter asked his manager to give his starter position to another operator, change his time to an early shift because he realized the need for a broader education. This was granted by Mr. Waldron, but one week later this operator's time was changed back to a later hour, thereby making it impossible to attend classes. Because this operator would speak up for his right he was picked on by the manager who had his pay envelope made up a number of times in order to fire him for the personal animosity that he had for this particular operator.[13]

The TUUL, the OWU, and Michelson shared a commitment to African American workers: they understood that these store employees shared the same dismal working conditions and grievances as their white coworkers, and, most importantly, a successful campaign—one that was already quite small—required their assistance. Black workers were among the many store employees laid off at Klein's that were union members. One distributed leaflet announced: "68 Negro and white workers were locked out of S. Klein Store, on Union Square, for organizing into the Office Workers Union (504-6th Avenue) for better conditions. They had been working 56 to 60 hours a week for $7 and $8. Although the N.R.A. ordered Mr. Klein to reinstate his employees, he has refused." Similarly, at Ohrbach's, "150 Negro and white workers" campaigned for "decent working conditions and a living wage."[14]

The Klein's-Ohrbach's movement, however, campaigned to improve African Americans' work conditions as menial workers *only*. It did not seek to advance them to sales and clerical positions. White employees were not so progressive as to risk their own job security for the advancement of blacks or for the implementation of merit hiring—a fact of which African Americans were likely very aware. Black employees, too, appear not to have pushed for integration but sought instead more freedom in their current roles. They likely were unwilling to undertake such a daunting struggle because they recognized that their white coworkers would not have supported this cause, or perhaps they simply had no desire to become sales or clerical workers or to take up that point at this particular moment. Nevertheless, the interracial relationship forged on the movement's front lines eventually became an essential component in the wartime and postwar efforts to integrate sales work in New York City department stores.

During the strike, white union members reported gaining a greater respect for their black coworkers. They began to notice black operators' "militant manner and fighting spirit," solicited their support, and elected an African American operator to the strike committee.[15] Harlem race worker

George Carter and other local blacks also lent their support to the cause and attended some of the weekly rallies in Union Square, especially when they learned that store officials had instructed their remaining employees to "insult all Negro patrons, so they won't come back again" in an effort "to break the strike and split the ranks of the workers."[16]

Yet despite the interracial nature of the Klein's and Ohrbach's strikes, which was a critical component of their success, these protests never received the support of the black nationalist-leaning "Don't Buy" movement. Racial discrimination in hiring was not included as a point of contention, to the disappointment of "Don't Buy" leaders; it was frankly a measure too radical for white employees to even consider. In late April 1935, Benjamin J. Davis Jr., then editor of the *Negro Liberator*, criticized the OWU for not taking a stance on discrimination against Negro workers. He noted that "in the last Ohrbach strike there was no demand for the Negro workers and patrons of that store. I was informed by one of the strikers that the General Manager of both Ohrbach's and Klein's instructs all employees to 'insult Negro patrons so that they won't come back again.' It was a bad omission that [this] point was not raised during the strike struggle."[17]

In response to this criticism, the OWU created and distributed a leaflet to Harlem's black community declaring, "Our employers have many ways of keeping us divided, in order to divert us from the real issues, in order to keep our wages down, etc." It continued: "This problem is acute in Harlem. Negro clerks and office workers who are competent (as we can see in Koch's) are barred from this type of work, because of the deep rooted prejudice instilled in us by our bosses, and in order to keep the Negro people a rung lower in the economic ladder." The OWU promised to secure white-collar work for African Americans, "without firing any of those employed at present," and equal pay for equal work. Additionally, this leaflet highlighted the union's success in forcing the store executives at Ohrbach's to give Negro workers representation on its Junior Executive Board.[18] No evidence in extant OWU records, however, suggests that the union kept its promises. Perhaps the union never truly believed in integration; or maybe the OWU strategically kept its distance from black nationalist campaigns, believing that associating with radical black militants would hinder its progress. This likely left blacks—those involved in and outside the movement—wary of white communists as a result.

Nevertheless, the OWU strikes demonstrate the possibilities interracialism held in white-collar labor struggles. Although the movement's victory was quite limited and temporary, as prestrike difficulties resurfaced as early as April 1935,[19] demonstrators proved not only that department store workers specifically and white-collar workers generally could be organized but also that, together, black and white workers could be effective in improving work conditions. At Klein's, strikers were rehired and provided back pay. Ohrbach's agreed to reinstate workers with full seniority rights and to not lay off strikers until all other store employees had a twelve-week layoff first; it also agreed to an 8–10 percent wage increase for all employees, a forty-hour workweek, a one-hour lunch break, a twenty-minute relief period, employee elevators, additional lavatories, and extras placed on a preference list for permanent employment. And, despite still being confined to menial service positions, African American service workers were provided direct representation on the store's Junior Executive Board and a new supervisor of elevators (Thomas was hired to replace Waldron).[20]

In May 1935, approximately two months after the movement's end, Ohrbach's OWU branch reported that black elevator operators "are now treated as any other department in the store" and that all discrimination "either in the department or in the store" had been eliminated.[21] These observations from white employees suggest an overall improvement in black-white relations as a result of the strikes. Although it is unlikely that blacks and whites became fast friends, they likely grew to respect the other as both coworkers, deserving of a simple "hello" and "goodbye" when they encountered each other, and formidable allies with shared work experiences and grievances. However, the authors of this report also reveal that white employees had a limited understanding of racial discrimination in the workplace. They had reduced it to the acts of ignoring African Americans and failing to provide adequate representation among store officials. Once again, it becomes glaringly apparent that Davis's criticisms of the movement had fallen on deaf ears; no challenges were made to promote African American workers in these stores for several more years.

The Klein's-Ohrbach's strikes and the victorious sit-down strikes at major department stores and five-and-dime chain stores in Detroit, New York City, Philadelphia, and other cities in 1937 and 1938 helped expand unions' presence and recognition in the retail industry. In 1938, Local 1-S of the URWDSEU contracted to organize Macy's nonselling workers. Nonselling departments were the first targeted by this labor organization because these departments predominantly employed men in manual jobs and had fewer turnovers than sales. Men, union leaders reasoned, were more open to labor organizing and considered more invested in keeping and improving their jobs because of their family obligations. Six hundred workers in receiving, packing, order filling, supply, and cafeteria departments were the first to join Local 1-S and to campaign successfully for a forty-five-hour, six-day workweek. Two years later, when Marcella Loring Michelson was elected the union's new organizer, membership expanded to include passenger elevator operators, freight elevator operators, housecleaners, tailors, and seamstresses.

At this time, Local 1-S also began recruiting sales and clerical workers, the majority of whom were women. Initially, women were ignored because they were expected to marry and leave the workplace, and thus, in the eyes of union leaders, they had less of a stake in the labor movement. Furthermore, as union vice president William Atkinson argued, "ladies in selling [were] reluctant to join a union and the younger ones . . . don't want to pay dues. And they don't realize what the benefits that they have as far as grievance procedure is concerned, their sick benefits, their retirement . . . and pension."[22] Michelson, however, felt that this was only part of the story and began courting women workers: "A lot of women, married women, thought they [were] only [going to work] in department stores for a moment . . . for extra pin money. But when it really came down to it, they needed—they weren't working just for pin money, they were working because they needed to work." Being a woman herself, Michelson contended, was extremely beneficial in the recruitment of women workers: "It was easier for a woman to walk around certain departments in the store, where a man would not be allowed or it would be unusual to find a man." The clerical divisions were even harder to unionize. But like their selling coworkers, Michelson and other union leaders were able to assure them that joining the union would be a benefit.[23]

As Local 1-S grappled with its involvement in pushing for women's rights, it took a much stronger and definitive stance on racial discrimination. With its leaders being strong supporters of the Communist Party, although not necessarily party members, Local 1-S welcomed African American employees, all of whom labored in nonselling departments. Of these workers, passenger elevator operators leveraged the union most successfully to maintain their position and improve their working conditions. Working as an elevator operator was one of the few decent paying department store jobs available to African Americans. William Atkinson recalled that, during the Depression, his starting salary at the age of eighteen was $18.00 per week. Operators twenty-one years of age received $22.00 per week. By 1946, operators earned as much as $39.75 per week. "In those days," Atkinson declared, he was able "to feed my mother and my grandmother [which] was something else, too."[24] As a result, once hired, many operators remained at the store much longer than other black employees. In 1944, elevator operator James Labitue celebrated his thirtieth anniversary, Arthur Love observed twenty-five years, Friendly James marked twenty years of service, and James Cumberbatch was honored for twenty-four years. Cumberbatch served as an elevator operator well into the 1970s; in 1974, he celebrated fifty years on the job.[25]

All of Macy's passenger elevator operators were black; and, like Pullman Porters, they occupied a complex, contradictory existence. On the one hand, they were symbols of servitude, second-class citizenship, and the denial of manhood rights. Tasked with manually operating store elevators, they were seen and heard only when providing basic directives such as "door closing" or "first floor." On the other hand, for the black men who secured this work, elevator operating was praised, as it reflected their respectability, enhanced their urbanity and sophistication, offered decent wages and hours, and held the promise of social mobility. In the black community, several store operators were featured in the black press and touted as "race men." Many of these men held high school degrees (some also had college degrees), had served in the armed forces, and were community leaders. Elevator operator Atkinson was a high school graduate from a middle-class family. His mother was a former schoolteacher and a graduate of the University of Michigan, and his father was an engineer in the Department of Navy and designed the bows of warships. Operator Leon Johnson earned a bachelor of arts degree from Morris Brown University in Atlanta and attended Meharry Medical College for one year before coming to Macy's in 1922.[26] Others were community activists. Labitue, for example, ran against future mayor Fiorello H. La Guardia for alderman in 1912, was the party's lieutenant of his district, campaigned under Herbert Straus to elect Herbert Hoover as president, and was involved in the Knights of Pythias, the Elks, and the Masons.

Black elevator operators' grievances and demands were often prominently featured in the union newsletter. Of the existing newsletters, race is never discussed or used to describe workers. Only through newspaper records are passenger operators identified as African Americans. Further, union newsletters reveal that none of the black operators' demands involved challenging the racial order of department store work. Instead, like black workers at Klein's and Ohrbach's, they only made requests that bettered their day-to-day labors during their early years in the union (1940–1941). They appealed for the installation of fans in the elevators and the dispensing with uniform hats during the hot summer months. Other demands included the provision of sweaters to shield them from the "constant drafts on the main floor" in the winter and that the store, not the operators, be responsible for purchasing their gloves, since they were a required element of their uniform. Operators also asked for a resolution to the lunchtime crowding of employee elevators, a formal salary review (which the store had failed to conduct "for years"), and the observance of seniority when overtime was extended.

Their participation in the union resulted in two major accomplishments: the store provided operators with winter sweaters and extra employee elevators during the lunchtime rush. Additionally, the union provided African American workers, who were typically treated as second-class citizens, with a sense of belonging and community. After an elevator department's union meeting, workers commented, "Never before have the majority of men in this department been able to discuss their problems— how they affect us and how to remedy them. Until we became union-minded such a thing was frowned upon and discouraged in every way. We never really knew each other and never trusted anyone. Now that we have the union to help us, we know whom to trust and we fear no one." Also, the union used inclusive language such as "we" and referred to elevator operators as part of the "non-selling or service group of employees." Their concerns were addressed as one unit, alongside freight operators, restaurant and tearoom employees, and warehouse and deliverymen. Correspondingly, their successes were announced and celebrated in the same fashion.[27]

Social events were held that included all union members, regardless of race and color. At parties, elevator operators, packers, collectors, and clerical and sales workers danced the mambo, jive, and waltz; and a basketball team was organized that invited all male workers to participate. (This is particularly striking considering that at many department stores, notably those in the South, such events were segregated by race.) These events built camaraderie, increased black union involvement, and lessened racial strife (perhaps helping temper whites' opinions of African Americans as servile, docile, and unintelligent, and African Americans' feelings that the union was a "white man's cause"). As a result, these changes laid the foundation for the strong interracial unionism needed to improve workers' conditions. This is best evidenced in *Sparks*, Macy's employee newsletter (managed by white workers). A strong correlation appears between the unions' development and the number and types of articles that featured African American workers. Before Local 1-S, African Americans typically appeared in the newsletter when they celebrated an employment anniversary. And in these

FIGURE 6 *New York, New York. R. H. Macy and Company Department Store during the Week before Christmas,* 1942. Library of Congress Prints and Photographs Division, LC-USW3-013120-D.

cases, blacks were portrayed as "friendly store servants" in a photograph or brief note. Later, as contact between black and white workers increased in the space of the union, lengthier, more detailed coverage was provided. Black employees were now described as intelligent, poised, and thoughtful. For example, in January 1942, *Sparks* applauded operator Robert Smith for his customer service. According to the news story, as Smith was running an elevator during the Christmas rush, "on one of the floors he was about to pass, he noticed an elderly, crippled lady and her companion. Appraising the situation with intelligence and sympathy, Mr. Smith stopped the car, turned around to the people in it, and asked them if they would please make room for the customer. They complied with alacrity."[28]

When the nation entered World War II, Local 1-S, like other retail unions, found its course in the department store business complicated as the industry—let alone the country—underwent profound changes, most notably regarding consumption and labor. First, consumption took on new significance, emerging as a way for Americans to support the war effort; and, as a result, department stores became sites to partake in patriotic consumption. Many sold war bonds, stamps, American flags, and other merchandise that demonstrated their loyalty. Macy's sold film reels of the Japanese attack on Pearl Harbor, Douglas MacArthur, and the bombing of Manila. It also offered its customers the opportunity to purchase food boxes for the "boys abroad" (figure 6). Gimbel's provided "customers a chance to buy 'patriotic envelopes' and stamped envelopes mailed from 17 American [military] bases." The retailer also "encouraged customers who were 'knitting like mad for that man of yours in the service' to buy yarn in regulation colors" from them.[29] Department stores also leveraged their influence to inspire customers to shop but not overshop, to give to the Red Cross, to conserve rubber, gas, paper, and metal by saving these items and visiting stores via mass transit or walking, to sew their own clothes, and to grow their own Victory Gardens.[30]

Second, department stores suffered a significant loss of labor. Since the federal government judged retail work as nonessential to the war defense, nearly all male employees eligible for combat were drafted. Many female workers resigned to work in defense industries and other industries, such as banking, that were liberating their hiring policies. In an effort to cope with this labor shortage, merchants experimented with different forms of retailing. Many adopted self-service forms of retailing. In a 1943 talk sponsored by the National Retail Dry Goods Association, Franklin Lamb, president of a firm that manufactured shelving fixtures, expressed the reasoning behind this selling method: "To meet the present conditions, it becomes necessary to deliberately break up the practice of forcing assistance on customers. . . . The fewer salespeople on the floor simply do not have the time for anything but stock-keeping and giving asked-for help to customers." Some stores presented all merchandise on the selling floor—sometimes piled up on tables or arranged on clothing racks—for customers to examine and choose what they wanted. With this approach, salesclerks answered questions, replenished merchandise, retrieved sizes or items stored in the stockroom, and acted as cashier once customers independently found their desired items. Other retailers began using "open merchandise displays," where sample goods were openly displayed on the selling floor, giving customers the opportunity "to examine without intervention of sales workers." If a customer wanted to purchase a particular item, he or she would locate a salesclerk, who would retrieve the item from the stockroom.

This approach necessitated that workers and consumers continue to interact but permitted stores to rely on fewer, and often novice, sales workers.[31]

As the war revolutionized the industry, it also transformed the labor movement. Retail unions found continuing the work and strategies adopted in the prolabor milieu of the 1930s to be quite difficult. First, they lost a cadre of organizers and members. And second, retail unions, like other labor organizations of the time, demonstrated their support for democracy abroad and at home by vowing not to strike or engage in any confrontation tactics during wartime. As a result, they were left without their most effective method of protest—the ability to strike and picket.

But these changes did not drive the department store movement to a standstill. Instead, retail unions took advantage of wartime patriotism and changing labor dynamics to advance their goals. Because of the loss of white men, a new leadership rose to power: African Americans and women were promoted into union leadership roles. Elevator operator Atkinson was elected vice president of the predominantly white Local 1-S before being drafted (a position he reclaimed on his return). By May 1946, other African Americans were voted into office: three African American presidents, one black financial secretary, and at least one black officer each term.[32] Under this new leadership, Local 1-S and other New York store unions established temporary antidiscrimination committees composed of black and white members. These committees were tasked with implementing and monitoring fair employment practices in local department stores. They were of particular importance because retailing was not a defense industry and therefore did not fall under the purview of President Franklin D. Roosevelt's Executive Order 8802 and the Fair Employment Commission.

From its inception, Local 1-S's antidiscrimination committee recognized that it "had a two-fold job: to fight for equal rights and legislation to guarantee those equal rights and also to fight at home in Macy's against the discriminatory practices there."[33] Alongside local civil rights and community organizations, Local 1-S pressured Macy's to end its Jim Crow practices. Often relying on the empty threat of demonstration, the union persuaded the retailer to relax its discriminatory hiring practices during the war. Management was surprisingly amenable to hiring a few African American sales and office workers. It likely figured that this course of action was wisest, as it thwarted any discord that might disrupt the flow of business, enabled managers to cope with wartime labor shortages, and demonstrated their support for democracy. Public opinion, as exemplified by the rise in consumer activism and support for retail unions in the 1930s, coupled with government initiatives and court rulings that favored desegregation and labor rights, also influenced Macy's decision. All American citizens were expected to make massive sacrifices, and retailers were not exempt. By demonstrating their commitment to American democracy through merit hiring, retailers probably believed they could win back the public approval of big retailing that black consumer movements, government investigations, and union activities of the 1930s had destroyed. Additionally, store officials may have considered that advancing African Americans, even if only a few, and women—essentially, a meaningful portion of their remaining workforce—would dissuade their employees from leaving the store for factories that offered higher pay.

At Macy's, Bloomingdale's, and other department stores founded by and/ or managed by Jews, the decision to hire African Americans in positions of responsibility was also likely tied to executives' own racialized ethnic background, history, and present circumstances. As many scholars have explored, the Second World War was a watershed moment in Black-Jewish relations. It heightened American Jews' sensitivity to and sympathy for the plight of African Americans, and vice versa. Both groups recognized a kind of shared history and experience as a result of anti-Semitism and race discrimination, or what one scholar calls "parallel patterns of oppression," as well as the contradictions of America's democracy abroad and at home. Jewish Americans and African Americans, as a result, "developed communication along the lines of basic civil rights and marked a degree of mutual interests and understanding" that advanced the black freedom movement.[34]

In the fall of 1945, in a political climate committed to racial equality, as epitomized by the passage of the Ives-Quinn bill and the formation of New York's State Commission against Discrimination, Local 1-S voted to make its antidiscrimination committee permanent and intensified its pressure on Macy's to hire sales and clerical workers regardless of color, religion, or national origin. One of the permanent committee's first victories occurred "when most of the Christmas hiring had finished" later that year. "There were not many jobs available and management had an out," a committee report detailed. But pressure from the committee forced management "to make some token hirings and so by Christmas time there were at least 8 Negro salesclerks in Macy's."[35]

Several months later, Local 1-S won sales jobs for Lucille Valentine and Jack Miller. Valentine was promoted from packer to saleswoman in the housedresses department at "no reduction in salary and with greater earning opportunity than before."[36] Miller became Macy's first Negro salesman. After years of service as an elevator operator and upon his return from the war, he applied to the Employment Office for a transfer to a sales department. Store unions were particularly concerned with the "policy by which service men and women [would] return to their jobs once the war [was] over."[37] Union leaders Loring Michelson and Sam Kovenetsky contended that Miller "had taken our [war] Victory quite literally. He had personally participated in bringing this Victory and he was understandably anxious to share in its advance." For several months, store officials evaded and resisted Miller's request, but he remained undeterred. Finally, Miller was offered a sales job, but with a significant reduction in salary: his wages of $39.75 per week, which he earned as an elevator operator, were cut to $33.00 per week. "In spite of the loss of earnings that Mr. Miller would suffer, he chose to accept the position in the belief that the principle involved was far more important than the money involved." The antidiscrimination committee admired his act but was unwilling to "accept without vehement protest this act on the part of Macy's." Hoping to secure Miller an increase to his former earnings, it asked store president Jack Strauss for a meeting and rallied union members. The committee's effectiveness in securing the raise, however, is not documented in extant historical records.[38]

In 1946, union leader Atkinson also advanced to sales. After defending his country in the war, Atkinson returned to Macy's. During his reinstatement interview, the interviewer invited Atkinson to resume his prewar work as an elevator starter. To this offer, he "pitched," "Lady, look, I fought a war for democracy, and that's what I was promised: a better world. . . . Now I want a better job." Surprised, the interviewer implored employment manager Helen Hyde to finish the meeting. Hyde said, "Oh, Mr. Atkinson, it's so nice to have you back. I know you'll be happy to have your job, but the interviewer tells me that you're not happy with that." She then asked Atkinson what job he wanted. As Local 1-S vice president, Atkinson was familiar with the responsibilities and salaries of all department store positions and knew salesmen in the furniture department earned the highest pay. So he said, "Furniture." Hyde refused. Atkinson then said, "Rugs," and again Hyde refused. His third choice was the radio department. Atkinson had gained experience with radios during his service in the war, but he was informed that there were no openings in this department and was assigned to work as an elevator starter. One week later, Hyde called Atkinson and offered him a sales position in the toy department. Not long after, he learned of an opening in radios, applied, and, as a result of his training and seniority, became a salesman in the radio department.[39]

In 1947, Local 1-S's antidiscrimination committee, along with the New York Urban League (NYUL) and the State Commission against Discrimination, likely helped integrate Macy's Executive Training Squad. Mary Dean was one of the first African Americans accepted into the squad and then appointed junior assistant manager of men's department and women's handkerchief department. She was promoted to senior assistant manager of the handbags department in 1948 and elevated to manager of men's and women's handkerchief department in January 1951. Dean hailed from exceptional origins, as the daughter of civil rights activist Channing Tobias, wife of William Dean of the United Nations, and mother of two children. She earned her bachelor of arts degree from New York University and a master of arts degree in fine arts from Columbia University, taught at Paine and Bennett Colleges and at Atlanta University, and served as director of arts and crafts of the National United Service Organizations during the war.[40] Another alumnus of Macy's Executive Training Squad was Frederick D. Wilkinson, a World War II veteran, a graduate of Howard University and Harvard Graduate School of Business Administration, the husband of former psychologist Jeane Ann Lee, and father of three. Wilkinson's first appointment was as junior buyer of socks. He was promoted to buyer of men's shirts and furnishings in 1962, administrator and manager of Macy's branch store in Jamaica, Queens, in 1968, and later became the retailer's first African American vice president.[41]

Other antidiscrimination committees made similar progress. In 1946, thanks to these committees, most New York stores had hired token blacks in sales and office positions, although none of these new hires were assigned to "choice merchandise" departments such as furniture, where they could earn large commissions. Under the leadership of an African American president, Bloomingdale's local union pressured store management to hire four black salesclerks. Gimbel's had hired one African American salesclerk (out of 1,700 total sales workers). Hearns appointed six blacks to sales positions (its total sales workforce was 2,000 persons). In 1947, the *Chicago Defender* reported that Macy's, the city's largest store, led in black employment "with an estimated number of 10–20 . . . [although, the] Union (CIO) didn't believe the number exceeded 15. They work in buttons, hosiery, curtains, socks, hardware, and radio." That same year, Gimbel's hired two additional black sales workers, celebrating a not so impressive three hires of color in white-collar work, while Saks Fifth Avenue reported employing one African American sales worker. By the early 1950s, however, the local committees had expanded the hiring of African American white-collar workers in these retail establishments: in 1951, twelve black sales workers were hired at Bloomingdale's; and between October 1952 and February 1953, five out of eighteen blacks hired at Gimbel's and Saks Fifth Avenue were assigned as office clerks.[42]

New York department stores accepted merit hiring but that did not mean they welcomed it. Several stores placed limitations on the process of integration using "hidden discrimination in hiring and promotion."[43] To combat this, Local 1-S's antidiscrimination committee familiarized itself with the hiring process: working with the Negro Labor Victory Committee, the YWCA, the NYUL, and several local churches, the union identified African American applicants and then assumed the responsibility of training job candidates on the Macy's interview process. This process always began with a preliminary interview and was followed by an employment test and a hiring interview. An applicant who passed these stages was sent to the Employment Office to apply for open sales positions.

Local 1-S schooled applicants on appearance, manners and alertness, the art of interviewing, and the employment test. All applicants were instructed to make no mention of the union during the interview, and, should the interviewer refer to stock, packing, or other menial work, they were advised to "pleasantly but firmly stick to selling (or clerical)." Candidates also were told that if they are asked to take an employment test, upon completing it they should ask to see the corrected examination. This was of particular importance, according to Local 1-S, because those in charge of hiring at Macy's often failed black applicants, even when they had passed, in a covert effort to evade integration. Finally, all applicants were ordered to report back to the antidiscrimination committee after they had applied. Constant communication between the two parties, the union believed, would ensure that any misinformation provided by Macy's management was quickly corrected. Management, it advised potential applicants, "give . . . misinformation as is their want to put you off till there are no jobs left." Also, once a candidate verified that he or she had applied for a position of responsibility at Macy's, Local 1-S contacted the store's Employment Office about the candidate's application status and "if we get no satisfaction, then we plan to go to arbitration on violation of contract and also submit each individual to the state commission against discrimination."[44]

As the union worked to circumvent these and other barriers, Macy's employed other unscrupulous tactics. Although the retailer pledged to hire

African Americans in sales and office positions, it promised to uphold this pledge only as long as workers of color demonstrated that they were "capable of doing the job."[45] But, as proven by the store's interview process, "capable" could be so situational and malleable that few African Americans fulfilled this qualification. And, for those deemed "capable," Macy's instituted a 10 percent quota on black hires in all of its departments. This quota, according to the union, ensured that "a Negro may be hired to-day for a job, he will not be hired tomorrow even though there are still openings."[46]

Macy's also adopted a new pay scale to discourage African Americans from seeking positions of responsibility by providing that African Americans in white-collar positions actually earned less than those employed in menial jobs. Many black employees were unlike Miller and Atkinson; they were unwilling to transfer to sales or clerical jobs if that meant taking a pay cut. Of the few available union records documenting the organization's identification of potential job applicants of color, Anna Smith was the only other employee that expressed an interest in doing this. In 1945, Smith had worked as a stockclerk for three years and hoped to transfer to sales because she found stock work to be too strenuous. During her interview with union officials, Smith indicated that she earned $31.25 per week in her current position and was willing to accept a lower salary only if necessary and with the promise that she would eventually earn this much or more in the future. Unfortunately, despite having the ability and intelligence to be trained, Smith had no previous experience in sales and was thus deemed an unfavorable applicant by Local 1-S.[47]

Local 1-S's antidiscrimination committee, and others, pushed for more than racial equality in the workplace, even as the Taft-Hartley Act created massive national strife within union ranks. (Local 1-S ended its affiliation with the Retail, Wholesale and Department Store Union [RWDSU], which supported the Act in 1948, and rejoined the CIO as an independent union as a result of this strife.) Since the inception of the union's antidiscrimination committee, it had maintained an education campaign to purge any vestiges of prejudice among its members, the public, and store officials. This campaign relied heavily on public meetings on the various manifestations of race discrimination and tactics for ensuring its end, as well as the creation and distribution of antidiscrimination pamphlets, articles, and the like. In 1943, the union joined black city councilman Benjamin J. Davis to protest the sale of "mugging night sticks" in Macy's on three grounds: first, the "daily newspapers have made the term, 'mugging' synonymous with Negroes and that the sticks therefore represented incitement against

Negroes"; second, "that any white woman who possessed one of the weapons could attack any Negro whose looks she did not like and later plead defense against possible 'mugging'"; and third, "that sale of the nightsticks possibly violated police department regulations concerning carrying weapons by civilians."[48]

In 1949, with its wartime "no-strike" pledge having long expired, Local 1-S and the NAACP campaigned against the selling of the film *Little Black Sambo*, which the store eventually removed from its shelves, and held demonstrations to force the removal of a store window display featuring a "doll representing a baby born on the 'Amos and Andy' radio program." The window display also presented a "caricature of a Negro man in the style used by those who spread race hatred." Three years later, the antidiscrimination committee demanded that management stop conducting business with foreign vendors that used "nigger" to designate the color "black" on their merchandise and invoices. The committee stipulated that business could resume once this color designation was replaced.[49] Similarly, the antidiscrimination committee for Local 2, Gimbel's local union, charged Rose Amos, union member and office worker, with making "slanderous remarks" and using "vile language" and "racial slurs against her African American and Jewish co-workers." Local 2's joint general counsel dismissed Amos from the union in 1951.[50]

Retail unions also campaigned against race discrimination outside the confines of department stores. The executive board of Local 1-S issued a formal statement expressing its opposition to segregated baseball leagues in 1942—five years before Jackie Robinson broke the Major League Baseball color line. Unions wrote newspaper articles and letters to their congressmen condemning racial discrimination, giving particular attention to the mistreatment of blacks in the South. They also protested terrorism directed against African Americans in Freeport, New York, and Columbia, Tennessee; campaigned for the termination of May Quinn, an educator charged with teaching her students anti-Semitism and other "un-American attitudes"; rallied against the Veteran Administration's denial of accreditation to the United Negro and Allied Veterans; and worked to prevent the election of another racist to fill senator Theodore G. Bilbo's seat.

The department store movement benefited from New York City's vibrant and powerful retail unions. Communist labor organizers helped create these unions, while the principles and activities of civil rights groups in the 1930s and 1940s, as well as the prolabor milieu of the time, shaped the composition, goals, and strategies of local department store unions. Local 1-S, in particular, provided African American workers with an inside vantage—one that suitably complemented black consumerism, leveraged their labor power, and won white support—to dismantle discriminatory employment and consumption practices. In just a few years, the labor movement in the department store industry opened many doors formerly closed to African American workers and consumers in New York City. Had more department store unions throughout the country modeled themselves after New York unions, the department store movement would have likely found far more widespread success, happened sooner rather than later, and been more lasting.

Chicago Unions and the Department Store Movement

The prevalence of unionization in New York's retail industry, coupled with the vibrancy of black activism surrounding issues of production and consumption before and during World War II, significantly shaped the nature and direction of the department store movement in New York. In Chicago, the involvement of unions was not as widespread or profound, even though the URWDSEU and the USEU of the CIO represented many of the city's department stores and accepted African American members. In downtown stores, however, these labor organizations generally took neither a strong nor an active role in the implementation of merit hiring in Chicago's retail industry. But in their representation of the South Center Department Store in Bronzeville (figure 7), the URWDSEU and the USEU, specifically, advocated on behalf of store workers of color, helping improve their pay and work conditions, and indirectly broadened the goals of the larger department store campaign.

Jewish real estate developers and entrepreneurs Harry M. Englestein and Louis Englestein owned South Center Department Store. However, the store opened with an integrated sales force led by African American Richard Jones in 1928. Jones was not only the face of South Center but also a paradigm of how department store work could provide middle-class status. (Many store customers, in fact, earnestly believed that Jones owned and ran the business.) Jones started at South Center in 1928 as assistant to the store president. He steadily moved up to general superintendent and subsequently became vice president—in both positions he managed and supervised store operations and employees. In 1942, Jones resigned and joined the army. He returned to South Center four years later and was eventually appointed vice president in charge of personnel and public relations—a position he held

SOUTH CENTER DEPARTMENT STORE, 47TH ST. AT SOUTH PARKWAY, CHICAGO.

FIGURE 7 *South Center Department Store, 47th Street at South Parkway* (Chicago, Illinois, 1928). Original Curt Teich Postcard Donation, Newberry Library, Chicago, A118873.

until 1954, when he was selected as director of U.S. Operations Mission to Liberia and subsequently U.S. ambassador to Liberia. Jones once again returned to South Center in 1959 as vice president in charge of personnel and public relations. After less than a year, he left to become the executive vice president of Victory Mutual Life Insurance. Jones would come back to South Center once more in 1963, where he assisted in the reorganization of the store under different ownership until September 1966.[51]

Over time, South Center employed more African Americans in nontraditional jobs than whites. In 1952, for example, Bernadine Carrickett joined the South Center team, becoming the first African American style counselor and women's buyer in Chicago. A graduate of Fisk University, Carrickett began her career as a secretary to a furrier and later became a parts inspector in a factory during World War II. Sometime after the war, Carrickett worked as a commentator at local fashion shows and was the first African American woman to appear regularly on television and radio as a fashion commentator for a Loop shop. At South Center, Carrickett made "five trips a year to the dress marts of New York, where she select[ed] and purchase[d] clothes which . . . intrigue[d] her customers." She maintained a clientele of "about 50 socially prominent women, who [bought the] special creations" she purchased during her New York trips. Much of Carrickett's success was the result of her ability to understand her clients and influence their buying habits. She recognized, for example, that black customers were style and quality conscious, were "inhibited about wearing the color red," and did not "purchase materials in dark brown because of the difficulty of blending the color with their complexions."[52]

The black press frequently commended South Center for its hiring practices and for being a major retail establishment that served and treated black customers with respect, as its practices facilitated the creation of a "leavening group within the Negro population." Working at South Center offered many African Americans entry into the middle class—a group, according to black journalist Roi Ottley, that was college educated, registered Republicans, affiliated with the Episcopalian or Presbyterian Church, and leaders in their community. As Ottley detailed, "They move smoothly and complacently within the Negro community, earning a livelihood from the Negro market. . . . They may have a slightly lower economic status than white persons belonging to the identical class, but in the world in which they live, they have a sheltered and relatively secure position, and enjoy as well various forms of distinction." He continued, "In a word, they provide the vanguard of the race's economic and cultural progress, and . . . as such, they represent the most stable element on the south side."[53] South Center also "ethically" sold African Americans brand-name merchandise and welcomed them to attend classes and events on homemaking, child care, interior decorating, and personal appearance classes that spoke directly to their specific experiences, needs, and wants. Moreover, the store sponsored tournaments at Parkway Community Center, essay and art contests in nearby schools, and special classes in swimming and ice skating on the Midway.[54] All of this, many believed, facilitated the rise and proliferation of a black middle class.

The Englesteins saw themselves as masterminds of a "noble experiment"— a humanistic business endeavor that enabled African Americans to climb the socioeconomic ladder. But, like good businessmen, they saw African American workers and shoppers as commodities, untapped resources in the consumer market ready to be exploited for profit. The mass migration of black southerners to northern cities in the first half of the twentieth century had given birth to the "Negro Market." In the urban North, blacks found better jobs and wages and subsequently spent their new money on consumer goods. Downtown department stores in Chicago virtually ignored this growing black population, but the Englesteins saw a window of opportunity. Like Henry Ford, the Englesteins understood that to profit from the "Negro Market," they would have to employ African Americans in steady, well-paid jobs and encourage them to buy merchandise sold by their establishment. They tailored their marketing and business strategies to meet the needs and desires of the city's sizable and rapidly expanding black community, and, of course, earn their disposable income—which by the end of the Second World War "made up a lucrative $8 billion to $10 billion market" that, one fair employment activist claimed, "was larger than Canada's and potentially equal to the entire U.S. non-European export market."[55]

South Center, thus, was created to be simultaneously a shopping venue, a leisure site, and a community center. It housed Madame C. J. Walker's hair salon and school, the latter occupying an entire floor of South Center where it trained women and men interested in becoming hair stylists and independent business owners. The Englesteins' department store also served as the site for several community events such as the *Chicago Defender*'s Cooking School in the fall of 1939, a competition that featured cooking demonstrations by Eloise Keller, and music auditions sponsored by the National Auditions of Negro Music and Dancing, a group led by attorney Nathan K. McGill and musician Noble Sissle.[56]

The Englesteins also designed advertisements that spoke directly to their targeted clientele and were prominently featured in black media (which is particularly noteworthy, as few major retailers advertised in black publications or on black radio programs). A 1948 advertisement for hair antiseptic in the *Chicago Defender* detailed the product specifications and addressed concerns specific to African Americans. The ad promised that the hair antiseptic was the "finest medicated tar scalp formula your money can buy" because "your hair and scalp deserve fine care." Here the store addressed black consumers' desire for quality goods and name-brand products.[57] The advertisement also promised to refund consumers' money should they find the product unsatisfactory. For African Americans, this provision was tremendously important for two reasons. First, among downtown department store owners, black hair was considered greasy, dirty, and unsanitary; for this reason, ostensibly, African Americans were not permitted to try on or return hats because whites feared that their hair would contaminate the item. Second, having the option to return a product or receive a refund on an unsatisfactory product was unheard of. African Americans were expected to purchase items without trying them on or testing the product to ensure satisfaction.

In addition to demonstrating concern for black consumers, advertisements often referenced South Center's employment of African American sales workers. The hair antiseptic ad, for example, instructed consumers to purchase the serum "from Miss J. Jackson at the drug counter in the South Center Department Store."[58] At the end of this two-paragraph advertisement with a graphic image of an African American woman fussing with her hair, the store once again directed customers to head directly to Miss J. Jackson's drug counter to solve their hair woes.

Harry Englestein not only hired and sold to African Americans but also promoted himself and his store as advocates of black welfare and advancement, leveraging a type of paternalism that enabled him to woo black customers and gain their confidence and loyalty. (This paternalism, however, did not necessarily extend to his employees.) He often donated money and time to black churches, institutions, and organizations. In April 1935, for example, Englestein presented $2,000 in checks to ministers and leaders of local charitable institutions, including Provident Hospital, Ebenezer and Pilgrim churches, and the South Park Branch of the YWCA.[59] He also led the South Central Community Council, which, alongside the *Chicago Defender*, pressed the city government to build a fieldhouse and institute a recreational program in Washington Park for local black residents.[60] In 1948, Englestein worked with South Side merchants "to discuss ways of increasing community confidence in neighborhood business. In a unanimous resolution they decided to compete in price, quality, assortment, and service with Loop and other outstanding stores."[61]

In an address to executives and employees of the store, Mary McLeod Bethune saluted South Center for being "an outstanding institution" that "brings together people of all races in a common battle for justice and equality among men. . . . They have not asked for black people and white people, but just people who could produce" and help set "the tempo of the future."[62] Those who worked day in and day out at the department store—80 percent of whom were African American in 1948—generally held a different opinion, however. South Center's black employees were victims of the same race ideology that afflicted downtown department stores. As one observer noted, South Center's black employees "have been booted around and have been the most under-paid in the city."[63] They received lower wages and fewer benefits and opportunities for advancement than white employees at this and other Chicago department stores.[64]

As a result, South Center employees sought union representation. The earliest documented incident of South Center unionism occurred in May 1942, when approximately 80 percent of the store's workforce "walked out over the question of the right to be represented by a union" of their choosing. Workers vied for Department Store Employee Unions Local 291 of the URWDSEU-CIO, while store owner Harry Englestein favored Local 73 of the Building Service Employees Union (BSEU) of the AFL—a union that had already established a strong foothold in several State Street stores. Englestein "was willing to bargain with a union, it is said, but sought to secure AFL affiliation." The BSEU, but more specifically the AFL, the *Chicago Defender* accused, would safeguard Englestein's power and control. "The AFL [had been] brought into the store by [Englestein]," the paper insisted, "who preferred to sign a three-year back-door contract with the AFL giving the employes a $1 increase for three years rather than deal with a bonafide [*sic*] CIO union and grant REAL increases. He preferred an organization that had practiced color discrimination for years."[65]

But workers remained wholeheartedly committed to Local 291. In fact, during the strike, the union "not only claim[ed] a majority but . . . represent[ed] a majority of [South Center's] employes," according to Local 291's business manager.[66] The strike lasted only five weeks, but the dispute continued for nearly a year. Finally, in late December 1942, it was decided that an election would be held no later than January 15. This election presented employees with the opportunity to cast their vote for their preferred bargaining agent and thus bring an end to the jurisdictional dispute.[67] Extant records strongly suggest that Local 291 won the election and continued to represent South Center workers until late 1948, when leadership was "shifted over to [USEU] Local 329 of the AFL in the hope that its additional bargaining power would gain . . . [them] substantially more."[68]

And more they got. According to the South Center Unity newsletter, in late November 1948, "one hundred workers at the South Center Department Store joined our Local. They were dissatisfied with their long negotiations with management and a measly wage offer of $1. Within 9 days Local 329 was able to boost the ante to a $3 raise, another $1 step-up the next year, and approximately $85 in back-pay to each member."[69] At this time, employees also aggressively demanded an end to race discrimination in job appointment and wages. With the notable exception of Richard Jones, whites had held most of the supervisory positions since the store opened, even if only in name, and received better wages and benefits, while African Americans worked in sales, offices, and maintenance positions at depressed wages and without many of the amenities extended to their white coworkers. Additionally, white employees, even those eligible to join the union, were forbidden from doing so and, as nonunion people, were paid higher wages and received better benefits. This design benefited management and was used to impede the maturation of a powerful interracial union. They demanded the "inclusion of so-called 'assistant buyers' in [the] union." Union organizational director Sidney Lens explained, "Their rates are much higher than those of union members. These people are in reality salespeople, all white. [Harry] Englestein . . . is very touchy on this subject; claims he had trouble getting white help to come to that neighborhood, etc. Outside of one or two the assistant buyers are not really supervisory."[70]

South Center employees also engaged in a lengthy battle to secure higher wages and commissions, a five-day, forty-hour workweek, paid leave, insurance, breakfast and supper money, and stronger seniority protection. Eager to meet this end, workers often called attention to Chicago's ever-increasing cost of living and justified their demands by paralleling their conditions to those of their counterparts in other comparable retail establishments as well as to industrial laborers—both of whom earned more than South Center employees and were offered better benefits. Industrial laborers, the union pointed out, were guaranteed a minimum rate of thirty dollars per week and a five-day, forty-hour workweek by law. To add insult to injury, the organization learned that South Center "wage scales are lower than in comparable stores in the rest of the city."[71] And it did not have to go far to prove this claim: "Every other contract of our Local Union," South Center employees showed, "has a 5-day 40 hour-workweek. Most outlying stores such as Goldblatt's, Wieboldt's, Hillman's [a grocery chain], and others, and many Loop department stores, also operate on a 5-day 40-hour workweek."[72]

Adding fuel to a raging fire was the continued wage disparity between black and white workers. In 1950, the starting wage for African American workers was $0.53 per hour. Wages were not much better for those who had devoted twenty years of service to South Center: they earned only $32.50 per week and a supper stipend of $0.75, while whites received higher wages and $1.50 supper allowance.[73] In an open letter to the public, the union explained "that [this] is evidence of racial discrimination. . . . Not only must they eat less on the job, they must continue the habit when they take home their less than $30 weekly wage. All of this, remember, while the cost of living in the Negro ghetto goes higher and higher."[74]

After three months of difficult talks, South Center employees had inched closer to their ultimate goals. They negotiated $27.50 for a forty-two-hour workweek for all employees; newly hired and incoming workers would earn $24.50 per week for forty-two hours' work during their probationary period and receive the aforementioned pay thereafter.[75] More specifically, workers were promised "a $2 overall increase, $2.75 for all employees with five years or more of service with the company, $2 increase on the minimum, a one-half percent increase on commission rates for the shoe salesmen in addition to the $2 raise, a retrospective date on the aforementioned to February 1, 1950, an increase on supper money to $1, and an attempt to mutually adjust the workers' 6th day (one-half day of work) so that the time worked is in the morning rather than the present afternoon schedule," with the intent of providing "an unbroken half day."[76] In return, the union agreed on a "no strike" clause, which provided "during the term of this agreement and for a period of 30 days after the expiration of this agreement, there shall be no strikes, work stoppages, diminution of work, slowdowns, suspension of or interference with work on the part of the Union or any of its members, nor shall there be any lockout on the part of the Employer on any account whatever."[77]

Harry Englestein also promised that, should the store show moderate profits in 1950, he would give workers a five-day, forty-hour workweek in 1951.[78] But, as many expected, when the time came, Englestein reneged. He did, however, offer to shorten the workweek but only if "the forty hour week was to be at the same hourly pay as the forty-two hour week, plus a picayune 2½ [cents] per hour."[79] Workers rejected his offer. Management then proposed a one-dollar raise, as opposed to a wage decrease. Once again, employees rebuffed the proposal. They insisted that management could afford to provide a larger pay raise given that merchandise prices had increased 10–15 percent and that management regularly donated large sums to black churches and organizations.[80]

Unable to reach a peaceful settlement, South Center employees made preparations to strike. They consulted their union's national office for approval. The general president William L. McFetridge agreed not to veto any strike action but asked workers to partake in mediation before demonstrating. With the intervention of a mediator, a settlement was reached in April 1951. The terms were a "five-day, forty-hour week, raises of $3 for selling and $3.50 for non-selling, over and above the reduction of hours, a $4 and $4.50 boost in minimum wages and other fringe issues," including improved commissions in the furniture department, and a $1 attendance bonus to be provided as part of their regular wages. In a letter to Mc-Fetridge, Lens celebrated, "The money and workweek provisions are exactly what we asked for when we began negotiations and we're proud to say that this is the first independent outlying department store with a five day week."[81]

Despite this victory, tensions continued to mount between management and workers, and finally exploded to enormous portions in 1952. Complaints about the store's feeble incentive system, supervisors (and in one instance a stockperson) selling in direct competition with salespeople, and, of course, "the main issue of MORE MONEY?" persisted.[82] Workers' pay rates, they complained, were roughly $12 per week less than in downtown and other neighborhood stores.[83] Hoping to end the wage discrepancies once and for all, a committee of South Center union representatives consisting of Virgie Mosley, Julia Blackwell, and Gladys Stevens, accompanied by their spokesman Sidney Lens, met with store executives Robert Mackie and Louise Connolly to demand "(1) changes in unit, (2) changes in hours and premium pay, (3) contract conditions, and (4) wages," specifically a pay increase of $4.20 per week, in late March.[84]

A couple of weeks later, in early April, another meeting was held. However, only Lens was invited. Here, Mackie shared that officials were unwilling to agree to any demands until the union discharged union steward Virgie Mosley, who, management alleged, "is running the store." A longtime employee, Mosley had worked at South Center since it opened. In 1941, after nearly fourteen years of service, Mosley helped form the store union and remained central to its operation. Her dedication to workers' rights and the union was celebrated among store employees and customers but often placed her at odds with management. Mackie and his wife, in particular, held a strong dislike for Mosley, which often played out on the sales floor. For example, on one occasion, when Mosley learned that Mrs. Mackie, then a supervisor in the female accessories department, was mistreating personnel and insulting customers, Mosley organized a boycott, whereby all employees in Mrs. Mackie's department stopped working until she corrected her behavior.[85] The union rejected the entire counterproposal, which, in addition to demanding the dismissal of Mosley, also provided for the extension of the present contract only if seniority was abrogated from contracts, and granted all store employees the right to sell.

By late April, negotiations had reached an impasse and the union had unanimously voted to authorize its committee to strike, should that become necessary. The two sides attempted mediation,[86] but ultimately their inability to reach an agreement led to a strike. Picketing commenced on May 15 at 7:00 A.M., with 80–90 employees out of 150 total and quickly gained the support of the entire South Side community. Local shop owners openly sympathized with the movement. Reverend A. P. Jackson of the Liberty Baptist Church visited the picket; other ministers called to wish workers luck, and "at least ten ministers" told their congregations to respect the picket lines. Leaders of the CIO Transport Service Employees pledged their support. And the *Chicago Enterprise* and *Chicago World* newspapers wrote supportive editorials.[87] Not everyone, however, was so encouraging. Days before the picket, the wife of one employee wrote to Mosley's husband, asking that he "let" his wife "quit." She stated: "Please let your wife quit so my husband won't have to lose his job. I am sick and we have a family. If we don't pay our rent we will [be] put outdoors. He need [*sic*] his job."[88]

Two and half hours into the picketing, the demonstration hit a snag when "For Rent" signs were posted in the store windows and newspapers released the story that South Center was going out of business because it could not meet the union's demands. Management reported that employees wanted exorbitant wage increases of $74,000. Union leaders accused the company of spreading false information. Workers wanted $15,000 in wage increases; the store was willing to provide only $7,000. The 1952 strike, however, was not the first time Englestein threatened to sell the store. In April 1947, after employees went on strike for an eight-dollar raise on their twenty-two-dollar minimum wages, he posted a "For Sale" sign in the window and began negotiating to dispose of stock.[89] The same tactic was also employed during a labor dispute in 1950.

However, unlike the previous incidents, the posting of the "For Rent" signs was not a trick or gimmick. Englestein was, in fact, preparing to sell South Center Department Store. He commented, "I'm not kidding, this is the end. An auctioneer will inventory the business today and I'll sell it to the highest bidder." Immediately, union members voted to end the strike and began entertaining the possibility of forming a corporation to buy the business and rent space in the building. Ten days later, on May 26, the committee met with Englestein. He affirmed that he would sell the store but only if the union agreed to the conditions offered in April, including the dismissal of Mosley, and made this a condition of the sale.[90]

Workers dug in their heels and filed a complaint with the National Labor Relations Board (NLRB). In their charge, they alleged that Harry Englestein engaged in unfair labor and bargaining practices and failed to pay employees their regular and vacation pay during the months the store prepared to close—despite spending $23,000 preparing for the anniversary sale and $6,710 on eleven full-page advertisements in one newspaper alone during the settlement process and as he prepared to sell South Center. Eventually the NLRB ruled in favor of the employees and ordered Englestein to pay a settlement of $4,000. This settlement was distributed among sixty-seven employees. (During the dispute, several workers secured other work, likely making them ineligible to share in the settlement; these workers, however, continued to aid in the cause.)[91]

South Center employees also applied for unemployment compensation with the NLRB. They claimed that they had been forced out of work, insisting that, once the store announced its closing, workers ceased all protest activities and were ready and available to work. Instead, Englestein relied on extra employees and supervisors to take inventory and prepare for the sale of South Center. Upon learning this, Lens wrote Englestein to call his attention to "the fact that this is work that should be done and is ordinarily done by the regular crew. Demand is hereby made that this inventory work be assigned to members of the union at the store who ordinarily do it." Further, he claimed that Englestein's "failure to use them" was a "discriminatory act."[92] In June 1952, with Englestein unwilling to employ union members, the Illinois Division of Unemployment Compensation ruled that South Center employees were eligible for unemployment compensation because their unemployment was due to the company's decision to terminate its operations, not a work stoppage due to a labor dispute.[93]

South Center employees finally returned to work in late June, when Morris Berman and Morris Bloomberg of Meadows Mercantile Corporation purchased and reopened South Center Department Store. Prior to the reopening, the new owners signed a contract with Local 329, welcoming the return of Englestein's former employees, including Mosley and those who demonstrated, and providing a four dollar increase for all store employees.[94] Nearly one month later, management reported that sales were up 5 percent compared with the same period during the previous year.[95]

The acquisition of South Center by Berman and Bloomberg did not end the struggle for fair employment. Throughout the 1950s, the South Center union continued to press for higher wages and better benefits and work conditions. In 1963, ownership changed once again when African American cosmetic mogul S. B. Fuller and *Chicago Defender* owner John Sengstacke purchased the department store, renaming it Fuller Department Store. Sengstacke remarked, "This is just the first of many examples to follow of Negroes crossing political and all other lines to cooperate on the basic matter of working together in business. We should have been doing this years ago. This is just the beginning."[96] But soon thereafter, as Fuller began to face serious financial trouble, the store fell on hard times. Things only got worse "when a Chicago social worker accused him of extending credit to welfare clients, which was against welfare regulations. The social worker urged his customers on welfare not to honor their debts to his department store, which cost more than $1 million and eventually led to him losing the store."[97]

. . . . . .

Although the department store unions discussed here most directly affected those laboring or seeking to labor in New York and Chicago stores, their efforts were widely felt and would shape the direction of department store campaigns in the 1950s and 1960s. Perhaps their most important influence was simply to demonstrate the potential for labor organizations' participation in the department store movement beyond those two cities. That influence was also prefigured as early as 1942 in the *Atlanta Daily World*'s delighted reaction to the success of union efforts to institute merit hiring at Macy's. "We believe," the editors wrote, "that right here in the South, especially in metropolitan centers like Atlanta, New Orleans, Birmingham, Memphis, and Nashville, much practical good [could] be accomplished through such a policy. Certainly there would be a substantial increase in the patronage of Negroes to such stores, and too, such stores would be making wholesome contribution to interracial understanding and appreciation for the true worth of Negro talent and ability." By the 1960s, unions—retail, garment, and otherwise—would be involved in sit-in demonstrations at F. W. Woolworth Company stores in the American South.[98]

The department store unions in New York and Chicago in the 1940s and 1950s also pioneered in their willingness to tackle racial discrimination on behalf of both workers and consumers in the marketplace, rather than ignore the latter issues or bequeath them to prominent civil rights organizations. These unions sometimes worked without the assistance of civil rights organizations, and sometimes they worked closely with these organizations to shape the contours of this movement. Regardless of which approach they took, department store unions were able to capitalize on their unique vantage as insiders—a vantage that permitted them to not only dismantle racially discriminatory hiring practices but also foster camaraderie between white and black workers. This camaraderie, in particular, allowed African Americans to transition into sales and office work without too much resistance and contest any future impediments to their success and advancement.

Although the postwar era saw the precipitous decline in the idea of unions and the New Deal bargaining system, the acceleration of household consumption—stimulated by the collapse of the "old regime" of sharecropping and tenancy and continued urban migration within as well as out of the South—swelled the pent-up consumption demands of African Americans. As a result, activists targeted department stores and other places of consumption in unprecedented ways and intensity. They launched notable department store campaigns in Pittsburgh, Philadelphia, Washington, D.C., and Charlotte, among other cities, throughout the remainder of the twentieth century. But the movement did more than just spread. More and more, it addressed the concerns and needs of African Americans as both consumers and workers, skillfully forcing onto the American public their demands for full and equal access to the employment, recreations, and conveniences of the modern, urban middle-class life increasingly associated with American citizenship. Ironically, however, black demands for access to all of this came at the cusp of the beginning of the decline of the kind of shopping experience traditionally associated with department stores, underscoring that the movement was concerned with not only democratization but also broad access to a kind of class-marked experience—being served as well as owning goods.

4 The Department Store Movement in the Postwar Era

In May 1945, as the Allies cemented their victory over Germany, celebrations erupted throughout Europe and the United States. Crowds took to the streets and strangers kissed in elation, while cheers and parades welcomed servicemen and servicewomen returning home. African Americans, too, partook in the festivities. But as they happily reunited with their loved ones and commemorated the occasion, they were occupied by questions about what the forthcoming state of peace would hold. "What are our chances of getting a job after the war? Have they stopped jim crowing us from restaurants and amusement places like they used to before the war?" returning soldiers asked.[1] Had the nation learned anything from its battle against fascism? Will the inroads made in the workplace and the marketplace endure? What measures must we take to prevent undesirable outcomes?

African Americans and their white allies certainly had reason to worry. After World War I, blacks employed in war agencies and defense industries were laid off. Black unemployment and economic deficiencies skyrocketed as a result. Reconversion after the second global conflict did not produce the same outcomes, as "most African American men hired during the war retained their toehold in northern labor markets." Skilled black male workers—the majority of whom were employed in war agencies and production—were hard hit by postwar layoffs, however. They struggled to secure comparable work, as a result of racial discrimination and segregation, and labor market segmentation. Black female workers had an especially tough time. "Many employers used a two-tiered seniority system, with women at the bottom. In the rush to provide employment for returning veterans, even the most progressive unions displaced women workers," forcing them to return to domestic and other service sector jobs that offered no benefits or security.[2]

At department stores, merchants fired black workers to provide employment to returning white veterans and white saleswomen who had left for higher-paying defense work during the war but were discharged thereafter. Others simply tightened their grip on racially discriminatory practices, believing that returning servicemen of color, now more confident and vocal about the abuses of American racism, needed to be put back "in their place." For example, in 1944, Brys Department Store in Memphis dismissed its eight black elevator operators and hired white operators in their stead. The white operators were promised eighteen dollars per week—six dollars more than the store had paid its black operators—and the installation of stools in each elevator car (a comfort not provided black operators) to prevent exhaustion from standing all day.[3] In New York City, a hub for department store integration during wartime, few stores expressed an interest in increasing their employment of African American sales and office workers and executives, when talking with the New York Urban League (NYUL) of Women Shoppers in late 1945.[4] And, at Thalhimers, returning servicemen of color found that neither the skills that they acquired in the armed forces nor the sentiments of a war for democracy translated into better work opportunities. Robert Scott was assigned to his old job as deliveryman, despite serving as a personnel clerk in the armed forces; Powell Williams returned to his delivery department after working as head telephone operator for the U.S. Army; and Bishop Gordon was restored to the maintenance department after serving as a private first class and the assistant to the chaplain in the Marine Corps, where he led religious services and assisted with clerical tasks.[5]

In response, countless men and women, blacks and whites, expressed their profound disappointment that, while the war against fascism may have been won, the war against American racism, or rather the war for democracy at home, was far from over. Department stores remained key battlegrounds and took on greater significance as black purchasing power had reached an unprecedented level of $8–$9 million by 1947 and the relationship between consumption and citizenship had changed.[6] American citizens were now told that it was their civic responsibility to spend, a drastic turnabout from wartime instructions that they should refrain from frivolous spending and conserve their money. In the late 1940s, "the growing dominance of Keynesian economics within influential business, government, and labor circles put more emphasis on the power of total consumer spending—to determine everything from employment to economic growth."[7] Racial restrictions, however, continued to limit African American access to and participation in the consumer sphere and by extension their citizenship; but postwar ideas about consumption and citizenship positioned African Americans to challenge racial segregation and discrimination in the marketplace like never before.

For the most part, the department store movement remained a fight for jobs in the immediate postwar era, taking on consumer issues as it saw fit. This phase of the movement marked a period of preliminary testing that would eventually lead to militant protests in the 1950s and 1960s. Under the leadership of the National Urban League (NUL) and the American Friends Service Committee (AFSC), the movement relied on intercultural education and moral exhortations. Emblematic of racial liberalism and the early civil rights movement, the NUL and the AFSC believed that if respectable blacks and white community leaders simply asked store officials to hire African Americans in sales and clerical positions, they would, and after that "their attitudes about integrated workplaces and African Americans generally would change," helping them "topple barriers in other industries and locations."[8]

The NUL and the AFSC were armed with new allies and weapons in their fight to end race discrimination in the workplace in the postwar era: the law and science. In March 1945, seven months before the war officially ended, New York became the first state to enact a fair employment law to promote merit hiring and investigate charges of employment discrimination. New Jersey (1945), Massachusetts (1946), and Connecticut (1947) soon followed suit, and by 1960, thirty-five states and over two hundred cities had ratified fair employment commissions and laws, all the while legislative bills calling for a permanent Fair Employment Practices Commission (FEPC) died in the U.S. Congress in 1945 and again in 1950. In 1948, the Massachusetts Fair Employment Commission received a complaint that a Boston store refused to hire an experienced African American woman in sales and instead wanted to employ her as an elevator operator. Over the course of the commission's investigation, it discovered that this Boston store, in fact, did not employ any African American salespeople, and subsequently pressured store officials to hire fourteen black saleswomen and two black salesmen. The New Jersey Fair Employment Commission not only investigated complaints of employment discrimination but also held conferences with business leaders to persuade them to integrate their workforces. The commission touted that after one convention, a merchant hired three black salesclerks and expressed a willingness to hire more should neighboring stores also adopt merit hiring.[9]

Social scientists supplied the second weapon: scientific proof that the hiring of African American sales workers in department stores would not harm business.[10] The psychologist Gerhart Saenger and the sociologist Emily Gilbert investigated white customers' reactions to African American sales workers at large New York City department stores. They found that while prejudice informed whites' reactions to the employment of black sales personnel, it did not affect their buying habits or result in a loss of customers, as many department store managers had long claimed. Study participants, even those most resistant to integration, did not eschew buying from African American salesclerks and even testified that the service provided by these workers of color was of the same quality as that provided by white sales personnel. For many, the need or desire to purchase merchandise overrode their prejudice against black clerks, while the proliferation of self-service retailing minimized worker-customer interactions and eased their acceptance of integrated sales forces.[11] Another study conducted by John Harding and Russell Hogrefe revealed that white employees at "two leading department stores in a large Eastern city" did not quit when African Americans were hired in sales and clerical positions; instead, they remained and cordially worked with their new coworkers of color. "Equal status work contact," Harding and Hogrefe stated, "produced a large increase in willingness to work with Negroes on an equal basis"; but shared work, they also found, did not yield any "significant change in willingness to accept other relationships with them."[12]

As the NUL and the AFSC tackled job discrimination, the Congress of Racial Equality (CORE), the National Association for the Advancement of Colored People (NAACP), and others struggled to end the "Jim Crowing" of African Americans in public accommodations. In early 1945, the Baltimore *Afro-American* celebrated that in New York and other northern cities, "many restaurants and amusements which were formerly closed to him, now [are] catering for his money."[13] Black purchasing power had grown enormously and merchants wanted their share, of course. Merchants also were motivated to serve blacks in states and locales that had ratified legislation outlawing discrimination in public accommodations and amusements by the mid-1940s.

But the *Afro-American* overstated the situation and may have been overly optimistic. Many public accommodations gladly accepted black dollars, but a great many still refused to serve African Americans either entirely or with dignity or respect. And in this economic milieu, one that encouraged spending, it did not take long before racial conflict erupted between white workers and black customers in retail establishments. CORE and the NAACP—while lending support to labor initiatives—leveraged the new relationship between citizenship and consumption and new antidiscrimination laws to publicly advocate on behalf of black customers and challenge race discrimination in stores. CORE, in particular, embraced more militant tactics, boycotting and protesting retailers that treated their customers as second-class citizens, while the NAACP sought redress in the courts, filing lawsuits on behalf of African Americans whose consumer rights had been violated.

Now that blacks had some answers to their initial questions on postwar life, what should they expect from the department store movement? Would the movement—one that appeared to have virtually split black employment from consumption in the immediate postwar era—be effective? How quickly would progress be made? And how might the movement, which mobilized impressive campaigns in Philadelphia, Chicago, New York, and other northern and western cities, impact blacks in the South?

Integrating Department Store Work in the Era of Racial Liberalism

From the mid-1940s through the early 1950s, the NUL and the AFSC believed that integration would be simple, that people were inherently decent and reasonable, that people of color simply needed to be taught respectability and provided occupational training, that racists needed only to be educated about African Americans and meet "respectable" blacks, and given all this, American racism would fall. They felt certain that protest and demonstrations would portray African Americans as antagonistic, combative, and intimidating, and do little more than agitate and repulse whites. They "reasoned" that once white employers and customers met respectable black people, they would feel comfortable hiring them in the "highly visible" and skilled role of sales worker and in the white space of the selling floor. Then whites' "attitudes about integrated workplaces and African Americans generally would change" and help "topple barriers in other industries and locations."[14] They would eventually learn that their plan had its faults: persuasion meetings were an important element in the integration process, but relying almost solely on this tactic would prove tedious and mostly produce tokenism. Persuasion required the real threat and actualization of protest, if any substantial transformation were to occur in the workplace.

The NUL's involvement in the department store movement is not surprising. For the first half of the twentieth century, the placement of African Americans in skilled and semiskilled blue-collar jobs and white-collar occupations, as well as black community development and housing, was a primary concern for the league. According to NUL historian Touré F. Reed, the league promoted social science theory over structural remedies for discrimination and advocated behavioral modification and voluntarist arrangements as the keys to elevating the social and economic condition of African Americans and "bridging physical and psychological divisions between the races." The NUL "offered blacks moral and vocational training intended to enhance their efficiency and attentiveness in both workplace and community," and "encouraged employers, unions, and landlords to open jobs and housing to blacks."[15]

The league's employment initiatives began at its inception in 1910. Its attention to blacks in white-collar jobs, including department store sales and clerical positions, however, did not garner much momentum until the 1930s, when its branches provided adult education and vocational training— sometimes in concert with black universities and colleges and federal agencies—and maintained local job registration bureaus. The league's New York branch was so invested in this cause that its job bureau registered white-collar workers all day, every day, and allocated only one day a week to the placement of domestic and menial workers. Still, in the face of a sluggish economy and pervasive Jim Crow laws, the NUL, specifically its New York and Chicago branches, succeeded in placing a handful of African Americans in sales and clerical jobs in businesses and the public sector. The organization experienced greater success in the 1940s, "when new possibilities were engendered by the combination of expanding job opportunities heralded by the Second World War and the League's improved financial status."[16]

In the postwar era, the league, with financial backing from the Rosenwald Fund, created the Pilot Placement Project in 1948. According to Reed, "Pilot differed from its predecessors in two significant ways[: it] represented the first successful attempt to standardize the job placement activities already being carried out by League locals[; and it] finally equipped the NUL with the tools to erect a national system of 'clearance' allowing the League to direct skilled Afro-Americans to jobs equal to their talents and training, irrespective of location."[17]

The Pilot program aimed to place "qualified" and "specially trained" African Americans, many of whom had been laid off after the war, in occupations traditionally closed to them and reflective, or rather a reaffirmation, of their middle-class status. Not only did it seek to improve the material condition of African Americans, but the program also sought to create a "substantial middle class" that could "carry the load of the great masses below them" and dispel whites of their preconceived notions of black inferiority and fears about race integration and equality.[18] To meet this end, Pilot pursued four time-honored actions: first, it located African Americans trained in a number of fields requiring technical and professional education; second, the program targeted private businesses in need of trained, professional workers and gently persuaded them to hire qualified blacks; third, league members screened and placed black workers in jobs equal to their talents; and, finally, they held follow-up conversations with employers and new hires to determine job performance and reception.

Many NUL branches applied this approach to department stores, which were thriving, profitable, and key sites of American middle-class formation in the mid-twentieth century. In 1946, the league determined that 4,100 department stores existed in the nation, 304 of which were located in thirteen major metropolitan areas with significant black populations. Each of these stores, the organization also learned, employed hundreds of workers and sold billions in merchandise every year—both figures, the NUL presumed, would soar in the postwar years.[19] Armed with this information, branches prepared for battle: they conducted additional research on their local department stores, sent influential community members to meet with store officials and heads of local merchandising associations, recruited white organizations and leading industrialists, launched sticker and letter-writing campaigns, held training courses in merchandising and retailing, and pushed for stores to integrate during the Christmas and Easter shopping seasons (when the demand for workers was great)—and only when all else failed did they organize mass demonstrations.[20]

NUL branches often collaborated with other organizations, including newly established antidiscrimination employment commissions, to dismantle racial barriers in retail and other industries. For example, the NYUL joined forces with the New York State Commission against Discrimination, which was established by the 1945 Ives-Quinn Antidiscrimination bill and facilitated the upward mobility of countless black women. Together, and in only a few years, they had reduced the number of African American women working as domestics from 64 to 36 percent and increased the presence of black women in sales and clerical jobs from 3 to 13 percent.[21]

One of the most highly publicized and successful NUL department store campaigns involved the Pittsburgh Urban League (PUL) in partnership with the Pittsburgh Interracial Action Council (PIAC), an organization of blacks, whites, Christians, and Jews "interested in solving local interracial problems on a practical level." In early 1945, the PIAC set out to place "qualified"

African Americans in sales positions and end discrimination against black customers who were routinely denied the courtesy of trying on clothes in the city's "Big Five" department stores—Kaufmann's, Horne's, Frank and Seder, Rosenbaum, and Gimbels. Initially the PIAC believed that ending race discrimination would be "none-too-difficult" given the wartime actions of New York and Boston department stores. However, its hopes were quickly dashed when, upon meeting with store officials, the organization learned that officials pontificated about, and may have even believed in, fair employment and customer service but refused to integrate out of fear of alienating their white employees and customers. The PIAC then polled white salesclerks and customers, hoping that its findings would dispel the prejudices and fears of the retailers. The PIAC poll revealed that 85 percent of the buying public did not object to being served by "qualified clerks whose skins happened to be tinted," and 75 percent of white clerks "expressed their willingness to see qualified Negroes in these jobs." The organization also had customers and salespeople pledge their support in writing. But when the PIAC presented its findings to store officials, none were swayed to make any changes.[22]

By 1946, "it [had become] painfully obvious that the stores intended to kill the[se] peaceful efforts by simply ignoring them." Subsequently, the PIAC recruited the support of the PUL, the NAACP, Congress of Industrial Organizations (CIO), the *Pittsburgh Courier*, unions, and over a dozen other civil rights organizations and formed the Committee for Fair Employment in Pittsburgh Department Stores. With a combined membership of more than 5,000 people, the committee distributed handbills in front of store entrances, on downtown street corners, and on trolleys and buses entering and leaving Pittsburgh's shopping district. Thousands of postcards and telegrams protesting the "un-Americanism of the hiring policies" flooded stores. Protesters tied up telephone switchboards with calls urging managements to integrate, while others canceled their charge accounts.[23]

But store officials continued to ignore and resist the committee's peaceful persuasions. The committee took the "drastic step" of organizing picket lines and telegraphed the mayor to inform him of its intentions. The mayor begged the committee to delay picketing until he could convene a meeting with store representatives and the committee. The two parties met four times throughout January 1947. At each meeting, store officials offered to study the problem, to the dismay of the committee, while picketers stood outside, prepared to start demonstrating if their demands were not met. Finally, after the fourth and final meeting in late January, with news of the movement widely publicized by the national news media, the "Big Five" conceded and released the following statement: "There will be no discrimination in up-grading and employing Negroes from this day forward. Because of different problems which exist in the stores there will not be . . . simultaneous hiring. Negro applicants will take the same chances as whites. They will be hired and upgraded on their ability and fitness for the job. Negro employees already on the job will be given all the opportunities that white employees are given for upgrading. While there is still the problem of customer acceptance to be studied in certain stores, the practice will be that of no discrimination."[24] The "Big Five" also agreed to consult the committee with the selection and hiring of African American salesclerks and follow its advice on how to correctly integrate them on the selling floor.

As a result, ten black salespeople—most of whom were employed as temporary workers—were initially hired in four of the five department stores. Only one store complained that customers objected to its new hires; the remaining stores "professed to be pleased with the results." Two of these "pleased" stores were Frank and Seder and Kaufmann's. Frank and Seder hired an African American student from the University of Pittsburgh's Bureau of Retail Training to supervise the store's men's and boy's clothing department. The new supervisor managed eighteen to twenty-five employees "along with other matters connected to selling." Another student from the University's Bureau of Retail Training reportedly performed well "in various phases of selling and supervision at Kaufmanns."[25] The committee also negotiated the promotions of several African American menial workers. Some workers welcomed the opportunity to work on the selling floor because of its meaning and the promise of advancement. Others, however, were disappointed to learn that a promotion did not translate into higher pay or more regular work and, as result, chose to remain in their current positions.[26]

During this period, and nearly 300 miles east of Pittsburgh, the AFSC headquarters in Philadelphia was also anxious about racial progress and shared a similar mission and approach to that of the NUL. In 1943, the Quaker organization established the Race Relations Committee to focus on race and democracy. It, and the AFSC more broadly, eschewed radical activism and strongly advocated education as an effective path to racial equality. Specifically, it insisted that "the best way to bridge gulfs of prejudice and fear is not so much to take them directly as to bring various groups together in common work, recreation, and workshop."[27] As the Race Relations Committee developed, soldiers were returning to civilian life, leading to increasing concern about the economic difficulties facing African Americans in the postwar years and the founding of the Jobs Placement Program in early 1945. The program, according to one scholar, "was well timed, arriving just as business leaders and scholars were extolling 'social responsibility'—which included hiring nonwhites." It was headed by University of Pennsylvania professor Frank Loescher and sought "to provide employment opportunities for trained Negroes of skill and promise in fields not traditionally open to Negroes—when all races may work creatively and harmoniously together." The AFSC's Jobs Program also aimed to "create [a] better understanding" between the races and change "the white man's attitudes and beliefs [about African Americans] . . . by giv[ing] white clerical, technical, and professional people the experience of working with Negroes of similar backgrounds and interests."[28]

Several months later, in October 1945, the program formed the Committee on Fair Employment Practices in Department Stores (CEPDS) in Philadelphia. The committee was a diverse coalition that married the goals and efforts of the AFSC's Race Relations Committee and Jobs Placement Program, CORE, the Pennsylvania NAACP, the Council for Equal Job Opportunity, the Armstrong Association of Philadelphia, the Southwest-Belmont Branch of the YWCA, the Women's International League, the American Jewish Congress, the Fellowship of Reconciliation, Friend's Committee on Race Relations, the West Philadelphia Civic League, the United People's Action Committee, the Germantown YWCA, and the Fellowship House. One year later, the Retail Clerks International Protective Association joined the CEPDS.[29]

Starting the CEPDS, however, did not mean that the Jobs Placement Program became unconcerned with other types of work. Instead, activists hoped that, by focusing on a single occupation, the program might "create sufficient publicity" and "rivet public attention on racial discrimination in employment and thus possibly assist the legislative efforts then underway." The committee worked to create positive publicity by quietly convincing store officials that the hiring of African American sales and clerical workers not only would be well received by their customers and staffs but also would be "safe . . . [and] profitable." In other words, the department store committee believed that by simply asking store officials to adopt merit hiring and promising no mass demonstrations or bad publicity—that would be inconvenient and harmful to store profits and image—department stores would gradually employ African Americans in sales and clerical positions. The committee then presumed that, once hired, African Americans would be accepted, or simply go unnoticed, as long as they performed well. Management, in turn, would see the proverbial light, abandon its prejudiced attitudes, and hire more blacks in positions of responsibility. Thereafter, the committee believed, interracial tensions in and outside the workplace would be alleviated.[30]

Initially, the committee targeted Philadelphia's most prominent downtown department stores: Strawbridge & Clothier, John Wanamaker's, Gimbel Brothers, N. Snellenburg, Lit Brothers, Bonwit Teller, Stern's, and Frank and Seder. The first five stores lined Market Street, a historic and major thoroughfare in the city, while the remaining three were located within walking distance. Strawbridge's and Wanamaker's were the oldest and, with Bonwit's, represented the high end of retailing; Gimbel's, Snellenburg's, and Lit Brothers were mid-to-upscale stores; and Stern's and Seder's were modest retail institutions. All of these stores welcomed African American patrons in all areas of their business, including dressing rooms and public restrooms, because they were legally obligated to under the conditions set by the 1935 Pennsylvania Equal Rights Law. But in practice, black customers were often not well received or treated fairly. African Americans were welcomed in Stern's and frequented it more regularly as a result, while Strawbridge's, Wanamaker's, and Bonwit's openly expressed disdain toward blacks and did not have a significant black customer base.[31]

Between 1945 and 1948, the Philadelphia committee partook in a series of "friendly conversations" with store officials. Initial conversations sought to reassure officials that the committee was in no way trying to wreak havoc but was simply gathering information in behalf of their "Negro friends" who were looking for employment. In subsequent conversations, the committee gingerly pressured officials to place African Americans in white-collar jobs. It often came armed with evidence to support its cause. Some of this evidence included social science research, committee-sponsored surveys and studies, and opinion polls. One poll involving 956 shoppers revealed that 60 percent were agreeable to African American salesclerks, 32 percent disliked the prospect, and 8 percent were unsure. Another study on small stores with interracial sales and clerical staffs concluded that everyone "worked amicably together" and their integration was in no way detrimental to business.[32]

Despite this information, the majority of store officials rejected integration, insisting that it would repel "customers," a term they used to refer exclusively to white people, and damage store profits. But a few stores were intrigued. They "seemed impressed by the examples of department stores in other cities such as New York, Boston, and Hartford, Connecticut, which [had] hired Negroes without unfavorable reaction on the part of their customers and other employees, and . . . seemed thoughtful when the difference between the ideal of equality of opportunity in the United States and the fact of inequality [was] pointed out."[33]

On a scale of most agreeable to least, Stern's stood at one end and Wanamaker's was on the other end. Stern's was most open to integration and seemed willing to do so immediately. Its Jewish owners, the AFSC surmised, were not only inspired by the Quaker tradition but also valued the profits earned from black patronage. However, Stern's was unwilling to take this step unless other Philadelphia department stores did the same. Wanamaker's, on the other hand, proved much more difficult to convince. In January 1946, Marjorie Swann and William K. Hefner, CEPDS and CORE members, interviewed Wanamaker's personnel manager and the manager's assistant about the store's hiring policies. Both officials explained that "they had been gradually working Negro employees into all capacities of the store and that now there were only [two] capacities closed to Negroes: (1) office help, and (2) sales clerks." But they had no plans to open these fields because of the prospect of negative customer response. Black stock clerks, wrappers, and cashiers hired during wartime proved irresponsible, they argued. Their decision, retailers insisted, was bolstered by the Market Street Store Association's agreement not to hire African American sales personnel. Wanamaker's personnel manager, however, believed "that in time [blacks] would be accepted . . . but not in the near future. . . . Such a change must not be rushed or come about under pressure."[34]

Negotiations with the remaining six department stores were equally as frustrating. Several stores placed the responsibility of integration on the Philadelphia Merchants Association; the association, then, placed the issue back on the stores. In the early spring of 1946, having grown tired of this back-and-forth, Loescher and CEPDS chair Charles Shorter asked Strawbridge's president Herbert J. Tily to arrange a meeting between the CEPDS and Howard Cooper Johnson, Strawbridge's vice president and Philadelphia Merchants Association president. Tily promised to set up the meeting and be in touch.

Tily, however, failed to keep his word. Two months later, after many unsuccessful attempts to speak with Tily and Johnson, Loescher finally reached Johnson on the telephone. Although Loescher was hoping for a face-to-face meeting, he was ultimately pleased to have an opportunity to convince Johnson that the Merchants Association should encourage downtown stores to adopt merit hiring. Loescher thoughtfully detailed the predicament of black workers in Philadelphia, tried to assuage Johnson's fears that integration would alienate white customers, and explained the procedure involved and the benefits reaped by New York and Boston department stores that began employing African Americans in sales and offices during wartime. He then asked Johnson for advice on how to get Philadelphia stores to follow suit. But, as he was asking, Johnson abruptly interjected, stating that neither the Department Store Committee nor the AFSC had "any business telling employers what they should do." Loescher tried to explain that these groups were only trying to help and invited Johnson to meet with committee representatives. Johnson refused. Loescher then tried to arrange a time for the committee to present its concerns before the Merchants Association. "Absolutely not," Johnson replied.[35]

At this juncture, Johnson boasted that he was a "birthright Friend," implying that this status provided him with special influence that could be leveraged to endanger Loescher's job. Loescher pressed on and tried to impress on Johnson the gravity of the situation, explaining that if "a peaceful means of working this out are not found, there could be such situations as happened in New York where pressure methods were used on stores, such as picketing." Johnson's temper flared and he angrily accused "the AFSC of threatening Strawbridge and Clothier." Loescher adamantly denied making any threats and tried once more to convince Johnson to consider meeting with the CEPDS. As their telephone exchange continued, Loescher discerned that he was only upsetting the vice president and politely ended the conversation about thirty minutes after its start.[36]

By late summer of 1946, the CEPDS had met with every Philadelphia department store but had made little progress. Then, in early September, it tried a new approach: the committee sent Mosetta Freeman to apply for open sales jobs. Freeman was a junior college graduate with three years of work experience as a supervisor in a mail-order house. Her application was accepted at Strawbridge's, Snellenburg's, and Stern's, but none of these retail establishments called her for an interview. She also applied for a sales position at Seder's, where the personnel officer told her that the store "hired colored" but there were no current openings and she was never called for an interview. Lit Brothers was the sole store to invite Freeman for an interview. But, as she learned during their meeting, the retailer was interested in hiring her only to work at the fountain in the store basement. Freeman graciously declined and asked about clerical openings. Once again, she was told that there were no current openings but would be notified when a position became available. And, again, she never was.[37]

The committee, however, remained undeterred. In late September it sent four more black women to apply for advertised sales and clerical positions, only to run into similar roadblocks. Strawbridge's stated that it had "no openings for salesgirls" and offered one woman a job as a packer and another a job as a stock clerk. Strawbridge's, Seder's, and Lit Brothers told the two other women that they did not hire blacks for sales and office positions, only in the stock department, and refused to consider ending their discriminatory hiring policies. The committee widely publicized the experiences of these women, hoping to pressure and embarrass merchants. But again, it did not produce the desired effect.

After one year of relentless campaigning by the committee, Gimbel's was the only department store that amended its hiring policy. Sometime in the autumn of 1946, and unbeknownst to the CEPDS, Gimbel's hired a black cashier in its oilcloth department. For nearly eight or nine months before this hire, the committee had been holding routine persuasion meetings with store management, but it was the threat of mass demonstration that pushed the retailer to hire a black sales worker. Before Labor Day, the retailer placed a job advertisement in the newspaper, stating that it was looking to hire 24 saleswomen. One day later, 1,200 people flooded the store's personnel office; 400 of these applicants were African American. Astoundingly, Gimbel's met with all the applicants and quickly got them out of the personnel office.

African Americans, however, reacted unfavorably to the newspaper advertisement and management's perfunctory consideration of their applications. Their reaction sparked fear that Philadelphians of color might retaliate with pickets and boycotts, and compelled store executive Arthur Kaufmann to take action.[38] He called a meeting with department heads and salespeople to assess their sentiments about desegregation. Gimbel's sales forces, in particular, loathed the idea. But their ill feelings did not govern the retailer's decision. Instead, Kaufmann promoted a current employee of color to the oilcloth department, believing that the implementation of fair employment would be a good public relations and financial move. The oilcloth department was a unit that would least upset white customers, management trusted, and its supervisor had been trained for the priesthood and reportedly "had no prejudice." So successful was Kaufmann's plan that the store later hired an African American saleswoman in its rug department, located in the store's basement, and black clerical workers in its personnel office.[39]

Not long thereafter, and keeping to its word, Stern's hired two African Americans in "customer contact work."[40] The AFSC was elated with these victories and sent its gratitude and appreciation to Gimbel's and Stern's managements. But these breakthroughs failed to inspire other department stores to follow suit. Instead, they had the opposite effect: the remaining six retailers dug in their heels and adamantly refused to integrate. The committee magnified the campaign's visibility as a result. On June 18, 1946, the CEPDS held a dinner for department store executives at the Barclay Hotel. Only half the invitees attended and heard keynote speaker Elmo Roper, public opinion expert and market researcher for *Fortune* magazine, present "scientific evidence" proving that the employment of African American sales and clerical workers had no ill effects on businesses. Roper "urged stores, collectively or individually, to begin immediately promoting qualified Negroes." The CEPDS also encouraged department store customers, black and white, to write letters expressing their support of merit hiring and affix "I should like to see qualified Negroes included in your sales force" stickers on their letters and bill payments.[41]

Very little appears to have resulted from these tactics until the autumn of 1947, when Wanamaker's store manager informed Loescher that store executives "would be disposed to upgrade and hire Negroes in clerical and sales positions if petitions with large numbers of signatures of their charge customers could be gathered, since fear of negative customer reaction is their major objection."[42] Immediately, the CEPDS implemented a multiphased plan of action designed and spearheaded by CORE. During the 1947 Christmas shopping season, thousands of black and white Philadelphians mobilized: they collected countless petition signatures, distributed campaign literature in front of stores, on street corners, and at a booth in City Hall, and publicized the movement in local and union newspapers and on local radio stations; the AFSC, CEPDS, and CORE wrote their members asking for their individual support and encouraged them to recruit other civic groups to which they belonged; a delegation of committee members met with Republican mayor Bernard Samuel and asked that he convene a meeting of store executives (a request he declined); and a special committee of Friends groups was formed to put pressure on Strawbridge's, specifically. The CEPDS and CORE also considered launching picket lines outside discriminating department stores and jamming telephone lines—as the Pittsburgh department store campaign had done one year earlier—but extant historical records suggest that these tactics were likely not pursued.[43]

Wanamaker's remained unmoved, although a letter from the store's management stated that it was still thinking about integrating its workforce. Other stores, however, remained silent on the issue. In fact, not until February 1948, when the city council approved a municipal Fair Employment Practices Commission (FEPC) ordinance, did the remaining department stores address their racial practices. The ordinance established a city-level committee that would ensure the implementation and protection of fair employment in Philadelphia and eventually forced the remaining department stores to end their discrimination policies and hire at least one African American salesclerk. But the decree was not without problems. It ultimately favored business, not workers, as it mandated that the FEPC could start an investigation into discriminatory employment practices only once someone filed charges and then it allowed the complainant a mere sixty days to make a claim.

Less than three months later, in April 1948, the CEPDS "officially disbanded," stating that "it felt that its initial job was completed." Although the committee had not realized the victory it envisioned, and instead achieved only tokenism, it resolved "that there was and is much latitude for improvement in regard to employment of Negroes in department stores but that before more pressure could be brought to bear on them, it would be necessary to bring all Philadelphia's utilities, businesses, and industries to the level which the downtown stores have achieved."[44]

The AFSC, however, remained committed to integrating department store work and promoting racial equality and interracial understanding. It met with Philadelphia's store executives, who had recently integrated their staffs, hoping to assuage the fears and tensions that often arose with integration. Some store executives complained that their black employees carried a chip on their shoulder and were not competent to complete their job duties, while others griped that African Americans in sales and office positions were not appropriately dressed and groomed. Another group of executives recommended that African American workers should not take the initiative in social situations; rather, they should let invitations to after-work gatherings come to them, cooperate regardless of their preconceived notions of the job and its responsibilities (in other words, be willing to sell as well as dust merchandise), be on time, and be sure to inform management of lateness and sickness.[45] These complaints were commonplace, mirroring managements' grievances about white workers as well. But, when directed against blacks, they elucidate officials' racial bias and their efforts to justify discriminatory employment practices by perpetuating the myth that qualified black applicants did not exist.

Likewise, some white customers objected to being served by persons they deemed inferior; the same was true on the other side of the counter in regard to white employees who preferred to work with their own. A few workers even went so far as to threaten to quit if minority employees were not terminated. For example, in the late 1940s, white workers at a Philadelphia Woolworth's demanded that management fire a newly hired African American woman or face a walkout. Similarly, at Gimbels in Philadelphia, white employees refused to work with a "very efficient and personable Chinese girl" and forced management to transfer her.[46] Not all white employees who threatened to quit, however, forced the reinstitution of race segregation. More often than not, when whites threatened to quit, managers refused to concede to their racist demands, and these workers begrudgingly remained. Other disgruntled employees resorted to other tactics. Some ignored and refused to engage African American coworkers, some provided new hires with incorrect information to make trouble, and some openly gossiped about and ridiculed employees of color.

African American workers were often afflicted with imposter syndrome as a result. They rarely trusted their white coworkers, and vice versa. Each group viewed the other as the "other," and, with the weight of historical and social pressures and assumptions, cultivating racial harmony was challenging and often complicated by the competitive nature of sales work. Because workers, who despite sharing a counter and department, "compet[ed] with each other for advancement[,] . . . the development of genuine friendships among co-workers" was encumbered.[47] The division of labor along department lines also made forging strong ties between the races difficult. As the historian Susan Porter Benson observed of the prewar era, sales forces split along lines of ethnicity, religion, age, and education, but "the major divisions within the store were almost invariably among department lines. Retailing students frequently remarked that the saleswomen's primary loyalty was to the department."[48] But African American "firsts" were typically assigned to departments where they worked alone or had little contact with white employees and customers and consequently experienced difficulty building interracial relationships.

It is not clear whether the Friends organization fully understood the situation, as its retort to these tensions involved restructuring its applicant preparation program in a way that appears to have addressed whites' complaints alone. Thus, similar to NUL adult education and vocational training initiatives, the AFSC venture evolved into an intensive six-week job-training program to school black applicants on their attitudes and behaviors, on good grooming habits, and on choosing conservative clothing in complexion-flattering and harmonizing color combinations. The program also instructed applicants on the best ways to interact with their new employers, coworkers, and customers.

· · · · · ·

The AFSC continued its work in Philadelphia while expanding its geographical reach. In the spring of 1950, it sent Thomas Colgan to establish an AFSC Job Opportunities Program in Chicago. His arrival marked the start of the Friends' three-year campaign to integrate employment in State Street department stores. Like the leaders of the Chicago Urban League (CUL) and CORE, Colgan surmised that the strategy of integrating State Street department stores would have the greatest effect on employers not only in Chicago but also throughout the state of Illinois. He explained that these grand emporiums "were symbolic of discrimination in Illinois. We felt we ought to attack the symbol."[49]

Carson Pirie Scott was selected as the AFSC's first target. In 1948, without a single African American employed, Carson's began flirting with the possibility of implementing an integration program, but had nothing to institute such a measure. Extant historical records suggest that the retailer's decision to integrate its workforce was a humanistic endeavor, and that might be true. But it is more likely that the retailer wanted to avoid protest and bad publicity and appreciated the financial gains that typically came with the adoption of merit hiring. Nevertheless, two years later, in 1950, after hearing rumors that management might be receptive to the idea, Colgan met with store vice president Sam Carson. Carson immediately suggested that Colgan work with C. Virgil Martin, assistant to the store president, to devise an integration program tailored to their needs. Soon the AFSC was charged with finding Carson's a suitable job candidate to break its color barriers, with two stipulations: first, applicants had to be college graduates, and second, they were to have been "the first in something."[50]

The AFSC invited the CUL, the Illinois State Employment Service, and local community activists, including Ora Higgins, to refer qualified blacks. Twelve applicants were referred and interviewed. Of these applicants, seven were selected to participate in a "leaderless conference," where the AFSC and store representatives would observe and evaluate them. Only five applicants, however, attended the conference. In a one-hour roundtable discussion, the job candidates grappled with the sole question: "As the first Negro to be employed by a large retail establishment, what are the problems you would expect to encounter and how would you overcome them?" As Colgan described, "What followed was one of the most exciting experiences I have had to date. At one point, during the conference, [one of the evaluators] asked me if it was possible to get 5 jobs. We were all greatly impressed by the intellect of the applicants and their realistic approach to the problem. Although the selection was difficult to make, we all agreed that [Charles Sumner 'Chuck'] Stone [Jr.] was [the] number 1 applicant."[51]

Just two months after Colgan first made contact with Carson's, Stone was quietly hired as Martin's administrative aide. Stone met all of Carson's needs: he was one of the first African Americans to graduate from Wesleyan University and a veteran Tuskegee Airman.[52] Stone eventually went on to earn his master's in sociology from the University of Chicago. Later he wrote and edited influential black publications in New York, Washington, and Chicago, helped found the National Association of Black Journalists (and served as its first president), and was the first black columnist for the Philadelphia Daily News.[53]

As a result of Stone's placement and Carson's favorable reception to this new hire, the retailer hired an additional sixty-eight blacks in jobs ranging from "an Administrative Assistant, Comptometer Operator, Clerk-Typist, to Stock Clerks, Watchmen, and Furniture Handlers" by September 1950.[54] So committed was Carson's to integration that when F. H. Scott learned that one of his employees said she would quit if they "send a Nigger down to her area," he quickly informed her, "Well, I got your job because there's going to be a Nigger down there as you call it in the next couple of days and I'm telling Mr. Martin to put one down there. And I just have your resignation." Flabbergasted, the employee responded, "Mr. Scott you wouldn't do that to me." He said, "Look, if Mr. Martin doesn't have a Nigger down there in a couple of days he's fired." Although the employee was not fired, Martin "had a unit control person [of color] down there that afternoon" and the employee "never opened her mouth."[55]

Carson's was intensely proud of its integration program; but, like other retailers that had integrated their workforces, it was never comfortable publicizing its contributions to the department store movement and preferred to present the public with a fait accompli.[56] In fact, when John Sengstacke, publisher of the *Chicago Defender*, heard rumors that Carson's employed a number of African Americans in nontraditional jobs, he called

Martin to inquire. Martin responded by inviting Sengstacke to visit the store with one of his reporters. Soon thereafter, Martin and Sengstacke "had lunch together in the men's grill and then . . . walk[ed] through the store." They "walked through the control area, through some of the sales audit area," then Sengstacke turned to Martin and said, "Why didn't you tell me about this? You've got a lot of my people here." To which Martin replied, "John, remember I asked you to come with your reporter, because I'm going to ask you to do one thing—not to write this up for about another four to five months because we're just not ready for all of the exposure that we're going to get." Martin also promised that, should he find out that anyone was going to write about it, Sengstacke "will have the first break on it."[57]

As Carson's integration program progressed, the AFSC continued its involvement. The organization regularly met with store officials and employees, black and white, to "review" the retailer's integration program. During one visit in October 1950, officials praised the program, touting that "they were not able to put the brakes on the program because many department managers have had such excellent experience with these new employees that others are requesting more all the time." But officials also shared some concerns about the program, which were fraught with racial overtones. To Colgan, Carson explained that, several months earlier, management discovered that two black employees were selling marijuana, and one of the store detectives had a police record. Worried that black criminals were among the store's ranks, officials investigated the backgrounds of its African American employees and learned that eight of its then forty-eight black workers had police records for shoplifting, drug distribution, and murder. Carson's then prohibited the employment of South Side residents "because of the crime incidence, poverty, and health." This policy, in effect, disqualified many black Chicagoans since the city's segregation patterns restricted their housing options mostly to the South Side.[58]

Neither in his meeting with Carson nor in his confidential reports did Colgan comment on management's overwrought fears of black criminality or its failure to consider that whites with criminal backgrounds also likely worked in the store. Perhaps as a result of his own prejudices, Colgan agreed with Carson and was unable to recognize problems with marking African Americans as criminals. A more likely explanation is that Colgan was cognizant that management's concerns about black criminals were symptomatic of a larger issue threatening to impede integration: whites' biases and prejudices toward African Americans. This explanation, in particular, makes sense, as a few weeks later the AFSC held three roundtable discussions segregated by race and occupation to assess and improve the integration process at Carson's.

The first roundtable discussion was held in early November 1950. Charles Stone and eight other black employees met offsite, at a local YWCA, and candidly shared their experiences working at Carson's. They recounted how management failed to introduce them to other employees, provide them with a general orientation of the store, or make provisions to have a white employee take them to lunch. For these employees, not being introduced bred "resentment, feelings of insecurity, [and] doubt of the intent of management and aggression." Only one black employee was provided some orientation to the store: a white bundle man took the initiative of introducing the new worker to the department and ate lunch with him for the first week. Colgan observed that "this created an atmosphere [where] Jimmy [wanted] to continue working. He seemed to be about the best adjusted in the group and commended Carson's for their excellent policy."[59]

Black workers also criticized the color line that divided labor, space, and social activities. Black porters worked separately from white porters, and employee locker rooms were segregated by race. On numerous occasions blacks were asked not to use the restrooms. To make matters worse, several black employees heard rumors "that the Christmas party would not be held this year," which some, including the AFSC, presumed "was . . . because Negroes were being employed in the store and the fear of their participation in the party. They note[d] . . . many social activities among the white employes. For example, just two weeks ago a group was organized to present a play. However, no Negro was invited."[60]

The second roundtable discussion invited department managers to share their opinions and concerns. Like their employees of color, they felt that African Americans were not properly introduced and suggested that the store president should have announced the new policy at a "top level conference" of supervisors. Then they could have discussed the policy with their subordinates. Managers also agreed that current employees should be notified of all new hires before their first day and recommended that a sponsor orient all new employees, black and white, to the store.[61]

Generally, the managers were receptive to integration, but they also believed merit hiring should have its limits. Almost all agreed that blacks should be employed first as menial workers and "when they prove their value be promoted to better jobs. This included promotion to sales at Christmas time. However, it should be done a few at a time." Others shared their fear that African Americans carried "horrible diseases." Another mentioned that all blacks looked alike, while one said that "they sort of jiggle when they walk." Regarding the issue of segregation, store officials discussed one white employee's refusal to occupy a locker with an African American worker. "Everyone present agreed that lockers should not be segregated in this fashion. There was also agreement that a white person should not be forced to occupy a locker with a Negro." And at least one person felt that, because of the new hiring policy, Carson's "was losing much of its prestige and perhaps many of Carson['s] customers would object and leave."[62]

Many white employees also alleged that Carson's adoption of merit hiring was "ruining the reputation of the department store" in the third roundtable discussion. Several employees, however, shared that working with African Americans changed their opinion about the race. A stock clerk charged with forty stock boys, twenty of whom were black, shared "that prior to working with Negroes he was prejudiced, but now through the association he found that he was all wrong." He added that, "in examining his background, [he] could not understand why he was prejudiced since his parents did not provide this teaching." A number of white clerical workers also reported that they had developed friendships with their new coworkers of color.[63]

The roundtable discussions allowed activists and store management to evaluate internal responses to integration and improve interracial social- ization in the store. In late January 1951, the AFSC celebrated that "white and Negro employees are beginning to socialize in the store. Many mixed groups were reported in the lunchrooms. Negro employees are being wel- comed to join the drama group for the spring play." That same year, the AFSC also instituted Applicant Preparation Workshops in Chicago, hoping to increase the number of "competent" black workers at Carson's and other establishments. The workshops were led by Ora Higgins and mobilized the strengths of the Wabash Avenue YMCA, Dunbar Trade School, and the Illinois Distributive Education Program of the Board of Education. One hundred and ten applicants applied to participate in the program, and after a series of psychological tests and personal interviews, sixty-eight were chosen. The workshops aimed to "help the young people learn which fields held the greatest promise for the development of their particular aptitudes, how to discover the requirements of specific jobs and how to present their personal qualifications in the most favorable light." They also sought to instill students with "a sense of social responsibility" and equip them with the skills and mind-set needed to "handle . . . tense situations on the job."[64]

The CUL also participated in the preparation of African Americans applying to sales positions; and, by 1952, it had established a sales clinic that promoted and trained blacks, particularly those in high school, for opportunities existing in all facets of sales.[65]

But problems persisted. In 1951, store detective Delano Ross and clerical worker Florence Plant—both black firsts—charged that African American employees at Carson's were denied equal opportunities for advancement. After four years with the store, Ross complained, "I have been hearing that I'm the best man in the department for four years. But eight assistants have passed through my office and only one outranked me in educational background. I'm still just a dick." Seeking to address this issue, Ross made six appointments with the personnel director Elizabeth Hatch in a three-week period. Hatch canceled or rescheduled all of these appointments. Similarly, Plant criticized the exclusion of African Americans from the store's executive training program. She charged, "I've reached my peak in pay—$55 a week—after two years. . . . Young kids are here two weeks and go into the training program. And they start at a salary that took us two years to get." Both Ross and Plant reported that Carson's maintained two salary scales: one for blacks and one for whites. Whites generally made five dollars more a week than blacks.[66]

When questioned by the AFSC Job Opportunities Program, Hatch adamantly denied these accusations and placed the blame on African Americans for not advancing. "The average Negro," she commented, "doesn't believe that he can advance on merit. Despite a firm stand by management, he doesn't think he really can get to the top." She also disclosed that six African Americans had completed the store's executive training program during a three-year period, two of whom were still at Carson's. Ross and Plant, among others, disputed Hatch's claims. They held that most black employees were willing to pursue the steps necessary to achieve as much, but the store's integration program "[left] a great deal to be desired" and even accused the retailer of systematically blocking their attempts to advance. In late 1953, an AFSC officer corroborated these observations, noting that "there are Negroes in most training classes being held at the store all the time [but] there are fewer in the selling classes. . . . [It was unclear as to whether] the store [was] purposely holding the number down." He also discovered that Carson's had no immediate plans for extending integration to its other locations in Skokie and Evergreen Park, Illinois; Hammond and Gary, Indiana; and at 95th and Western Avenues. Even two years after this, its downtown store employed only eleven African American sales workers; the majority of its workforce of color remained in clerical and menial positions.[67]

As Carson's tried to fix, and arguably disguise, the glitches in its integration program, stories of its success had reached other nearby retailers and influenced Mandel's, Fair Store, Charles A. Stevens & Company, and Wieboldt's to adopt fair employment. But, like Carson's, these stores, too, were reluctant to extend their new policy to sales departments, where they might risk alienating their targeted clientele. They assigned an overwhelming majority of their new employees of color to offices, where they could quietly and covertly execute their integration programs, and occasionally used African Americans in sales during rush seasons.[68] The picture was even bleaker for African Americans seeking executive and managerial jobs. "Virtually no Negroes are employed in upper level management jobs," the CUL uncovered. "Two of the major mail order houses, Spiegels, and Aldens, have Negroes filling fairly responsible positions in the personnel department, and the former has a Negro buyer. Carson Pirie has Negro executive trainees, and Goldblatts has a Negro Assistant Buyer. The Fair Store employs a Negro as a comparison shopper."[69]

In the 1950s, Carson Pirie Scott had quickly "[become] a symbol of fair hiring in Chicago" and had "[made] a profound impression on business in Chicago."[70] Yet, Marshall Field and Company, the city's most prestigious department store, was not swayed and remained "the symbol of discrimination," according to the AFSC.[71] Marshall Field had a philanthropic relationship with Chicago's black community, supporting the Parkway Community Center, a social service center once directed by Horace Cayton. However, it historically maintained a color line in hiring that was hard, fast, and notorious. Since 1945, it had held the following sentiment about black workers: "Negroes are employed in considerable number by our corporation in various divisions. But it is our considered opinion that the addition of Negroes to our retail store payroll at this time would serve to *create* racial tension in this area rather than otherwise." It continued, "Meanwhile, as a business institution, we *can* take our stand on the side of racial understanding and cooperation, and can support all projects that seem sound toward that end. We shall continue as a matter of policy to support such projects financially, and in other ways that may present themselves—including the service and good offices of our directors, company officials and personnel groups." But the retailer adamantly refused to change its policy for fear of "fan[ning] the flames of controversy."[72]

In 1951, however, Marshall Field's reportedly began flirting with the idea of ending its discriminatory hiring policy. But when presented with Richard S. Dowdy Jr. in 1952, Field's did not budge or even consider breaking its color line. Dowdy held a bachelor of arts degree and a master of arts degree in economics from Duquesne University. His résumé included experience working as an accountant, a postal clerk, and a salesman for North Carolina Mutual Life Insurance and serving in the air force from 1944 to 1946.[73] In 1952, Dowdy wrote Marshall Field's personnel department, seeking employment in finance, control, and merchandising. Intrigued by his qualifications and experience, yet reportedly unaware that Dowdy was African American, Field's invited Dowdy for an interview and "intimated" that the company might be able to offer "a beginning job at a beginning salary." With this, Dowdy traveled from his hometown in Pittsburgh to Chicago "prepared to accept such an offer even though, in doing so, I might place myself at a disadvantage—economically." He recounted, "I received a cordial reception by Marshall Field. There were two interviews on two different days. . . . (Both were rather lengthy and rather informal, with several off-the-record disclosures made in each.) In gist I was told that the only thing standing in the way of my being hired was the fact that Marshall Field and Company—the department store—did not hire Negroes. I was told that this situation while very lamentable was nevertheless true."[74]

Afterward, Dowdy filed a complaint with the Commission on Human Relations in Chicago. In its investigation, the commission learned that, according to Field's, the retailer employed several hundred blacks in a variety of jobs at operations other than the Chicago store, and "at one time or another the Chicago retail store has had in its employ three or five Negroes, who were very light in complexion, and probably not identifiable as Negroes." Management admitted that "this small representation of Negroes does not constitute evidence of merit employment practices," but it "has given long and careful attention to the question of employing Negroes in their Chicago retail store." It was concerned, however, "that the employment of dark complexioned employees would negatively affect the 'character, atmosphere and flavor' of the company, and would, therefore, be harmful to the firm's competitive position." Field's went further: it opined that "the company's refusal to employ Negroes does not constitute racial discrimination as appearance, including the color of skin, for that firm [is] a legitimate standard of selection and that they would not consider a dark skinned person to be fully qualified for a position in the store; in this respect the company believes that it is 'discriminating' rather than discriminating *against* any group." In the end, the commission sided with Dowdy and recommended that the store, "in cooperation with other appropriate agencies, take such action as may be deemed advisable and applicable to effect a change in the apparently discriminatory practices of Marshall Field and Company."[75]

In June 1953, approximately one month after the commission handed down its decision, Field's finally embraced fair employment. But the retailer's embrace was far from wholehearted and complete. Its board of directors voted to adopt an Employment on Merit program on all levels *except* sales. Scheduled to begin on the second of July, the program provided for employment of fifty nonwhite persons. As stipulated in the program's procedures, the progress of these new hires would be observed for three months and then evaluated to determine whether additional integration would be pursued. Several months later, in the fall of 1953, Field's had hired "thirty some odd" workers of color in its mail-order houses and warehouses, and had just begun to hire African American clerical workers in its main store on State Street. It also hired "one credit interviewer, one telephone sales girl, one file clerk, and one secretary to a buyer."[76] Nearly one year later, however, Field's employment of African Americans declined to twenty-three; of these workers was Mildred C. King, who worked in telephone sales in the main store's personal shopping service department.[77] By 1955, Field's had hired approximately ninety African Americans; but by the end of the year, forty-three of these workers had resigned or had been forcefully displaced, leaving just forty-six blacks employed at its main store on State Street, mail-order house, warehouse, and other sites of operation in the Chicagoland area.[78]

By the end of the decade, Field's employed approximately one hundred African Americans at its eight sites of business, and still the overwhelming majority labored as kitchen workers and elevator operators.[79] Records suggest only one or two worked in sales—a number that indicated that Field's was still far from integrating its sales departments. Officials provided numerous excuses to defend their persisting racist hiring policies: they cited that "they have some divisional managers who are extremely prejudiced," they argued that Carson's made a mistake in assigning Charles Stone to the personnel department, they complained that "many of their most difficult and prejudiced employees are in sales," and they insisted that the majority of the store's customers favored keeping the store's sales force all white, with only one or two approving of black sales clerks.[80]

It was not until the mid- to late 1960s, as a result of persistent pressure from civil rights and government agencies, that Field's hired African American sales workers beyond a token few. By late 1969, the retailer reported employing 356 black salespeople (9.4 percent of total sales workers) and 1,149 black nonsales workers (15.8 percent of total nonselling workers) in its Chicago store, and 437 black salespeople (4.3 percent of total sales workers) and 1,297 blacks in nonselling positions (13 percent of total nonselling workers) in its Chicago and suburban stores combined.[81]

But Field's race problems did not stop there. African Americans often complained that the retailer discriminated against blacks in its advertising and displays. For example, in December 1968, one former Christmastime employee and longtime shopper of Field's expressed her displeasure to see that while Goldblatt's and Carson's window displays include black mannequins and employ black models for advertisements, Field's "follows no such policies."[82] Other customers also were upset by the absence of black mannequins in the store's window displays and were even more disheartened to find that in the store's 1969 Christmas Toy Catalog, of the sixty-six children featured in fifty-six pages, none were black, Mexican, Asian, or Indian.[83] Field's reportedly lost many of its loyal customers to its competitors during the 1968 and 1969 Christmas shopping seasons as a result. But evidently, this economic loss was not great enough to convince the retailer to make any immediate changes. Several more years—arguably a decade or so—would pass before Marshall Field could be considered fully integrated and accepting of African Americans. Even then, however, an undercurrent of racial conflict and tensions remained.

Demanding First-Class Citizenship for Black Consumers

The NUL, its branches, and the AFSC may have advanced black employment in the northern and western department store industries in the 1940s and 1950s, but these advances did not automatically translate into gains for African American customers in these very same stores. Racial barriers in the northern public accommodations could be "hard and fast" like those in the South, "but, at the same time, they could also be surprisingly and unpredictably flexible."[84] Rarely did African Americans encounter "White Only" or "No Colored" signs north of the Mason Dixon line; instead, it was only when blacks sought service that they learned the proprietor's race policies, and, even then, those policies might vacillate depending on from whom and when black customers sought service. Also, civil rights legislation—although not always obeyed—could provide some degree of protection and recourse. By the 1940s, eighteen northern and western states had enacted laws barring discrimination in public accommodations and amusement.[85] "Fourteen of these statutes outlaw discrimination because of race and color, seven include religion or creed, four specify national origin or alienage, and four indicate no specified ground of discrimination."[86] By 1955, New Jersey, New York, Massachusetts, Rhode Island, and Connecticut had established state commissions to hear and adjudicate complaints of discrimination.[87]

The push for antidiscrimination legislation, however, was not simply a northern phenomenon. Civil rights activists in Kentucky pushed for anti-discrimination legislation as well. But this legislation focused specifically on department stores. It aimed to ensure that "all citizens [had] the privilege of making purchases in any mercantile establishment in the state." The bill proposed to provide that "no person shall, on account of race, be refused service or the right to purchase garments or similar good at any mercantile establishments, or be denied any privilege accorded to other prospective customers." Unfortunately, Kentucky's House of Representatives voted fifty-three to forty-three against its ratification in March 1946.[88] Nearly two years later, African American representative Dennis Henderson introduced four civil rights bills into the House of Representatives. One of those bills would have required "open[ing] full facilities of department stores and their beauty shops to Negroes."[89] But again, it was rejected because white legislators feared that such a measure would have "produced immediate changes in racial practices."[90]

While the Kentucky campaign failed, an examination of locales where antidiscrimination commissions and laws were successfully instituted reveals that the black consumer experience remained fraught with insults and injuries. Some proprietors of businesses and public accommodations blatantly ignored the law; others served customers of color but refused to treat them with respect and dignity. In the mid-1940s, an adolescent Dick Gregory and his older brother visited department stores in downtown Chicago, eager to spend their earnings from their summer jobs on a government floor project. Their excitement quickly faded, however, as they encountered the white sales staff. Gregory recalled:

We were treated like dogs. We go into a place and a salesman would hurry away from his white customer. "What do you boys want?"
"Hat."

"What color?"

"Brown."

"What's your head size?"

"Don't know."

"You have to know."

"I'll try it on."

"Like hell you will."

To make matters worse, store detectives shadowed Gregory and his brother. The irony, Gregory observed, was that while African Americans "couldn't touch, couldn't try things on," stores "put our money right next to white folks' money in the cash register."[91] But even under these conditions, consuming in department stores, whether downtown or in black communities, could be a positive experience. For example, when Gregory returned home from his shopping excursion, he and his brother "spread out our clothes on the floor for everybody to see. There were more shirts and socks and underwear on that floor than in the whole wide world." Further, he wrote, "I felt a lot better going back to high school that year, wearing new clothes, feeling clean on the outside."[92]

Being humiliated, ignored, and treated as criminals does not capture the totality of many black shopping experiences. Shopping in white-owned stores, whether downtown or in black enclaves, also meant that African Americans often encountered racist merchandise. As discussed in the previous chapter, during World War II, Macy's sold "mugging night sticks," a product that threatened to elicit violence against blacks, who had become synonymous with mugging in the press, before labor and civil rights activists forced the retailer to remove them from its shelves. In the 1940s, Gimbel's sold the nursery book *Pinky Marie*. This racially offensive book, as described by the *Afro-American*, deals with the adventures of a "colored girl" named Pinky Marie Washington Jefferson Jackson, who has hair "just like Baa Baa Black Sheep, with his thick wool all scrumbled-scrambled up." Both of her parents, Mr. and Mrs. Washington Jefferson Jackson, were "as black—as black—as black." Her father had "kinky, black hair all over the top of his round black head," while her mother's hair remained unknown "because she always wore a big red-and-white hanky tied around her head."[93]

Under the direction of CORE, the NAACP, and middle-class women's groups, black consumer activism forced Gimbel's and other retailers that violated African Americans' civil and consumer rights to remove racist goods from their shelves and to respect and recognize blacks' human dignity. Similar to the NUL's and AFSC's department store campaigns, the struggle to end race discrimination in public accommodations was "fought little by little, place by place, in countless small skirmishes that went largely unnoticed outside a small circle of activists and readers of the black press. . . . Activists chipped away at the customs that separated the races until the sight of blacks at northern lunch counters, hotel lobbies, theaters, and amusement parks was not unusual—at least in the big cities"[94]

A significant proportion of the activism on behalf of black customers was levied against unscrupulous white retailers operating *in* black communities. In postwar Harlem, where blacks had already pressured the Office of Price Administration to enforce price controls during wartime, the Consumers' Protective Committee, the Harlem Housewives League, the Consolidated Housewives League, and the Consumers' Unit No. 1 used political lobbying and direct action protest to stop duplicitous selling practices, including overcharging, shortchanging, short weighing, and pulling-in ("a system whereby stores paid people to stand outside their businesses and aggressively pull shoppers inside").[95] One domestic worker complained that the price of food in Harlem was double that in her employer's neighborhood, while the cost of a dress was often three or four dollars more on 125th Street than downtown.[96] Another African American customer was charged "$24 for a pen and paper set" at a shop on 125th Street. To his dismay, "the next day the buyer saw an advertisement in a daily paper which stated that the same set could be purchased for $12 at many different stores downtown. The customer took his set back to the store which had sold it to him, and when he protested about the difference in price he had paid for it and what other stores charged the 125th Street merchant hurriedly refunded him his money."[97] In response to such stories, the aforementioned Harlem organizations and others investigated complaints of insults and injustices, educated clerks on how to treat black customers, and demanded that they do so.

The NAACP and the black press also were heavily involved in protecting and supporting the rights of black consumers, and they participated in consumer protests. The NAACP aided numerous individuals who filed complaints with the organization, stating that they had been denied service in stores and restaurants, and turned away from hotels. They met privately with business owners, and, when that failed, which it often did, they employed nonviolent activism and filed suit against Jim Crow establishments in violation of newly implemented state and local statutes. The black press, such as the *New York Amsterdam News*, provided black consumer groups with a forum with which to encourage community members to patronize Blumstein's Department Store, W. T. Grant, and other local retailers that had proven records of treating African Americans fairly and courteously.[98]

It is noteworthy that, while retail establishments were often sites of northern protests because of their mistreatment of African American consumers, lunch counters in discount stores in downtown shopping districts rarely were targets. Southern lunch counters in five-and-dime stores were frequently sites of protest in the civil rights movement; in fact, they are some of the most remembered, celebrated, and successful challenges to race discrimination. In the North, however, these eateries generally welcomed African Americans; they "were places of convenience and anonymity, not intimacy. But local customs, even in chain stores, varied. In Topeka, Kansas, for example, blacks were expected to stand at lunch counters even if seats were vacant."[99]

Once retailers softened their racial policies, they began to cater to the particular needs and desires of African American shoppers. Colm Tóibín's *Brooklyn*, a novel about an Irish immigrant woman living and working as a saleswoman in Brooklyn in the 1950s, illustrates this point. The fictional Bartocci's, a department store loosely based on Macy's, decides to welcome shoppers of color as more African Americans have moved into the surrounding area. To court these customers, the store begins to sell nylon hosiery in red, sepia, and coffee—shades desired by black women and complementary to their skin tones—at a separate counter, "away from the other normal stockings." Management recognizes that the store may "lose customers but we're going to sell to anyone who will buy and at the best prices." It instructs its sales staff to perform their duties as if nothing has changed and "to be polite to anyone who comes into this store, coloured or white."[100]

· · · · · ·

Integrating Pittsburgh's, Philadelphia's, and Chicago's department store sales forces may have been immediately viewed as the movement's biggest successes during this period of preliminary testing. And for many reasons, they were. The lessons yielded, however, also were a major feat, as they would be much more plentiful and instrumental in shaping the movement's future direction and that of the civil rights movement. First, activists learned that while the strategy of persuasion could achieve some success, it was mostly tokenism and did little to realize immediate or mass change.

"Decent people," as the borough president of Manhattan called them, were not persuaded to simply "do the right thing." It was, as activists correctly gleaned during this period, all about profits. The second lesson for activists, therefore, was that persuasion and political lobbying were most effective when supported by mass demonstrations and boycotts that leveraged both African Americans' purchasing and labor power. Finally, leaders realized that with this approach, employment discrimination, consumer discrimination, and the segregation of public accommodations could be best confronted concurrently.

5 Worker-Consumer Alliances and the Modern Black Middle Class, 1951–1970

· ·

In early 1951, when the Coordinating Committee for the Enforcement of D.C. Anti-Discrimination Laws (CCEAD) began protesting Hecht Company, the department store campaign had ostensibly abandoned the labor-oriented initiatives of the 1940s and fixated on the democratization of consumption. Hecht's was an archetypal southern department store, despite being located on the periphery of the solidly Jim Crow South. It welcomed everyone in its merchandise departments but prohibited African Americans from enjoying the pleasure of being served at its lunch counter, thereby fastening onto them a badge of servitude. The CCEAD, a multiracial civil rights group committed to the enforcement of two "lost laws" prohibiting discrimination in Washington public accommodations, copied the tactics and strategies of early department store campaigns to demand the desegregation of this space. It began by flooding management with stickered bill stubs and pledge cards. The protest quickly evolved into a mass demonstration supported by over one hundred civic, labor, and church groups and featured "respectable, well-behaved" blacks picketing three times a week and sitting in the store's lunch counter every Saturday. After nearly one year of unrelenting opposition, Hecht's integrated its lunch counter in January 1952.[1]

The Hecht's campaign was one of the earliest lunch counter demonstrations to sweep across the American South. In the years before and after the renowned Greensboro sit-in (in fact, as early as 1943 but more commonly in the 1950s and 1960s),[2] blacks had grown weary of having to travel several miles to eat lunch or use a restroom when working in and visiting downtown districts. From D.C. to Charlotte to Nashville, they organized widely publicized sit-ins and picket lines to force the desegregation of public accommodations and democratization of the transactional nature of customer-business interactions as a result.[3] But African Americans had other goals. What began as protests aimed at restructuring the physical space of the public sphere and procuring the right to experience the indulgences of customer service often grew into organized endeavors to dismantle the formidable barriers to black economic emancipation. These endeavors maintained a broad understanding of the black community's shared interests and involved challenging segregation and discrimination in the marketplace on behalf of black customers *and* workers. Some southern campaigns, such as the Washington, D.C., effort, realized merit hiring once African American customers achieved equal access to and treatment in stores. Others, like the Charlotte sit-in movement, negotiated the hiring of blacks in sales and clerical jobs behind the scenes, away from the prying eyes of consumers and the press, during the throes of protest.

The proliferation of sit-ins and picketing in the postwar era marked a new phase in the department store movement. The movement decreased its reliance on moral suasion and education, and it readily embraced very public forms of resistance. Early reformers learned that moral suasion alone produced limited results. To be effective, moral suasion required the threat and actualization of protest as well as the support of government authority such as the federal and state Fair Employment Practices Commissions (FEPC). The movement also now involved an increased amount of clandestineness, which was needed to challenge segregation and discrimination in the workplace since "the narrowing of public discourse" and governmental policies had contributed to the dismantling of the labor movement in the Cold War era. "The rise of anticommunism shattered the Popular Front coalition on civil rights, while the retreat and containment of the union movement [as exemplified by the passing of the Taft Hartley Act in 1947] deprived black activists of the political and social space necessary to carry on an independent struggle," particularly one that attended to labor-related and economic inequalities.[4]

Still, conditions were ripe for democratizing labor and consumption following the Second World War. First, by leveraging anticommunist sentiments and the new international gaze on the nation, black activists pressured President Harry S. Truman to address domestic racism and shape a political milieu that was progressively becoming pro–civil rights. He then mandated the establishment of a committee to investigate civil rights, encouraged Congress to enact civil rights legislation, and outlawed discrimination in the military. Efforts, albeit unsuccessful, also were made to establish a permanent FEPC; while the Legal Defense and Educational Fund of the National Association for the Advancement of Colored People (NAACP) succeeded in outlawing white primaries, restrictive covenants, and racial segregation in railroad dining cars and, most notably, in public education. The extension of civil rights continued over the next twenty-five years, under the direction of President John F. Kennedy, who issued

Executive Order 100925 and initiated a drive for civil rights and voting rights bills, and President Lyndon B. Johnson, under whom these bills were realized and a national program to end poverty was executed.

Second, in the "golden age" of capitalism, a period of steady economic expansion that began after the war and lasted until the early 1970s, consumerism was celebrated as the "essence of American freedom."[5] This ideology underscored the injustces blacks had long suffered in the marketplace and, at the same time, presented them with new opportunities for fighting segregation and discrimination in this sphere.[6]

Third, white economic dependence on African American workers and consumers grew as the black population of the nation's major cities rapidly expanded and black purchasing power increased. In the postwar era, millions of blacks continued to stream into cities, lured by dramatic growth in industrial and white-collar employment and the relaxation of racial barriers that had previously barred their employ. Now better employed, although often not in positions of responsibility, and better paid, African Americans saw their purchasing power swell from $8–$9 billion in 1947 to $30 billion in 1969, marking black consumers as a group deserving of recognition and consideration.[7] At the same time, millions of whites (and later a smaller but significant number of middle-class blacks), assisted by federal mortgage and construction programs, relocated to rapidly expanding suburban areas. By 1960, with the exception of New York and Los Angeles, the country's ten largest cities were more than 20 percent African American.[8]

Finally, now more urban, waged, and skilled, African Americans leveraged their power as both workers and consumers to build worker-consumer alliances and challenge racialized patterns of labor, consumption, and urban landscapes. They recognized that, because of the postwar assault on the labor movement, consumption was a promising avenue for realizing full and equal status in the nation. They also rightly reasoned that the power of labor could be resuscitated when leveraged in tandem with black purchasing power. In other words, consumer protests could make demands on behalf of, and thus advance, the agendas of black customers *and* workers simultaneously.

Thus, black worker-consumer alliances were grounded in a notion of linked fate. Linked fate, the political scientist Michael Dawson argues, supposes that the "historical experiences of African Americans have resulted in a situation in which group interests have served as a useful proxy for self-interest."[9] In other words, because race has been a decisive factor in determining African American life changes, the collective interests of the race typically override economic polarizations of the group. Linked fate fostered an acute sense of loyalty and awareness that the race's economic enfranchisement was intimately tied to its members, and vice versa, and thus stimulated both individual and collective political action.

In the 1950s and 1960s, this meant that, because all blacks, regardless of their own or their family's social and economic status, were treated as second-class citizens in the marketplace, most, if not all, African Americans were invested in dismantling Jim Crow and improving their and the group's socioeconomic position. Black communities' wholehearted support for the integration of department store sales staff perfectly illustrated the political consciousness described by "linked fate." While it most immediately benefited the more urbane and educated black middle class, virtually all blacks, regardless of class, trusted that opening white-collar work would benefit everyone involved. Middle-class blacks hoped to secure this skilled work to escape menial labor and affirm their class position, while those of the working class believed that one day they would move into white-collar employment and acquire middle-class status as well. And even if they did not achieve middle-class status, the increased social recognition of other blacks would benefit the status of the race as a whole. Moreover, nearly all blacks expected that the placing of African Americans in sales would enhance the black customer experience, and vice versa.

Alliances cultivated between black waitresses and their customers and later black saleswomen and their customers were integral to southern department store campaigns. Nationally, waitressing had been an occupation reserved for white native-born and immigrant women. But in the South, because whites "were more accustomed to intimate social relations with black servants in both the private and public realms,"[10] a large contingent of African American women toiled as waitresses at segregated lunch counters and restaurants in stores.[11] Segregated eateries were emblematic of the profound contradictions of American consumer culture: although situated in the "democratic space" of the department store, they were Jim Crow spaces that reinforced white supremacy and black inferiority. Indeed, such lunch counters may well have become targets for civil rights protests because they rendered America's racial contradictions so visible in everyday life.

At the same time, these lunch counters reinforced the communal solidarity of black consumers and laborers, which would empower subsequent civil rights protests. There is evidence that black waitresses went above and beyond their assigned duties to provide their customers of color with outstanding service and special amenities, effectively enabling African Americans to at least momentarily shed their badges of servitude and experience the pleasures of being served. For both parties, exchanges such as these bestowed human dignity, prestige, status, and a sense that they, as African Americans, belonged not only in the elegant, modern world of downtown stores but also in the American democratic polity.

When black waitresses were promoted to sales, which was often the result of the power of worker-consumer alliances in lunch counter demonstrations, the relationship between these two groups deepened. Just as they had at store eateries, African American workers empowered shoppers of color—many of whom were their former lunch counter customers—to realize and perform respectability and citizenship. Black saleswomen cultivated interpersonal relations to sell goods to customers of color, thus providing them with a first-class experience, even in the midst of the de-skilling and degradation of sales work and the loss of comprehensive customer service. Black salespeople also routinely performed acts of defiance, bending and breaking rules they deemed unfair or discriminatory, in behalf of black consumers.

As a result of these relationships—and consistent with the growing link between class identity and the mid-twentieth-century consumption regime more generally—a *modern* black middle class emerged at lunch counters and on selling floors.[12] Worker-consumer alliances and the protest campaigns they shaped facilitated African Americans' move out of agriculture and service into white-collar employment from the 1950s to the 1970s. These alliances also democratized customer service practices in the "consumers' republic," with the understanding that where and what African Americans purchased was fundamental to claiming, expressing, and receiving treatment as members of a more privileged stratum. In other words, only when permitted to work, shop, and eat freely in the consumer sphere did African Americans fully claim middle-class citizenship. They were then expected to express their status through respectable behaviors and manners, even as their consumption of goods and services affirmed their status. All of this could be achieved in the world of the mid-twentieth-century department store.

Consequently, the success of southern department store campaigns in advancing the black conditions of labor and consumption reinvigorated movements to end economic discrimination throughout the country, inspiring the creation of the Selective Patronage program, Southern Christian Leadership Conference's Operation Breadbasket, and others that relied on intraracial solidarities and confrontational and militant strategies. Southern campaigns reminded activists—many of whom had traveled south to occupy lunch counter seats—that retail institutions and other workplaces throughout the country were beset with their own set of discriminatory practices. The "Don't Buy" campaign, persuasion, and unionism had increased blacks' presence and improved their position in the northern stores in the previous decades, but they had failed to fully integrate the retail industry. So, in the 1960s, activists drew on and revitalized the tradition of protest to advance black employment in department stores. This time, however, black workers were more involved and protesters' demands were more forceful and exact. They pushed for quotas and affirmative action programs, hoping to establish the scaffolding needed to ensure long-term racial and economic justice.

But their efforts were thwarted as suburbanization heightened and urban decay pushed department stores away from center cities, making white-collar jobs even scarcer. By the late 1960s, as the "golden age" of capitalism came to a close and black nationalism and black power rose to prominence, the thrust of black consumer politics shifted. Activists now focused their energies on advancing a separate black economy and guaranteeing low-income customers "the right to a decent standard of living in the Consumers' Republic."[13]

Southern Department Store Campaigns:
Washington, D.C., and Charlotte, North Carolina

In the post–World War II era, Washington, D.C., bore a striking resemblance to a northern city in terms of industrialization and urbanization. Yet despite having relatively few Jim Crow laws, the nation's capital was very much a southern city in terms of race relations. Segregation and racism were endemic, and its civil rights movement to integrate the public sphere was patterned after those of the American South. The 1950s and 1960s marked a period of significant civil rights agitation on several fronts, including employment, biracial patronage of restaurants and places of amusement, housing, education, and welfare and police procedures. The city's department stores became sites of conflict as activists pushed first for integrated eating facilities, then expanded their efforts to include white-collar positions.

Hecht Company was one of these sites. Founded in 1895, Hecht's was the "youngest" of the city's grand emporiums and "among the least prestigious during its first three decades of operation. Its target audience came from the lower end of the market: white- and blue-collar persons of moderate income."[14] The store also was extremely popular among African Americans. Even in the segregation era, black customers, Alice Ross recalled in 2006, believed that Hecht's "treated you a little bit nicer" than other department stores.[15] It was the most accommodating in letting black customers try on and return clothes and open charge accounts. The store had long refused to serve its loyal black customers at its basement lunch counter, however, reserving it for its white customers only; and the store was hesitant to employ African Americans in positions of responsibility. These discriminatory practices triggered a series of sit-in demonstrations in D.C. department stores that spanned the next ten years.

On February 19, 1951, Hecht's sponsored a full-page advertisement in support of World Brotherhood Week. The advertisement featured a message from Eric Johnston, economic stabilization administrator and general chair of the weeklong event. The message, which was positioned beneath a picture of black and white hands clasped in friendship, read:

> We talk about building bridges of brotherhood around the world in answer to the communist pretensions, and that's a splendid vision. But brotherhood begins on a man to man basis at home and not a mass to mass basis across the oceans. Without that footing it is idle talk and an empty vision. We can't afford to blind ourselves to the disturbing and undermining racial and religious antagonisms in America. They will defeat our good intentions for a world brotherhood until we cast them out and live as brothers in our states, communities, and neighborhoods—not for a single week in any year, but day by day and year by year.[16]

Hecht's advertisement caught the attention of the CCEAD, the civil rights group behind the *District of Columbia v. John R. Thompson Co., Inc.* case. Led by Mary Church Terrell and Annie Stein, the CCEAD was committed to the reinstatement of the antidiscrimination laws of 1872 and 1873. These laws were passed when the District Legislative Assembly governed the city and required "all eating-place proprietors to serve any respectable, well-behaved person regardless of color, or face a $100 fine and forfeiture of their license for one year."[17] In 1901 the antidiscrimination laws were omitted from a recodification of the District of Columbia Code, imposing racial segregation. That omission notwithstanding, the underlying Reconstruction-era laws were never overturned. The city's failure to repeal these laws provided the CCEAD with the legal basis to challenge segregated public accommodations, including those at Hecht's department store.

To the CCEAD, the advertisement suggested that the company "might be ready to change" and build "bridges of brotherhood."[18] Almost immediately thereafter, a group that included Terrell and Stein met with Harry Schwartz, Hecht's personnel director, to address the discrepancy between the store's policy of segregated lunch counters and the brotherhood advertisement. Schwartz explained that the ad was a "purely commercial gesture" but "agreed to discuss possible change in policy with the officials of the store."[19] After a series of meetings, Schwartz announced that the lunch counter would continue to be reserved for white customers only and broke off negotiations. The *Afro-American* reported that "Mr. Schwartz was 'rather rude' to the delegation and told them flatly that there would be no change of policy unless 'pressure is exerted.' . . . He conceded, however, that if the committee could prove that Hecht's would not lose any business by lowering the racial barriers a change might be considered."[20] The committee, with the support of over one hundred civic, labor, and church groups, immediately moved to commence "an active boycott campaign with stickers on bill stubs and pledge cards as the major technique" (figure 8).[21]

For weeks, thousands of pledge cards and letters inundated Hecht's office, but the company refused to change its policy. By the summer of 1951, it had become evident that the boycott was not having the desired effect and the CCEAD began to pursue a more aggressive strategy. In June, the committee sent volunteers to a sit-in at the lunch counter at the store's 7th and F Street, N.W., location. In a letter to a Hecht's boycott supporter, Stein wrote that the sit-in was organized "like a picket line, with two-hour shifts. We had between 15 and 20 people sitting down at a time all through the day on Saturday. The manager would come over and say, 'We don't serve colored here' and we'd say, 'That's all right, we'll wait.' He didn't take a chance on throwing us out, because after all it really is the law now that they may not discriminate. Now the store is closed on Saturdays and we are continuing the sitdowns [sic] on Fridays." On one occasion, the famed African American singer and dancer Josephine Baker joined sit-in demonstrators and tried to get served at the lunch counter. Even then, Hecht's refused to integrate.[22]

On July 20, the boycott was reinforced with picket lines, which marched in front of Hecht's three times a week, calling customers' attention to the store's segregation policy.[23] Picketers were required to obey a dress code designed by Stein, who reasoned that since the antidiscrimination laws

FIGURE 8 *Fair-Minded Americans Stay Out of Hecht's* leaflet. Coordinating Committee for the Enforcement of the D.C. Anti-Discrimination Laws Records, 1949–1954, Historical Society of Washington, D.C.

required service to "any respectable, well-behaved person" (qualifiers for "legitimate" consumer), picketers must dress and act as such. In other words, African American protesters were expected to consume and display material goods and behaviors that reflected middle-class black respectability as evidence that they were deserving of full citizenship. Organizers likely mandated that protesters look like modified, budget-friendly versions of respected black figures such as Josephine Baker (the "World's Best Dressed Woman" according to *Jet* magazine in 1951), Lena Horne, federal judge Jane M. Bolin, Jackie and Rachel Robinson, and congressman Adam Clayton Powell Jr. and his wife Hazel Scott (who was described as "a typical housewife" in a 1947 issue of *Ebony* magazine).[24]

Given this premise, the picket line became virtually a site of identity formation. On his first day on the picket line, Marvin Caplan, a CCEAD member, recalled that even in the sweltering heat of August, demonstrators looked to be "dressed for church or some other formal occasion. They wore ties and jackets. A couple of them wore felt hats. The half-dozen women on the line, both black and white, were even more fashionably dressed. . . . All of them wore pretty summer dresses and summer hats."[25] Not everyone was able to observe the dress code, however. In a letter to Stein, Alice Trigg, chair of the boycott, wrote that on one picket line a woman had "a dress on up to her knees and she was no small or good looking person at best, with a slip hanging about three inches all around, and the way she was rocking on those heels I wondered when she would sprawl." Before Trigg had an opportunity to speak with the woman about her inappropriate attire, a fellow protester stopped her. The protester surmised that the woman likely was wearing her "working attire," as "lots [of demonstrators] came from work . . . [and because] white people were always giving [blacks] that inferior feeling and [they] would be playing right into their hands" if they asked the woman to leave the picket line for her attire.[26] Although this working-class woman was not reprimanded for her dress, others like her were probably instructed on the finer points of middle-class consumption and behavior via observation or direct conversation with a CCEAD leader or member.

In Washington, D.C., the scholar Beverly Jones argues, "picketing became not only an effective device for forcing Hecht's to negotiate but also an instrument of education."[27] Not only were protesters coached on being middle class, but black and white passersby were informed about the injustices perpetuated against the store's "respectable, well-behaved" customers and persuaded to join the boycott. One woman vowed not to buy much-needed curtains for her new apartment until Hecht's submitted. She stated, "I can't afford to pay cash for curtains. But Hecht's is the only place where I have a charge account. But I'll be darned if I'm going to let Hecht's get away with making Negroes go hungry."[28] Another protester sitting-in at Hecht's lunch counter recounted the following story:

A high-ranking [white] officer sat down next to me. The clerk offered to serve him, but the officer stated that "this other man was here before me, serve him, I am in no hurry." The waitress replied, "He can not be served because he is colored." The officer ordered a coke. When it was brought, he ordered another and another, until there were six cokes in front of me. The waitress called the manager, who could do nothing about the cokes that had been already served to me. But he did order the waitress not take another order from the white officer.[29]

On the whole, the picketers received enormous public support. A 1951 progress report of the boycott from the CCEAD stated, "The response of the public is good. Nearly 90% of the colored trade is kept out of our line, and about 5% of the whites came up to our pickets to pledge their support."[30] The committee received both words of support and money from individuals and businesses, including North Carolina Mutual Insurance of Durham, the United States ambassador of Monrovia, Liberia, and the American Psychological Association.

Not all African Americans, however, backed the boycott. Some continued to shop at Hecht's, going on days when the CCEAD was not picketing.[31] Picketers observed that a number of black customers still patronizing Hecht's during the boycott were Howard University students (which was quite ironic given that Howard students had been actively engaged in the D.C.'s "Don't Buy" movement in the 1930s and initiated one of the earliest sit-ins in 1943).[32] In response, Stein and Terrell contacted the university, requested that students support the cause and offered to speak with student organizations about the committee's efforts to end segregation and discrimination in D.C. restaurants.[33]

Even with a few African Americans crossing the picket line, the D.C. campaign was effective in significantly reducing Hecht's profits. To fight the picket, the store held "fabulous sales" on days when demonstrators were present. But sales did little to lessen the store's financial loss. By the end of the summer, hoping to broker a compromise and end the boycott, Hecht's offered African American patrons service at two stools at the sherbet counter.[34] When protesters rejected this offer, the lunch counter manager proposed that they order their food at the lunch counter and sit at the sherbet counter. Viewing this as "ridiculous" and a different manifestation of Jim Crow, the CCEAD continued its campaign. In December 1951, just before a major Christmas protest, Stein addressed members of the CCEAD in the Laundry Workers hall. She opined that Hecht's was losing an enormous amount of business and predicted that Hecht's would capitulate to their demands by early 1952 (figure 9).[35]

Just as Stein predicted, on January 14, 1952, almost one year after the first meeting between the CCEAD and Hecht's and a nearly $6 million loss to the store, Hecht's quietly integrated its lunch counter.[36] The store could not afford to suffer any additional financial loss or lose African American customers, especially since D.C.'s black population had already increased by nearly 50 percent between 1940 and 1950 and was fast becoming the city's racial majority.[37] The store made no formal announcement, however. By some accounts, even when questioned about the integration of its lunch counter, some officials insisted that the store had never discriminated against its black customers, while others refused to admit that Hecht's had changed its policy. But word of Hecht's new policy was eventually leaked by some of the store's black employees. Caplan recalled, "One Saturday, in about the middle of the month, a black porter came out to sweep the pavement while the line was in progress and softly and casually mentioned to a couple of the pickets that they didn't need to picket anymore. The store, he said, had changed its policy." Three days later, an African American woman was able to buy a sandwich and a cup of coffee from a white waitress without being ignored or rebuffed. And not long after, Terrell, Stein, and three black women reporters from the *Afro-American*, the *Pittsburgh Courier*, and the *Associated Negro Press* enjoyed lunch at the counter.[38]

The disclosure of Hecht's policy change by an African American porter hints at the importance of the worker-consumer dynamic in this boycott. In this protest, among others, many black employees supported efforts to integrate stores' dining facilities. In their time away from the workplace, they attended committee meetings, donated money, helped create flyers, and spread the CCEAD's message about Hecht's and its discriminatory policy. Others acted as secret agents. While on the clock, they obeyed the rules of respectability (regarding dress and conduct) set by the committee and listened for any information about store management's plans to undermine the demonstration; they later reported their findings to committee leaders.

FIGURE 9 *Even at Christmastime* leaflet. Coordinating Committee for the Enforcement of the D.C. Anti-Discrimination Laws Records, 1949–1954, Historical Society of Washington, D.C.

Black employees, especially the waitresses at Hecht's lunch counter, occupied a particularly difficult position. While they supported the desegregation movement, they were forced to ignore protesters, many of whom were their families and friends, in order to keep their jobs and support their children. Unionized waiters and waitresses were instructed by their unions to cooperate with the committee and did so to whatever extent restaurant policies allowed them. Extant records, however, do not reveal the true number of unionized waitresses of color at Hecht's. Committee members wondered how a black waitress could have "enough nerve to refuse a colored patron," but expressed some sympathy that these women had to consider their jobs and families.[39] Management told all African American employees that "they did not realize what this is all about and they should keep quiet." It threatened "that all persons seen talking with the 'strikers' would be dismissed."[40]

This "no talking" policy infuriated many black employees, especially waitresses who stood on the front lines, although on the other side of the counter, of the boycott. Three waitresses were fired after speaking to sit-in demonstrators, while another waitress was reassigned to a behind-the-scenes position after "allegedly" talking with committee volunteers. One African American waitress was so outraged by the treatment accorded to blacks that she refused to serve all people of color as long as her own were ignored. On July 13, 1951, while a group of CCEAD members were seated at the lunch counter and being ignored, a woman from India approached the counter. The waitress declined to serve the Indian woman, "stating that if she is to be forbidden to serve colored Americans simply because of their color, she would not serve other persons of color." In her stead, the lunch counter manager waited on the woman and, after she finished her lunch, personally escorted her out of the store to prevent the group of CCEAD members from explaining the situation to her.[41]

Once free to eat at Hecht's lunch counter, and inspired by the strengthening of the standard nondiscrimination clause written into all employment contracts executed by the federal government in September 1954, Washington activists focused their energies on broadening African Americans' job opportunities. There had been significant growth in the region's job openings. Yet most positions—both skilled and "a whole gamut . . . [that] required little training"—were closed to African Americans. As a result, from 1954 to 1957, the President's Committee on Government Contracts, the National Urban League, and the NAACP, among others, persuaded and prodded employers, including the Chesapeake and Potomac Telephone

Company and General Services, Inc. (an operator of cafeterias and snack bars in government buildings), to integrate jobs formerly reserved for whites and provide on-the-job training.[42]

Department stores also were targeted. In 1958, nearly one out of every two residents was African American, yet they made up only a negligible portion of the city's sales force. One activist observed that "two or three sales girls" in five-and-dime stores formed the entire black sales force in downtown D.C.[43] That same year, after failed attempts to persuade department store owners to hire black sales help for the 1957 Christmas season, the Committee on Equal Employment Opportunity (CEEO) organized a one-day consumer boycott—"Day of Prayer for Merit Hiring and Abstinence from Shopping"—to force the city's major department stores to hire African American salesclerks and adopt merit hiring practices.

The one-day boycott, which corresponded with the committee's ongoing "We Believe in Merit Hiring" sticker campaign, was unlike any other.[44] With the support of nearly two hundred black ministers and their parishioners, the committee asked the city's black population to observe March 27 as a day of prayer and to abstain from shopping. The committee did not aspire to garner much fanfare, nor did it seek to "start a stampede away from the downtown shopping areas." Rather, it hoped that the one-day action would serve as a "gentle, but firm nudge to the big shop-owners" and communicate that "if Negroes are not good enough to work behind the counter, they are not good enough to stand on the other side, either, as customers."[45]

In the days before the boycott, fears abounded among the city's white business and civic leaders that the protest would create "considerable misunderstanding and division within the community."[46] Hoping to assuage these fears, district commissioner Robert E. McLaughlin met separately with department store executives and the CEEO to prevent the boycott. He proposed that the issue be delegated to the Commissioner's Council on Human Relations. This group in turn proposed that it advise the district commissioners on race relations and quietly work toward integrating department store sales work.[47] The CEEO rejected this proposal, and on March 27, led by Reverend E. Franklin Jackson, the organization's chair, black Washingtonians participated in the Day of Prayer for Merit Hiring and Abstinence from Shopping.

In this stay-away campaign, protesters abstained from shopping in the district's five major department stores and, in place of picketing and other forms of demonstration, attended services at the city's black churches at noon and 8 P.M. to pray for success. African Americans stayed out of Hecht's,

Woodward & Lothrop, S. Kann Sons & Co., Lansburgh's, and Julius Garfinckel & Company. The exact number of participants is unknown. However, observations from boycott organizers and store officials and employees indicate that the campaign "cut significantly into stores' usual business." Black customers were conspicuously absent from the selling floor and the day's sales reflected as much. Jackson estimated that the boycott kept approximately 90 percent of the usual black shoppers from stores.[48] One organizer observed that at Hecht Company, a store "usually pretty crowded with Negroes," only seven black customers wandered the aisles. Similarly, a white female model at Hecht's noted that, during her six-hour shift, she saw no "more than one in 50" African Americans. At Woodward & Lothrop, one store official stated: "There have been some Negro customers in here so far. But I saw many more shopping the first few days of the week."[49]

Unfortunately, the shopping ban did not achieve the desired effect. While the committee chair expressed optimism that stores would soon be hiring African American clerks in the days after the ban, store officials resisted the adoption of merit hiring.[50] Most officials were irritated by the ban and used it as another excuse for not hiring African American salesclerks, while others minimized the economic loss of the one-day boycott. One official blamed blacks for their absence on the selling floor (the typical excuse being that no qualified African American sales workers existed), commenting: "We were gradually getting ready to hire Negroes as sales help. We already employ them in office work and just about every other capacity. There was no bitterness at all up until now, but with this thing dragged out into the open, I just don't know how long it'll be before we hire them as clerks." The president of another store explained: "I won't say when we would have hired them but if we were going to do it in April, we sure wouldn't do it now. This thing stirs up our customers and our own sales help and we would be losing face if we put Negroes in sales jobs any time soon."[51]

The 1958 movement adopted the boycott strategy to "gently" push store officials to integrate their sales forces. Unlike the CCEAD's campaign, this movement did not directly utilize black store workers, build an interracial coalition, or aggressively attack discriminating department stores on multiple fronts over a prolonged period of time. Instead, the CEEO leveraged the power of the Negro market for only an abbreviated period of time. With this approach, the organization failed to significantly diminish store profits and reputation, draw attention to store officials' economic dependence on African American customers, and convince officials that white consumers would patronize integrated establishments.

True to their word, department store executives did little more than hire a few token black sales workers until pressured by lengthier and more dramatic boycotts in the 1960s. These boycotts organized by the Congress of Racial Equality (CORE) threatened to do much more damage than a one-day shopping ban and benefited from the growth and success of highly publicized southern sit-ins, such as the Greensboro sit-in. In 1959 CORE began meeting with Lansburgh's store executives, hoping to persuade them to employ more blacks in sales. Lansburgh employed about two hundred black workers out of a total workforce of 1,000 in its downtown store. Only eleven of its African American workers were salesclerks, and seventeen were in clerical positions. At the insistence of CORE, store executives provided the organization with a list of twenty-five blacks who were set to be hired in sales departments. But soon thereafter, CORE discovered that over half of the applicants on the list were former employees and that the store had no intention of hiring any new African American sales workers. Finally, in December 1961, after three years of failed promises and little progress, CORE set up picket lines in front of Lansburgh's. A few months later, in February 1962, picketing ceased when the two parties reached an agreement on the store's merit hiring policy.[52]

The same year that CORE targeted Lansburgh's, it also launched a merit hiring campaign against Hecht's flagship store on 7th and F Streets, N.W. CORE charged that this Hecht's "engaged in token hiring, placing its few black employees in strategic positions to suggest that there were others."[53] A survey "by teams of observers"—some of whom were reportedly black store employees—revealed that African Americans made up 44 percent of the shoppers on weekdays and 47 percent on Saturdays. Yet the store employed only five black salesclerks out of a total of 270 in the downtown store; on the other hand, *all* of its janitors, maids, lunch counter waitresses and cooks, and parking lot attendants were African American. Whites accounted for all of the twenty store managers, all of the eight office clerks, and every parking lot cashier. CORE eventually persuaded Hecht's to hire thirty-five African American salesclerks and one assistant buyer.[54]

In February 1964, Hecht's was once again charged with violating fair employment practices. Few African American women held permanent sales jobs, no African American sales personnel were assigned to "prestige" or commission departments, and blacks with seniority and experience were not being promoted to supervisory positions. Unable to quietly convince store officials to even acknowledge that a problem existed, CORE organized pickets at Hecht's downtown and Parkington (in Arlington, Virginia) locations.[55] Not long after picketing began, Hecht's and CORE reached an agreement in March 1964, whereby "the company promise[d] to increase the opportunities for Negroes by a considerable measure." Store officials assured CORE "that fair employment policies will be supervised and vigorously enforced."[56]

Between 1950 and 1970, these campaigns helped increase the number of nonwhite sales workers in the city's retail industry by approximately 300 percent, from 1,314 sales workers to 4,027.[57] While the integration of sales work and dining facilities in Washington, D.C., appears to have been the product of separate campaigns run by different organizations, these movements actually overlapped and were interrelated. United by racial solidarity, the desegregation of public accommodations and white-collar employment in the retail industry relied on worker-consumer alliances. The link between consumption and protest was visibly manifested in "the politics of respectability" that protesters embraced, as they sought to project an image of African Americans as conservatively dressed and behaved citizens who deserved the equal treatment and status befitting their behavior. A more direct link was made evident when black shoppers withheld their purchasing power to damage store profits and reputations. Meanwhile, workers used their unique position to observe, resist, and report incidents of racial discrimination and whispers of merchants' plans to retaliate against protesters. These alliances proved so effective that, once on the selling floor, African Americans expanded their efforts to raise black workers' wages, living standards, and working conditions, and contributed to long-term structural changes in the department store industry.

· · · · · ·

Just as protesters in Washington, D.C., turned their attention to fair employment, the sit-in movement commenced in Charlotte, North Carolina. Unlike the Washington campaign, which focused on consumer rights and then fair employment, however, the Charlotte sit-in movement tackled these issues simultaneously. On February 9, 1960, moved by the Greensboro demonstration, Johnson C. Smith University (JCSU) students staged sit-ins to protest segregated eating facilities at S. H. Kress Company and F. W. Woolworth. Within a few days, approximately two hundred students expanded their presence to W. T. Grant Company, McLellan's, Liggett Drug, Belk's, Ivey's, and Sears, Roebuck, and Company. W. T. Grant, like the other targeted retailers, immediately closed both of its lunch counters (one for whites and the other for African Americans), hoping to suppress the demonstration. Yet despite its best efforts, well-dressed and mannerly

FIGURE 10 Woman carrying picket sign, "Equality Is Right, Give It to Us," during W. T. Grant protest, 1960. Courtesy of the *Charlotte Observer* and Robinson-Spangler Carolina Room, Charlotte Mecklenburg Library.

protesters, whose numbers steadily increased in subsequent days and months, occupied lunch counter seats reserved for white patrons and patiently waited for service. Others picketed the storefront and ceased shopping at the establishment (figures 10 and 11). Protesters defiantly withstood venomous verbal and physical assaults. After several contentious months and hundreds of thousands of dollars lost, the store capitulated to the protesters' demands and became the "only integrated lunch counter where blacks could eat in downtown Charlotte." By July 1960, six of the remaining stores targeted by protesters had followed suit; and on July 9, fifteen African American students, in accordance with a prearranged plan, were served at seven Charlotte lunch counters for the first time. Sears, the eighth and final store, announced its dining room had been integrated for two months on October 28, 1960.[58]

Hoping to avoid any additional conflict and violence, news of the desegregation of Charlotte's lunch counters was delayed per an agreement between the city's mayor James Smith and the local press.[59] Additionally,

FIGURE 11 Sit-in protesters in downtown Charlotte, 1960. Courtesy of the *Charlotte Observer* and Robinson-Spangler Carolina Room, Charlotte Mecklenburg Library.

all news coverage of the Charlotte sit-in demonstration ignored the integration of W. T. Grant's sales force—an equally important accomplishment of this movement.[60] In 1960, Doretha Davis was quietly promoted from waitress at W. T. Grant's twenty-seven-seat "Negro-only" lunch counter to sales clerk, becoming the city's first African American saleswoman.[61] Her promotion, as was the case with many African Americans who were hired as salesclerks during the civil rights era, was the direct result of the lunch counter sit-in. Although the hiring of Davis did not make for an integrated sales force, her promotion marked a major feat of the Charlotte sit-in movement. It set in motion the gradual transformation of the selling floor whereby, after her hiring, more African American sales workers were employed and even more African American consumers were recognized as citizens deserving of equal access to and treatment in the retail industry.

The Charlotte sit-in protest did not receive the national attention that the Greensboro demonstration did, nor was it one of the more dramatic sit-ins during the civil rights movement. But it was the first sustained demonstration for racial equality in the city. In 1960, Charlotte was reputed to be a "model of racial moderation." Home to nearly 210,000 people, 28 percent of whom were nonwhite, this southern city was in the early stages of the integration process.[62] This process, however, was by all appearances to-kenism. Most accommodations and services had opened their doors to African Americans, often without court orders or much conflict.[63] Whenever the black community threatened to file a lawsuit or protest, the city's white elected officials and business elites quickly acted to quell any potential racial conflict with token concessions, aiming to preserve a strong business environment and protect Charlotte's image.[64] As a result, African Americans freely voted and were quite influential in local politics, local department stores integrated their restrooms in the years after the *Brown* decision, and the newly built public library quietly welcomed black patrons in 1956. Charlotte also became one of the first southern cities to desegregate its bus service and voluntarily desegregate its public schools.

But the city was far from integrated. So, on February 9, 1960, JCSU students initiated a sit-in demonstration at eight downtown stores, believing that retail establishments were ideal sites for challenging racialized patterns of consumption and urban landscapes. Initially, only "some hundred students" participated in the movement.[65] But in the days and months that followed, the movement picked up support. It received the endorsement of nearly the entire JCSU student population. The Pastor's Fellowship of Charlotte, an interdenominational association of Negro ministers, and the Gethsemane AME Zion Church held freedom rallies for the students and their supporters. The Negro Methodist Ministerial Alliance backed the students.[66] Black professionals and business leaders organized caravans of Cadillacs to transport JCSU students from campus to the downtown stores.[67] African American domestics laboring in the homes of prominent white families reportedly eavesdropped on conversations and related any relevant information to sit-in leaders. And, when merchants refused to engage in any sort of meaningful negotiations, black Charlotteans initiated an Easter shopping boycott and wore old clothes to Easter Sunday services to signal their support of and participation in the movement.

The student-led movement also enjoyed the backing of many white residents. On one occasion, two white women seated at a booth at Liggett Drug Store offered their seats to African Americans. The counter manager quickly interrupted and asserted that the counter was closed and no one was allowed to enter.[68] Other white shoppers, alongside black protesters, canceled their charge accounts at targeted stores.[69] The Unitarian Church of Charlotte and the United Presbyterian Church joined picket lines. The Mecklenburg Christian Ministers Association, which represented three hundred churches and four hundred members, "unanimously called for an end to racial discrimination in both city and county" in March 1960. One month later, sociology students at Belmont Abbey College surveyed 1,300 people in Charlotte, Greensboro, and Atlanta about their willingness to patronize integrated stores and lunch counters. Fifty-eight percent of those surveyed stated that they would not patronize integrated lunch counters; however, 65 percent would shop in other departments even though counters were integrated.[70]

But these consumer-driven actions alone did not account for the sit-in's success. The mutual recognition of African American workers and consumers that their fates were intricately tied was crucial. Lunch counters were sites where this recognition often surfaced and developed into worker-consumer alliances.[71] In stores with black-only counters, this process began before the commencement of sit-in demonstrations. Black lunch counters had long served as sites of black middle-class engagement and formation. For example, black teachers often held meetings at the black lunch counter in W. T. Grant's basement. Prior to their scheduled meetings, they would contact Davis and ask her to "make it nice . . . really first-class." Davis would then meet with the cook to design a menu with "some hot food and vegetables," despite store rules dictating that the black counter serve cold or concession stand–like food on paper plates and the white counter serve hot meals prepared in the kitchen and plated on fine china. (In fact, the kitchen was located upstairs to ensure that white patrons were always served hot meals.) On the day of the event, Davis "would bring all this food down" to the black counter, without the assistance of an elevator, and serve the meals on fine china.[72]

The special treatment Davis extended to these teachers points to the significance of worker-consumer alliances in the construction of a modern black middle class. Despite their economic proximity to working-class laborers, black teachers, along with ministers, qualified as middle class because they fulfilled the clean work, education, and respectability requirements that defined this class in the nineteenth and twentieth centuries. But consumption was required to be firmly positioned in the middle class. For African Americans, being served at the lunch counter in a manner resembling the service provided to white customers not only improved the convenience and pleasure of engaging the world of consumption but also tempered the restraints that thwarted their full membership in the middle class and American democracy. In other words, through the menu and décor, workers like Davis provided black patrons with an opportunity to taste and perform the defining characteristics of luxury consumption, including abundance, wealth, superiority, and equality. Additionally, being served in this manner was testimony to black and white customers and the store (management and workers included) that respectable blacks were a discerning clientele that belonged and should be valued in all departments.

During the sit-in movement, lunch counters were on-site locations where African American customers and store workers strategized. Initially, students wanted only, in the words of sit-in leader Charles Jones, "to come in and place my order and be served and leave a tip if I feel like it."[73] But after connecting with black store workers, student protesters realized that to secure first-class citizenship in the marketplace, they would need to negotiate the promotion and advancement of both consumers and workers. Frequently, students congregated at W. T. Grant's black lunch counter and inquired "about situations in the store . . . [and] salespeople and their attitudes." Davis and other lunch counter employees provided protesters with inside information on how to organize the sit-in. On several occasions she helped students determine the best time to protest at the lunch counter in order to attract participants and onlookers: "And I would say, 'Come in about 12:00 or 1:00 [P.M.].' Walk in. The counter's full." Davis informed students of anything she heard about the store's intentions and plans to handle protesters, and shifting attitudes among management, workers, and customers. This inside information and the bond forged between workers and protesters led to the desegregation of W. T. Grant's lunch counters.[74]

Not all black workers, however, were so willing to get involved in the movement, revealing that many feared the consequences of getting involved and the moments where linked fate was challenged, threatened, and possibly weakened. Dorothy Howell, a waitress whom Davis supervised, recalled that some "had mixed emotions about [the sit-in]. We knew it was coming, so we just kind of sat back and watched the fireworks."[75] Similarly, during the Greensboro sit-in, "a black woman working at the lunch counter scolded the students for trying to stir up trouble."[76]

Despite the reluctance of a few, worker-consumer alliances led to the desegregation of not only eating facilities—that would now serve as places for respite for black workers and consumers—but also sales work.[77] Selling was a major economic activity in Charlotte, yet blacks held only a negligible portion of sales jobs. At the height of protests, as pressure to fully integrate the consumer sphere mounted and profits plunged, W. T. Grant's management approached Davis about a sales position in the lamp department—a department had been extinct and reopened to test out integration. Initially

Davis was reluctant to be a pioneer. But demonstrators strongly encouraged her to accept the position. One gentleman, a certified public accountant, advised, "You go ahead. . . . Write down what you need to know [about sales work and] give it to me and I'll work out a plan."[78] Once she received her promotion, black customers, many of whom were her former customers at the lunch counter, flooded W. T. Grant to show their support for the desegregation of the selling floor and for Davis. She recalled,

> We black people, we [had] to stick together. I had no white clientele, because they would come in and if they walked in they would not let you help them. They wouldn't let me help them. And word went out that I was out there. They had hired a black sales person in retail and to support them. And all my support came from . . . my people, and they spread the word around that Mrs. Davis was in sales now. No other store had black sales people. And that's why it really meant a lot for us to stick together as black people.[79]

Black customers not only purchased merchandise from her department; they also brought in items from other departments so she could record the sale. Others visited Davis's department simply to provide moral support.

With their patronage, Davis became one of the store's highest-selling sales workers and was eventually promoted to the jewelry department—a big-ticket department typically manned by experienced white saleswomen. Years later Davis left W. T. Grant to work at Lucielle Vogue, a local women's clothing boutique, and her customers followed. Davis was assigned to the sportswear department, but few African American women, like the teachers she once served as a waitress, desired sportswear. According to Davis, "Back then people dressed, they didn't wear sportswear much. Everybody dressed. The teachers looked just like you look when you go to church on Sunday." Davis asked the store manager to be reassigned "upstairs," where the more elegant clothing was sold. He refused, insisting that "those old [white] ladies have been up there for years and they just don't want nobody up there, no competition and so forth." Davis subsequently solicited her loyal customers to "start asking for me and if they tell you that I cannot go upstairs, you walk out." They did exactly as she instructed. The outcome of this worker-consumer cooperation, however, is unclear in extant records. But one can imagine that it eventually persuaded management to reassign Davis to the "upstairs" department for the sake of increased store profits.[80]

As black customers buttressed black workers, salespeople like Davis empowered consumers of all classes by enabling them to perform and embody a middle-class lifestyle, if only in the confines of the store's four walls. Harkening back to skilled, interpersonal selling (an aspect of selling that was gradually losing favor as technology altered the nature of sales), early black sales workers provided customers of color with shopping experiences traditionally extended to wealthy whites: they remembered names and previous purchases and acted as personal stylists and servants. And, when their departments did not have merchandise that met customers' liking, they researched, ordered, and showcased items that they knew would appeal to their black clientele. In newly integrated stores, many black customers celebrated the difference. No longer treated as second-class citizens or forced to locate and purchase an item on their own, many testified that they were now warmly greeted, advised on their purchases, and gently coaxed into buying complementary items by a highly skilled salesperson of color.

Ora P. Lomax provided the same outstanding service to her customers. As a tester in Richmond's department store campaign, Lomax integrated sales and management staffs at several downtown department and boutique stores, including Raylass Department Store, Lerner, La Vogues, and the May Company in the 1960s and 1970s. She also was hired as the first African American salesperson at Clinique in Miller & Rhoads. Here, as was her pattern and that of many "firsts," Lomax exceeded management's expectations. Management believed that Lomax would not be able to sell Clinique, because it was a cosmetic line for white women. But Lomax "learned how to mix" foundations and concealers to perfectly match the broad range of skin tones found among African American women. She recalled, "There was something they had there I would mix the colors to make it brown and then so it wouldn't come up on black skin ashy and I was selling it. They were buying it, those who were dark skin. I could mix their colors and it would look nice on them."[81] Providing this special and differential treatment to black women proved so successful that management asked Lomax to take on the Clinique men's line as well. Crowds of black men—many of whom were likely the husbands and sons of her female clients—came to see Lomax, and she would instruct them on what products to use and how to use them.[82]

African American sales workers also went above and behind their job descriptions to safeguard racial fairness. Some bent or broke store rules they deemed unfair or discriminatory. For example, when one worker in the customer service department of an upscale New York department store learned that "black customers' files were flagged with a special code to indicate race," they "messed it all up," ensuring that the store would "never [be] able to get those files back together again."[83]

Others protected customers from being scammed by retailers and violated by store security. While working at Newman's in Richmond, Lomax "went to bat for . . . [a] young black man," who had been falsely accused of stealing and subsequently beaten by an African American security guard. Lomax overheard the security guard tell a nearby white man: "This is the way you have to treat niggers." She recounted, "When he said that, something just clicked with me. . . . I boycotted the store, I went to Human Relations Commission down at City Hall and I protested against it. I got that man." As a result of her actions, Newman's fired both the security guard and Lomax. Lomax, however, was rehired the next day, likely after management reflected on her "good" sales and reputation in the store's coat shop.[84]

Generally, African Americans praised the integration of sales and other white-collar work. However, a few preferred to be served by white workers because the psychology of racism bred thoughts and feelings that white clerks provided better service or that being served by a white person provided a sense of superiority (a reversal of traditional service interactions). These consumers likely held an individualistic, not a group-centered, view of life chances, revealing the ways in which race and racism have hindered the making and stability of linked fate in the department store movement. For example, in 1933, one Harlem store owner reported, "I got myself some enemies five years ago when I hired my first Negro salesman. Today white customers come in and will allow the boys to render them service. But when Negro customers come in they are nasty toward the boys and refuse to be waited upon until a white salesman is available."[85] Thirty years later, in the 1960s, scholars of the *Racial Policies of American Industry* at the University of Pennsylvania documented similar instances in other retail settings. In one case, some African American physicians "expressed the feeling that they were being given second class treatment because they were called on by black detail men. In another case, a black salesman hired to sell hotel space to groups, found that Negro groups resented being dealt with by a black."[86]

· · · · · ·

In the months that followed W. T. Grant's integration of its lunch counter and sales force, demonstrations continued, with a few incidents of violence and arrests.[87] In May 1960, mayor James Smith's Committee on Friendly Relations, a biracial group tasked with arbitrating the sit-in negotiations, secured a hiatus in the demonstrations. The committee hoped the hiatus would produce a settlement. But by late June, negotiations between the students and store officials had stalled. All but two stores, Ivey's and Belk's department stores, were willing to appear before the mayor's committee and make the concessions necessary to end demonstrations. Students then resumed sit-ins at targeted retailers and initiated a boycott of all downtown businesses. They also began making plans to conduct a major demonstration on July 4. When store executives heard about this plan, they immediately requested a meeting with the mayor's committee, where they finally agreed to integrate their lunch counters. Less than one week after this resolution was reached, on July 9, fifteen black students were served at seven Charlotte lunch counters where the sit-ins had occurred.

The effectiveness of these worker-consumer alliances inspired other antidiscrimination campaigns in Charlotte. Successful campaigns were launched against segregated schools, restaurants, theaters, hotels, and hospitals. In early December 1961, JCSU students reinitiated protests against Ivey's and Belk's department stores. Both stores had integrated their lunch counters in 1960 but refused to open their store restaurants to African Americans. Not long after picketing commenced, Mayor Stanford Brookshire's Committee on Community Relations, a biracial committee charged with solving the city's race problems, intervened. It persuaded Ivey's and Belk's to desegregate their restaurants in exchange for a promise from students that they would take all future complaints to the mayor's committee before returning to public demonstrations.

One year later, and two years after Davis became Charlotte's first black salesclerk, Brookshire and his Committee on Community Relations persuaded local store executives to hire African American sales personnel.[88] Sharing the opinion of black workers and consumers, city officials held that opening public accommodations and employment to African Americans only made good economic sense. It enabled blacks to make a stronger contribution to the economic health of the community. Together, local government support and black protest enabled African Americans to finally start making substantial headway in retail employment in February 1963. In this single month, blacks were hired in positions of responsibility at Seymour's, S. H. Kress and Co., Woolworth's, Grant's, and A&P stores. In March, Mellon's department store and West Side pharmacy each hired three African American sales clerks.[89] Additional black hires continued, with Belk's being among the last to integrate its sales force in the late 1960s.[90] Over the course of this decade alone, black Charlotteans in sales rose nearly

150 percent, while those selling in the retail industry increased approximately 200 percent.[91]

Worker-consumer alliances in the D.C. and Charlotte campaigns contributed to the dismantling of the formidable barriers to black economic emancipation. But these campaigns are only two of many southern movements in the mid-twentieth century that leveraged the powers of both African American workers and consumers. In Savannah and Atlanta, Georgia, for example, student-led movements compelled the desegregation of eating facilities and restrooms and the implementation of fair employment practices. One of the most publicized demonstrations occurred in Atlanta in October 1960, when Martin Luther King Jr., alongside student protesters, sat in at the Magnolia Room in Rich's Department Stores and was subsequently arrested.[92]

The Rebirth of Northern Campaigns

The success of the southern campaigns breathed new life into the national movement for black economic freedom. African Americans—many of whom resided in the North and traveled south—occupied lunch counters and picketed storefronts, seeking to dismantle southern apartheid. Others who did not go south organized sympathy protests and launched regional boycotts of chain stores that had refused service to black southerners. Increasingly, however, these demonstrations compelled many African Americans throughout the nation to self-reflect. Among those who traveled south, Reverend Leon Sullivan admitted, "We realized that the North and East had the same problems that were just as acute."[93] Northern civil rights campaigns of the 1930s and 1940s had succeeded in establishing antidiscrimination legislation and institutions in these regions, something that southern activists were struggling to secure in the 1950s and 1960s. But antidiscrimination bureaucracies did little to close the "enormous gap in affluence, status and power" that existed between African Americans and whites. "The gains of the postwar period gave them a sense of the possibility of change, but the magnitude of change—small—engendered bitterness," one scholar observed.[94] Frustrated and bitter, northern blacks were disheartened by local governments' failure to solve the problem of racial inequality in employment, housing, and school discrimination as promised. They were equally troubled by deindustrialization and the out-migration of major firms such as RCA, General Motors, and Ford, which had once employed blacks en masse and now facilitated the rapid destabilization of urban black communities.

Inspired by the southern freedom struggle but wary of traditional civil rights liberalism, African Americans residing in blighted inner cities organized campaigns that sought to change their economic fortunes. The Negro American Labor Council and the Trade Union Leadership Council aggressively denounced racism in trade unions. They challenged the lack of black union leadership and exclusion of black workers in white-dominated skilled trades. Other campaigns skillfully merged the distinguishing tactics "Don't Buy," persuasion, and sit-in movements while drawing on elements of Black Nationalism (notably the Nation of Islam, which had been growing rapidly since the 1950s) to end racial discrimination in the private labor markets and attend to urban decay, juvenile delinquency, and black deviancy generally. Northern blacks reignited their battles against race discrimination in department stores and other retail establishments, understanding that, while they had made headway in the first half of the twentieth century, the battle remained unfinished. Additionally, they broadened their reach to other private industries, employing the tactics of the department store movement. All of this marked the rise of a more conspicuous and targeted national black economic freedom movement in the 1960s. For example, in the summer of 1960, Reverend James R. Robinson, executive secretary of CORE, announced that the organization had developed a national employment movement patterned after the "students' non-violent, yet direct action approach." CORE's employment movement identified available jobs and met with managers to negotiate the hiring of blacks in positions of responsibility; and, when management failed to comply, sit-ins and picket lines were initiated.[95]

Arguably, however, the most transformative northern campaign was the Philadelphia Selective Patronage Movement. Founded in 1961 under the leadership of Reverend Sullivan and four hundred ministers, the Philadelphia movement embraced a different model of black consumer protest than what was used in southern campaigns. It was "explicitly rooted . . . in the city's black working-class neighborhoods rather than in the Center City offices of the liberal reform organizations"; it employed militant language and confrontational strategies; and it cultivated intraracial solidarities, like the black worker-consumer alliances that characterized southern department store campaigns, and eschewed alliances with white liberals, to break racial barriers to white-collar jobs in the city's private industries.[96] The Philadelphia movement insisted that implementing fair employment required the specification of a percentage or exact number of trained African Americans that would be hired. To meet this end, the campaign first identified companies that discriminated against black workers. Often campaigners, with the assistance of black workers, surveyed local businesses to glean information on their hiring practices. They observed and received details from management on the racial composite of menial and nonmenial workers, the (differential) treatment of workers of color, and black consumer traffic, buying patterns, and dealings.

Violators of fair employment were then visited by an appointed spokesperson and negotiating committee. During these meetings, without using the word "quota," ministers requested that executives integrate a "minimal acceptable standard" of jobs in categories of employment historically reserved for whites by a predetermined date. If executives agreed, no further action was taken with the exception of occasional check-ins to ensure that integration was on task. However, when a company refused to meet with campaign representatives or failed to comply with their request, ministers exhorted their congregations to withhold their "patronage" from offending businesses. They consciously avoided using the word "boycott" and instead adopted the euphemism "selective patronage," hoping to inspire, and not alienate or antagonize, businesses to hire African Americans and keep activists impervious from prosecution. Once businesses surrendered to the demands of the Philadelphia movement, ministers instructed their parishioners to resume patronizing these companies and help them recoup their customer base and profits.[97]

Because the Philadelphia movement leveraged the powers of the Black Church, workers, and consumers, it achieved tremendous success. As scholars of the civil rights movement have skillfully detailed, the church was central in the lives of African Americans. It gave ministers the ability to reach and involve black Philadelphians of all classes on a weekly basis. It "also gave the ministers access to a broad range of women's social and community networks that would prove crucial to spreading the word about boycotts."[98] As a result, the Philadelphia movement secured skilled and white-collar work for about 2,000 African American workers in the private sector and convinced a total of three hundred companies, including Tastykake Baking Company, Pepsi-Cola, Sunoco, and A&P, to embrace fair employment.[99]

None of the targeted companies, however, were department stores. But the Philadelphia campaign inspired those concerned with the African American condition in the retail industry. In 1962, under the leadership of Martin Luther King Jr., the Southern Christian Leadership Conference established Operation Breadbasket. Modeled after Sullivan's selective patronage program, Operation Breadbasket "negotiate[d] . . . [for] more equitable employment practices." One of its earliest protests was directed against Rich's department store in Atlanta. In late November 1963, hundreds of Breadbasket members, the Committee on Appeal for Human Rights, and the Student Nonviolent Coordinating Committee picketed Rich's downtown location during rush hour. They demanded the retailer hire more African American personnel and promote current African American workers to white-collar positions. Just one day after the protest began, it was halted after making "a real breakthrough"—"253 of 1,816 Negroes working in 16 downtown stores had won employment in 'nontraditional' jobs as clerks and salesmen."[100]

After four years in the South, Operation Breadbasket expanded its reach to the urban North. In 1966, King inaugurated Chicago's Operation Breadbasket to end discriminatory hiring practices in businesses that primarily served African Americans and/or were located in black neighborhoods. The organization's first target in Chicago was Country Delight Dairy. Over the next two years, it protested four other dairies, Coca-Cola and Pepsi-Cola, and a number of supermarket chains. In its first fifteen months, Chicago's Operation Breadbasket achieved spectacular success: it "created 2,000 new jobs worth $15 million a year in new income to the African American community."[101] While the Chicago branch concentrated on the food-related companies, Operation Breadbasket in New York created new jobs at commercial bakeries, soft drink bottlers, and dairies but also Mays Department Store, Abraham and Strauss, and Martins Department Store. In 1970, Reverend John L. Scott, executive director of the New York Operation Breadbasket, celebrated that, "in terms of new jobs and increased salaries they have increased the annual income of the black community by $16 million. They have caused companies to deposit $20 million annually in the black banks of New York City and have secured contracts for black service companies and some black business such as advertising and employment agencies."[102]

In Pittsburgh, the United Negro Protest Committee (UNPC) employed selective buying campaigns against three of the city's major department stores. The UNPC was a grassroots coalition of interracial civil rights, religious, and civic organizations, including the NAACP and the Greater Pittsburgh Civic League. It aimed to end job discrimination and place African Americans in positions of responsibility. One of its early successes involved Kaufmann's department store. In early 1966, the UNPC threatened to initiate a selective buying campaign against Kaufmann's. Faced with the prospect of consumer boycotts and massive picketing, the retailer quickly complied with the committee's demands and adopted an affirmative action policy that promised to increase the employment of African Americans as sales workers, delivery drivers, warehouse and garage workers, and beauticians.[103]

The organization's "major breakthrough," however, came a few months later. In 1962, the UNPC began talks with executives at Joseph Horne Co. and Gimbels department stores. These meetings failed to do much more than place one or two token African Americans in positions of responsibility. Four years later, Horne's and Gimbels remained two of the city's most notorious violators of fair employment. Horne's employed 3,550 people, 167 of whom were African American. Only 29 of the store's African American employees held "positions of responsibility." Similarly, Gimbels employed 2,327 workers, 151 of whom were African American. And of these black employees, only 35 held nonmenial positions. Neither store had any black truck drivers, helpers, warehouse employees, or clerics.[104]

In April 1966, over Easter weekend, exasperated by years of hollow promises and unable to secure a written agreement, the UNPC under the leadership of James McCoy, chair of the aforementioned organization and the NAACP's labor and industry committee, initiated a selective patronage campaign. The organization demanded "*at least 500 more Negroes* hired by both stores in the normal time in which the stores expand and lose employees either through retirement or resignation."[105] It ordered not only jobs in sales and clerical work, which had long been the principal goal of the various department store campaigns throughout the nation, but also "jobs in crafts, and in numbers that reflect more than tokenism."[106]

The campaign involved two major forms of demonstration: a community enlightenment program and strategic picketing. The community enlightenment program sought to educate African Americans about the purpose and significance of the campaign. Ministers sermonized about the campaign to their congregations, handbills and placards were distributed at church doors, and speeches were given at church groups, block clubs, and other organizational gatherings in Hill District (the epicenter of African American life and culture in Pittsburgh). Black Pittsburghers were encouraged to cease shopping at these retail establishments, write letters of protest to management, cancel their store charge accounts, and join the picket line.

Picketing dramatized the campaign. Lines swelled with members of black and white Pittsburgh communities, Duquesne University students, and local celebrities such as Pittsburgh Steeler John Henry Johnson and NAACP president Byrd Brown. The campaign also received the support of the

Catholic Interracial Council, the Clearing House on Open Occupancy, and the Lincoln Park Community Center. Demonstrations were executed at strategic times, Monday and Thursday evenings and on Saturdays, to provide black professionals an opportunity to be "identified as supporters for the NAACP and the UNPC struggle for better jobs" and to maximize their effect. Observers recalled scenes of empty stores and storefronts crowded with protesters marching with signs that read "This Company Is Unfair to Negroes," "Stop deliberate tokenism in employment now," "Negroes want upgrading on jobs, too," and "This company practices token employment." These demonstrations convinced "about two-thirds of those who were about to enter either Gimbels or Horne's not to go in."[107]

The Pittsburgh Human Relations Commission attempted to suppress the consumer boycott and help both sides reach an agreement. News reports indicate that both sides were open to signing a written agreement (certainly a step forward as previously neither Gimbels nor Horne's agreed to do this), but they were unable reach a compromise. Store representatives insisted they had always been willing to hire African Americans. But they sought only qualified, college-educated African Americans, and these individuals "are at a premium and retail stores cannot offer them enough money to keep them so they get jobs with large industries."[108] The UNPC viewed this excuse as company "foot dragging" and intensified its efforts. Gimbel's suffered incredible profit loss as a result and sought an injunction against the UNPC and the NAACP. But the store quickly learned that the injunction did little to impede the campaign.

In early May 1966, after three weeks of protest, the UNPC's selective patronage campaign ended with a "memorandum of understanding" signed by UNPC and NAACP officials and Horne's and Gimbel's representatives. The memorandum, a twelve-point agreement, provided for "open hiring and promotion practices as well as no retaliation against any employee for filing charges or testifying in protection of his rights by Title VII of the Civil Rights Act of 1964." It also stipulated that these retailers would "step up efforts to recruit Negroes for all open jobs and contact the Urban League, the UNPC, and the NAACP when openings arise." To ensure that both department stores fulfilled their part of the signed agreement, the UNPC and the NAACP were scheduled to meet with store officials every two months for six months and then every third month thereafter. Also, anytime a problem arose or when the UNPC received complaints from black employees, it intended to meet with management to iron them out.[109]

It is unclear as to whether the UNPC succeeded in opening five hundred positions to African Americans. However, its demand for a specific number of hires suggests that more than token hiring was accomplished. Other selective buying campaigns against department stores proliferated in the urban centers, followed a similar pattern, and achieved results similar to those of the UNPC's Pittsburgh campaign. And although many of these campaigns shuddered at the word "quota," they were in effect insisting that companies fulfill a quota. This approach, coupled with the introduction of the Equal Employment Opportunity Commission in July 1965, facilitated the rise of affirmative action programs in the retail industry and increased businesses' accountability regarding minority hires and placement.

· · · · · ·

By the mid-1960s, activists on the front lines of the civil rights movement had discarded their respectable church clothes in favor of blue jeans. For activists, jeans held several meanings. They symbolized a separation from the pretensions and values of the establishment by obliterating social class distinctions, and they reflected the realities of mobilizing rural black southerners who had become the movement's principal focus. The wearing of denim, one historian has noted, signified African Americans' conscious rejection of "a black middle-class worldview that marginalized certain types of women and particular displays of blackness and black culture. . . . [Their new attire] presented an ideological metamorphosis articulated through the embrace of real and imagined, southern working class and African American cultures."[110]

But, ironically, pulling on a pair of jeans also marked African Americans' immersion, or rather integration, into the logic of consumer capitalism—the system that continued to simultaneously constrain and liberate them. Jeans, like Coca-Cola and automobiles, were mass-produced consumer goods, symbols of modern American consumer culture, and features of common life. Yet, as manufacturers sought to capitalize on their widespread appeal, jeans, once a democratizing item of clothing, became "designer" goods, now re-marked and remarketed to signify social distinctions and new social identities.

This transformation denotes a shift in black class formation and activism. African American class was now marked less by the transactional nature of consumption and more by the consumer good itself; meanwhile, black activists, who recognized that middle-class living in the postwar era was dependent on access to credit, orchestrated campaigns to end credit discrimination against low-income customers.

Worker-consumer alliances, and intraracial solidarities generally, facilitated the emergence of a modern black middle class that could now purchase such class-marking consumer goods as designer jeans. These alliances were central not only to the southern retail movements but also to the democratization of the consumer sphere. Focusing on strengthening black economic power, worker-consumer alliances empowered black workers and consumers to freely act and perform in the consumer republic and subsequently nurtured a modern black middle class. These alliances engendered feelings of superiority, confidence, human dignity, prestige, and status. They provided blacks with a sense of belonging in American consumer culture and democracy, although these feelings were often fleeting and unstable because of the continuous metamorphosis and persistence of race discrimination.

In these worker-consumer campaigns, however, individual ambition is difficult to separate from the collective or communal interest. Arguably this was the brilliance of these alliances rooted in linked fate. Individuals such as Davis and Lomax wanted rewarding, quality jobs, the freedom to eat and rest in the privileged space of downtown, and the status and prestige that accompanied being served. In a way, these desires were self-serving. They were about survival, convenience, and belonging. Simultaneously, such desires suited and were similar to those of the collective whole. As a whole, the black community wanted jobs and access to the consumer republic that would challenge white supremacy and notions of black inferiority and improve the condition of its members. Furthermore, the black community believed that realizing social and political equality required their economic empowerment.

But, as the next chapter explores, their efforts were thwarted as suburbanization, rioting, and urban decay pushed retailers to abandon downtown centers. Even worse, these movements—in both the North and the South—contributed to the devastation of a separate black economy, which had long provided freedom and dignity to its workers and consumers, and reinforced white commercial enterprises and "the legitimacy of the capitalist order as a way of organizing economic life."[111] Yet, despite these setbacks, which are undeniably significant and still require attention and mobilization, retail campaigns succeeded in dismantling major racial barriers in employment, consumption, and urban landscapes, thereby conferring middle-class citizenship to countless black workers and consumers in the twentieth century.

Toward Wal-Mart

The Death of the Department Store Movement
. . . .

In the hours and days after the assassination of Martin Luther King Jr., cries of sorrow and fury mingling with the sound of shattering windows filled the air, while thick plumes of black smoke from raging fires engulfed Washington, D.C. "Small groups of youths," grieving the sudden and tragic loss of the civil rights leader, raced through store aisles, turning over displays, "harass[ing] clerks" and customers, and "snatch[ing] merchandise" at the city's "two biggest department stores"—Hecht Company at 7th and F Streets, N.W., and Woodward & Lothrop at 10th and F Streets, N.W.[1] Just a few miles away, insurgents pillaged and destroyed the building and contents of Sears, Roebuck, and Company at 911 Bladensburg Road, N.E. (figure 12).[2] Chaos reigned. Retailers frantically closed store doors and boarded up windows, desperate to protect themselves and their businesses from looting, bomb threats, and arson. "Frightened and angry police and national guardsmen . . . shot protesters and looters; sniper fire, stray bullets, and accidents took many lives as well."[3] The unrest lasted four days and precipitated the arrests of 4,352 people by the National Guard, the provision of medical treatment for 961 injuries, and the deaths of 6 people. Residents directed much of their frustration, anger, and sorrow toward retail establishments that had a history of discriminating against African American workers and consumers. They damaged an estimated 909 businesses and 238 housing units, of which the majority were units "that contained mixed commercial uses and living quarters."[4]

A few commercial enterprises, however, sustained little or no damage. Insurgents left untouched commercial establishments with which they were unfamiliar, those that had instituted fair employment and customer service policies, and businesses that advertised their grief over the loss of King.[5] Upon learning this, Woodward & Lothrop "set a large color portrait of Martin Luther King, surrounded it with ferns and beside it a sign that said: 'We are saddened that he lost his life in the crusade to win equality for all through peace.'" Thereafter the store was left virtually unharmed.[6] But the damage was already done: the civil disturbance sliced sharply into retail

FIGURE 12 Firemen fighting fire at Sears store on the corner of K and Oates Streets, N.E., after the riots of 1968. General Photograph Collection, Historical Society of Washington, D.C., CHS 11276.

sales and patronage during the historically lucrative Easter shopping season. Sears suffered $2 million dollars in damages and later sought to recoup those losses by suing the District of Columbia, contending that city officials neglected to protect the store.[7] Woodward & Lothrop lost an estimated $1 million dollars in sales compared with its previous Easter sales, while Hecht's downtown-store sales "were off between 35 and 40 [percent] during the racial upheaval."[8] Three months later, sales had yet to fully recover. In July 1968, D.C. store sales totaled only $366 million—$21.6 million, or 5 percent, less than the previous year.[9]

Nationwide, King's murder ignited civil disturbances in over 160 American cities and resulted in widespread destruction, the death of 22 people, and the injury of more than 1,100 others.[10] Incidents of urban conflict and turmoil, however, were not isolated to April 1968. Throughout the 1960s and into the early 1970s, "widespread looting and arson . . . plague[d] urban commerce . . . reaching beyond the well-known examples of Watts, Detroit, and Newark to touch smaller [American] cities."[11] Scholars and politicians have generally accepted that urban disturbances were, at their core, revolts against exploitative retail practices, as well as protests against "police brutality and inadequate employment, housing, and education." Others, however, have theorized that rioters sought to drive out white businesses, nurture black capitalism, and take control of downtown—the space where they resided and worked.[12]

Scholars, contemporaries, and politicians may not agree on the motives and anticipated outcomes of midcentury urban revolts, yet most agree that "the riots finished downtown shopping."[13] But the end of downtown shopping was neither immediate nor unprecedented in 1968. Center cities were already in rapid decline since the close of the Second World War for a host of reasons: as a result of the sit-in demonstrations and boycotts of the 1950s and 1960s, which induced blacks and whites to avoid downtown shopping areas; the bourgeois exodus to suburban communities; deindustrialization; the internationalization of manual and low-skill work; the degradation of service jobs; repeated race riots; poor and underserved schools; the federal government's refusal to provide mortgage capital for inner-city neighborhoods; and the erection of massive public housing projects in American cities.[14]

Retailers were, in turn, profoundly affected by the deterioration of downtown centers. They suffered staff and customer shortages because middle-class white suburbanites refused to travel to cities, fearing that they were dangerous havens of so-called undesirables—the poor and black. Consequently, middle-class whites chose to work at and patronize suburban stores. The loss of white employees and clientele opened new doors for African Americans, by forcing retailers to change their employment of and the way they served the black community. For example, in 1969, Woodward & Lothrop in Washington, D.C., announced that it had adopted fair employment and promised to promote on the basis of "merit, not race, religion, national origin, or sex." It also "incorporated black mannequins into its window displays and featured black employees and their accomplishments in the company's in-house *Woodlothian* magazine." Not long thereafter, store officials instituted equal pay for equal work and permitted African American employees to use any restroom and enter the store using the front door.[15]

But these gains were not enough to restore Washington's troubled and battered downtown, nor did they mean that the department store movement had weathered the storm. By the 1970s, Sears, Hecht's, Woodward & Lothrop, and other D.C. department stores had closed their upper levels and/or reduced their hours and staff in their downtown locations, enabling them to continue business in downtown D.C. until the 1980s and 1990s. However, not all retailers fared so well: Landburgh's, for example, was forced to permanently close its doors in 1973. Surviving stores concentrated on their more lucrative branches in suburban shopping centers that were virtually inaccessible via public transportation to city dwellers—many of whom were "members of depressed socioeconomic groups"—and were thereby protected from protests that threatened to disrupt business.[16] The Supreme Court decisions in *Lloyd v. Tanner* (1972), *Scott Hudgens v. National Labor Relations Board* (1976), and *PruneYard Shopping Center v. Robbins* (1980) established that malls were private property and therefore had a legal right to prohibit protest.

With the deterioration of urban centers and the relocation of major retailers to "the outer edges of the whitest part of suburbia," both of which threatened to undo civil rights gains, the department store movement was faced with new challenges.[17] The situation became direr as discount retailers proliferated in the mid-1960s. New competition from discount stores prompted American department stores to restructure their labor and consumption practices in their efforts to remain relevant and profitable. Operating under a low-overhead, high-volume, and low-price policy, discount retailers attracted customers from all segments of the income distribution. They also were less dependent on sales workers, relying instead on intense advertising to sell products and menial laborers to process orders. In response, department stores adopted a business strategy that closely modeled that of their new competitors: they sold more volume and cut prices, consolidated departments, broadened their marketing beyond their traditional customer base, and centralized managerial power. Department stores also expedited a process that they initiated during the Second World War: they reduced labor costs by degrading and de-skilling sales work and, as a result, increased their reliance on low-wage, unskilled, part-time workers who, ironically, were none other than blacks, women, students, and the chronically under- and unemployed—all groups retailers viewed as cheap and controllable.

Not only did department stores' new business strategy degrade sales work, but it also degraded the consumption experience. For much of the twentieth century, consumption had been just as much about the practice of being served as it was about acquiring goods. However, as service was devalued or even disappeared, the significance of goods intensified and the price declined. Everyone could now purchase brand-name goods at lower prices in discount and midlevel department stores on a regular basis. But customers increasingly took on the duties previously undertaken by the sales worker: they had to educate themselves on products through advertising and word of mouth, instead of being educated or coerced by skilled salespeople; and they had to identify and locate desired merchandise, often without assistance. They basically did everything, except process the order (which, in recent years, of course, is a task that grocery store customers have taken on). High-end department and specialty stores such as Nordstrom, Saks Fifth Avenue, and Neiman Marcus, however, continued to adhere to the traditional standards of selling and buying, but their targeted clientele is no longer the middle class; instead they cater almost exclusively to the upper classes.

Transformations in work and consumption, thus, forced the department store movement to modify its tactics, approaches, and reach. Civil rights action directed against Sears, Roebuck, and Company in the 1960s and 1970s illustrates the movement's new direction. Leaders continued to use traditional forms of protest against downtown stores but more forcefully pushed for the elimination of racial discrimination in hiring and promotion in suburban branches, as well as the extension of credit to working-class blacks—both of which they hoped would continue to advance black economic freedom in the final decades of the twentieth century. Individuals filed lawsuits under Title II and VII of the Civil Rights Act of 1964, which respectively outlawed discrimination in public accommodations and workplaces based on race, color, religion, sex, and national origin. The movement also welcomed the support of the U.S. Equal Employment Opportunities Commission (EEOC), another progeny of the 1964 act, and President Lyndon B. Johnson's War on Poverty, with the hope that grassroots activism coupled with government oversight and legal action would finally end discrimination and exploitation in the marketplace.

New Challenges, New Workers, and New Modes of Consumption

The three decades following the Second World War were a transformative period for American department stores, as they found themselves confronted with two major questions: Should they remain committed to downtown centers, spaces that many of them had called home and in which they had reigned for nearly a half century? Or should they abandon their home to seek respite from civil unrest, follow their preferred markets, and compete with discounters that were beginning to threaten their power and profitability? Some tried to pursue both paths; some chose the latter approach;

and others went out of business—sometimes by choice but often as a result of the difficulties associated with modernizing their operations and diminishing sales.

All of these courses had tremendous implications for African American workers and consumers. First, stores that opened suburban branches, hoping to remain competitive in an industry that was moving farther and farther into suburban and rural areas, adopted practices that caused the resegregation and de-skilling of sales work in their establishments. Second, retailers, like Sears, Roebuck, and Company, tried to keep their center city locations open and thriving while expanding into the suburbs. Yet, despite their best efforts, they were unable to resuscitate decaying urban environments and eventually deserted cities and, by extension, black and brown populations in favor of middle- and upper-class white suburbs. This, coupled with the closing of local department stores, left thousands of black urbanites un- or underemployed and forced to patronize exploitative neighborhood businesses that devalued them as workers and customers and carried a much smaller inventory of goods (often of subpar quality and sold at exorbitant prices).

The Discount Revolution

Suburbanization changed the location of American retail,[18] while discount stores drastically altered the art of selling and buying. Discount stores existed as early as the 1950s, but most were short-lived (with the exception of E. J. Korvette), carried little merchandise, "possessed little customer appeal," and, as a result, were of little consequence to traditional emporiums. In 1962, however, Kmart, Target, Woolco, and Wal-Mart opened their doors in March, May, June, and July, respectively. Within three years, these discount stores had "[surpassed] in sales volume all of the conventional mode department stores combined."[19] Their success lay in their compliance with the principles of high volume, fast turnover and low overhead, and low prices. They expanded their merchandise lines to model those of department stores, sold below the manufacturers' suggested retail price, operated a strict self-service model, employed fewer workers, offered fewer services, welcomed new technology that quickened the checkout process, and built on large stretches of cheap land on the outskirts of major cities and nearer to distribution centers.[20]

Less than thirty years later, discounters had displaced department stores as the nation's top retailers. Their ascent was facilitated by the repeal of fair trade legislation that had once given suppliers the authority to specify minimum retail prices and prohibit these types of stores from peddling brand-name goods. While Wal-Mart would become "the *tour de force* of twenty-first century retailing," Kmart had held that title for the better part of the late twentieth century. (This fact was not lost on Sam Walton, founder of Wal-Mart, who was known for frequently visiting Kmart, studying its approach, and perfecting and applying it to his own stores.)[21] S. S. Kresge and Company launched Kmart—currently, a subsidiary of the Sears Holding Company—as "a complete department store" and "as one-stop shopping units" for the entire family.[22] Housed in "functional modern buildings" that "exclude unnecessary frills,"[23] Kmart stores sold a wide array of brand-name merchandise at lower prices than department stores, "filling in its inventory with private label goods only when brand-name products were not available."[24] Many branches included supermarkets, pharmacies, automobile service and tire centers, patio and garden shops, furniture marts, fashion apparel (including clothing lines created by celebrities and sold exclusively at Kmart), fine jewelry and silverware, complete footwear assortments, and sporting goods departments and even housed an in-store restaurant (Kmart Chef and later K-Café, both of which were low-cost versions of the elegant dining areas of traditional and fashionable department stores) to provide customers respite and to encourage them to shop longer and more often.[25]

Kmart's banality signaled the increasing importance of acquiring goods and the declining significance of service and the aesthetics of displaying and selling merchandise—two major aspects that had characterized the shopping experience for decades. But for their customers in the 1960s and 1970s, most of "very modest income and very modest expectations," stores like Kmart offered quality merchandise at lower prices.[26] While African American customers appear to have been virtually ignored by officials during this period, it is likely that Kmart was a site of consumption where they did not feel like imposters and maybe even felt like valued participants in the marketplace. As the historian Ted Ownby notes, "Recent chain stores . . . never asked customers to go to the back door; nor have the employees who greet each customer used condescending terms in addressing particular customers."[27] In their way, they provided a uniform shopping experience in that discount retailers were "friendly in not being unfriendly and democratic in offering everyone the same not particularly personal experience."[28]

Another critical component of Kmart's success was its drastically low labor costs. From 1960 to 1977, discount stores' labor costs made up only

11–13 percent of total sales, whereas department stores paid out as much as 30 percent of their sales income to their more highly skilled, unionized labor force.[29] Discount store employees were overwhelmingly part-time, less skilled, nonunion workers, such as high school or college students, retirees, individuals working a second job, and those willing or desperate enough to work part time and for low wages and benefits. These workers had virtually no expertise in customers' needs and desires and no knowledge of salesmanship or of the products they sold; they were far from skilled in the art of selling or expected to actually sell merchandise. Instead, store officials relied exclusively on advertising and low prices to do this work. Their employees, as such, were essentially cashiers and stock clerks who needed only the skill of speed. Speed was required to refill and organize stock and quickly and efficiently ring up and check out customers. (These tasks were further expedited by retailers' reception of new technology such as point of sale systems, optical character recognition devices such as scanning wands, and electronic recording devices.)

The historian Thomas Jessen Adams explains that discount retailers, most notably Wal-Mart, "engaged in the relentless drive toward lower labor costs and greater management control over production characteristic of capitalism since its inception," producing intensely antilabor store environments. Wal-Mart elected to have each store owned and operated by different companies, rather than a single corporation, to evade the Fair Labor Standards Act of 1938 and to pay employees less than minimum wage as well as impede union organization. Similarly, Kmart leased different departments to smaller companies, which sold preapproved Kmart items. The terms of these leases stipulated that although the smaller companies were separate employers, Kmart retained control over hiring and product. Workers in these leased departments, for example, "wore name tags identifying them as Kmart employees and had to learn and follow all Kmart work policies." This arrangement divided employees and hindered the establishment of a single union, thus weakening bargaining power; instead, several different unions covered different workers in the store. Additionally, these fragmented workplaces "disabled cross-shop consciousness and solidarity."[30]

Discounters pursued intimidation and paternalism to promote shop floor totalitarianism and discriminated against African Americans, women, and the disabled when they believed it would increase profits. Retailers fired workers engaged in union activity under the guise of small, petty infractions, and they rewarded other employees for antiunionism with raises, promotions, and paid vacations. Kmart went so far as to create a security department in the 1960s and 1970s that was tasked only with identifying and suppressing union activity in all Kmart stores. Other retailers administered lie detector tests and employed spies to instill "fear and subservience to management."[31]

Department stores saw their profit margins and dominance slipping in the 1970s and 1980s as a result; and so they began adopting the same principles and methods of retailing as the discount giants to remain competitive in the marketplace. Sears, Macy's, J.C. Penney, and others centralized managerial policy, reduced the autonomy of local managers, cut prices, consolidated departments, advertised heavily in catalogs and newspapers and on radio and television, invested in technology, and expanded their marketing to other groups besides middle-class whites. Sears, for example, lowered its prices by 15–50 percent in its women's apparel departments "to attract more cost [conscious] female consumers." It also began selling national brand-name products in addition to its own private label merchandise.[32]

Not to concede ground, or rather profits, to discounters, Marshall Field and Gimbels renewed their commitment to budget basements, while Nordstrom opened its Nordstrom Racks and matched its competitors' prices on any item to appeal to price-conscious shoppers. Macy's eliminated its bargain basement and created budget sections throughout the store. It replaced the bargain basement with the Cellar, an "attractive complex of departments selling housewares, gourmet food and candy with a barroom type of restaurant and contemporary fashion shops." The retailer also added apparel lines to cater to a larger market: it opened junior clothing departments, expanded the Club House (a higher-priced women's sportswear department for working women), and began selling the Liz Claiborne clothing line to attract upper-class women between the ages of 25 and 40. It also modernized its credit operations to monitor charge customers' shopping behavior and to facilitate the dissemination of promotional materials.[33]

This, however, was not all. Many department stores restructured their workforces to reduce labor costs and increase volume. At Sears, managerial salaries ceased being based on their efficiency in "keeping the margins between operating costs and sales as large as possible." Managers were now paid in accordance with overall sales volume. Selling also changed substantially. Fewer and fewer full-time hours were offered, while department store sales work, in general, no longer held the promise of providing individuals with a career. Increasingly, sales work became the temporary and part-time occupation of the less educated, housewives in need of extra money or something to do while their children were in school, and the youth. Employees received less training in sales and merchandise; they were typically provided a half-day or one-day training session on assisting customers in locating goods (not identifying goods that suited their customers' particular taste and style), persuading shoppers to open a store credit account, and using the computerized cash register for purchases, returns, and exchanges.[34]

In being divested of their traditional responsibilities, status, and prestige, department store employees saw their wages and hours reduced, their commissions eliminated, and opportunities for promotion decreased. In the 1980s, one African American saleswoman with extensive selling experience recalled, "When Sears hired me, I was hired with a salary plus commission. About two years ago, they decided no more commission. Now it is strictly hourly." And yet her duties increased. She explained, "When I was first hired here, my job was to sell mattresses, drapes, and luggage. Now, carpets have been added on to it, and small appliances have been added on to it. We used to [have] a crew that just put out the stock and refinish the shelves and all that stuff. Now, we still have them, but the sales associates are now expected to put out stock too."[35]

Not all retailers made such dramatic changes to their business approach. Higher-end department stores such as Nordstrom, Saks Fifth Avenue, and Neiman Marcus were located in upper-class neighborhoods in cities and suburbs to appeal to nearby whites and deter African American workers and customers. They relied on white workers versed in the art of selling and were content with being top retailers among their targeted clientele.[36] At Nordstrom, for example, sales workers were knowledgeable about the merchandise and experienced in advising and building relationships with customers. One men's apparel salesman "could take a swatch from a bolt of fabric that was going to be tailored for a suit and coordinate a complete wardrobe of shirts and ties, all the way down to the cufflinks." His customers saw him "as an ally. They heeded his advice on where to get a good haircut or what style of glasses to wear. . . . Their wives saw [him] as the mediator who could interpret their views to their husbands."[37] Experienced sales workers, most of whom worked on commission, identified and satisfied shoppers' needs. They coordinated complete wardrobes using designer brand and upscale, private (store) label apparel, shoes, and accessories. Customers, in turn, could display and perform not only who they were but also who they wanted to be both in and outside the store.

Fierce competition from discount retailers, however, was not the only impetus for the transformation and resegregation of retail work and consumption in the latter half of the twentieth century. This period also saw the deterioration of urban centers—a process motivated by federal policies that supported suburban home ownership and commercial development, and worsened by the race riots in the 1960s. It was disastrous for downtown economies, retailers, and urban black communities. Hoping to restore American cities, the federal government, with the backing of the department store industry, implemented urban renewal programs. According to the historian Vicki Howard, across the country "downtown retailers saw urban renewal as a means of 'salvation'—specifically a strategy for fighting competition from the new discount stores that sprang after World War II. Urban renewal was also a means of reclaiming their traditional role downtown."[38]

Department store executives at Edward Malley Co. in New Haven,[39] Macy's in New York City, Rich's in Atlanta, Filene's and Gilchrist in Boston, and Gimbels and Wanamaker's in Philadelphia, among others, took leading roles in local urban renewal projects. Sears, Roebuck, and Company also led renewal programs in city neighborhoods where it maintained stores. The retailer "was plagued with shoplifting and found it difficult to convince its best sales people to work in decaying neighborhoods. Even steady customers were reluctant to go to some stores." Executives hoped that "an urban renewal effort might change this situation, protecting the company's sizeable investment in retail facilities, and it would also mean increased sales of Sears products to be used in the clean-up campaign."[40] But, as the retailer ultimately learned, it was ill equipped to contend with the deep-seated social problems that plagued American cities.

Arguably, Sears's most notable revitalization project concentrated on Chicago's North Lawndale community, the home of the company's headquarters from 1906 to 1973. In the 1950s and 1960s, despite being bombarded with civil rights unrest, Sears had emerged as one of America's top retailers, eventually beating out its major competitor Montgomery Ward. But the company's fortune did not reflect the course of the neighborhood where it was headquartered. As Sears progressed, North Lawndale regressed. The North Lawndale neighborhood is located on Chicago's West Side and was in dire shape by the 1960s. In the 1940s and 1950s, the neighborhood underwent a "rapid and complete ethno-racial transition" as a result of the Second Great Migration. Available entry-level, unskilled jobs, affordable housing, and public transportation made Lawndale an enticing alternative to the overcrowded, overpriced, crime-ridden South Side. Coinciding with and arguably as a result of this influx, more than 75,000 white residents abandoned the neighborhood. Lawndale's Jewish residents opted for suburban living in Skokie and Highland Park after the Supreme Court outlawed restrictive covenants in 1948 and mass-produced suburbs put home ownership within reach for millions of middle-class citizens.[41] The result was that, by 1960, North Lawndale "turn[ed] from almost 90 percent Caucasian to more than 90 percent African American"—a significant percentage of whom were unemployed and undereducated.[42]

Lawndale had become a neighborhood of so-called undesirables and undesirable elements. It was, in a word, a ghetto. Residents, civil rights activists, city officials, and local business leaders reasoned that the source of the problem laid with young African Americans who had received poor schooling and were ill prepared for, and thus without a productive place in, the job market and society. Delinquency, crime, and street gangs proliferated and alienated "respectable" black and white residents as a result.

As this community declined, Sears's executives considered relocating its headquarters to downtown Chicago to escape the poverty and unrest of the West Side. But to the surprise of many, after much deliberation, the retailer decided not to abandon North Lawndale. Many executives felt morally obligated to respect former president and CEO Julius Rosenwald's philanthropic legacy and commitment to Chicago's black community. Others had been raised in and had fond memories of the neighborhood; they were overwhelmed with nostalgia at the thought of moving. At the same time, the logistics and cost of relocation were weighed, as well as the possibility that moving would garner bad publicity. There is even a slight possibility that executives also sympathized with African Americans who, through civil disturbances and protests, voiced their frustration, anger, and sadness about being repeatedly and forcefully denied first-class citizenship. Eventually, the retailer concluded that staying to rebuild North Lawndale could be a boon to its profits and reputation among the people it served.

The company's urban renewal program was grounded in the belief that "saving" this ghetto hinged on "saving" its black residents. This process, they conceived, would involve transforming the West Side's undesirables of color into respectable workers and consumers. In 1954, Sears (and other private sources) made monetary donations to the burgeoning Greater

Lawndale Conservation Commission (GLCC), an interracial, not-for-profit community organization tasked with "mak[ing] Greater Lawndale an outstanding neighborhood for modern living and work."[43] Sears remained the organization's largest backer for the next two decades. Together, Sears and the GLCC counseled Lawndale families on "property, propriety, and personal matters; becoming better citizens by knowing the obligations and responsibilities as well as the rewards of citizenship; living in a complex urban area; becoming productive members of the economy; [and] becoming informed of the citizens' role in law and order."[44]

The Sears-GLCC relationship resembled businesses' and middle-class blacks' responses to the Great Migration in early twentieth-century Detroit and Chicago. Ford Motor Company, for example, cultivated close alliances (that often involved material rewards) with the leaders of Detroit's black community, most notably black clergymen, heads of black fraternal organizations, and the city's two principal race advancement organizations—the Detroit Urban League and the local branch of the National Association for the Advancement of Colored People (NAACP). These relationships enabled the company to recruit and shape a black workforce that embraced a pro-management stance and resisted unionism in the first few decades of the twentieth century.[45] Similarly, in Chicago, "most employers of large numbers of migrants recognized that they could most effectively shape the work habits of migrants by seeking the advice and aid of black Chicagoans who shared their objective of creating an efficient black work force."[46] According to the historian James Grossman, employers sought the assistance of Black Chicago's Old Settlers (African Americans living in Chicago before the Great Migration and often of the middle and upper classes), the Chicago Urban League, and the Wabash Avenue YMCA. Separately, as well as together, these groups worked to transform southern blacks into productive, proficient, and respectable employees and residents of the city.

Nearly forty years later, Sears and the GLCC, too, encouraged and supervised black Chicagoans' deference to middle-class norms of behavior. Supported by the retailer, the GLCC held tea parties, fashion shows, and fund-raisers to create bonds and solidarity among residents and raise funds needed to build a community center, health clinics, and other infrastructures. It also sponsored block clubs to monitor community norms and advocate for city services. These clubs created codes of conduct that mandated that residents keep their property clean, behave respectably and courteously, be as quiet as possible at all times of the day, and be "good neighbors" and refrain from criminal activities.

Consumption, or more specifically "respectable" consumption, was a key aspect of Lawndale's urban renewal program. One proponent likened the process to being a gentleman. He espoused, "There is a saying in French, which translated goes something like this: 'A gentleman is 50% dress, 50% address.' And Lawndale unfortunately today is 50% poor dress and 50% poor address. To keep people who want dress and address, Lawndale has to be given prestige."[47] Not surprisingly, Sears and the GLCC believed that prestige could be taught and conferred through consumption and relied on African American women to meet this end. They understood that women typically handled their family's shopping and, in the specific case of the black family, were often the primary breadwinner and head of household as well. Executives and community leaders also appreciated the role of women in raising children—ideally, middle-class citizens—tending to the beautification and maintenance of the home, and shaping the direction and dimensions of the black freedom struggle.

The GLCC, thus, attended to this reality. Black women sat on the organization's board of directors and various subcommittees, and launched the Ladies' Auxiliary in 1957 (an action-oriented arm that provided moral and financial support to the organization).[48] According to one scholar, "The Ladies' Auxiliary capitalized on women's traditions of socializing and sharing responsibility to accomplish their priorities." As it matured, the committee proved to be "peripheral to the [GLCC] only in name."[49] It planned and executed GLCC initiatives, revealing the woman-focused nature of Lawndale's urban renewal project. For example, the commission regularly disseminated tips on buying and decorating a home. In February 1958, the Ladies' Auxiliary held an event called "Color Comes Calling." This event was "an instructive and entertaining 30 minute talk and demonstration" that enlightened its audience on "(1) simple, basic, color rules; (2) how to blend colors with drapery, upholstery and wall combinations; and (3) how to use colors you like and enjoy to reflect yourself."[50] The auxiliary also sponsored several programs and competitions, including Cleaner Lawndale Operation Pride and the Community Good Neighborhood Award, which encouraged residents to improve and maintain their property. While informing and creating a need and desire for a middle-class life, and all of its accoutrements, Sears concurrently advertised its household wares in the *Lawndale Journal*, inviting residents to decorate their homes with rugs, paint, windows, bath ensembles, and appliances sold at its Tower Store. Thus, from the GLCC events to Sears's advertisements, Sears sold goods in a way that echoed early department store sales techniques—the employment of skilled saleswomen, advertisements, and displays to educate its customers on "good taste" and convince them that they could buy a "virtuous" home and life.[51]

Sears and the commission also sponsored fashion shows, galas, cotillions, and other social activities at the Sears Community Center and the Sears YMCA. The fashion shows, in particular, featured clothing and accessories modeled by black women and youth from the neighborhood and were available for purchase at Sears. During the Christmas shopping season, the GLCC gave tours to "underprivileged children of the Greater Lawndale area . . . to acquaint them with Sears, Roebuck, & Co. and give these children a chance to see Santa Claus and individually talk to Santa Claus."[52]

All of these events were designed "to illustrate that women and girls can be attractively as well as modestly and decently attired," and to court and educate current and future shoppers of color.[53] These objectives were reinforced with store advertisements. In the 1960s, Sears increased and refined its advertisements to black Chicagoans, publicizing wares that would mark a shopper as modern, respectable, smart, stylish, and of course prestigious. For example, a 1963 ad for "High Style Hats" illustrated "the latest fashion design hats in the newest fall colors" and instructed the reader to "charge it on Sears revolving charge account."[54] In January 1966, Sears advertised a coat sale. It claimed, "Spectacular Clearance of Cloth Coats and Luxuriously Fur-Trimmed Coats at Big Saving with a Full Winter Ahead!" Coat types and prices were categorized into two groups: "Casual and Dressy Cloth Coats" that were "smartly styled" "in . . . quality fabrics" and "all warmly lined. Many with zip-out lining" and "Lavishly Fur-Trimmed Coats" with "such luxurious furs as natural mink, blue dyed Norwegian fur, dyed Persian lamb . . . on the finest fabrics."[55] Again, the buyer is instructed to charge her purchase.

Instruction in middle-class consumption was not solely about taste making; it also was about creating middle-class citizens. In 1962, under the advisement of Mark Satter, a Chicago attorney and former GLCC board member, the commission initiated and developed a consumer education program. According to Satter, "We do not plan an abstract academic discussion, but rather a down to earth dollars and cents program with emphasis on precisely how much can be spent for the major articles we buy . . . and how to determine the amount we can pay for rent, ways to learn the value of homes we buy and general day to day consumer education in all fields affecting minority communities of the city of Chicago." The program also attended to the pitfalls of making large purchases and the dangers of bankruptcy.[56]

But it was not enough to imbue African Americans with middle-class tastes and behaviors. Blacks needed the means with which to buy and live a Sears-designed middle-class life. So, in the 1960s, Sears and the GLCC implemented employment programs that targeted African American women and youths (figure 13). This decision is particularly striking given that Lyndon B. Johnson's War on Poverty had been influenced originally by decades-long scholarship that blamed women for the rise of familial and urban ills and thus sought to help men "assume their proper place as income providers and head of households" and regain their "masculine dignity."[57] At the same time, however, their decision was sound. Sears's employment programs were linked to both the anti–juvenile delinquency efforts of the late 1950s and early 1960s and the War on Poverty's principal goal (one that arguably emerged after much criticism on the policy's historical assumptions and foundations) of eliminating economic and social deprivations by raising poor people to the middle class.[58] Further, Sears already had a history of working with and assisting African American women and understood women's value in building, shaping, and controlling black families and neighborhoods. (This appreciation, also held by the War on Poverty's Community Action Program, tapped into the nation's deep tradition of local governance and community participation.) Additionally, the retailer was in dire need of trained office workers, and, given that it viewed clerical work as women's work, it is no wonder that it focused on developing jobs programs for black women and girls in Lawndale. Finally, men were typically relegated to manual work—a field that provided on-the-job training and did not require instruction in respectability.

In 1961, Sears cosponsored the Jobs for Youth program—a "hardcore" employment initiative for high school dropouts or potential dropouts, people often regarded as juvenile delinquents and members of "street corner society"—with the Weiboldt Foundation, Chicago Boys Clubs, Chicago Youth Centers, the YMCA, and the federal government. The program brought together the skills and efforts of the school system, industry, youth-serving agencies, city and state governments, and responsible adults and youths to encourage troubled young people to reenroll in school and to provide instruction on navigating the worlds of school and work. Over the course of seven weeks, program participants were tested on their level of abilities and provided academic tutoring by the Northwestern Student Tutoring

FIGURE 13 Ted Bell, photographer, *Vern Bailey, Catalog Personnel at Sears-Main (West)*, CULR_0002_0078_0861_007, ca. 1969, Chicago Urban League Records, series 2, box 78, folder 861, University of Illinois at Chicago Library, Special Collections.

Project and mentorship from a "group of matured citizens." They also received counseling to help them understand and resolve their problems, and afforded internships at businesses and industries in the community. Graduates of the program were invited to join the Jobs for Youth Alumni Club, which aimed to maintain and broaden the activities of graduates. Some of the club's activities included social meetings, "helping others" projects, cultural programs, and supporting and assisting each other.[59]

Six years later, the retailer instituted the Sears Clerical Training Job Opportunities in the Business Sector (JOBS) project, an employment program for African American women that was likely associated with or influenced by the antipoverty programs Job Corps and Neighborhood Youth Corps. The YWCA of Metropolitan Chicago, the Youth Opportunity Center of the Illinois State Employment Service, and the Illinois Department of Vocational Education and Rehabilitation also supported the project. The Clerical Training JOBS project aimed to prepare black women for "good jobs." It required job applicants to complete twenty weeks of job training that "included 35 hours a week of classes in typing, shorthand, receptionist and switchboard skills, calculator and business machines, business math and English." Classes also instructed women on "personality development— the fine points of grooming, charm, and personal hygiene." One year into the project, the training program had grown significantly: "Six full time workers" now trained women between the ages of seventeen and twenty-one "in job skills, personality development, and how to apply successfully for a job. . . . While undergoing training, the young women receive[d] a small salary." By the end of the program, "enrollees" had secured "work in offices where the clerical unity had working-training agreements."[60]

On June 23, 1967, the first class of thirty-three students graduated. At graduation, "most of the trainees . . . had been tested and interviewed for employment" by the "companies that helped [the JOBS project] by donating training equipment."[61] In 1968, after the third class completed the program, Sears publicized that 105 women had graduated from the program and that 88 of these graduates had been hired as clerical workers throughout Chicago.[62]

Few, if any, clerical graduates of color appeared to have been hired by Sears, despite promises to the contrary and cries that the company needed trained office workers.[63] However, Sears did hire several graduates from the Jobs for Youth program. For example, in 1974, with the program now called the Youth Motivation Program, Sears celebrated the success of two young black high school dropouts: Cheryl Redmond and John Swoope. After four years and numerous promotions at Sears, Redmond was promoted to a senior clerical assistant tasked with supervising other unit members and assisting a buyer. Swoope was encouraged to return to school after spending almost a year as a mail messenger for Sears. Presumably after graduating from high school and the youth program, he was appointed as a division head for the Business Service Centers in Department 731P. Swoope credited the program as the reason why he earned his high school diploma and gained a sense of work ethic: "I've been working for Sears for four years now, and I've missed only one day of work in all the time. I've had a number of jobs and promotions and now I have 18 people to supervise. . . . Right now, I feel I'm as good as I once was bad."[64]

When publicizing the news of Redmond and Swoope, the retailer was quite self-congratulatory as if it was the primary source of their success. But few other black hires are named in extant records, suggesting that Sears's job program, like those of Carson, Pirie, Scott in Chicago and Bamberger's in Newark in the early 1960s, was not without faults. Like Sears's program, Carson's and Bamberger's programs encouraged high school dropouts and potential dropouts to remain in or reenroll in school and earn their high school diploma. Students who agreed to this plan were hired as part-time store clerks, messengers, or warehouse workers. Few secured gainful employment in department stores after graduation, however—the direct result of retailers' unwillingness to fully embrace workplace integration and the changing nature of retail during this period. Thus, as one scholar observed, these programs "had little impact on department store work forces since they were not primarily intended to make these employees permanent, full-time workers."[65]

Sears and other retailers continued to make "some commitment to hire the hardcore," owing to encouragement from the JOBS program and the National Alliance of Businessmen organization throughout the 1960s and into the 1970s. But again, their commitment and subsequent initiatives did little to permanently diversify white-collar work in the department store industry. A disproportionate share of "hardcore" blacks, thus, was mired in service and warehouse positions. Students complained that these jobs offered little room for growth and that the cost of going to work—transportation, clothes, babysitters, and the like—was significantly more than what they earned. In fact, the earnings provided by the welfare system were often more than what they could earn at these entry-level jobs.[66]

Unfortunately, Sears, the GLCC, and their urban renewal initiatives did little to improve the overall condition of North Lawndale and its residents;

moreover, the gains made were upended by civil disturbances in 1965, 1966, and 1968. According to the historian Amanda I. Seligman, the riots did not "set off a precipitous decline in the West Side's fortunes"; instead, they "exacerbated existing problems and widened established cleavages in race relations, the local economy, and employment."[67] In August 1965, in the midst of protests against a city fire department station in West Garfield Park for its refusal to employ African Americans, "an out-of-control fire truck killed a young black woman. The picketers smashed windows at the firehouse and nearby stores" and set a few fires, causing an estimated $20,000 in damage.[68] Two more riots occurred in 1966. In June, a police officer shot a man in Humbolt Park, a largely Puerto Rican neighborhood. Incensed, local residents broke windows and looted retail establishments. And in mid-July, the Chicago police turned off fire hydrants that were keeping youth cool in the sweltering summer heat on the Near West Side. Rioting subsequently ensued and quickly expanded into East and West Garfield Park and North Lawndale. Ten people were wounded, twenty-four were arrested, and "looting and arson damaged more than $2 million worth of property."[69]

The most damaging civil disturbance on the West Side, however, was by far the King riots in April 1968, which caused $14 million worth of physical damage, nine deaths, and injuries to forty-six civilians and ninety police officers. Many commercial enterprises were destroyed by window breakings, looting, and arson, and never reopened after the riot ended. "Blocks and blocks of residential property remained vacant lots—unoccupied and unkempt—into the twenty-first century. . . . Over the next several decades, the populations of North Lawndale, East Garfield Park, and West Garfield Park halved. Black families with means moved elsewhere in the city, leaving only the poorest families behind and making the West Side the epitome of inner-city desolation."[70]

In the end, Sears's efforts failed. Its Lawndale project failed to curb poverty and crime, while its job programs did little to improve black employment. So, in 1973, with most other businesses having abandoned the West Side of Chicago, Sears closed its Lawndale headquarters as well, and reopened downtown in the newly finished Sears Tower on South Wacker Drive.

Legal Battles between the EEOC and Sears, Roebuck, and Company, 1973–1986

Sears's urban renewal ventures should have furthered the department store movement's objectives. But even as the retailer tried to mediate and encourage black middle-class life and aspirations in Chicago, it bitterly refused to sincerely democratize its labor and consumer practices. Throughout the 1950s and 1960s, Sears fervently opposed black demands to integrate its "better job categories" in Chicago, New Orleans, Denver, Pittsburgh, Covington and Lexington, Kentucky, and other cities. The retailer capitulated only after unrelenting pressure from the Congress of Racial Equality (CORE) and other civil rights organizations, and even then its employment of African Americans in these positions was of a token nature.[71] Then, in 1969, Sears rebuffed the request of the National Welfare Rights Organization (NWRO) that the retailer grant welfare recipients the same right to credit that other consumers enjoyed. In response, the NWRO effected a large-scale campaign against the retailer. Its members, most of whom were poor black women, wanted the freedom to procure quality, durable, low-priced goods—especially adequate furniture, appliances, and clothing—that they were unable to attain at their neighborhood retailers or without credit at working- and middle-class department stores. Access to credit, these women insisted, would provide them with not only the means to buy but also the freedom to decide on their own what to buy, without the input of the state or the local welfare department. By 1979, the NWRO had pressured Sears into becoming one of the few large retail stores that granted welfare recipients charge cards.[72]

As one contemporary recalled, Sears was "a very tough company when it came to the civil rights movement."[73] So, in the wake of the 1964 Civil Rights Act—the legal achievement of decades-long black activism—many blacks sought assistance from the EEOC (others, such as Woodward and Lothrop workers, leveraged older labor laws and unionization).[74] African Americans had grown tired of jumping retailers' incessant hurdles toward fair employment, only to find new hurdles—such as interviewing but not hiring or hiring but not promoting, suburbanization, and the privatization of shopping malls—placed in the way. Title VII and the EEOC presented African Americans, and by extension the department store movement, with a new avenue to address wrongdoings in the workplace. For example, in September 1965, Charles J. Lawson and Lillian Campbell filed a complaint with the EEOC alleging race discrimination in the hiring of sales personnel at the Sears in Fayetteville, North Carolina. Lawson and Campbell "were told their applications would be filed and they would be called if needed. . . . Campbell alleges only one Negro salesgirl is employed in the store and most departments are segregated." Again, in early November 1965, Bettie J. Covington and Nancy Armstrong filed a similar complaint against Sears's mail-order center in Laurinburg, North Carolina. Covington and Armstrong tried to apply for sales work twice on September 20 and "were told the manager was out. They charge this is a device to avoid interviewing Negro applicants and stated that Negroes are only employed in menial jobs."[75]

In all of these cases, the commission concluded that Sears had not violated Title VII of the Civil Rights Act because no vacancies were allegedly available at the time of application. The agency ignored the fact that African Americans made up 1–2 percent of the workforce in these stores, and, of those employed, most worked in manual jobs that required little to no skill. But these and other charges were not filed in vain. In a pro–affirmative action milieu and emboldened by its recent victory against AT&T, the EEOC, driven by the flood of complaints and unremitting civil rights activism, took action and pressured the retailer "to improve their performance in employing women and minorities."[76] In response to this pressure, Sears instituted an affirmative action program that was designed to force the integration of the "territories and sovereign Parent departments." It was developed using information obtained from a distributed questionnaire about minority and women workers. It required managers to consider the race, sex, and national origin of applicants and employees in making all employment decisions. The program sought to meet several goals: first, "to attract [local minority and women's groups] and where their present level of skill or knowledge might not be sufficient, to assist them through training programs"; second, to "balance our work force in all job categories, reasonably reflecting the population composition of the area surrounding each Sears employment unit"; third, "to hire and promote minorities into jobs where previously they may have been underrepresented"; and fourth, to provide "equal pay for jobs of substantially equal skill."[77]

Another goal of the program involved educating employees on its purpose and progress. In employee newsletters, brochures, and handouts, management frequently addressed worker concerns about affirmative action. For example, in one newsletter, program director Ray J. Graham spoke of white men's fears that they might lose their opportunities. He stated that white males have "simply lost their monopoly on them. What we're aiming for is a policy of inclusion, not exclusion. . . . [The] competition for jobs will now be a lot stiffer . . . but we still promote people on their ability to do a job." Graham also answered the question about whether the program was in reality reverse discrimination. Borrowing an analogy from an AT&T executive, Graham compared affirmative action to "a continental road race from New York to Los Angeles between two cars, one black and one white."

He relayed a story of how the white car's route was uninhibited but the black car's path was littered with "nails, tacks, glass, boulders, and trees." Essentially, the goal of the program was to ensure not only that the path for both cars remained clear but also that the black car had an opportunity to "catch up with the white car."[78]

After five years, Sears published the progress of the affirmative action program in its annual report. Comparing 1969 and 1973 statistics on female and minority representation, the 1973 annual report showed that black employment increased from 7.6 to 11.1 percent. Black workers' presence improved in all positions of responsibility (officials and managers, professional, technicians, sales workers, office and clerical, craftsmen, and operatives) and decreased in manual fields of laborer and service worker. Most notably, minorities increased 178.3 percent in the category of officials and managers; 5.8 percent of Sears's officials and managers were African American, Asian, American Indian, or Spanish-surnamed American. The percentage of women workers did not increase; in fact, it decreased by 1 percent—but their presence improved in the following job categories: officials and managers, professionals, technicians, sales workers, office and clerical, and operatives. The company reported that the percentage of women in the officials and manager category increased 70.2 percent, with this group representing 27.6 percent of the company's total officials and managers.[79]

Yet despite this marked progress, minorities and women continued to be discriminated against and filed complaints with the EEOC seeking resolution; records suggest that nearly 1,500 complaints were made from 1965 to 1979.[80] The company blamed the intervention of the federal government and women and employees of color for being unqualified and uninterested in jobs that would diversify the workplace. It also claimed that its affirmative action efforts faltered because its decentralized structure made the implementation and supervision of its program difficult. According to one scholar, "Memos about affirmative action that came from [headquarters in Chicago] were often suppressed in the territories, and though there was eventually some hiring of minorities at the store level, the personnel department found that college-educated black employees were being relegated to the candy department or the shipping docks, without any plans for moving them along."[81]

As a result, in 1973 the commission indicted Sears for violating the 1964 Civil Rights Act and began an investigation into the charge. The next year, as the EEOC and the company negotiated a settlement, Sears added the Mandatory Achievement of Goals (MAG) Plan to its affirmative action program, hoping to accelerate the representation and promotion of minority and female employees. Per the MAG Plan's terms, unit managers at all levels were required to fill all "vacanc[ies] caused by the departure or promotion of a woman or [a] minority . . . [with] somebody of the same group. All other vacancies must be filled on a one-for-two basis," meaning a woman or minority group member must be hired for one out of every two openings that occur. The affirmative action manual provided the following example of how the retailer projected the MAG Plan would proceed: "You anticipate 6 full time commission sales openings. However 2 of them are minorities and women, with the remaining four being white men. MAG requires that the 2 be replaced 'in-kind' prior to making any other assignments to that job classification and *then* the one out of two (50%) rule applies to the remaining 4." The manager then would hire four women and/or minorities and two white men.[82]

Sears Roebuck touted that minority groups had made "dramatic gains" as a result of the company's affirmative action program, specifically the MAG program, and insisted that the EEOC's charges were insincere.[83] In 1975, in large part as a result of its MAG program, Sears was named one of thirteen winners in the 1975 annual Corporate Social Responsibility Awards competition sponsored by *Business and Society Review*.[84] Two years later, in January 1977, the company learned that, thanks to its MAG program, it was outpacing the national workforce in hiring and promoting women and minorities and decided to permanently install this operation. In its 1976 annual report, the company revealed that African Americans had "moved into 13.4 percent of the jobs, up 5.8 percent from 1969." They held 6.4 and 5.8 percent of the top-level posts as "officials and managers" and "professionals," respectively. Also, blacks occupied 11.9 percent of sales positions and 12.8 percent of office and clerical positions. Women had made similar progress according to Sears. They "represented 35 percent of 'officials and managers.' In the 'professionals,' they held steady at 48.6 percent of the jobs, up from about 15 percent in 1969."[85] By January 1980, only a few months after the EEOC filed suit, black representation in sales, clerical, and managerial positions had increased slightly: 7.4 percent of "officials and managers," 9.6 percent of "professionals," 11.4 percent of sales workers, and 13.8 percent of office and clerical workers were African American.[86]

However, the MAG program was not without its fair share of problems. Gordon Weil revealed that "the company reports that 'several members of management have been dismissed, and others have been disciplined as a result of the program' or rather their failure to participate in the program."

Ray Graham, the "man who head[ed] the [Sears] affirmative action program in Chicago," recollected "visiting balky store managers in the South and telling them they would have to accept the program or leave."[87] Additionally, another scholar noted, "in practice . . . the MAG program had loopholes: if a qualified woman or minority could not be found a white man could be hired, and women's groups alleged that employees were not always told about the program or how to apply for one of the relevant job openings."[88]

Sears's equal opportunity initiatives went beyond hiring and involved supporting minority economic development. It funded Tower Ventures, Inc., a Minority Enterprise Small Business Investment Company created by the Department of Commerce, and invested in minority-owned banks. Tower Ventures was created to assist "socially and economically disadvantaged Americans" in their efforts to own and operate small businesses; it was especially helpful to small firms that could supply Sears with goods and services. This program offered basic services for businesses and provided "long-term capital by lending funds to these businesses, guarantee[d] loans made to them by third parties, and help[ed] them locate management and technical assistance."[89] One of these minority-owned businesses was Nor-Way Printing. In 1983, Sears contracted the company to handle some of its printing. Nor-Way Printing owner Wayne Williams recounted that the retailer did not restrict the type of printers used to create Sears brochures or impose any unreasonable deadlines and paid its bills in a timely manner—all problems small businesses often faced when working with large corporations. Williams credited Sears with helping him expand his company: in 1983, Sears's first order was 100,000 brochures; by 1986, a single job for Sears was 18 million copies. With this, Nor-War Printing moved into a new and larger plant in the winter of 1986.[90]

Other department stores implemented similar programs to support minority economic advancement during this period. Neiman-Marcus, for example, established a policy whereby it promised to purchase only from businesses that maintained good records in minority hiring and promotion. This upscale retailer complemented this measure with its own fair employment policy.[91]

Sears Roebuck, thus, insisted that women and minority workers had made tremendous gains as a result of the company's affirmative action initiatives. The EEOC, however, disagreed, and rightly so. Accusations of race and sex discrimination abound. For example, in 1973 and 1974, the NAACP Legal Defense Fund filed charges of discrimination against Sears's Catalog Distribution Center and Retail Store at 495 North Watkins, and Sears's

Broad Street Retail Distribution Center in Memphis, Tennessee. It alleged, "The company discriminates against an identifiable aggrieved party and against all Blacks—male and female in terms of recruitment, initial employment, assignments, promotions, training, job classifications, demotions, terminations and in terms and conditions of employment. The company terminates black employees with high seniority, replaces them with new non-blacks and retains non-black employees with low seniority during reductions in forces." After investigating these charges, the EEOC concluded that not only were African Americans "underrepresented" in Sears's "aggregated Memphis workforce"[92] but also the majority were concentrated in part-time positions and manual labor jobs. Further, the commission determined that black workers were systemically discouraged from and denied transfers and promotions, and discharged "in disproportionately large numbers in comparison to their presence [in the] Memphis workforce."[93] These charges became the basis for the commission's Memphis race discrimination suit.

Civil rights organizations and individuals not only leveraged the powers of the federal government to challenge workplace discrimination; they also continued to organize and participate in demonstrations. In 1974, the Indiana Black Caucus, with the support of the Chicago-National Organization for Women (NOW),[94] voted unanimously to boycott "Sears for moving its fifty-year old store in central Gary, Indiana, to a suburban shopping center inaccessible by public transportation." Relocation, NOW leaders argued, would result in the loss of city revenue, the reduction of the black retail workforce, and the confinement of those hired, most notably black women employees, to "the dirtiest, lowest-paid, least-skilled jobs."[95]

It is not surprising, then, that the EEOC and Sears were unable to peacefully resolve their dispute, as each party held drastically different views on the conditions of black and women workers. So, in early 1977, the EEOC issued a Commission Decision that there was "reasonable cause" to conclude that Sears violated Title VII. Not long after, efforts to reach an out-of-court settlement resumed. But again, conciliation failed, especially after Sears, represented by Charles Morgan (founder of the southern regional office of the American Civil Liberties Union), filed a class action suit on behalf of retailers with fifteen or more employees in late January 1979. In the wake of *Regents of the University of California v. Bakke* and *United Steelworkers v. Weber* in 1978, the Sears suit directly challenged various agencies and individuals of the federal government, including the EEOC, on the legality of affirmative action. The company charged that the government had no clear national policy. Specifically, it argued that "the myriad of Federal antidiscrimination statutes and regulations" conflicted with one another and were impossible to comply with, and that government policies themselves had created "an unbalanced workforce dominated by white males."[96] Sears further complained that the federal government had "failed to enforce civil rights laws, including education and housing provisions, intended to provide industry with a well-qualified workforce."[97]

Some African Americans—most prominently Nathaniel Wright Jr., a black power advocate, Episcopal minister, and scholar—applauded Sears for bringing attention to the government's violation of antidiscrimination laws and its dysfunctional approach to civil rights and black participation in all aspects of American life. Arguing that the black community should support the Sears suit, Wright praised the company's philanthropy, especially concerning black education, its voluntary implementation of an affirmative action program, and the MAG initiative.[98]

Others were not so supportive. For example, Vernon Jordan, then president of the National Urban League (NUL), "appreciate[d] the bind Sears [found] itself in." Specifically, he wrote, "government orders have been inconsistent and contradictory. Given the employment picture, you can't have affirmative action for everybody. That's why it is necessary to have effective affirmative action for those most in need of special efforts—Black workers struggling to overcome the negative heritage of persistent exclusion from jobs, trades, and professions." Jordan, thus, concluded, "That's why both the government and the private sector have to redirect their efforts. If the Sears Suit results in such a clarification, it will have served a good purpose, but if it becomes part of the attack on the principles of affirmative action in the post-Bakke era, it could have harmful effects. Given the negative mood of the country . . . I am afraid this suit will give aid and comfort to the enemies of affirmative action."[99]

Many feared that the Sears suit would weaken or, worse yet, end affirmative action programs in the United States. Several civil rights activists vehemently opposed the Sears suit and implored the company to withdraw it and pushed President Jimmy Carter to have the suit dismissed. The NUL and its Chicago branch viewed the Sears suit as "another example of the effort to strengthen the forces that oppose affirmative action" and as "a legal effort to circumvent rather than to meet the company's responsibility to show concern for those who remain excluded."[100] The NUL, however, also "agree[d] that Sears has a valid point in complaining about the difficulty of satisfying the multiple federal laws and directives and that resolving their conflicts and focusing our affirmative action goals are worthy pursuits." Apparently, the organization ultimately hoped the end result of the suit would be the "consolidation of EEO enforcement into a single, cabinet level department," a process it "hoped to work with Sears towards meeting this end."[101]

Jesse Jackson, then national president of Operation PUSH, referred to the lawsuit as "a mixture of Kool-Aid and cyanide." He wrote,

> The Kool-Aid side is that Sears raises some legitimate questions about conflicting regulations (though even this charge is less true since the President's reorganization message to Congress and the Uniform Guidelines issued by the EEOC in 1978); castigates the Federal Government for its failure to enforce civil rights laws (which is beyond dispute and thus, weakens its moral authority to challenge private industry); and documents how the Federal Government planned an imbalanced work force.
>
> The cyanide side is the present conservative climate in which this suit was filed; the right-wing and racist elements that have endorsed it; the political message it sends to the President, the Congress, and the Courts; its prayers for relief which far exceed its basic complaints and its potential for polarizations.

Jackson, like Jordan and other civil rights leaders and organizations, including the NAACP, feared that the Sears suit held the potential for augmenting the *Bakke* decision. The NAACP Executive Committee argued that this lawsuit was part of a larger effort to undo civil rights laws and affirmative action. More explicitly, it stated that "the Sears suit is part and parcel of the northern strategy of nullification and interposition."[102]

The Sears suit sparked some activism: PUSH circulated a petition, with the hope of obtaining 250,000 signatures, asking Sears to drop the suit; Jackson organized a national coalition of groups representative of civil rights organizations, along with groups of women, minorities, and individuals with disabilities, to "confront the issue of the Sears Suit . . . [and bring] national pressure on the current administration for full employment";[103] and this national coalition held an Emergency National Leadership Conference in late February 1979 to discuss the class action lawsuit brought by Sears, "the legislation which is under attack and possibly map strategies and courses of action that may be taken with respect to this suit."[104]

Approximately five months after Sears's suit against the EEOC was filed, it was dismissed. Within months, on October 22, 1979, the EEOC filed five lawsuits against Sears, charging that the retailer had violated Title VII of the Civil Rights Act of 1964. Three of the suits were based on race, one on race and national origin, and one on sex. Of these lawsuits, the sex discrimination case was the only case to go to trial; it was tried during a ten-month span from 1984 to 1985 in the U.S. District Court in Chicago. The EEOC charged Sears with systematically failing to hire women for commission sales positions on the same basis as men, refusing to promote women working in noncommission sales to commission sales positions on the same basis as men, and paying female supervisors less than their similarly situated male counterparts. The agency used elaborate statistical data and qualitative evidence on Sears's hiring procedures, not testimony, to support its charges. Specifically, it compiled and analyzed disparities between the female proportion of commission sales hires and the female proportion of sales applicants. For example, between 1973 and 1980, women made up 61 percent of the full-time sales applicant pool and 66 percent of its part-time sales applicants at Sears. Yet women were only 27 percent of the full-time commission sales hires and only 35 percent of the part-time commission sales hires—except in Sears's "Midwestern territory," where women made up 52 percent of part-time commission sales hires—during this period. The EEOC also examined statistical differences between the expected and actual proportions of women among employees promoted from noncommission to commission sales positions for both part- and full-time women, and the character differences between male and female commission sales applicants that may or may not determine their success. Much of Sears's defense involved disputing the EEOC's statistical data.

Historians have been particularly enthralled with the sex discrimination case, in large part because of the use of expert witnesses to parse out statistical evidence and working women's history during the trial. Two well-known feminist historians, Rosalind Rosenberg and Alice Kessler-Harris, testified as expert witnesses on behalf of Sears and the EEOC, respectively. They offered conflicting historical interpretations of white women in the workplace and the factors—employers and workers—involved in shaping patterns of employment around sex. Rosenberg argued that women and men hold different "expectations concerning work, in their interests as to the types of jobs they prefer or the types of products they prefer to sell." Women's expectations surrounding work were shaped by their socialization into domestic roles that caused them to value their home and family over work and made them resistant to the idea of working in male-dominated fields. In other words, Sears's lack of women in commission sales, Rosenberg concluded, was the direct result of women not desiring this type of work. Conversely, in support of the EEOC's insistence that Sears had refused women opportunities to work in commission sales, Kessler-Harris argued, "What appear to be women's choices, and what are characterized as women's 'interests' are, in fact, heavily influenced by the opportunities for work made available to them. Where opportunity has existed, women have never failed to take the jobs offered. . . . Failure to find women in so-called non-traditional jobs can thus only be interpreted as a consequence of employers' unexamined attitudes or preferences, which phenomenon is the essence of discrimination."[105]

In the end, despite the EEOC's strong statistical evidence of disparities and Kessler-Harris's convincing argument, though without live testimonies from complainants (instead, the EEOC read depositions into the record), the court sided with Sears and Rosenberg's historical interpretation of women's relationship to work in January 1986. Presiding U.S. District Court judge John Nordberg agreed that the onus of sex segregation lay with women and their lack of interest in commission sales jobs. He also praised Sears's affirmative action program and sharply criticized the EEOC for pursuing the case. The Sears decision was a devastating defeat for women workers; the EEOC achieved neither a monetary settlement nor better jobs or working conditions for the women it sought to protect. Unsuccessfully, the agency appealed the court decision in April 1986. Two years later, the U.S. Court of Appeals upheld Judge Nordberg's ruling (only one judge dissented).[106]

For African American women, the sex discrimination case was particularly upsetting. Many who filed charges overwhelmingly specified that they had been discriminated against because of their race *and* sex. However, as the historian Venus Green notes, "the EEOC, legal statutes, and NOW unconsciously harmed African American and other 'minority' women by erasing their color. Guided by a 'gender-first' ideology that prioritized gender and a narrow concept of equality that often limited expectations to achieving male privileges the state and women activists inadvertently reinforced for African American women much of the discrimination they sought to abolish."[107]

By design, then, the majority of black women's complaints were classified as sex discrimination cases only, while those involving black men were categorized as race cases. But the EEOC did not just mishandle black women's intersectional identities and oppressions; it also failed to engage those who had been active in major antidiscrimination movements such as the long-standing department store campaign (an aspect that even its expert witness Kessler-Harris neglected). The department store campaign had succeeded over the previous decades because blacks, men and women, from different classes and backgrounds were bound by the common goal of black economic advancement. Consequently, because the EEOC separated the interests of black women from those of their male counterparts and ignored the elements that had facilitated the success of the department store campaign, among other reasons, the commission lost the Sears race discrimination cases. This loss, in turn, spelled the end of the department store campaign.

Vertis Laval's story illustrates some of these problems. In 1975, Laval accused the Sears store on Ponce de Leon Avenue in Atlanta, Georgia, of race/color and sex discrimination. She stated that while she was on maternity leave, the retailer laid her off and retained the services of "less senior whites."[108] The EEOC, however, found no reasonable cause to believe that Laval was discriminated against on the basis of her race, despite her insistence to the contrary and because it lacked the statistical evidence to support her allegation. Instead, it concluded that "because all persons on Pregnancy Leaves of Absences are women, and such persons are not protected from layoff during these absences, this policy impacts exclusively upon women to their detriment." As a result, the agency invited Laval to join its sex suit.[109]

Even when African American women charged only race discrimination, the EEOC reclassified or entirely dismissed their complaints, especially when they did not easily fit into the parameters set by the agency. In March 1972, Shirley Mims charged:

> I have more seniority than the white girls in Department 6 [at the Sears Warehouse at 4640 Roosevelt Boulevard, Philadelphia, Pennsylvania], but I am constantly given the dirty jobs or being transferred from one to another to fill in. I did not receive a pay increase between August 1970 and December 1971. When I asked why, my supervisor told me that I was not performing in a Clerk 2 capacity and as a result on January 4, 1972, I was demoted from a Clerk 2 to a Clerk 1. My supervisor realizes this is not my fault because I have often asked why I was being transferred out when I have more seniority than the white girls. But he saids [sic] that [he] is doing what the Manager has directed him to do. In addition on March 1972 I was transferred to the floor to pick orders, while the two white girls with less seniority, and no high school education stayed with their desk jobs. I feel I am being discriminated against because of my race in terms and conditions, Seniority, Demotion and Wages. Other Black females are being transferred to unwanted jobs, [w]hile white girls are not. New white female employees start out in Sears with better and higher paying positions.

In another complaint, Mims alleged that Sears "retaliated against her by exerting pressure to get her to withdraw her original charge of discrimination."[110]

The EEOC determined that the Sears warehouse disproportionately assigned African American women, many of whom were high school graduates with clerical skills, to manual laborer positions, while their white counterparts, "none [of whom] were high school graduates [or] had commercial training," were assigned to clerical jobs. Yet, the agency pursued Mims's charge as only one of sex discrimination, finding that, upon her return from maternity leave, she was demoted to a job where she performed "lower rated" manual work, and while it "did not result in an actual decrease in her wages, the reclassification had the effect of lowering her eventual salary maximum."[111]

As exemplified in Mims's case, the commission did not completely disregard the special plight of African American women. Instead, it appears that these working women of color presented the agency with a conundrum: How could it redress violations where race and sex discrimination were not only intertwined but also very apparent? In a few of these cases, the commission appears to have pursued both charges, albeit separately. Its heavy reliance on statistical data, not witness testimony, likely permitted this course of action. For example, in April 1975, Carolyn J. Triplett alleged that the Sears Catalog and Distribution and Retail Store at 495 N. Watkins in Memphis, Tennessee, "maintains a maternity policy which discriminates against me and other female employees by failing to treat maternity leave for pregnant females in the same manner as leave for temporary disability is treated for male employees. Due to the operation of this discriminatory policy, and because I am a Black female, I was refused reinstatement when I attempted to return from maternity leave."[112]

After investigating her charge, the commission made two major conclusions. First, it found that "Sears fails to provide for pregnant employees the same retention-of-service-date benefits provided for employees with other temporary disabilities," in violation of Title VII. Second, statistical data convinced the EEOC that Sears discriminated against Triplett because she was black. It argued, "The 1970 Census data show that blacks comprise 31% of the Memphis Standard Metropolitan Statistical Area (SMSA). However, this facility's workforce in 1973 was only 26% black, increasing to 31% in 1974, an indication blacks as a class had not been employed in proportion to their presence in the population. Hence, it is reasonable to infer that blacks would tend to have less service than Anglos since they had been previously excluded." But the commission did not stop there. It continued, "Moreover, Respondent's nationwide lay-off statistics for 1973 provided in response to Commissioner's Charge 750-74-C5000, show that blacks as a class are 'RIFed' [reduction in force] disproportionate to their presence in the Respondent's workforce. Blacks were 15.8% of Respondent's workforce nationwide but comprised 34% of the employees laid-off in 1973. This pattern is replicated in the charged facility. In 1973 blacks comprised 27% of the facility's regular employees, but constituted 62% of the regular employees laid-off." Based on this, the commission invited Triplett to join in its "collective effort" to resolve the matter.[113]

Lesser known and virtually absent from historical scholarship and memory, yet just as upsetting, are the race discrimination cases. The EEOC filed four suits alleging discrimination against minorities in hiring at two retail stores in New York City, one in Montgomery, Alabama, a Catalog Merchandise Distribution Center (CMDC) in Memphis, Tennessee, and two stores and a CMDC in Atlanta, Georgia. These suits sought to effectively end Sears's discriminatory employment practices, ensure the permanent implementation of affirmative action programs to eliminate the company's unjust practices, and provide victims of discrimination with back pay with interest.[114] The major point of contention in these cases involved how fair employment should be gauged. Sears insisted that the percentage of black hires should be weighed against the percentage of African Americans in the civilian labor force. The EEOC, on the other hand, contended that the percentage of African American hires should be weighed against the percentage of African American job applicants.

In the six years prior to filing suit, the EEOC studied employment practices at Sears stores throughout the nation. Yet its race discrimination cases were flawed from the very beginning. The commission insisted that the retailer "maintained a nationwide pattern of exclusion of minorities from management positions continuing at least until July 24, 1969." The EEOC further argued that there was "a continuing pattern of discrimination in the hiring and lay-off of minorities throughout Sears' southern territory and discrimination in the hiring of minority salespersons in certain stores in the New York City and Washington, D.C., areas." Yet a memorandum authored by Issie L. Jenkins, the EEOC's acting general counsel, touted, "Sears has been in the vanguard of the affirmative action since 1974 and, with respect to minorities, possibly as early as 1969." She added, "Sears had ceased discriminating against minorities and had also implemented substantial accelerated affirmative action programs some years before the 180-day period commenced" on August 30, 1973.[115]

These two opinions underscore the confusion surrounding the EEOC's objectives and standards for assessing fair employment. For example, in its motion to dismiss, Sears argued that the Montgomery store located at 1920 South Court Street did not discriminate against individuals on the basis of race. Instead, it hired more minorities than those in the local civilian workforce in the 180-day period after the commissioner's charge was filed. Sears held, "From March 1973 to August 1973, the Montgomery store hired 145 persons, of whom 50, or 34.5 percent were black. According to the EEOC, blacks constituted approximately 27.9 percent of the civilian labor force. . . . Since 1973, blacks have been hired at an equally impressive rate: during that period, the rate has never fallen below 32.9 percent even though the workforce of the Montgomery store decreased 9.3 percent from February 1966 to January 1978."[116] The EEOC, however, was not swayed. Its statistical evidence revealed that during this three-month period, 23.4 percent of white applicants were hired, while only 8.6 percent of black applicants were hired. The commission concluded "that such evidence establishes an issue of material fact as to whether an unlawful employment practice occurred within 180 days" of the commissioner's charge.[117]

Again, in the New York case, the EEOC held that the "defendant's hiring practices cause white applicants to have a much higher success rate than blacks and Hispanics, a fact which we believe to indicate discrimination in light of the few qualifications required for most defendant's jobs such as sales." The commission found that, at the Brooklyn facility, "blacks were 36.5% of the applicants in the six-month period in 1973 . . . [and] even in 1978, they were only 25.3% of total applicants, only slighter higher than their 24.5% composition of hires in those six months of 1973, and were only 19.1% salesworkers." Regarding Hispanic workers, the organization revealed that its case against Sears was "less compelling, for in 1978, they comprised 7.0% of the total employees and 5.8% of salesworkers, of which both figures are above their 3.8% composition of applicants for the six month period." Thus, it concluded, "one would expect the Hispanic composition of applicants to be increasing during this period" and yet it had not.[118]

The hiring practices at the White Plains store were quite analogous. Between February and July 1973, African Americans made up 25.7% of all applicants. Yet, "even in 1978, they were only 16.4% of total employees and only 12.9% of salespersons." Similarly, during the same period in 1973,

"Hispanics were 3.5% of applicants. . . . In 1978, Hispanics were only 0.2% of total employees and 0.0% of salesworkers."[119]

Sears, however, was pleased with this growth in African American and Hispanic employees. In 1973, the retailer set a "black long range goal" of "only 20%" and a "Hispanic long range goal" of 10 percent for its Brooklyn store. According to the retailer, its employment of African Americans had, in fact, increased, even as the overall employee population at this facility had decreased from 934 persons in February 1973 to 722 persons in January 1979. But, it celebrated that its number of black employees had risen from 138 (14.8 percent of its workforce) to 181 (25.1 percent), while black officials and managers rose from 7 (8.8 percent) to 21 (28.8 percent) during this period. The number of Hispanic employees also increased: from 1973 to 1979, Hispanic employees went from 26 (2.8 percent) to 48 (6.6 percent). The affirmative action goals for the White Plains store were set at 14.0 percent for African Americans and 1.0 percent for Hispanics. It not only met but proudly exceeded those goals: in February 1973 the store employed 594 workers, 75 (12.6 percent) of whom were African American and 13 (2.2 percent) of whom were Hispanic; it employed 62 officials and managers, 3 of whom were black and none of whom were Hispanic. By January 1979, while its workforce had reduced to 574 people and 58 officials and managers, African American workers increased to 92 (16 percent) and Hispanic workers rose to 15 (2.6 percent); and black officials and managers increased to 7 (12.1 percent) and Hispanic officials and managers rose to 1 (1.7 percent).[120]

Both parties made similar arguments in the Atlanta and Memphis cases. Statistical data were the sole ground on which the race cases were fought. In fact, the EEOC did not conduct any personal interviews with workers and officials, nor did it conduct on-site inspections of the stores and CMDCs named in the complaint. The only investigation conducted was "the statistical surveying done in preparation for the Commission Decision," EEOC representative Aimee Gibson confirmed.[121] This survey aggregated statistical employment data at 168 Sears facilities—a mere sampling of the retailer's total stores and warehouses. The SMSA was used to analyze these data. This approach, according to the commission, "followed the procedures in Section 11 of the EEOC Compliance Manual." But attorneys for Sears claimed that the EEOC overlooked the directives in the aforementioned section, which instructed investigators to "interview or depose various respondent officials, expert consultants, charge parties, and other witnesses . . . [and] make on-site inspections of the respondent's facilities." Thus, Sears concluded, the statistical information provided the EEOC with a limited assessment of hiring and employment practices at these local establishments.[122]

In addition to failing to thoroughly investigate race discrimination in Sears's stores and warehouses, the EEOC never singled out any of the targeted facilities in its early interactions and negotiations with Sears, nor did it attempt to conciliate the issue. According to Sears, "There was no good faith bargaining on the issue; quite simply, there was no bargaining at all." Further, the retailer claimed that "EEOC representatives never revealed or discussed what specific practices at the facility named in this Complaint allegedly discriminated against black applicants. There was no attempt to discuss hiring or other employment practices or statistics at this facility." This failure "thus deprived Sears of its statutorily-guaranteed right to settle the individual issues against it in an informal, out-of-court manner."[123]

These missteps were quite costly. In the Montgomery case, for example, they bolstered Sears's claim that race discrimination was not a problem at the Montgomery store; in fact, the retailer presented evidence that only two employees had ever filed discrimination charges against that location. Store manager Earl Dewey Kitchen submitted an affidavit testifying to this. Kitchen had been "active in local, regional, and national groups whose goals have been to improve the status of blacks in society" since 1964 when he served on mayor Earl James's biracial committee. As a member of this committee, he "discuss[ed] and propose[d] solutions to racial problems and defuse[d] local racial tensions in the City of Montgomery." Kitchen testified: "To the best of my knowledge, information and belief, only two employment discrimination charges *ever* have been filed against the Montgomery store. Only one, filed in 1972, involved alleged hiring discrimination on the basis of race." The EEOC closed this charge in 1974, he averred, "because it could not locate the charging party." He further stated, "The other charge involved an allegation of reverse discrimination filed by a white employee." This charge was still under review at the time of his affidavit.[124]

The flaws in the EEOC's case against Sears's Montgomery store resulted in its dismissal in May 1980. Presiding Federal judge Robert E. Varner admonished the EEOC for charging Sears with discrimination on the basis of race, sex, and national origin in its original complaint in 1973 but citing only one facility when filing the discrimination case in Montgomery. Varner rebuked the commission's strategy and approach and "failure to seek conciliation."[125] He ruled, "Sears was thereby put to the expense and effort of investigating and preparing to defend against all those general charges at each facility. Some six years later that all-encompassing charge has resulted in a suit charging the Montgomery-Sears store with discrimination against blacks." Further, Varner said, "this court can think of no better example of a situation where the requirement of verification should be more vigorously adhered to in order to prevent the EEOC's across-the-board, catch-all pattern of practice charges against nationwide employers, only to turn around and bring suit in one particular facility on the limited basis and issue of discrimination." The judge also ruled that the EEOC was required to "conciliate charges" before bringing suit against alleged violators and had failed to obey this provision.[126]

One month later, the New York case was dismissed. Presiding Federal District Court judge Kevin Thomas Duffy contended that the suit was invalid because a commissioner whose appointment had expired signed the charge. Duffy did add that "the commission can institute this action again, providing it does so properly."[127] The judge also commented that, in establishing the commission, "Congress was concerned with the rights of individual citizens. It would appear that in this case the commission failed to demonstrate the same concern."[128]

All of the Sears race suits—which were "considered the government's broadest race discrimination case against a major employer" at the time— were settled by late spring 1981. Negotiations began not long after the 1980 presidential election, an occasion that confirmed the nation's political turn to the right. By then, the Montgomery and New York cases had been dismissed, the Memphis case was on the verge of being dismissed by the magistrate judge, and the Atlanta case was still in progress. The settlement was announced in June 1981. "Both sides applauded the settlement," *Washington Post* contributor Merrill Brown wrote.[129] But the negotiated settlement, as observed by the *Chicago Tribune*, "amount[ed] to a victory for the defense." The settlement required the company to make only "minor adjustments" to its affirmative action program for the next five years.[130] It did not provide "for any back pay or other monetary compensation to alleged victims of Sears employment practices."[131] Instead, the settlement required only that the retailer pay more attention to the disparity between the number of black and Hispanic applicants and the number of black and Hispanic hires, and record this information in quarterly reports "for 18 months after specified reporting periods."[132] These terms were "directed at ensuring that the employer will implement procedures to monitor its own hiring practices in ways that should assure compliance with the law," said J. Clay Smith Jr., acting chair of the EEOC in 1981.[133] Additionally, the settlement barred the EEOC from filing class-action suits against Sears on behalf of alleged discrimination victims for the next five years, although individuals were permitted to seek judicial relief.

In the end, several factors accounted for the commission's loss. First, the EEOC was outspent and outstaffed by Sears. Second, these cases silenced minority workers: they prioritized statistical evidence (with each side claiming the other's statistics were flawed and inadequately analyzed), not witness testimony; they did not directly engage African Americans and civil rights organizations leaders, those who had been waging antidiscrimination campaigns in the retail industry for decades; and they ignored, or perhaps were simply baffled by, the complexities of black intersectional identities and victimization. Many scholars have blamed the lack of witness testimony for the EEOC's failure. And certainly, it played a part. This choice was somewhat understandable given the commission's limited resources, the difficulty of calling witnesses because of the lapse of time between when individuals filed their charges and when the cases were adjudicated, and its success in exclusively using statistical evidence to win the AT&T case. But, as the nation turned to the right, affirmative action was confronted with continuous efforts to dismantle it that demanded that complainants provide more and more evidence to support their claims.

The litigation of these cases was only part of the problem, however. The settlement, particularly that of the race cases, coupled with changes in the retail industry, reinforced discrimination against black workers and made achieving socioeconomic mobility and (perceived) democracy through sales work more arduous. In fact, the settlement may have hastened the reconsolidation of race discrimination in the workplace, as it provided Sears with no clear or exact procedures on how to attract minority candidates, defined affirmative action as a numbers game only, and ignored the structural problems that bred employment discrimination.

Surprisingly, unlike campaigns against the retailer in the 1950s and 1960s, the Sears affirmative action cases did not garner much attention from nor did they impel mass demonstrations by African Americans—elements that could have altered the cases' outcome. Several reasons likely account for the lack of grassroots activism. First, Sears had a long history of goodwill toward the black community, which produced loyalty among African Americans and likely tempered their frustration and willingness to protest the retailer's practices. Second, black civil rights activists, much like the workers involved in the cases, may have felt alienated from the process. And third, demographic changes in the black community in the postwar era harmed collective activism. In the 1960s and 1970s, the gap between the middle class and the lower class in the black community had widened and hindered the execution of a large collective effort or denunciation of Sears. On one hand, the exodus of industrial jobs from U.S. cities, the expansion of black urban neighborhoods beyond municipal limits, the legal end to employment discrimination, and rising incomes as African Americans entered more white-collar and professional jobs facilitated a surge of middle-class blacks living in the suburbs and more prestigious urban neighborhoods. Their lower-class counterparts, on the other hand, remained bound to inner cities. Even in areas where blacks of the middle and lower classes resided in proximity, members of the middle class segregated themselves, embracing respectable behaviors, community institutions, and employment as well as patterns of consumption that distinguished them.

Not only did the gap between the middle and lower classes widen, but their desires and needs diverted as well.[134] This, in effect, tremendously weakened the power of linked fate between African Americans that underpinned earlier struggles. Although black unity on overall goals and aspirations did not disappear, its support of the means to achieve those goals weakened. According to the political scientist Michael Dawson, "On issues of taxes, partisanship, the role of the government, fiscal policy, and the like, blacks remain on the left and unified—more unified across class than whites, but on issues of the strategy, tactics, and norms of the black quest for social justice, large cleavages can be detected."[135]

In spite of these obstacles, dozens of new complaints and lawsuits alleging discrimination on the basis of race, gender, and age continued to be levied against Sears. Most were dismissed, quietly settled out of court, or were simply unsuccessful.[136] The retailer's good fortune ended, however, with the class action lawsuit *Samuel Carroll et al. v. Sears, Roebuck, and Company.* In 1977, after being denied promotions, Samuel Carroll and Charles W. Grant charged that "Sears' discriminatory employment practices disadvantage blacks in the areas of hiring, training opportunities, promotion, compensation, and terminations"; that company testing procedures "disparately affect black employment and promotion"; and "that black employees at Sears have been victims of disparate treatment." The Louisiana District Court ruled that the plaintiffs had failed to prove any class-wide discrimination or disparate treatment against blacks in 1981. Two years later, the Court of Appeals for the Fifth Circuit in Louisiana upheld the district court's decision "with respect to hiring, job assignment, training, and termination" but reversed the district court's ruling on promotion. It found that Sears discriminated in the promotion of African Americans to managerial and other salaried positions and "instruct[ed] the district court to fashion a remedy for discrimination in promotion that is consistent with the holding of this opinion."[137]

Given resounding evidence that Sears downgraded positions once they were occupied by African Americans, the Louisiana Court of Appeals was troubled by the retailer's failure to promote African Americans to top managerial positions. The plaintiffs showed, for example, that when black employee Monroe Smith was promoted to installation manager, the position was no longer a salaried one. However, white employees who had held the position before and after Smith were provided salaries rather than hourly wages. Further, as depositions exposed, "Sears never had a salaried black employee during the period covered by this lawsuit even though there were 22 to 26 such positions in its workforce. Of the division managers, the total number of blacks varied from 14.5 percent in 1974 to 18.7 percent in 1977 even though the workforce was 26.8 percent black in 1974 and 34.3 percent black in 1977. For the category 'other managers,' only 2 of 49 were black in 1974, and there were no blacks of 28 in 1977."[138] Sears's remedy to this problem is not specified in extant records. However, it is likely that some small changes were made to thwart any further legal troubles.

· · · · · ·

Throughout the 1970s and 1980s, Sears remained the nation's leading retailer, but holding on to this position grew increasingly difficult as time progressed. Discrimination lawsuits, competition from discounters (notably Kmart and Wal-Mart) and specialty stores, inflation, and several bouts of economic recessions in the 1970s and early 1980s alienated customers and ate into store profits. The situation became more troubled as Allstate Insurance Company, which Sears had established in 1931, sustained enormous underwriting losses. Then, in late May 1975, the retailer experienced a 60.8 percent loss in profits in a single quarter. In response, Sears reorganized its merchandising management to give headquarters tighter control of operations and acquired financial control of its merchandising suppliers—a strategy that had already proved quite profitable for leading discounters.[139]

But Sears's efforts to improve business did not have the desired effect, and by 1991 Wal-Mart had replaced Sears as the top retailer. Sears moved into second place with Kmart following in third. Wal-Mart earned its new position by capitalizing on weak unions and waning government regulations, maintaining intimate relationships with its suppliers, and "perfect[ing], integrat[ing], and systematiz[ing] technological and marketing ideas put in play by [its] competitors." The discounter operated with "a few thousand highly skilled managers and professionals who contract out nonessential services to cheap, specialist firms" and was compulsive about keeping wages and labor costs at a minimum. It also resisted the trend to build in suburban areas in the 1970s and 1980s. Instead, Wal-Mart "expanded like molasses, spreading through tier after tier of rural and ex-urban counties," ironically serving the kinds of areas that the Sears catalog once targeted.[140]

Wal-Mart also was highly centralized. It created a system that gave executives immediate and complete oversight of every step of the retail process—from when a product was packaged and shipped from the factory to the store through its purchase at one of its locations. For example, in 1983 Wal-Mart appropriated universal product code scanning—a system being used only by grocery stores at the time—and tied it to an ordering system linked to headquarters, distribution centers, and manufacturers.[141] Within five years, the retailer had a satellite communications network, whereby owner "Sam Walton [gave] pep talks to hundreds of thousands of employees" and "a buyer could demonstrate for department heads in every store the precise way to display new products."[142]

The retail game changed profoundly in the last decades of the twentieth century, as urban decline, suburbanization, discount retailing, and a conservative, antilabor political climate transformed work, consumption, and citizenship. To its credit, however, the department store movement did succeed in ending blatant race discrimination and segregation in the marketplace. The demographic composition of department store selling and buying was certainly more diverse than ever. But, as a result of historical conditions beyond the movement's control, sales work no longer conferred middle-class citizenship by the end of the century. It had become, in effect, a dead-end job laden with some of the same shortcomings and pitfalls that African Americans had worked for decades to overcome. Now, only if African Americans leveraged this work to earn a college or graduate degree and secure professional work could they attain middle-class status.

Correspondingly, department store consumption had lost its grandness and prestige. It became less service oriented and more about the acquisition and display of brand-name and designer goods—merchandise that required and signaled some degree of affluence and status via the product itself rather than the manner and context in which it was acquired. Consumption, then, became more and less democratic: on the one hand, discounters offered everyone—regardless of race, age, gender, and class—the opportunity to purchase low-priced brand-name goods in a shared space where no one received skilled and targeted service; and, on the other hand, when considered in conjunction with the degradation of work and the increased stratification of department stores (lower class versus middle class versus high-end stores), inequalities became more marked and social mobility more difficult to realize in this new marketplace.

Thus, as African Americans prepared to enter the twenty-first century, they were once again left to redefine and reimagine their relationship with American consumer culture and democracy. Would it continue to be a battleground for equality and a site for claiming and performing citizenship? Might it ever be a place where America's racial democracy one day becomes simply and only democracy? These and other questions remain to be answered.

Epilogue

· ·

In the late 1980s, my mother left the world of a department store sales-woman for a career in banking. She did not abandon her role as a depart-ment store consumer, however. She remained a faithful shopper of midlevel and upscale stores, buying accoutrements that both displayed and reaf-firmed her middle-class status. Two decades later, and a few years into her retirement from Bank of America, boredom drove her back into retail—not at Hecht's, where she once worked, but at a small bridal shop in Westmin-ster, Maryland. Three days a week she dresses in stylish outfits and travels forty-five minutes from her home in Baltimore to this suburban commu-nity in Carroll County to help brides-to-be find the "perfect" dress. She does not earn much and would likely make more as a saleswoman at a midlevel or upscale department store; but she does not do it solely for the money, as she explains. Here, unlike at most department stores, she can use her fashion and sales expertise to style women of all races, sizes, ages, and economic backgrounds and make them feel "good, like equals."[1] She ap-preciates the relationships she has cultivated with her clients, the camara-derie that she is a part of in this all-female workplace, and, of course, the money that she earns that allows her to contribute to her family's household and continue her shopping habit (although today, she, like so many, pa-tronizes Amazon and department stores via their online sites more than visiting the stores themselves).

The world of retail, too, changed during this period. Both the department store and the shopping mall where my mother once worked shuttered. Golden Ring Mall was the first to go. In the 1980s and 1990s, poverty and crime in the surrounding area increased as the demography changed; two of the mall's three anchor stores—Montgomery Ward and Caldor—went bankrupt and closed. The erection of more upscale shopping centers in Baltimore County and the extension of a major highway that eased shoppers' access to them also contributed to the older stores' demise. All of this caused a significant decrease in patronage, particularly by members of the middle class. By the early 1990s, Golden Ring Mall had deteriorated into a "dead mall," a shopping center with high merchant vacancies and low consumer traffic, and eventually closed in 2001.[2] Sold to new owners, the mall was demolished and replaced by an open-air shopping center called the Centre at Golden Ring. Wal-Mart, Home Depot, and Sam's Club (a Wal-Mart operation), not department stores, anchor the mall and attract thousands of customers daily. Five years after Golden Ring Mall closed, Hecht's went defunct after Federated Department Stores acquired the May Department Store Company, Hecht's parent company since 1959, and began the process of creating a "nationally recognized department store chain under the Macy's nameplate." Hecht's, as well as Strawbridge and Clothier, Kauffman's, Filene's, and Famous-Barr, was converted into a Macy's as a result.

· · · · · ·

The department store movement succeeded in opening this world to African Americans and provided them with the means with which to make claims to middle-class citizenship, but it certainly did not foresee the dramatic decline of these retail institutions. The struggle for racial equity in work and consumption, thus, continues. Racial discrimination in the retail industry persists in ways that are consistent with early forms of discrimination—not hiring African Americans in skilled and status positions and limiting black consumers' mobility in and access to the retail institution. Discrimination is also shaped by and reflective of the changing nature of American retailing, employment, and consumption in the twenty-first century—in that African Americans are hired in sales vis-à-vis cashiering and denied managerial and supervisory positions, for example.

Generally, African Americans have made tremendous headway in sales work and even achieved middle-class status in the post–civil rights era. The sociologist Mary Pattillo-McCoy has argued that "a contemporary profile of the black middle class reveals that higher-paid professionals and executives do not predominate as they do among the white middle-class. Instead, office workers, salespeople, and technical consultants—all lower-middle-class jobs—make up the majority of black middle-class workers."[3] In 1976, for example, "one out of every four black women in the labor force was engaged in clerical or sales work, compared to one in ten in 1960. . . . The distribution of black middle-class workers [thus] had come to resemble the distribution of whites: a large stratum of clerical and sales workers, a smaller stratum of professionals, and an even smaller stratum of managers and small businessmen."[4]

African Americans' presence in sales and office work grew in the late twentieth century and into the twenty-first century. In 1995, African Americans accounted for 7.8 percent of all sales occupations; they were 11.4 percent of 6,613,000 sales workers in retail and personal service.[5] By 2014, out of nearly 33.5 million people occupying sales and office jobs, 12 percent, or approximately 4 million, were African American; approximately 3.3 million Americans were working as retail salespersons, a little over 12 percent were African American. In department stores and discount stores, specifically, blacks made up 18.9 percent of 2,131,000 total employees.[6] In 2017, blacks made up 13 percent of the 33,566,000 total sales and office workers in the United States. They accounted for 12.8 percent of the 3,235,000 total retail persons. In department and discount stores, out of 2,069,000 total employees, African Americans made up 20.6 percent.[7]

The gains made by African Americans as consumers, however, are arguably better known. Widely publicized sit-ins and picket lines at department stores and five-and-dimes forced retailers to grant African Americans access to the marketplace on the same basis as whites. They can now freely try on and return clothes, partake in meals at store eateries, and access credit. Public accommodations, thus, are "the most integrated institutions in the U.S. today. . . . One who goes to a café in a Southern town today would find blacks and whites (who attend or work at largely segregated schools, live in segregated residential areas, and attend different churches) sitting at adjacent tables or even the same table, seemingly without even noticing. The demonstrators who were treated as criminal trespassers when they engaged in sit-ins at lunch counters are now treated as heroes."[8] They—and Title II of the Civil Rights Act of 1964, which solidified their activism into law—restored the common-law principle that "innkeepers, smiths, and others 'who made profession of public employment' were prohibited from refusing without good reason to serve a customer."[9] Title II also "gave many white businesspeople cover to do what market forces would have nudged them to do anyway, absent the emotional force of racial prejudice and the fear of retaliation by white bigots."[10]

Some scholars and contemporaries have downplayed the success of integrating public accommodations, arguing that these "institutions . . . are relatively peripheral both to the American socio-economic order and to the fundamental conditions of life of the Negro people."[11] Increasingly, however, scholars are seeing things differently. "Gavin Wright points out that desegregation was accompanied by marked economic progress in the South . . .

and this progress helps explain the 'dramatic decline in Southern white support for strict segregation between 1961 and 1968.'"[12] Randall Kennedy, too, has insisted that "the ethos of the law has helped to change the hearts and minds and conduct in a fashion beyond what many sit-in protesters would ever have initially imagined."[13] Similarly, I have pointed out that the desegregation of department store work and consumption had far-reaching consequences, as it did much to advance the black economic condition—of labor and consumption—in workplaces, public accommodations, and the home sphere.

African Americans' struggle in the marketplace, however, is unending. The changing nature of retail work and consumption and the persistence of race discrimination continue to present challenges, some that resemble those of the early and mid-twentieth century and others that are entirely new and shaped by industry transformations. Since the mid-twentieth century, department stores have been steadily declining as a result of new competition, technology, and globalization; they have consolidated, leaving few family-owned and independent department stores in business; and they have experienced the degradation of once-skilled work and have had to close stores and lay off hundreds of thousands of workers, an overwhelming majority of whom are minorities and women. In short, the grounds on which African Americans once struggled for economic freedom and mobility have changed and the process of securing middle-class citizenship as a retail worker and consumer is now more difficult and arguably impossible.

By the late twentieth century, few stores resembled their former selves. Long gone was the golden age of department stores. Department store sales and clerical work were now "dead-end jobs" and "lower-middle-class jobs" stripped of their former responsibilities, status, and prestige. Sales workers are cashiers and stock people, for all intents and purposes. One historian observed, "Like other service-industry workers, [salespeople have experienced] a continuation of the trend toward part-time work, pressures for increased productivity, closer surveillance through computers and industrial espionage, and low pay."[14] The nature of consumption has also changed—or more accurately, deteriorated—from full-service shopping to self-service shopping: no longer is all merchandise housed in glass cases or out of reach from customers, no longer are sales workers dressed in all black or in their Sunday best, no longer are salespeople experts in the art of selling and the merchandise they sell, and no longer are these stores places where visitors have their every desire and whims fulfilled. Now, customers are more knowledgeable about identifying and locating their desired merchandise (in large part because of modern advertising) and are, thus, less reliant on sales clerks to assist them through the shopping experience.

As black people grappled with these transformations, stores relocated, not overseas like factories but to the suburbs, where mass transit did not extend, and stores could respond to their new competition, resume their discriminatory practices, and elude protests. Initially, downtown stores existed alongside suburban department stores. But by the 1970s, "as suburbs mushroomed downtown stores declined while branches proliferated and even eclipsed their parent stores." In Baltimore in the mid-1970s, Hochschild-Kohn closed its urban store and "became a purely suburban operation," thereby displacing a significant number of African American workers. Jordan Marsh & Company, a department store that had begun in Boston and eventually became a major retail chain throughout New England, ac-knowledged that its downtown Boston location was no longer its flagship store in the late 1970s. That title was transferred to its Warwick (Rhode Island) Mall branch. Similarly, in January 1983, J. L. Hudson, one of the nation's three largest department stores, closed the doors of its flagship in downtown Detroit on Woodward Avenue.[15]

In the twenty-first century, department stores face a new set of chal-lenges. Amazon, eBay, and other online retailers facilitated an increase of consumer expenditure, something much needed since the Great Recession, but also contributed to, and arguably hastened, reduced patronage of and the decline of brick-and-mortar stores and the loss of thousands of jobs. Also, department stores have "devalued their brand with constant dis-counting," hoping to weather this economic and retail milieu. "They're located in malls, which are not the hot shopping destination they once were. They're losing their most profitable brands, such as Ralph Lauren and Michael Kors, which are pulling out and, in some cases, opening stores of their own. And the middle-class population that used to sustain department stores is disappearing. Those families, now earning less, are turning toward discount retailers such as Walmart." Further, the tastes and expectations of American shoppers have changed, whereby they have increasingly shunned department stores in favor of fast-fashion retailers such as H&M, Zara, and Topshop.[16] As a result, J.C. Penney has closed nearly 200 stores since 2014, Macy's has closed over 150 stores since 2008, and, in 2017 alone, Sears, Roebuck, and Company closed more than 400 stores.

Making matters worse is the persistence of race discrimination in retail employment and consumption. Once denied sales and office jobs, African

Americans are now disproportionately represented in sales or sales-related positions like cashiers, customer service, and stock clerks—the lowest-paid positions in the retail workforce—and denied employment in management and professional occupations. In 2015, blacks composed 11 percent of the retail workforce, yet over 14 percent were cashiers and only 6 percent were managers.[17] In 2017, only 9.4 percent of first-line supervisors of retail sales workers were black, while 81.6 percent were white.[18] Also, compared with white workers, black workers are more likely to be employed part time and have on-class, unstable, and unpredictable schedules (despite wanting full-time and stable work), and paid less. One recent study reveals that full-time retail salespersons of color "are more likely to earn poverty-level incomes" and to be of the working poor. They are paid "just 75 percent of the wages of their white peers, amounting to losses up to $7,500 per year"; full-time cashiers of color are paid "about 90 percent of the wages of their white peers, amount[ing] to $1,850 in losses per year"; and "70 percent of Black and Latino full and part-time sales workers [are paid] less than $15 per hour, compared to 58 percent of White retail workers."[19]

Increasingly, then, retail is becoming less of a "steppingstone to better employment" and more central "to sustaining [black] homes and families."[20] Retail work, however, frequently fails to meet the needs of African American workers who—compared with their white counterparts—are more likely to be adults with children, to be the sole earner in their households, and to have some post–high school education (although the majority have a high school diploma or less). So, when paid less and confined to dead-end positions, many black workers find that retail work enables them to live on the bare bones of subsistence level but not thrive or climb the socioeconomic ladder in ways that retail work once promised.

In recent years, African Americans challenging race discrimination in retail employment have forgone consumer activism grounded in worker-consumer alliances—like their mid-twentieth-century predecessors—and instead pursued legal action. (This shift in approach is likely the result of the lack of strong unionization in the retail industry, the passage of the 1964 Civil Rights Act, and the splintering of the black community along class lines that has often made black activism difficult in the post–civil rights era.) In 2012, apparel retailer Wet Seal was charged with discriminating against its black employees. The federal race discrimination lawsuit claimed that "the company had a high-level policy of firing and denying pay increases and promotions to African American employees because they did not fit its 'brand image.'" In the spring of 2013, the company agreed to pay $7.5 million to settle the case.[21] A few years earlier, a class action suit was filed against Abercrombie & Fitch. The retailer had cultivated and profited from an "all-American and largely white" image. Black and Hispanic applicants charged that "when they applied for jobs, they were steered not to sales positions out front, but to low-visibility, back of the store jobs, stocking and cleaning up." One year after the suit was filed, Abercrombie & Fitch settled in an agreement that called for the company "to pay $40 million to several thousand minority and female plaintiffs" and hire a vice president for diversity and twenty-five diversity recruiters to "pursue benchmarks so that its hiring and promotion of minorities and women reflect its applicant pool."[22] The settlement also required the retailer to increase diversity in its advertisements and catalogs to encourage minorities to apply for jobs. These specialty retailers are not department stores, but these instances are nonetheless representative of the problems that continue to injure the industry and its workers of color.

Despite these major lawsuits, few structural changes have been implemented that would improve the condition of black retail workers. In fact, people of color and women—both of whom compose a significant portion of department store workers (with the aforementioned making up 40 percent and the latter accounting for 60 percent in 2017)—arguably suffer the most from the decline of these retail establishments. Yet politicians have virtually ignored the retail bloodletting. For example, in 2016, presidential candidates Donald J. Trump and Hilary Clinton gave a lot of lip service to the rebuilding of mining, manufacturing, and other industries that have historically employed burly white men. This, one journalist observed, "may represent an implicit bias against the working class of the modern service economy, which is more diverse and female; [while, mining and manufacturing jobs] [fed] into a national nostalgia for the mid-century economy, with its unionized workforce, economic growth, and high pay for men without much education."[23]

On the consumer front, because of black worker-consumer activism in the twentieth century, the department store is arguably more democratic than ever before: anyone can enter, anyone can touch the merchandise displayed on cold, metal racks and tables, and anyone can purchase goods— once attainable only by those of the upper and middle classes—with cash, credit, and store coupons. The department store, in effect, has become so democratic that it has lost its allure and much of its influence over the nature and direction of retailing. But even as stores became seemingly more democratic, the consumer sphere has become less so. As consumption has become less about service, it has become increasingly about goods and, as a result, has presented African Americans with new challenges or, arguably, different manifestations of old challenges. First, while "For Whites" and "Whites Only" signs no longer bar African Americans from gaining full access to the marketplace, now prices do that work. Wealth inequality—the result of historical and contemporary obstacles, including discrimination and segregation in housing, education, and the workplace and attacks on affirmative action policies—has prevented many blacks from buying pricey merchandise (or better yet, retail establishments and other business enterprises) that marks and creates class and wealth, and provides a sense of security, prestige, and citizenship in the late twentieth and twenty-first centuries.

Simply put, highly desired goods have become more expensive and hold greater meaning and power. Take, for example, the mania around Nike's Air Jordan sneakers in the 1990s. Air Jordan sneakers symbolized the popularity of basketball player and celebrity Michael Jordan, and the popularity of the sport itself, which seemed to open to poor people and held the promise of socioeconomic mobility. In his autobiography, hip-hop artist CeeLo Green admits to stealing sneakers and starter jackets, making "lots of people" unclothe and hand over these items, because he wanted to be somebody—or better yet, be somebody else.[24] Want for these shoes, however, often went beyond the crime of theft. "Teenagers," the historian Walter LaFeber has observed, "shot and sometimes murdered each other to steal Nike's Air Jordan sneakers and other athletic clothing. The shoes, which cost well under fifty dollars to make in Southeast Asian factories paying some of the lowest manufacturing wages in the world, cost up to three times that in stores. Customers of all ages willingly paid the huge profit to Nike because of Jordan's name, the highly advertised technology that went into the shoe, and the almost supernatural aura that seemed to surround Nike's world-famous Swoosh symbol and motto, 'Just Do It'— which, critics claimed, was exactly the advice gun-toting teenagers followed to obtain their Nikes."[25]

Second, even when people of color are equipped with the means to buy designer goods, discrimination against and racially profiling of these individuals in the marketplace have persisted. Since the 1990s, this practice has been referred to as "Shopping While Black." Shopping While Black occurs when store personnel, including owners, managers, salesclerks, and security guards, treat customers differently because of their race or ethnicity. This differential treatment involves providing substandard services to shoppers of color, subjecting them to verbal and physical attacks, and denying and/or degrading products and services. Shopping While Black incidents also include closely monitoring, questioning, searching, and detaining black and brown customers for suspicion of criminal activity such as shoplifting and credit card or check fraud.[26]

Retailers from Bloomingdale's to Lord & Taylor to Eddie Bauer have been charged with practicing racial discrimination.[27] In early November 2013, Macy's and Barneys in New York City were charged with falsely accusing three African American customers of credit card fraud and one of theft. At Macy's, Art Palmer was pursued and falsely accused of theft by the police after purchasing $320 worth of dress shirts and ties in late April 2013. Less than two months later, in June, actor Rob Brown was "handcuffed and detained while trying on a pair of Prada shoes, having just bought a $1,350 Movado watch for his mother. He was released without charges after showing multiple forms of ID." At Barneys, college student Trayon Christian and nursing student Kayla Phillips were accused of credit fraud. Christian, who has filed a lawsuit against the retailer, alleges that, as he tried to purchase a $350 Salvatore Ferragamo belt in April 2013, plainclothes detectives handcuffed him. Similarly, Phillips charges that "she was swarmed by four plainclothes cops [at a nearby subway station] in February after buying a $2,500 orange suede Céline purse at Barneys."[28] None of these four customers were officially charged with a crime, however. But their allegations sparked a national, albeit brief, discussion on consumer racism.

The practice of discriminating against African American shoppers, as we know, is not new, and so it is not surprising that the response of the black community in 2013 was reminiscent of the "Don't Buy" movements of the 1920s and 1930s, the persuasion campaigns of the 1940s, and the lunch counter sit-ins and picket lines of the 1950s and 1960s. Civil rights activist Al Sharpton threatened a holiday shopping boycott to force retailers to end racial profiling in the industry. To reporters, Sharpton stated, "We are not, I repeat not, going to go through the holidays and have people shop where they are going to be profiled. You can call it a boycott."[29] While this boycott never occurred, private meetings between Sharpton and other activists and store officials were held, and the New York attorney general Eric Schneiderman launched an investigation into the racial profiling in Macy's, Barneys, and other stores conducting business in the state.

The outcome, however, did not end consumer racism, nor did it do much to discourage it. In December 2013, not long after their practice of racial profiling was publicized, Macy's and Barneys posted the "Customers' Bill of Rights" throughout their stores, hoping to prevent future incidents and curb any further negative press. The document condemns profiling and states that any employee who engages in profiling "will be subject to disciplinary action, up to and including termination of employment."[30] In the summer of 2014, however, the attorney general's investigation concluded that minority customers were still profiled and surveilled "at rates far greater than those for white customers." At Macy's alone, 1,947 shoppers of color were detained at its Herald Square store and approximately 6,000 in total at the retailer's forty-two stores throughout the State of New York.[31] Because of these and similar findings, Macy's "agreed to pay $650,000 to settle a state probe into racial profiling complaints at its flagship Herald Square store" and released a statement declaring its commitment "to fulfilling the ideals of diversity, inclusion, and respect that our company aspires to achieve—every day, in every store and office, and with every customer and associate." The retailer also was required to "improve its employee anti-profiling training" and "hire an independent anti-discrimination expert who will regularly report to" the attorney general's office.[32] Barneys also "agreed to pay $525,000 to settle a discrimination case with the state attorney general . . . and also vowed to implement sweeping policy changes" in August 2014.[33]

Only two of the individual suits involving Macy's and Barneys have been settled, according to news reports. In July 2014, Brown's case was "settled in principle," according to Macy's; the terms of the settlement were not disclosed.[34] A few months later, in October, Barneys "quietly" settled the Phillips case "and insisted on a confidentiality agreement that bars her from publicly revealing how much money she received."[35]

Race discrimination is also a problem at shopping malls, particularly those in majority-white suburbs. As the scholar James W. Loewen found, "Mall managers don't want their shopping centers to get identified as 'too black,' which can prompt whites to shop elsewhere. Malls have died in response to the presence of young African Americans—even in solidly white middle-class areas—because white shoppers flee black youth. Also, a mall can easily lose its cachet; then cutting-edge retailers move to trendier locations. Suburban city officials also know that shopping malls often desegregate first, leading to white uneasiness that can fuel white residential flight."[36]

As a result, mall owners have pursued a variety of approaches "to discourage African Americans from visiting their malls: persuading public transportation agencies not to service the mall with bus routes from black neighborhoods, surveilling African American shoppers and making them uneasy, and having police follow black motorists." Additionally, as of late 2016, over one hundred malls and shopping centers have banned unaccompanied minors, young people under the age of eighteen, from these sites of consumption during specified days and times. These policies overwhelmingly target young people of color and arguably violate their rights under public accommodation laws. They require that minors must be accompanied by a supervising adult (someone over the age of twenty-one) on Fridays and Saturdays, during the day on school days, or any day after 5 P.M. Security guards and off-duty police officers are often stationed at mall entrances to check identifications, while others patrol these sites of consumption for violators.

Mall curfews trouble many consumers of color. Tony Fugett, president of the Baltimore County chapter of the National Association for the Advancement of Colored People (NAACP), expressed "[concern] that the policy discriminates against young people in general, and African American young people specifically."[37] Kim Rabuck, an African American contributor to the Socialist Worker website, wrote, "We are keenly aware of the thinly veiled racism, classism, and discrimination based on age or perceived age that will be perpetuated against our children." Rabuck cited an example where an Indian couple—a nineteen-year-old woman and a twenty-year-old man—shopping at the West Towne Mall in Madison, Wisconsin, were stopped and asked for their identification by a security guard, while their "younger white friend" who was accompanying the couple "was ignored as if she wasn't standing next to them, was not asked for ID, and not given a pamphlet."[38]

The issues with curfews become even more apparent when they concern young adults who work at malls. At the West Towne Mall, "proof of work status" is "required, and youth employees must go directly to the place of employment and must leave the property at the conclusion of their work shift if after 4:00 . . . or at any other time the policy is in effect."[39] This separation of work from consumption is a disturbing echo of an earlier moment of the black struggle for equal rights. As one opponent of the curfew has observed, "So stores can exploit young people as low-wage workers, but they cannot be present at the mall outside of that time when they're being exploited. It would appear that these employees cannot even go to the food court to eat during their breaks."[40]

Winning justice remains difficult, and, as I have stressed, the struggle is unending: Title II of the 1964 act does not cover all retail stores and requires plaintiffs to notify their state civil rights agency before filing suit and within a certain number of days of the incident; courts have narrowly interpreted the 1866 act and required plaintiffs "to produce evidence that they were denied the opportunity to complete a retail transaction."[41] Obtaining evidence can be challenging given that discrimination is often subtle.

Nevertheless, African Americans have remained undeterred. In addition to filing complaints and lawsuits, consumers of color also employ a variety of strategies to cope with and combat race discrimination, including (1) engaging in acts such as purchasing expensive items to legitimate their class, status, and belonging to others; (2) wearing their class (dressing, speaking, and acting in ways that convey middle- and upper-class status); (3) being loyal to businesses that provide quality products and services to minorities; (4) exiting and avoiding public accommodations that discriminate against shoppers of color; and (5) organizing protests, in conjunction with national civil rights organizations, against offending retailers.

It is unclear whether retail work and consumption will continue to be sites of black protest and socioeconomic advancement in the future. What is clear, however, is that they continue to hold the potential for being such sites, as consumption continues to be intricately intertwined with conceptualizations and realizations of American democracy. "Retail is one of the largest sources of new employment in the U.S. economy and the second-largest industry for black employment" in the twenty-first century of the United States.[42] Structural changes, however, are needed to protect and enable African American workers and consumers to continue to achieve modernity, middle-class status, and citizenship. Changes are needed in a variety of ways. Some experts argue that courts need to grant victims more leniencies regarding what is deemed admissible evidence in their efforts to prove discrimination. Others suggest that retailers raise wages and end wage disparities between the races, reduce uncertainty around scheduling workers, end hiring tactics that reproduce racial discrimination in the workplace (such as the use of credit checks), and provide diversity and racial sensitivity training to hiring, sales, and security personnel and actively monitor employment practices and customer-salespeople interactions by using mystery-shopping audits and "the demographic test." The hope is that, through increased federal and industry protections and employee training and monitoring, retailers will become more aware of racial biases and modify their behavior to ensure that all employees and customers are treated with dignity and respect.

Notes

Abbreviations in Notes

AFSC	American Friends Service Committee Archives
CHM	Chicago History Museum
CPL	Chicago Public Library
HML	Hagley Museum and Library
HSW	Historical Society of Washington, D.C.
JMM	The Jewish Museum of Maryland
LOC	Library of Congress
MHS	Maryland Historical Society
MWHS	Maggie L. Walker National Historic Site
NARA-CP	National Archives and Record Administration, College Park, MD
NPS	National Park Service
Sears Archives	Sears, Roebuck, and Company Archives
TL/RWLA	Tamiment Library and Robert F. Wagner Labor Archives
UIC	University of Illinois at Chicago Special Collections
UNC	University of North Carolina, Wilson Library
VCU	Virginia Commonwealth University Library, Special Collections
VHS	Virginia Historical Society
VRHC	Valentine Richmond History Center

Introduction

1. Jacqueline Dorsey Parker, interview by the author, June 10, 2013.

2. Parker, interview.

3. Lauren Thomas, "J.C. Penney to Close 8 Stores in 2018," *CNBC*, February 15, 2018.

4. Nathan Bomey, "Bon-Ton Stores Files Chapter 11 Bankruptcy as Department Stores Reel," *USA Today*, February 5, 2018.

5. This book broadly defines the term "department store." The term is used to describe large downtown and later suburban stores that sold household goods, furnishings, clothing, and dry goods; national chains such as Sears, Roebuck, and Company, Montgomery Ward, and J.C. Penney, which specialized in standardized mass-produced goods (the first two retailers started as mail-order catalogs, while the third sold only staple dry goods until 1930; the first two later added stores but never offered a wide range of amenities and services that characterized independent department and specialty stores); and specialty stores such as Lord & Taylor,

Saks Fifth Avenue, and Neiman Marcus, which typically carried less staple merchandise and more style goods like women's apparel. All of these retailers shared common business outlooks, were influential in creating and shaping a new culture of consumption in America, and promoted a racialized democracy.

6. According to the historian Susan Porter Benson, in the early twentieth century, "Macy's . . . treated customers to a range of services and touches of luxury as they shopped: the main floor columns of the store were made of marble, the escalators framed in 'burnished wood.' Marshall Field [in Chicago] displayed greater opulence, the galleries of the store's rotunda being supported by 'parallel rows of the classic white Grecian columns,' the floors covered with red marble, 'thick pile carpeting or Oriental rugs,' lighting by Tiffany chandeliers, the merchandise 'encased in polished mahogany and French glass counters.'" Benson, *Counter Cultures*, 82.

7. European department stores, particularly those in France, Germany, and Britain, share a similar history with those in the United States. Appearing in the mid- to late nineteenth century, these department stores facilitated the rise of a modern culture of consumption and influenced socioeconomic values and lifestyles. Some works on international department stores include Auslander, *Taste and Power*; Donica Belisle, *Retail Nation*; Benson and Shaw, *Evolution of Retail Systems*; Crossick and Jaumain, *Cathedrals of Consumption*; Lancaster, *Department Store*; Miller, *Bon Marché*; McBride, "A Woman's World"; O'Brien, "Kleptomania Diagnosis"; Parent-Lardeur, *Les demoiselles de magasin*; Pasdermadjian, *Department Store*; Rappaport, *Shopping for Pleasure*; Reekie, "Sydney's Big Stores"; Renoy, *Les Grands Magasins*; and Walton, *France at the Crystal Palace*.

8. Sandoval-Strausz, *Hotel: An American History*.

9. Wolcott, *Race, Riots, and Roller Coasters*.

10. Wiltse, *Contested Waters*, 2.

11. Wolcott, *Race, Riots, and Roller Coasters*, 4–5; and Wiltse, *Contested Waters*, 121–53.

12. Wolcott, *Race, Riots, and Roller Coasters*, 39.

13. In Chicago, during the First Great Migration, "Miss V—was refused service at the large State Street department store by one of the clerks." When local blacks complained, "the manager was interviewed and the clerk reprimanded and transferred. On the second visit, Miss V—received attention." Chicago Commission on Race Relations, *Negro in Chicago*, 320.

14. Korstad and Lichtenstein, "Opportunities Found and Lost."

15. Goluboff, *Lost Promise of Civil Rights*, 12. For the early civil rights movement, see Dalfiume, "'Forgotten Years' of the Negro Revolution"; Biondi, *To Stand and Fight*; Honey, *Southern Labor and Black Civil Rights*; Self, *American Babylon*; Sitkoff, *New Deal for Blacks*; Sugrue, *Origins of the Urban Crisis*; Von Eschen, *Race against Empire*; and Woods, *Black Struggle, Red Scare*.

16. Korstad, *Civil Rights Unionism*, 417. See also Goluboff, *Lost Promise of Civil Rights*; and Mack, "Rethinking Civil Rights Lawyering and Politics in the Era before Brown."

17. Nelson Lichtenstein, "Recasting the Movement and Reframing the Law," in Goluboff, *Lost Promise of Civil Rights*, 258.

18. Quoted in Wright, *Sharing the Prize*, 11.

19. Some of these cases included *Morgan v. Virginia* (1945), *Shelley v. Kramer* (1948), *Henderson v. United States* (1950), *Brown v. Board of Education* (1954), *Browder v. Gayle* (1956), *Boynton v. Virginia* (1960), *Bailey v. Patterson* (1962), *Heart of Atlanta Motel, Inc. v. U.S.* (1964), *Katzenbach v. McClung* (1964), and *Griggs v. Duke Power Co.* (1971).

20. Lee, "Hotspots in a Cold War."

21. MacLean, *Freedom Is Not Enough*, 77.

22. See Mills, *White Collar*.

23. From 1900 to the 1930s, the overwhelming majority of sales workers in American department stores were working-class women. Management worked to refine workers' class identity as a result, but was only partially successful: class training refined the working class and encouraged friendly worker-customer relations that improved store profits, on the one hand, while it simultaneously underscored workers' subordinate position (because it encouraged women to adopt a middle-class veneer but did not provide any of its rights and privileges) and bred resentment toward and strife with middle- and upper-class customers. Not until the economic crisis of the late 1920s and 1930s did middle-class women begin to seek department store jobs. Most of these women were either young college graduates or in their thirties with several years of department store experience; both groups wanted wealth and power. Also, during this period more and more department store saleswomen were married or once married and from middle-income homes. These women wanted to solidify their class position. They "sought a higher standard of nutrition, housing, or dress, the latest laborsaving appliances, vacations, or better education for their children, [and] the only answer was for the wife and mother of the family to go to work." Benson, *Counter Culture*, 213, 204.

24. Consuming respectable leisure activities, however, does not mean that new white-collar workers abandoned their working-class origins. Many continued to reside in working-class neighborhoods, attended "booze parties," and "tolerated unconventional sexual practices such as premarital heterosexual intercourse, prostitution, and homosexuality." Bjelopera, *City of Clerks*, 156, 157. See also DeVault, *Sons and Daughters of Labor*.

25. Benson, *Counter Culture*, 230.

26. See Mills, *White Collar*; Bjelopera, *City of Clerks*; and DeVault, *Sons and Daughters of Labor*.

27. Abelson, *When Ladies Go A-Thieving*, 5.

28. See Leach, *Land of Desire*.

29. The war and the years immediately thereafter witnessed "the start and peak volumes of the Second Great Migration, as close to 1.5 million black southerners left home" and moved to cities in the North and West. Roughly 1.1 million more African Americans followed in the 1950s. And by 1970, a total of nearly 3.4 million African Americans had left the region. Black populations in southern cities also expanded during and after the Second World War, when the war industries and later textile and other light industries relocated to the South. In 1940, 35 percent of the region's African American population lived in cities. By 1970, 67 percent of blacks

in the South were urban dwellers. James Gregory, "The Second Great Migration: A Historical Overview" in Kusmer and Trotter, *African American Urban History since World War II*, 19–38, 21; and Goldfield, *Black, White, and Southern*, 203.

30. Black men made tremendous strides as operatives, craftsmen, and foremen and as clerical and sales workers. In 1940, 12.5 percent of black men labored as operatives, 4.5 percent worked as craftsmen and foremen, and nearly 2 percent were employed as clerical and sales workers. By 1950, slightly more than 21 percent of African American men worked as operatives, nearly 8 percent labored as craftsmen and foremen, and approximately 4 percent worked as clerical and sales workers. African American women experienced the most gains in professional and technical, operative, service (excluding private household), and clerical and sales work. In 1940, approximately 4 percent of black women held professional and technical jobs, 6 percent worked as operatives, 10 percent were service workers, and a little more than 1 percent were employed as clerical and sales workers. Just ten years later, 5.6 percent of black women occupied professional and technical positions, more than 14 percent labored as operatives, almost 19 percent were service workers, and over 5 percent were clerical and sales workers. U.S. Bureau of the Census, *Changing Characteristics of the Negro Population*, 114.

31. U.S. Department of Commerce and U.S. Bureau of the Census, *Social and Economic Status of the Black Population in the United States*, 62.

32. Green, *Selling the Race*, 12, 132. Other examples of the commodification and marketing of black culture in the postwar era include the commercialization of black popular music, "Negro-appeal radio," and market products that were designed for and appealed to African Americans specifically.

33. Cohen, *A Consumers' Republic*, 190.

34. In these segregated spaces, black maids with white children in their care sat in the "For White" car, "passing" African Americans (or those mistaken for white) occupied seats in the first-class sections, and white men wanting to grab a quick smoke of a cigarette, cigar, or pipe visited the "For Colored" car, often seated or standing next to those they deemed their inferiors. See Hale, *Making Whiteness*, 121–97.

35. A minority highlighted class differences within the black community, hoping to dismantle segregation and discrimination. For example, John Mitchell Jr., editor of the *Richmond Planet*, argued that middle-class blacks "deserved special treatment and should [be] separate[d] from . . . common African Americans." Further, he "insist[ed] that if segregation must exist, it needed to be instituted along biracial class lines and remove 'white jail-birds, penitentiary convicts, dive keepers, white women of questionable character,'" as well as "low-lived and unclean" blacks, "from respectable society." Kelley, *Right to Ride*, 133.

36. Kelley, *Race Rebels*, 61.

37. Kelley, 75.

38. Cohen, *Consumers' Republic*, 190.

39. Many have criticized conspicuous consumption by African Americans as wasteful and an act of aping white society. Most notably, E. Franklin Frazier argued that "middle-class Negroes make a fetish of material things or physical

possessions" to escape their feelings of inferiority to whites and to convince, albeit unsuccessfully, whites that they are equal. Frazier, *Black Bourgeoisie*, 189.

40. Hale, *Making Whiteness*, 195; Ownby, *American Dreams in Mississippi*, 5; and Cohen, *Making a New Deal*, 154, 156.

41. Drake and Cayton, *Black Metropolis*, 557.

42. Leach, *Land of Desire*, 132.

43. See Wiese, *Places of Their Own*, 218. For additional information, see Pattillo-McCoy, *Black Picket Fences*; Mullins, "Race and the Genteel Consumer"; and Lacy, *Blue Chip Black*.

Chapter One

1. Marsha Orgeron, "'Making *It* in Hollywood': Clara Bow, Fandom, and Consumer Culture," *Cinema Journal* 42, no. 4 (2003): 76–97, 83.

2. Orgeron, "Making *It* in Hollywood"; *It*.

3. Jas. H. Collins, "Limiting Opportunity: The Man Who Wants to Be a Merchant," *Saturday Evening Post*, May 11, 1907, 13. According to Collins, "The department store grew out of the old dry-goods store. It is very new as yet. The greatest growth has come in the past decade. Ten years ago the departmental business of New York was perhaps not one-quarter of that of to-day. The old time dry-goods store of thirty years ago handled a few lines of textiles, and had two busy seasons—spring and fall. In between times there was stagnation, reduction of expenses, dismissal of clerks. It was the need for keeping busy every month in the year, and the necessity for keeping a clerical force intact that led to the addition of other departments. New lines were superimposed on dry-goods trade, and a cycle of business built up by advertising and special sales, that keeps a great store active the whole year."

4. Leach, *Land of Desire*, 6.

5. The term "fairyland of whiteness" is from Whitaker, *Service and Style*.

6. *Meriden Morning Records*, October 24, 1908, 7. See also Benson, *Counter Cultures*.

7. Abelson, *When Ladies Go A-Thieving*, 51–53.

8. Benson, *Counter Cultures*, 83.

9. Benson, 85. See also "Evaluation of Services to Customers."

10. Leach, "Transformations in a Culture of Consumption," 336.

11. Benson, *Counter Cultures*, 93.

12. Benson, 22. See also "A Common Type of Dry Goods Shopper."

13. The economists Thorstein Veblen and Simon Patten argued that during the Gilded Age mass consumption motivated all social classes to consume conspicuously. Americans aspired to the standards set by the elite, sought pleasure and release from degrading employment, and hoped to cross class lines (or better yet, diminish class and ethnic divisions entirely). See Veblen, *Theory of the Leisure Class*; and Patten, *Consumption of Wealth*.

14. Benson, *Counter Cultures*, 76–78. See also Cohen, *Making a New Deal*. Cohen argues that, in the 1920s and 1930s, white ethnics in Chicago leveraged the rise of consumerism and mass culture to strengthen their ethnic ties and communities. She

also argues against the homogenizing effect of consumerism: "Mass culture would not make them feel any less Polish, Jewish, or black or any less of a worker" (158).

15. Butler, *Saleswomen in Mercantile Stores*, 143–44. In 1910 Elizabeth Beardsley Butler, a pioneering social investigator of the Progressive Era, was commissioned by the Consumers' League of Maryland and the Russell Sage Foundation to secure information on the city's department stores for the preparation of a "white list"—a published list of stores that followed fair labor practices (i.e., fair wages, adequate work environment, and humane policies toward employees); consumers were encouraged to patronize only those stores and boycott others.

16. During this period, women seeking sales work were young college graduates or thirty-something with several years of department store experience or married or once married from middle-income homes.

17. Benson, *Counter Cultures*, 5, 209, 242.

18. Butler, *Saleswomen in Mercantile Stores*, 143–44.

19. Butler, 143–44.

20. Stern, *I Am a Woman*; Melissa J. Martens, "Expressions of Jewish Identity in Baltimore's Downtown Department Stores," in Decter and Martens, *Enterprising Emporiums*, 70; John Sondheim, oral history interview, November 17, 2000, Jewish Museum of Maryland (hereafter cited as JMM), Baltimore, MD; Benson, *Counter Cultures*, 209.

21. Martens, "Expressions of Jewish Identity in Baltimore's Downtown Department Stores," 70–71.

22. Sondheim, interview; Martens, "Expressions of Jewish Identity in Baltimore's Downtown Department Stores," 70.

23. Donovan, *Saleslady*, 110–11.

24. Benson, *Counter Cultures*, 236.

25. Benson, "'The Clerking Sisterhood' Rationalization and the Work Culture of Saleswomen in American Department Stores," 47.

26. Donovan, *Saleslady*, 111.

27. Bjelopera, *City of Clerks*, 157. See also DeVault, *Sons and Daughters of Labor*.

28. Hunter, *To 'Joy My Freedom*, 120; Green, *Race on the Line*.

29. Bjelopera, *City of Clerks*, 113–14.

30. I found no evidence of black workers participating in department store minstrel shows, although it may have certainly occurred.

31. Some of the key studies on whiteness and racial class formation include Brodkin, *How Jews Became White Folks*; Lott, *Love and Theft*; Roediger, *Wages of Whiteness*; Gubar, *White Skin, Black Face in American Culture*; and Rogin, *Blackface, White Noise*. For a critical perspective on these studies, see Arnesen, "Whiteness and the Historians' Imagination."

32. *Oriole Magazine* clipping, June 1951, folder Magazine Articles regarding Max Hochschild (1), Papers of Max Hochschild, 1854–1955; Hochschild-Kohn Anniversary Round Up, 1940, folder Subject Files—Anniversary, 1919–1958, n.d., Hochschild Kohn Collection, Maryland Historical Society (hereafter cited as MHS), Baltimore, MD. See also Whitaker, *Service and Style*.

33. Bjelopera, *City of Clerks*, 131. See also "A 'Telephony,'" *Strawbridge & Clothier Store Chat* 5 (October 15, 1911), 248, Hagley Museum and Library (hereafter cited as HML), Wilmington, DE.

34. "A 'Telephony,'" 248, HML.

35. Bjelopera, *City of Clerks*, 180.

36. William Atkinson, interview by Debra Bernhardt, June 26, 1981, tape recording, Tamiment Library, New York University.

37. Figures for black porters and helpers in 1890 do not include southern states. These data were unavailable, "owing to the fact that in 1890 the classification by race for several states and territories grouped porters and helpers with messengers and packers." U.S. Bureau of the Census, *Negroes in the United States, 1900*, 60; Greene and Woodson, *Negro Wage Earner*, 121; U.S. Bureau of the Census, *Negroes in the United States, 1910*, 34; U.S. Bureau of the Census, *Negro Population in the United States*, 526.

38. U.S. Department of Labor, *Negro Women in Industry*, 38.

39. Richard Dier, "400 of 10,000 Are Colored at Macy's Department Store," *Afro-American*, November 27, 1943.

40. Richard Dier, "Klein's Department Store Excludes Skilled Workers," *Afro-American*, January 15, 1944.

41. Leach, *Land of Desire*, 121; *Miller & Rhoads Extra: Richmond News Leader*, February 14, 1935, Valentine Richmond History Center (hereafter cited as VRHC), Richmond, VA; Kreydatus, "'You Are a Part of All of Us,'" 112.

42. Kreydatus, "'You Are a Part of All of Us,'" 115.

43. Mary Louise Williams, "The Negro Working Woman: What She Faces in Making a Living," *Messenger*, July 5, 1923. Dey's Department Store was located in Syracuse, New York.

44. Kreydatus, "'You Are a Part of All of Us,'" 110.

45. Bjelopera, "White Collars and Blackface," 482–83. See also "Some Elevator Don't's [*sic*]" 3 (August 15, 1909), 209; "Elevator Entrances and Exits" 3 (November 15, 1909), 294; "A Thoughtless Action" 4 (December 15, 1909), 12; "Elevator Courtesy" 4 (January 15, 1910), 27; all *Strawbridge & Clothier Store Chat*, HML.

46. Bjelopera, "White Collars and Blackface," 482–83. See also "Unlooked for Examples," *Strawbridge & Clothier Store Chat* 3 (October 15, 1909), 112, HML.

47. *Thalhimer Brothers, Inc.* (hereafter cited as *TBI*) *Talks, April 1950*, Virginia Historical Society (hereafter cited as VHS), Richmond, VA.

48. K. F. Lawrence to R. H. Macy & Co., July 11, 1907, and R. H. Macy & Co. to Lawrence, July 15, 1907, Record Group (RG) 10, Box 16, Reference—Harvard History Project, Documented History to 1930, pp. 2601-3443; Hower, History, 1919–1942, F1: Harvard History Project (1934), Documentary History of RHM & Co. up to 1930, pp. 2601–800, Macy's Archives, New York.

49. *TBI Talks*, June 1940, VHS, Richmond, VA; *Miller & Rhoads Mirror*, March 31, 1943, VRHC, Richmond, VA; and *TBI Talks*, July 1941, VHS, Richmond, VA. See also Kreydatus, "'You Are a Part of All of Us.'"

50. Kreydatus, "'You Are a Part of All of Us,'" 120.

51. "Frank Jackson Wins Promotion: Faithful Employee of Abraham & Straus Executive Assistant," *New York Amsterdam News*, June 20, 1928.

52. Kreydatus, "'You Are a Part of All of Us,'" 112.

53. *TBI Fights*, November 1944, VHS, Richmond, VA; *TBI Talks*, March 1942, April 1952, and August 1945, VHS, Richmond, VA.

54. "Domestic Help Runs Short as Women Take Men's Jobs," *Richmond News-Leader*, September 25, 1947. At Macy's in the early 1930s, the starting salary for black male elevator operators was twenty-two dollars per week. William Atkinson recalled that, because he was eighteen years old when he began working as an elevator operator at Macy's in 1931, he was paid eighteen dollars a week. See Atkinson, interview.

55. Hunter, *To 'Joy My Freedom*, 52–53.

56. *TBI Fights*, April 1945, VHS, Richmond, VA; *TBI Talks*, December 1946, April 1947, VHS, Richmond, VA.

57. *TBI Talks*, July 1945, June 1947, July 1952, and October 1952, VHS, Richmond, VA.

58. Atkinson, interview.

59. Kreydatus, "'You Are a Part of All of Us,'" 120.

60. *Macy's Sparks*, July 1943, Macy's Archives, New York.

61. *TBI Talks*, November 1945, VHS, Richmond, VA.

62. Greene and Woodson, *Negro Wage Earner*, 120, 313.

63. *Colored American Magazine*, May 11, 1901, 468–69; Greene and Woodson, *Negro Wage Earner*, 119–20. Sources disagree on what year Mattie Johnson was hired as a saleswoman for Siegel, Cooper & Co. In *Evidence of Progress among Colored People*, G. F. Richings contends that Johnson was hired in 1893. For additional information, see Richings, *Evidence of Progress among Colored People*, 537.

64. Richings, *Evidence of Progress among Colored People*, 537.

65. Mjagkjj, "A Peculiar Alliance."

66. Claude A. Barnett, Notes on Sears, box 406, folder: Notes for Autobiography, Claude A. Barnett Papers, Chicago History Museum (hereafter cited as CHM), Chicago, n.d.

67. "Ask Loop Stores to Begin Hiring Negro Salesclerks," *Chicago Defender* (National Edition), August 4, 1945.

68. *TBI Fights*, November 1944, VHS, Richmond, VA; *TBI Talks*, March 1942, April 1952, and August 1945, VHS, Richmond, VA.

69. Hine, *Hine Sight*, 103; Meyerowitz, *Women Adrift*, 36. On wages, see Chatelain, *South Side Girls*, 119. Dates and numbers vary slightly. According to one historian of the Chicago Urban League, "In 1918, [Sears, Roebuck, and Company] hired 600 girls temporarily during the Christmas rush to do clerical work in the entry office. Sears also opened a 'special division' in which it used 1,400 Negro girls. All of these employees 'were passed upon by the League's employment service before being employed.'" Strickland, *History of the Chicago Urban League*, 50–51.

70. Brown, "Womanist Consciousness," 624. See also Brown, "Constructing a Life and a Community."

71. T. J. Elliot Department Store was the black-owned store in Muskogee, Oklahoma. According to the Associated Negro Press in 1937, this "Frontier" department store was "the largest ready-to-wear store operated by colored people in the Southwest." Sixty-five percent of its customer base was white; the store grossed $15,000 annually and had a capital investment of $50,000. Like other black-owned department stores, the T. J. Elliot Department Store maintained a small staff: it had "3 people steadily employed, Oscar A. Amos, Mrs. Janie Douglas, and Mrs. M. A. Sadler." "Negroes Own Leading Frontier Store," April 8, 1937, box 260, folder 1, Claude A. Barnett Papers, CHM. On other black-owned department stores, see Richard R. Wright Jr., *Negro in Pennsylvania*, 86; *Who's Who in Colored America, 1930–1932*, 494; and "New Retail Store to Set Precedent," *New York Amsterdam News*, December 28, 1946.

72. "Business-Mad in Chicago, Thrilling Development since National League Met," *New York Age*, August 2, 1906, 2. See also *Report of the Eighth Annual Convention of the National Negro Business League*, 94–96.

73. *Report of the Ninth Annual Convention of the National Negro Business League*, 192.

74. *Report of the Fourteenth Annual Convention of the National Negro Business League*, 149–51.

75. Semmes, *Regal Theater and Black Culture*, 193; Reed, *Rise of Chicago's Black Metropolis*, 116; "Big Store Blazes New Trail in Interracial Relations," *Pittsburgh Courier*, April 18, 1936.

76. "Big Store Blazes New Trail in Interracial Relations."

77. "'Dick' Jones, Superintendent of South Center Department Store, Is Appointed to Board," *Pittsburgh Courier*, May 20, 1939; *Who's Who in Colored America, 1930–1932*, 249–50; *Who's Who in Colored America, 1938–1940*, 301–2.

78. "A. I. Hart and Company Celebrate Sixth Anniversary: Largest Department Store in East, Owned by Colored People, Has Enjoyed Unprecedented Growth; Begin with $700 in Small Space," *New York Amsterdam News*, October 10, 1923.

79. "Classes on Sales Opened in Chi Store," *Pittsburgh Courier*, July 14, 1934.

80. "Big Store Blazes New Trail in Interracial Relations."

81. "Big Store Blazes New Trail in Interracial Relations."

82. Addie Hunter, "Employment of Colored Women in Chicago," *Crisis*, January 1911, 24–25.

83. Crossland, *Industrial Conditions among Negroes in St. Louis*, 95–96.

84. Harris, "Whiteness as Property."

85. Drake and Cayton, *Black Metropolis*, 168.

86. Paul A. Kramer, "White Sales: The Racial Politics of Baltimore's Jewish-Owned Department Stores, 1935–1965," in Decter and Marten, *Enterprising Emporiums*, 37–65, 41.

87. "Fight, Fight, Fight," *Afro-American*, September 29, 1928.

88. Smith, *Here Lies Jim Crow*, 159.

89. Lou Frank, oral history interview by Melissa Martens, October 5, 2000, JMM, Baltimore, MD.

90. Powell, *Human Side of a People and the Right Name*, 292–93.

91. "Marshall Field & Co. Again Refused to Sell to Colored Girl," *Chicago Whip*, August 9, 1919.

92. "Stewart's, Newest Department Store to Close Doors to Race," *Afro-American*, August 10, 1929.

93. DuRocher, *Raising Racist*, 75–77. See also "Bounding Consumption" in Hale, *Making Whiteness*.

94. Edwards, *Southern Urban Negro as a Consumer*, 104.

95. Edwards, 106.

96. The historian William Leach has shown that credit and credit defaults also began to characterize white middle-class buying habits during this period. This occurred largely because of the production of more hard or durable goods, including sewing machines, furniture, and, during World War I, automobiles. Many "middle- and upper-class women . . . dependent on their husbands' or boyfriends' income, entered stores only to leave with a debt their male suitor could not bear." For example, in 1898, Frank H. Hebblethwaite "opened a charge account at Wanamaker's in New York City for his girlfriend Jireme G. Shear. In one afternoon she carried away a carload of goods, corsets, gowns, waists, drawers, gloves, and so forth." Hebblethwaite was "hauled into court" for failure to pay, and "required to pay $1,500 in arrears to the court." And in 1914, Emma Swift, "wife of theater impresario and composer Oscar Hammerstein . . . embarrassed her husband's credit accounts when she charged more than $5,000 worth of goods at Gimbels." Others took advantage of stores' generous return policies. Many women purchased mountains of goods and used them or kept them for an extended amount of time before returning them to the store. See Leach, *Land of Desire*, 125–28.

97. Hale, *Making Whiteness*.

98. Donovan, *Saleslady*, 160.

99. Newspaper clippings and correspondence relating to the Lynching of Matthew Williams, Courthouse lawn, Salisbury, MD, December 4, 1931, From the files of Governor Albert Richie, Maryland State Archives, Annapolis, MD. The historian Grace Hale posits another way African Americans were put "in their place." She argues that white southerners, in particular, reacted by marketing blackness through images such as Aunt Jemima to recommodify African Americans—this time as products to be consumed rather than as forms of production. Indeed, Hale argues, "black-figured iconography helped create an increasingly national market for branded and mass-produced consumer products by constructing the consumer as white. . . . Whiteness became the homogenizing ground of the American mass market." Hale, *Making Whiteness*, 168.

100. "Patronage of Race Not Wanted at Hochschild's: Race Patrons Not Wanted at Hochschild's," *Afro-American*, June 27, 1925; "Hutzler Bros. Color Line: Department Store Said to Allow Insulting and Discourteous Acts toward Its Colored Patrons," *Afro-American*, May 29, 1915.

101. "Mr. Wm. Goldsmith Denies the Allegation," *Afro-American*, December 31, 1910.

102. "Mr. Wm. Goldsmith Denies the Allegation."

103. "Marshall Field's Drawing Color Line: Members of the Race Find It Hard to Get Waited On; White People Have Begun to Notice It and Papers Comment on Same," *Chicago Defender*, June 10, 1916.

104. Edward Gutman, Edward Tucker, and Barbara Tucker, Oral History Interview 0459 by Barry Lever, March 13, 2001, JMM, Baltimore, MD.

105. Edith Parker, interview by author, February 8, 2012.

106. Maggie L. Walker, *Golden Jubilee: Historical Report of the R.W.G. Council, I.O. Saint Luke 1867–1917 (Fiftieth Anniversary)* (Richmond: Everett Wadley, 1917), 76–77, in the Maggie Lena Walker Family Papers Archives Collection, Courtesy of the National Park Service, Maggie L. Walker National Historic Site; and M. Ward Murray, "Chicago's Negro Department Store," *Colored American Magazine* 11, no. 1 (1906–1907): 29–35.

107. On "Colored dolls," see Mitchell, *Righteous Propagation*.

108. "Hart & Co. Blazing the Trail," *New York Amsterdam News*, December 20, 1922.

109. Brown, "Womanist Consciousness," 625–26.

110. "Our Duty: An Editorial It Is Hoped That Every Reader of the Amsterdam News Will Read and Act Upon," *New York Amsterdam News*, April 25, 1923.

111. "A. I. Hart and Company Celebrate Sixth Anniversary," *New York Amsterdam News*, October 10, 1923, 7.

112. "Harlem's Only Negro Department Store in Hands of Receivers; Liabilities Placed at $19,000; Stockholders Voice Confidence in President and Manager," *Afro-American*, January 4, 1924.

113. Cohen, *Making a New Deal*, 152.

114. Ownby, *American Dreams in Mississippi*. See also Hale, *Making Whiteness*.

115. For additional analysis on Marion Post Wolcott's photographs and consumption, see Ownby, *American Dreams in Mississippi*.

116. Drake and Cayton, *Black Metropolis*, 162. Also see Hobbs, *A Chosen Exile*.

117. Fauset, *Plum Bun*, 15, 16–17.

118. Olesker, *Journeys to the Heart of Baltimore*, 124.

119. Larsen, *Passing*, 156.

120. Smith, *Here Lies Jim Crow*, 158.

121. Hepp, *Middle-Class City*, 78–81, *op. cit.* 11.

122. "From Our Exchanges: Department Stores Draw Color Line," *Chicago Defender*, July 27, 1912.

123. Edwards, *Southern Urban Negro as a Consumer*, 97–98.

Chapter Two

1. Nannie Burroughs was referring to African American women in agriculture and domestic service, specifically. But her comments made in 1940 also capture the experiences of all black workers during this period. Jones, *Labor of Love, Labor of Sorrow*, 164–65.

2. The Boston Department Store also dismissed its black employees "with the explanation that white people wanted work too." Claude Barnett, "We Win a Place in

Industry," *Opportunity*, March 1929; Twelfth Annual Report of the Chicago Urban League, 1927–1928; "See New Irritations in Negro, White Job Competition: Heavy Losses in Jobs Balanced by New Work Opening Up," *Atlanta World*, December 2, 1931; "Race Loses Jobs to Whites," *Chicago Defender*, May 30, 1931; "White Girls Must Work," *Crisis* 41, no. 5 (May 1934): 139; "Why They Lost Their Jobs," *Afro-American*, October 24, 1931; "Accuse Legion of Discrimination in Unemployment Drive," *Atlanta World*, March 6, 1932; and "Urban League Sees Employment Shift: Slight Gains Revealed in Ghetto Sections of the Larger Cities," *New York Amsterdam News*, September 23, 1931.

3. Margo, "Schooling and the Great Migration."

4. On streetcar protests, see Kelley, *Right to Ride*.

5. August Meier and Elliot M. Rudwick, "The Origins of Nonviolent Direct Action in Afro-American Protest: A Note on Historical Discontinuities," in Meier and Rudwick, *Along the Color Line*, 323.

6. Skotnes, *A New Deal for All?*, 157–58.

7. For additional information on the black middle class in the first half of the twentieth century, see Drake and Cayton, *Black Metropolis*.

8. Richard Durham, "Don't Spend Your Money Where You Can't Work," Illinois Writers Project / Negro in Illinois Papers, 1942/01, box 41, folder 7: Agitation by African American Press for Equality of Employment Opportunities, Vivian G. Harsh Research Collection of Afro-American History and Literature, Chicago.

9. Hunter, "'Don't Buy Where You Can't Work,'" 83. See also Ottley, *New World A-Coming*, 113–21.

10. Hunter, "'Don't Buy Where You Can't Work,'" 87–88. Businessman William Linton and Yale Law graduates Joseph Bibb and Arthur MacNeal founded the *Chicago Whip* in 1919.

11. Joseph D. Bibb, "Work-Spend," *Pittsburgh Courier*, March 29, 1941.

12. The Chicago campaign never received the support of the *Chicago Defender*, the city's leading black newspaper. It ended in 1931 or 1932, after several merchants secured injunctions against picketing. See Hunter, "'Don't Buy Where You Can't Work,'" 101; and Meier and Rudwick, *Along the Color Line*, 317.

13. In January 1931, the *Chicago Whip* reported that it opened 5,000 new jobs. However, in January 1939, the newspaper stated that the "Don't Buy" campaign "resulted in over three thousand jobs for colored people right here in Chicago." See Hunter, "'Don't Buy Where You Can't Work,'" 93; Durham, "Don't Spend Your Money Where You Can't Work"; and Drake, *Churches and Voluntary Associations*, 244–61.

14. Drake, *Churches and Voluntary Associations*, 249; and Chatelain, *South Side Girls*, 118.

15. According to Meier and Rudwick, "Don't Buy Where You Can't Work" campaigns blossomed in at least thirty-five U.S. cities. See Meier and Rudwick, *Along the Color Line*, 315.

16. Cohen, *A Consumers' Republic*, 46.

17. Cohen, 55.

18. Howard, *From Main Street to Mall*, 85, 90.

19. Moreno, "Racial Proportionalism."

20. "White Pickets Aid as Negro Alliance Is Restrained," *Pittsburgh Courier*, December 30, 1933; "D.C. Alliance Pickets Halted by Injunction: Demands for Clerks 'Too Extreme' Say," *Pittsburgh Courier*, December 30, 1933; "Alliance Loses Injunction War, May File Appeal," *Pittsburgh Courier*, January 13, 1934; "Store Picket Injunction Hearing Jan. 2," *Afro-American*, January 6, 1934; George Streator, "Negro College Radicals," *Crisis* 41, no. 2 (February 1934): 47.

21. Moreno, "Racial Proportionalism," 418.

22. Norris-LaGuardia Anti-Injunction Act of 1932, 47 Stat.L.70 (1932).

23. "Alliance Loses Injunction War, May File Appeal."

24. Moreno, "Racial Proportionalism," 419. On the appeal, see "Alliance Files Appeal in Injunction Fight," *Pittsburgh Courier*, January 27, 1934; "Alliance Files Appeal against Injunction Writ," *Afro-American*, January 27, 1934.

25. In 1936, the NNA organized boycotts of the Sanitary Grocery Company stores, whose customer base was approximately 95 percent African American. The company (later renamed Safeway, Inc.) filed an antipicketing injunction against the organization and sparked a lengthy legal battle.

26. Pacifico, "'Don't Buy Where You Can't Work'"; Rowlandus H. Cooper, "Notes from Alliance Case Book," *New Negro Alliance Year Book 1939*, 25; Meier and Rudwick, "Origins of Nonviolent Direct Action," 330. See also New Negro Alliance v. Sanitary Grocery Co., 303 U.S. 552 (1938); and Martin Kilson, "Political Scientists and the Activist-Technocrat Dichotomy: The Case of John Aubrey Davis," in Rich, *African American Perspectives on Political Science*, 181–204.

27. Pacifico, "'Don't Buy Where You Can't Work,'" 71, 78; "New Negro Alliance," *Crisis* 40, no. 12 (December 1933): 288. See also Green, *The Secret City*.

28. Pacifico, "'Don't Buy Where You Can't Work,'" 71, 78.

29. Meier and Rudwick, *Along the Color Line*, 324.

30. Snyder, *Beyond the Shadow of the Senators*, 62.

31. Hunter, "'Don't Buy Where You Can't Work,'" 181.

32. Meier and Rudwick, *Along the Color Line*, 318.

33. Hunter, "'Don't Buy Where You Can't Work,'" 180.

34. Greenberg, *Or Does It Explode?*, 117.

35. "Thank You, Wanamaker Store," *Philadelphia Tribune*, October 20, 1932.

36. Two of its members were Effa Manley, an American baseball executive, and Avis Blake, wife of the famous jazz musician Eubie Blake. "2 Matrons Give Birthday Party," *New York Amsterdam News*, February 21, 1934; *New York Age*, February 24, 1934.

37. At this point, the association disbanded and joined the Citizens' League.

38. McKay, *Harlem Negro Metropolis*, 193; Greenberg, *Or Does It Explode?*, 120–21.

39. McKay, *Harlem Negro Metropolis*, 193.

40. Greenberg, *Or Does It Explode?*, 122.

41. "Blumstein's Patrons Assaulted," *New York Age*, July 21, 1934; and Muraskin, "The Harlem Boycott of 1934."

42. "Harlem Department to Hire Race Employees," *Chicago Defender*, June 9, 1934; and "The Spectator, 'In My Travels: With Pickets on 125th Street,'" *Afro-American*, June 30, 1934. Helen Sissle was one of the first African American saleswomen hired at H. C. F. Koch's Department Store, in June 1934. The daughter of Noble Sissle, the famous American jazz singer-lyricist-bandleader, she hailed from the black elite and was educated in France and Switzerland. *New York Age*, June 23, 1934; and Crowder, "'Don't Buy Where You Can't Work.'"

43. "Blumstein's Store to Hire Negro Clerks before September 1," *New York Age*, August 4, 1934.

44. Chatelain, *South Side Girls*, 118.

45. Cohen, *Consumers' Republic*, 52.

46. On Chicago's "slave market," street corners where African American women congregated to await white women seeking to hire black domestic servants, see Drake and Cayton, *Black Metropolis*, 246.

47. Chatelain, *South Side Girls*, 119.

48. McKay, *Harlem: Negro Metropolis*, 194–95.

49. William Conklin Brown, "Pleasantville—Jersey City—Red Bank New Jersey: In New Jersey," *Afro-American*, August 25, 1934.

50. "Fred Moore Charged with Color Bias," *New York Amsterdam News*, September 15, 1934.

51. "Fred Moore Charged with Color Bias."

52. Muraskin, "Harlem Boycott of 1934," 365–66.

53. See Williamson, *New People*; Williamson, *Crucible of Race*; Horton, *Free People of Color*; and Holloway, *Africanisms in American Culture*.

54. See Trotter, *Black Milwaukee*; Lacy, *Blue-Chip Black*; Landry, *New Black Middle Class*; and Frazier, *Black Bourgeoisie*.

55. *Philadelphia Tribune*, May 14, 1930; Nelson, "Race and Class Consciousness," 86. See also Drake and Cayton, *Black Metropolis*, 526–715.

56. Similar rulings and injunctions that halted the "Don't Buy" movement were made in Baltimore, Washington, D.C., Newark, Cleveland, and other cities. Moreno, *From Direct Action to Affirmative Action*, 39.

57. Edgar T. Rouzeau, "125th Street: 'After the Boycott—What?' All Harlem Awaits Answer," *New York Amsterdam News*, August 11, 1934.

58. Cohen, *Consumers' Republic*, 46. On the Harlem Riot of 1935, see Greenberg, "Politics of Disorder."

59. Greenberg, *Or Does It Explode?*, 125, 128, 130, 133.

60. Greenberg, 133–34.

61. Hedgeman, *Trumpet Sounds*, 76–78.

62. U.S. Department of Commerce and U.S. Bureau of the Census, *Social and Economic Status of the Black Population in the United States*, 74.

63. U.S. Department of Commerce and U.S. Bureau of the Census, *Social and Economic Status of the Black Population in the United States*, 74.

64. The Second World War and the shortage of manpower opened new employment opportunities to African Americans. According to Drake and Cayton, it

"resulted in the use of Negroes (at least temporarily) as bus drivers, operators, motormen on the surface and elevated transportation lines, as clerks in stores, waitresses in restaurants and at soda fountains, and in a variety of other situations where they had not been seen previously. Before the war, it would have been considered impossible to employ Negroes in some of these spots. Yet these colored employees have apparently been accepted, without serious incident, by both their white fellow-workers and the public. A concerted campaign to have Negroes employed as saleswomen in downtown department stores was conducted during 1943 and 1944, but met with little success." Drake and Cayton, then, surmise "that the public's reaction to Negroes in new or unusual job situations goes through three phases. First, there is surprise—perhaps shock. Second comes curiosity, and 'definition of the situation' (either acceptance or criticism), with or without further overt action. Third and last, there is complete acceptance." Drake and Cayton, *Black Metropolis*, 300.

65. Cohen, *A Consumers' Republic*, 84.

66. Cohen, 85, 86.

67. MacLean, *Freedom Is Not Enough*, 25.

68. On the NAACP and workplace discrimination cases, see Goluboff, *Lost Promise of Civil Rights*.

69. Howard, *From Main Street to Mall*, 113.

70. For additional information on the transformations undergone by department stores in the 1930s and 1940s, see Howard, *From Main Street to Mall*.

71. Carl Dunbar Lawrence, "Window Trimmer Miriam Andrews Sets a Precedent; Looks Ahead," *New York Amsterdam News*, March 17, 1945.

72. Some discrepancy exists regarding the name of G. Fox's first black personnel manager (meaning she was both African American and the manager of black personnel). *Opportunity* magazine reports her name as "Anaretha Shaw," while a 1984 history of black women in Connecticut and a 1986 article on Beatrice Fox Auerbach in the *Hartford Courant, Northeast Magazine* indicate that her name was "Martha Taylor Shaw." See Marjorie Greene, "Fair Employment Is Good Business at G. Fox of Hartford," *Opportunity*, April–June, 1948, 58–59, 73–75; *Black Women in Connecticut*, 7; and Linda Case, "The Very Private Life of Beatrice Fox Auerbach," *Hartford Courant, Northeast Magazine*, May 4, 1986, 13–23.

73. Greene, "Fair Employment Is Good Business at G. Fox of Hartford," 58–59, 73–75; memorandum from G. James Fleming, June 12, 1946, regarding "Employment of Negro Sales Clerks in Department Stores, Establishment: G. Fox and Company," American Friends Service Committee Archives (hereafter cited as AFSC Archives), Philadelphia.

74. While no known protests or agitation occurred, tension sometimes existed and played out on the selling floor. At G. Fox, African American saleswoman Delia Griffin recalled, "Well, there was one lady—she did make me mad. One lady—she came there, and you're supposed to buy anything unless you have your charge plate, right? So, she came and she wanted this little wallet, and she came and she said, 'I'd like this wallet, but I don't want you to wait on me.' So, I figured, well, she

didn't want me to wait on her because I'm colored, right? So, I said, 'Well, you can't buy it anywhere else. You have to buy it here because it has to be on my register.' I said, 'Well, the only way you're going to get it is I'll have to wait on you.' She said, 'Well, all right.' I said, 'Well, do you have your charge plate?' She said, 'No.' I said, 'Well, how are you going to get it if you don't have our charge plate?' She said, 'Well, my daughter has it, and she's shopping somewhere else in the store.' I said, 'Well, maybe if she'll come down here, I'll use her plate. If she's coming down here to meet you, I'll use her plate and sell it to you.' She said, 'No, I just want you to take my name. I'm some big someone from down South.' I said, 'Well, I'm some big somebody from up North!'" (Oral History Interview with Delia Griffin).

75. "Philly Youth Council Opens Jobs Bias Blitz," *Afro-American*, May 3, 1941.

76. "Launch New Campaign for Department Store Jobs," *New York Amsterdam Star-News*, June 13, 1942.

77. "N.Y. Department Store Employs Negro Clerks," *Pittsburgh Courier*, November 28, 1942; "Macy's Begins Hiring Negro Clerks," *New York Amsterdam Star-News*, November 21, 1942; Leroy W. Jefferies, "Integration of Negroes in Department Stores: Practical Approaches for the Integration of Negroes in Department Store Personnel," National Urban League, July 1946, folder Employment of Negroes—Cleveland Department Store Project, 1946–1948, Gary Urban League Records (hereafter cited as GUL Records), University of Illinois at Chicago Special Collections (hereafter cited as UIC).

78. S. W. Garlingion, "Macy's New Hiring Policy Stresses Equality to All," *New York Amsterdam News*, December 15, 1945; Venice T. Spraggs, "Foster Gets Key Personnel Post in World's Biggest Dept. Store," *Chicago Defender*, December 8, 1945; "The Way It Should Be, Reprinted from Fortune Magazine," October 1946, GUL Records, UIC Archives. See also "Lemuel Foster, a Macy Executive and Specialist on Race Relations," *New York Times*, June 25, 1981.

79. "Race Saleswoman Hired in Boston," *Atlanta Daily World*, December 24, 1944; "Department Stores in Boston Hiring Negro Saleswoman," *Pittsburgh Courier*, December 23, 1944. See also "Boston Big Department Stores Hire Saleswoman; Colored Reported Doing Splendid Job," December 20, 1944, box 260, folder 1, Claude A. Barnett Papers, CHM.

80. Memorandum from Fleming, June 12, 1946, regarding "Employment of Negro Sales Clerks in Department Stores, Establishment: Gilchrist Department Stores," AFSC Archives.

81. Harry W. Ernst, "Quaker, Negroes, and Jobs," n.d., AFSC Archives; Drake and Cayton, *Black Metropolis*, 741; "Ask Loop Stores to Begin Hiring Negro Salesclerks," *Chicago Defender*, August 4, 1945.

82. "What Race? Spiegel Doesn't Ask," *Chicago Defender*, June 26, 1965. Higgins served as an industrial specialist for the CUL from 1941 to 1945.

83. "Lauded," *Chicago Defender*, April 13, 1946. See also Roi Ottley, "Negro Woman Has Vital Role in Integration," *Chicago Daily Tribune*, May 23, 1959.

84. "What Race? Spiegel Doesn't Ask."

85. H. Jordan, "Narrative Report, 1952," October 2, 1952, Chicago Urban League Records, UIC. See also H. Jordan, "Narrative Report," January 3, 1953, Chicago Urban League Records, UIC.

86. Roy Wilkins, "The Watchtower," *New York Amsterdam Star-News*, February 13, 1943.

87. Greene, "Fair Employment Is Good Business at G. Fox of Hartford," 58–59, 73–75; memorandum from Fleming, June 12, 1946, regarding "Employment of Negro Sales Clerks in Department Stores, Establishment: G. Fox and Company," AFSC Archives.

88. Memorandum from Fleming, June 12, 1946, regarding "Employment of Negro Sales Clerks in Department Stores, Establishment: Gilchrist Department Stores," AFSC Archives.

89. Constance Curtis, "New Yorker's Album," *New York Amsterdam News*, September 11, 1943.

90. "Releases Survey on Salespersons," *New York Amsterdam News*, May 27, 1944.

91. Richard Dier, "Can't Keep Whites out of Harlem," *Afro-American*, September 8, 1945.

92. Cohen, *Consumers' Republic*, 83.

93. Quoted in Cohen, *Consumers' Republic*, 99. See also Drake and Cayton, *Black Metropolis*, 763.

94. Cohen, *Consumers' Republic*, 98.

95. "Refusal to Let Woman Try On Hat Costs Store $25," *Baltimore Afro-American*, February 6, 1943.

96. "Housewives in Fight to Finish," *New York Amsterdam-Star News*, April 12, 1941.

97. "St. Louis Women Refused Service in Downtown Cafes," *Chicago Defender*, July 15, 1944; "Women on Strike for Civil Rights," *New York Amsterdam News*, July 22, 1944; Mrs. Howard Woods, "Reject Jim Cafes in St. Louis Stores," *Chicago Defender*, September 16, 1944; and "1940s Civil Rights Demonstrations," in Wright, *Discovering African American St. Louis*, 13–14.

98. Roy Wilkins, "Watchtower," *New Amsterdam News*, June 15, 1940.

99. Quoted in Paul A. Kramer, "White Sales: The Racial Politics of Baltimore's Jewish-Owned Department Stores, 1935–1965," in Decter and Martens, *Enterprising Emporium*, 37–65, 48.

100. See Webb, "Jewish Merchants and Black Customers in the Age of Jim Crow."

101. Roy Wilkins, "Watchtower," *New Amsterdam News*, June 15, 1940.

102. Hayward Farrar, *Baltimore Afro-American*, 183.

103. "17 of 28 Stores Give Equal Service to All," *Baltimore Afro-American*, January 20, 1945.

104. "Our System," *Baltimore Afro-American*, January 13, 1945.

105. "14 Stores Added to Orchid List, Bringing Total to 44," *Baltimore Afro-American*, February 10, 1945.

106. Cohen, *Consumer's Republic*, 96.

107. On the Harlem Riot of 1943, see Brandt, *Harlem at War*.

Chapter Three

1. Korstad, "Civil Rights Unionism and the Black Freedom Struggle," 256. See also Korstad, *Civil Rights Unionism*; and Robert Korstad and Nelson Lichtenstein, "Opportunities Found and Lost." On the NAACP, labor, and the courts, see Goluboff, *Lost Promise of Civil Rights*.

2. Lichtenstein, *State of the Union*, 78.

3. Lichtenstein, 79.

4. Korstad, "Civil Rights Unionism and the Black Freedom Struggle," 256.

5. See Frank, "Where Are the Workers in Consumer-Worker Alliances?"; and Phillips, *AlabamaNorth*, 218, 223.

6. Opler, *For All White-Collar Workers*, 26.

7. A 1929 *Journal of Retailing* study of New York metropolitan stores found that managers in nineteen out of twenty-two stores permitted workers to wear either black or dark blue clothing with long sleeves and only "moderate or inconspicuous" trimmings and allowed tan and gray clothing during summer months. In 1930, some local retailers altered their dress code to provide sales workers with more liberties. Filene's, for example, allowed saleswomen to dress in "businesslike styles and neutral shades" after workers argued that their job performance was directly related to whether they felt that they were "dressed well and look[ed] smart." This argument, as the historian Susan Porter Benson has argued, "integrated [women's] rights as customers with their rights as workers." Sykes, "Dress Regulations in New York Metropolitan Stores"; Benson, *Counter Cultures*, 236.

Store managers closely supervised workers' interactions with customers. Workers often found this constant and intense observation to be nerve-racking, uncomfortable, and generally unpleasant. In his 1935 memoir, Nathan Ohrbach, founder of Ohrbach's, believed that each worker represented the store to the consumer. Thus, he made "it a practice to spend a good part of my time walking through the store . . . to afford myself the opportunity to hear how our floor people talk to our customers and what they say. Is this salesgirl trying to convince a customer that an obviously poor fitting dress 'is simply divine'? Is this salesgirl talking to a fellow worker while a customer is being neglected? Is another salesgirl telling a customer that a suit is all wool whereas it is really a mixture? Is still another salesgirl showing signs of becoming impatient and possibly discourteous?" Ohrbach, *Getting Ahead in Retailing*, 37–38.

8. Ormsby, "Other Side of the Profile," 21.

9. Devinatz, "Reevaluation of the Trade Union League," 50.

10. Trade Union Unity League, *Trade Union Unity League (American Section of the R.I.L.U.)*.

11. "S. Klein: 'On the Square' Store Plays Santa to Its Employees," *Newsweek*, December 29, 1934, 28–30; quoted in Opler, *For All White-Collar Workers*, 32–33.

12. Workers also struggled for control over the stores and Union Square. In the stores, they engaged in "monkey business" to disrupt business, slow down purchases, and discourage customers from shopping at these establishments. Acts of "monkey business" included releasing mice and pouring sticky substances on elevators to halt their movement and trap people inside. Strikers also gave children "Don't Buy at Ohrbach's!" balloons as they entered the store. Managers would confiscate the balloons, upsetting children and their parents. Outside the store, union members distributed leaflets, displayed signs and billboards, and held weekly rallies in the Square. Every Saturday, the busiest shopping day of the week, strikers held mass strike demonstrations. Each demonstration had a theme designed to solicit the support of various groups. Some themes included Catholic Day, Jewish Day, Writers' Day, and Theatrical Day. Protesters also confronted store owners at philanthropic events away from the stores and the Square. This approach, in particular, earned the labor movement press coverage and citywide support. Strikers confronted Nathan Ohrbach at a Brooklyn Hospital charity event, where he was being celebrated for his role as a great philanthropist. The publicity from this act of protest "turned the tide of the strike." More than ever, Klein and Ohrbach were acutely aware that their business and personal lives would continue to be disrupted until they agreed to protesters' demands. See Opler, *For All White-Collar Workers*, 34–41.

13. "Going Up," *Trade Union Unity: Official Organ of the Ohrbach Local of the Office Workers Union* 1, no. 1 (May 1935), Department Store and Office Workers' Organizing Collection, box 1, TL/RWLA.

14. Committee for Support of Klein & Ohrbach Strikers, "A Call from Negro and White Strikers of Klein's and Ohrbach," n.d., Department Store and Office Workers' Organizing Collection, box 1, TL/RWLA.

15. "Going Up," TL/RWLA.

16. "Clerks Told to Insult All Race Patrons," *Chicago Defender*, January 26, 1935.

17. "Clerks Told to Insult All Race Patrons"; Benjamin Davis Jr. to the Committee of Unemployed Office, Store, and Professional Workers, April 27, 1935, Clarina Michelson Papers, box 3, folder 2, TL/RWLA.

18. Office Workers Union, "To All Store and Office Workers on 125th Street, Negro and White!," c. 1935, TL/RWLA.

19. As early as April 1935, union leaders complained of layoffs and the return of "old pre-strike difficulties" at Klein's and Ohrbach's. Klein's workers lacked a strike fund and were reluctant to return to the picket line, and thus many of them chose to quit. Workers at Ohrbach's followed their example, except for twenty workers who returned to the picket line in 1936. See Opler, *For All White-Collar Workers*, 41.

20. "Going Up," TL/RWLA; "A Union Victory," *We Declare: The Official Organ of the A. & S. Local of the Office Workers Union* 1, no. 1 (July 1935), Department Store and Office Workers' Organizing Collection, box 1, TL/RWLA.

21. "Going Up," TL/RWLA.

22. William Atkinson, interview by Debra Bernhardt, June 26, 1981, tape recording and transcript, TL/RWLA, New York University.

23. Marcella Loring Michelson, interview by Debra Bernhardt, June 18, 1980, transcript, TL/RWLA, New York University.

24. Atkinson, interview.

25. "We Salute Four Anniversary-ites for '44," *Sparks*, January 1944; "Arthur Love Recognized for His 25 Years of Service," *Sparks*, April 1944; "Macy's G.I.'s," *Sparks*, November 1944; "Mr. James Marks 50th," *Sparks*, 1944, Macy's Archives, New York.

26. *Sparks*, March 1947, Macy's Archives.

27. *Union Sparks* 1, no. 24 (December 9, 1940); *Union Sparks* 2, no. 1 (January 6, 1941), Macy's Archives.

28. "Elevator Operator Commended by Customer," *Sparks*, January 1942, Macy's Archives.

29. "Macy's Has Been Selling Food Boxes for Men in Service" [display advertisement for Macy's], *New York Times*, April 1, 1942; "Gimbels Patriotic Envelopes" [display advertisement for Gimbel's], *New York Times*, January 25, 1942, quoted in Opler, *For All White-Collar Workers*, 121.

30. Opler, 122–23.

31. Opler, 126–27.

32. Vic Lopos, "National Negro Convention," May 30, 1946, Retail Wholesale and Department Store Union, Local 1-S, Department Store Workers Union Records, Tamiment Library.

33. Report from Anti-Discrimination Committee, July 25, 1946, Retail Wholesale and Department Store Union, Local 1-S, Department Store Workers Union Records, Tamiment Library.

34. Oscar R. Williams Jr., "Historical Impressions of Black-Jewish Relations prior to World War II," in *Strangers and Neighbors: Relations between Blacks and Jews in the United States*, ed. Maurianne Adams and John Bracey (Amherst: University of Massachusetts Press, 1999), 34–42, 40.

35. Report from Anti-Discrimination Committee, July 25, 1946, Retail Wholesale and Department Store Union, Local 1-S, Department Store Workers Union Records, Tamiment Library.

36. Report from Anti-Discrimination Committee, July 25, 1946.

37. Donald L. Pratt, "Store Unions Pay Rise Requests," *Women's Wear Daily*, December 27, 1944.

38. Correspondence from Samuel Kovenetsky and Marcella Loring to Jack Strauss, June 14, 1946, Retail Wholesale and Department Store Union, Local 1-S, Department Store Workers Union Records, Tamiment Library.

39. Atkinson, interview.

40. "Macy's Training First Negro Woman as Large Scale Buyer," *Chicago Defender*, October 18, 1947; "Negro Woman Named Manager at Macy's," *Atlanta Daily World*, January 21, 1951; "Tobias' Kin Promoted at Macy's Store," *Chicago Defender*, January 27, 1951; and "Macy's Moves Abroad," *Atlanta Daily World*, January 23, 1951.

41. Isadore Barmash, "Negro to Head Macy's in Jamaica," *New York Times*, February 16, 1968; "Macy's Promotes Negro," *Washington Post*, February 18, 1968;

"Buyer Gets Branch Manager Post with Macy's in N.Y.," *Chicago Daily Defender*, March 2, 1968; "Big Step for Frederick Wilkinson," *New Pittsburgh Courier*, March 2, 1968; and Wayne Leslie, "Frederick Wilkinson, Jr., 77, Executive at Macy's" [Obituary], *New York Times*, November 23, 1998.

42. Vic Lopos, "National Negro Convention," May 30, 1946, Tamiment Library; Lillian Scott, "N.Y. Stores Hire Negro Clerks and Business Goes On as Usual: Other Cities Please Note," *Chicago Defender*, November 15, 1947; and Opler, *For All White-Collar Workers*, 189.

43. Scott, "N.Y. Stores Hire Negro Clerks and Business Goes On as Usual."

44. Report from Anti-Discrimination Committee, July 25, 1946; Points at which a Negro may be rejected, n.d., Retail Wholesale and Department Store Union, Local 1-S, Department Store Workers Union Records, Tamiment Library.

45. "Macy's Points the Way," *Atlanta Daily World*, December 13, 1942, 4.

46. Report from Anti-Discrimination Committee, July 25, 1946; Points at which a Negro may be rejected, n.d., Tamiment Library.

47. Interview Notes on Anna Smith, n.d., Retail Wholesale and Department Store Union, Local 1-S, Department Store Workers Union Records, Tamiment Library.

48. "'Mugging Night Sticks' Are Withdrawn from Sale at Macy's," *New York Amsterdam News*, May 8, 1943.

49. Report from Anti-Discrimination Committee, n.d.; correspondence from J. K. Stearns, Chairman of Anti-Discrimination Committee, to Lemuel Foster, n.d., and correspondence from G. G. Michelson to Mr. Robert Gutter, October 13, 1952, Retail Wholesale and Department Store Union, Local 1-S, Department Store Workers Union Records, Tamiment Library; "Macyites Squelch Anti-Negro Display," *Union Voice*, March 27, 1949, quoted in Opler, *For All White-Collar Workers*, 189.

50. Opler, *For All White-Collar Workers*, 189.

51. Opler, 189; Johnnie A. Moore, "Personality Spotlight," *Chicago Defender*, November 7, 1959, and "Interview with Dick Jones, Manager of South Center," in Stange, *Bronzeville*, 103–5. See also Richard L. Jones's Resumes, 1949–1967, Personal Papers of Richard Jones in possession of Richard L. Jones III.

52. Roi Ottley, "Stylist Picks Fashions on S. Side: 1st Negro Woman in Field," *Chicago Daily Tribune*, March 4, 1956.

53. Roi Ottley, "Success Story of Middle Class," *Chicago Daily Tribune*, June 25, 1954.

54. Promotional Program for South Center Department Store, n.d., Personal Papers of Richard Jones in possession of Richard L. Jones III; and "A Negro Department Store," *Kiplinger Magazine*, September 1948, 43–44.

55. Delton, *Racial Integration in Corporate America*, 47–48.

56. Display Ad 15—No Title, *Chicago Defender*, November 4, 1939; Display Ad 11—No Title, *Chicago Defender*, July 14, 1934.

57. Display Ad 1—No Title, *Chicago Defender*, March 13, 1948. For more on African Americans' insistence on purchasing name-brand items, see Edwards, *Southern Urban Negro as a Consumer*.

58. Display Ad 1—No Title, *Chicago Defender*, March 13, 1948.

59. "Churchmen, Charities Heads Get Checks," *Chicago Defender*, April 6, 1935.

60. "Seek Seven Hundred Thousand to Build Improvements at Washington Park," *Chicago Defender*, April 13, 1935.

61. Photo Standalone 3—No Title, *Chicago Defender*, August 14, 1948.

62. Mary McLeod Bethune, "An after-dinner address delivered to a gathering of executives and employees of the outstanding South Center Department Store of Chicago, Ill.," September 22, 1947, National Association for the Advancement of Colored People Records, Library of Congress (hereafter cited as LOC, Washington, D.C.).

63. W. A. Deans, "Charge South Center Fooling Employes," *Chicago Defender*, December 26, 1942.

64. Because employees were "not allowed to tell their pay to anyone" and store financial records no longer exist, the exact nature of this wage discrepancy remains unknown. South Center News, n.d. (c. 1942–1948), United Service Employees Union Records (hereafter cited as USEU Records), UIC.

65. Deans, "Charge South Center Fooling Employes."

66. Deans, "Charge South Center Fooling Employes."

67. "South Center Employes to Select Union," *Chicago Defender*, December 26, 1942.

68. South Center Unity, November 9, 1948, Sidney Lens Papers, CHM.

69. South Center Unity, November 24, 1948, box 54, folder 11, Sidney Lens Papers, CHM.

70. Sidney Lens, correspondence to "Sandy," November 15, 1948, USEU Records, UIC Special Collections.

In 1949, union members expressed their dissatisfaction to the arbitration board. They protested the classification of six employees as supervisors even though their major duties were selling in departments with "only a total of four to seven employees," arguing that management purposefully misclassified these employees in an attempt to exclude them from the union and contractual benefits. The union requested that the arbitration board rule that these men were in the contractual union and should receive the wage increases and other benefits associated with their position. Further, the union asked that, should the board conclude that the six men were not in the contractual union, these supervisors be prohibited from selling because in doing so they deprived union members of commissions. The board concluded that the classification of these men as supervisors was "obviously an attempt to reduce the strength of the Union, weakening its bargaining power, divide the workforce, and avoid obligations provided for in the contract. These men are . . . ordinary salesmen. Classification of them as 'outside the unit' has caused ceaseless strife and discontent among the employees and should now be corrected." South Center employees also victoriously secured a five-and-a-half-day workweek and forced management to stop its "scandalous" approaches—forcing employees to submit to lie detector tests, "sternly" talking to workers, and retaining a "high-class personnel consultant" who "spoke down to the workers" and "made everyone feel that they were thieves"—to tackle the problem of inventory shortages. See Issue before the Arbitration Board, December 19, 1949, USEU Records, UIC Special Collections; Sidney Lens, correspondence to Robert Mackie, November 26, 1949, USEU Records, UIC Special Collections; and South Center Unity, January 24, 1949, and April 15, 1949, box 54, folder 11, Sidney Lens Papers, CHM.

71. Sidney Lens, press release, December 13, 1948, USEU Records, UIC Special Collections.

72. Local 329, Negotiating Committee for South Center Department Store Members, "A 1-way 'L' Ride and a Penny's Worth of Peanuts: An Appeal to the Public by Members of Local 329, AFL, Employed at the South Center Dept. Store," *Chicago Enquirer*, March 4, 1950.

73. South Center Unity, February 23, 1950, box 54, folder 11, Sidney Lens Papers, CHM.

74. Local 329, AFL, "An Open Letter," March 4, 1950, USEU Records, UIC Special Collections.

75. Agreement made between the USEU and South Center Department Store, April 27, 1950, box 18, folder 223, USEU Records, UIC.

76. Frank Socki Jr. to William McFetridge, March 20, 1950, box 18, folder 223, USEU Records, UIC.

77. Agreement made between the USEU and South Center Department Store, April 27, 1950, box 18, folder 223, USEU Records, UIC.

78. Frank Socki Jr. to William McFetridge, March 20, 1950, box 18, folder 223, USEU Records, UIC.

79. South Center Unity, March 6, 1951, USEU Records, UIC Special Collections.

80. South Center Unity, March 27, 1951, USEU Records, UIC Special Collections.

81. Sidney Lens, correspondence to William McFetridge, April 10, 1951, USEU Records, UIC Special Collections.

82. South Center Unity, February 1952, box 54, folder 12, Sidney Lens Papers, CHM.

83. South Center Unity, April 18, 1952, box 19, folder 228, USEU Records, UIC Special Collections.

84. Sidney Lens, statement, 1952, box 19, folder 226, USEU Records, UIC Special Collections.

85. Lens, statement, 1952.

86. Mediation between the two parties commenced on May 1. Englestein was the first to give his position: "He stated that the selling costs were too high and then gave a bill of particular for 40 minutes as to why the company wanted Mosley discharged," detailing her responsibility for the female accessories department boycott, as well as her involvement in a strike of South Center employees in 1941, an arbitration case during the 1950 Christmas season, and "a picket line of grocery workers for employees by a concessionaire a few years back." Again, it was reiterated that if the union agreed to Mosley's dismissal and "one or two other minor concessions," the company would provide all workers with a pay increase of fifty cents per week. Management made its final offer at the next mediation meeting. It stated that it would provide a raise of two dollars per week and a one-year contract,

or a two-dollar raise now, fifty-cent raise again in six months, cost-of-living increases at the end of twelve and eighteen months, and a two-year contract to expire on April 15, 1954, but again only if workers agreed to dismiss Mosley. Once again, workers declined management's offer. Sidney Lens, statement, 1952, box 19, folder 226, USEU Records, UIC Special Collections.

87. South Center Strike Bulletin, May 16, 1952, and June 3, 1952, USEU Records, UIC Special Collections.

88. Wife of an Employee (Anonymous), correspondence to Mr. Mosley, May 13, 1952, USEU Records, UIC Special Collections.

89. "Store Clerks Ask $30, Owners Threaten to Sell," *Chicago Defender*, April 5, 1947.

90. "We'll Buy Closed Store: Striker," *Afro-American*, May 16, 1952, box 54, folder 12, Sidney Lens Records, CHM.

91. Sidney Lens, correspondence to E. Maslanka, National Labor Relations Board, October 14, 1952, USEU Records, UIC Special Collections.

92. Sidney Lens, correspondence to Harry Englestein, May 28, 1952, USEU Records, UIC Special Collections.

93. State of Illinois, Division of Unemployment Compensation, Determination, June 1952, USEU Records, UIC Special Collections.

94. "Two Buy Store Closed in Union Wage Dispute," *Chicago Daily Tribune*, June 26, 1952; "Strike—Closed, Store to Open, Raise Won," *Herald American*, June 25, 1952.

95. "Sales Up 5 Pct. for S. Side Store," *Chicago Daily News*, July 24, 1952.

96. "Business," *Jet Magazine*, June 27, 1963.

97. "Fuller, S. B.," in Kranz, *African-American Business Leaders and Entrepreneurs*, 97–99.

98. See Pitrone, *F. W. Woolworth and the American Five and Dime*.

Chapter Four

1. Richard Dier, "N.Y. Service Men Told Chances of Getting a Job after War Not Bad," *Afro-American*, August 4, 1945.

2. Sugrue, *Sweet Land of Liberty*, 92.

3. "Whites Replace Negro Elevator Girls in Memphis," *Chicago Defender* (National Edition), August 19, 1944; and T. H. Runnel, "Negro Elevator Operators Fired," *Chicago Defender* (National Edition), November 25, 1944.

4. "Oppose Use of 'Pressure' to Gain Equality for Minorities," December 3, 1945, box 260, folder 1, Claude Barnett Papers, CHM; and "Stores By-Pass N.Y. Job Session," *Afro-American*, December 8, 1945.

5. *TBI Talks*, November 1945 and January 1946, VHS, Richmond, VA.

6. Susannah Walker, "Black Dollar Power: Assessing American Consumerism since 1945," in Kusmer and Trotter, *African American Urban History since World War II*, 376.

7. Cohen, *Consumers' Republic*, 129.

8. Cooper, "The Limits of Persuasion," 108.

9. Charles R. Perry, "The Negro in the Department Store Industry," in Bloom, Fletcher, and Perry, *Negro Employment in Retail Trade*, 31–32.

10. The American Jewish Congress's Commission on Community Interrelations, a community-based research organization, sponsored both studies. For more on the commission, see Jackson, *Social Scientists for Social Justice*; and Cherry and Borshuk, "Social Action Research and the Commission on Community Interrelations."

11. Saenger and Gilbert, "Customer Reactions to the Integration of Negro Sales Personnel." See also Saenger, "How Can We Fight Discrimination?"

12. Harding and Hogrefe, "Attitudes of White Department Store Employees toward Negro Co-Workers."

13. Dier, "N.Y. Service Men."

14. Cooper, "The Limits of Persuasion," 108.

15. Reed, *Not Alms but Opportunity*, 5–6.

16. Reed, 161.

17. Reed, 161.

18. NYUL Report, 1944, NUL Papers, Series 13, Box 19, quoted in Reed, *Not Alms but Opportunity*, 157.

19. National Urban League, "Integration of Negroes in Department Stores: Practical Approaches for the Integration of Negroes in Department Store Personnel," n.d., GUL Records, UIC. Note: Specifically, the NUL learned that in 1939 an estimated 750 workers were employed in each of the country's department stores and collectively sold approximately $7 billion in merchandise.

20. National Urban League, "Integration of Negroes in Department Stores."

21. Reed, *Not Alms but Opportunity*, 163. NUL branches in Cleveland, Minneapolis, and St. Paul also worked with antidiscrimination commissions to advance black employment.

22. K. Leroy Irvis, "Summary Report on the Campaign to Secure a Non-Discriminatory Hiring Policy in the Major Pittsburgh Department Stores," n.d., GUL Records, UIC Archives.

23. Irvis.

24. Irvis.

25. K. Leroy Irvis and Louis Mason Jr. (for the Committee on Fair Employment in Pittsburgh Department Stores), "Supplement to the Summary Report on the Campaign to Secure a Non Discriminatory Hiring Policy in Major Department Stores," December 1947, GUL Records, UIC Archives.

26. Urban League of Pittsburgh, "Inside the Facts for the Urban League Family," March 25, 1947, GUL Records, UIC Archives.

27. By 1952 the Race Relations Committee was renamed the Community Relations Community, signifying the AFSC's move away from education as the primary path to racial equality and toward an acceptance of "a wider scope of activism and an expanded understanding of 'race' and its complex interaction with other social issues." See Austin, *Quaker Brotherhood*, 144, 145.

28. Frank Loescher, "The Placement Service of the American Friends Service Committee: A Technique in Race Relations," *Occupations, the Vocational Guidance Magazine*, November 1946, AFSC Archives.

29. "Pamphlet Fights Bias in Stores," *New York Amsterdam News*, January 18, 1947.

30. Cooper, "The Limits of Persuasion," 106, 109.

31. Cooper, 111–12.

32. "Fair Employment in Philadelphia," box Social Industrial Section 1946, Race Relations Dept. (Placement Service) to Work Camps (Holly Ridge Conn.), folder Social Industrial Section, Race Relations Dept., Placement Service, General, 1946, AFSC Archives.

33. "Fair Employment in Philadelphia."

34. Department Store Interview with Wanamaker's Personnel Manager, Committee on Fair Employment Practices in Department Stores, January 24, 1946, box Social Industrial Section 1946, Race Relations Dept. (Placement Service) to Work Camps (Holly Ridge, Conn.), folder Social Industrial Section Race Relations Dept. Placement Service, Reports—Visit to Businesses, AFSC Archives.

35. Memorandum, Subject: Howard Cooper Johnson Telephone Conversation re Fair Employment in Department Stores, May 3, 1946, box Social Industrial Section 1946, Race Relations Department (Placement Service) to Work Camps (Holly Ridge, Conn.), folder Social Industrial Section, Race Relations Department, Placement Service, Correspondence, 1946, AFSC Archives.

36. Memorandum, Subject: Howard Cooper Johnson Telephone Conversation re Fair Employment in Department Stores, May 3, 1946. In referring to New York, Loescher may have been reminding Johnson of the highly publicized protest of Blumstein's Department Store in Harlem in 1934.

37. "Fair Employment in Philadelphia," box Social Industrial Section 1946, Race Relations Dept. (Placement Service) to Work Camps (Holly Ridge, Conn.), folder Social Industrial Section, Race Relations Dept., Placement Service, General, 1946, AFSC Archives.

38. Blauner's, Interview with Personnel Office, October 15, 1946, box Social Industrial Section 1946, Race Relations Depart. (Placement Service) to Work Camps (Holly Ridge, Conn.), folder Social Industrial Section Race Relations Dept. Place Service, Reports: Visit to Businesses, AFSC Archives.

39. Correspondence from Frank S. Loescher to Clarence Pickett, October 9, 1946; and correspondence from Clarence Pickett to Arthur O. Kaufmann (Gimbel Brothers), October 18, 1946, AFSC Archives.

40. "Fair? Employment in Philadelphia: A Report by the Committee on Fair Employment Practices in Department Stores," folder Social Industrial Section, Race Relations, Department Stores—Correspondence, 1947, box Social Industrial Section 1947, Race Relations Dept. (Placement Service—Department Stores) to Work Camps (Delmo Homes, Missouri), AFSC Archives.

41. "Fair? Employment in Philadelphia: A Report by the Committee on Fair Employment Practices in Department Stores."

42. Minutes, Committee on Fair Employment Practices in Department Stores, November 15, 1947, folder Social Industrial Section Race Relations Dept., Placement Services, Department Stores, Minutes 1947, box Social Industrial Section 1947, Race Relations Dept. (Placement Service—Dept. Stores) to Work Camp (Delmo

Homes, Missouri), AFSC Archives; Proposed Plan of Action of Committee on Fair Employment in Department Stores: November 25 to December 25, n.d., folder Social Industrial Section Race Relations Dept., Placement Services, Department Stores, Minutes 1947, box Social Industrial Section 1947, Race Relations Dept. (Placement Service—Dept. Stores) to Work Camp (Delmo Homes, Missouri), AFSC Archives.

43. Cooper, "The Limits of Persuasion," 121–23.

44. Department Store Committee, September 30, 1948, folder Reports 1948, box Social Industrial Section 1948, Race Relations Dept. (Placement Service, Forms and Form Letters) to Youth Projects (Institutional Service Units), AFSC Archives; Meeting Minutes, April 15, 1948, Box: AFSC Minutes 1948 Social Industrial Section to 1949 American Section (Executive Committee), Folder: AFSC Minutes, Race Relations, Committee on, 1948, AFSC Archives.

45. Julia A. Mayo, "A Narrative of Progress in Community Organizations: Report of the Philadelphia Applicant Preparation Workshop," May 1949, Bryn Mawr College, Bryn Mawr, PA, box: American Section 1949, Community Division, International Relations, Regional Offices, Peace Ed Portland to Race Relations, Job Opportunity, Applicant Workshops Philadelphia Applicants, folder: Prep Workshop, Philadelphia Reports 1949, AFSC Archives.

46. Wolfinger, *Philadelphia Divided*, 209.

47. In contrast, blue-collar workers, particularly those employed in occupations that required intense cooperation and contact, such as merchant seamen, accepted African Americans in the workplace and other social situations. Harding and Hogrefe, "Attitudes of White Department Store Employees toward Negro Co-Workers," 18–28.

48. Benson, *Counter Cultures*, 240.

49. Harry W. Ernst, "Quaker, Negroes, and Jobs," n.d., AFSC Archives.

50. C. Virgil Martin, interview by Cyrus H. Adams III, 1969, box 9, folder: C. Virgil Martin, Carson Pirie Scott Records, CHM.

51. Thomas Colgan, Report on Selection of Pilot Placement for Carson Pirie Scott, June 23, 1950, folder: Race Relations, Job Opportunities—Chicago, Visits to and Meetings with Business and Community Leaders, box: American Section 1950, Race Relations (Job Opportunities Program to Visiting Lectureship), AFSC Archives.

52. Martin, interview.

53. Martin Weil, "Charles S. Stone, Jr., Journalist and Professor Dies at 89," *Washington Post*, April 6, 2014.

54. "Report of the Industrial Department," September 1950, Chicago Urban League Records (hereafter cited as CUL Records), UIC.

55. Martin, interview.

56. Carson's integration process followed the recommendations of the social scientists Saenger and Gilbert. First, they suggested that the integration of sales and clerical workers transpire without public announcement or discussion. The public was confronted with a fait accompli. Second, because "the prejudiced customer often generalizes from the first Negro clerk he encounters," Saenger and Gilbert proposed that the first group of hired African Americans should be

overqualified in education, impeccable in their manners, and physically indistinguishable from whites to safeguard that prejudiced white customers have a good first impression of black sales and clerical workers. Third, they advised gradualism: African Americans should be assigned to low-sales, low-traffic, and nonintimate departments, such as the umbrella department, glove department, or any department located in store basements, until whites had grown accustomed to being waited on by African Americans and working with them in positions of responsibility. And finally, they stated, once successful, integration schemes should be widely publicized as safe, profitable, and well received. "Well received," thus, meant that black clerks, who were covertly hired and displayed, went virtually unnoticed and accepted with little to no criticism or protest. Saenger, "How Can We Fight Discrimination?" 547–48; and Saenger and Gilbert, "Customer Reaction to the Integration of Negro Sales Personnel."

57. Martin, interview.

58. Thomas Colgan, Visit with Pirie Carson, Vice President, Carson Pirie Scott & Company, October 20, 1950, folder: Race Relations, Job Opportunities—Chicago, Visits to and Meetings with Business and Community Leaders, box: American Section 1950, Race Relations Dept. (Job Opportunities Program to Visiting Lectureship), AFSC Archives.

59. Thomas Colgan, "Round Table Discussion of Negro Employees from Carson's," November 1, 1950, folder: Race Relations, Job Opportunities—Chicago, Visits to and Meetings with Business and Community Leaders, box: American Section 1950, Race Relations Dept. (Job Opportunities Program to Visiting Lectureship), AFSC Archives.

60. Colgan, "Round Table Discussion of Negro Employees from Carson's."

61. Thomas Colgan, "Round Table Discussion, Department Managers, Carson Pirie Scott & Co.," November 3, 1950, folder: Race Relations, Job Opportunities—Chicago, Visits to and Meetings with Business and Community Leaders, box: American Section 1950, Race Relations Dept. (Job Opportunities Program to Visiting Lectureship), AFSC Archives.

62. Colgan, "Round Table Discussion, Department Managers, Carson Pirie Scott & Co."

63. Thomas Colgan, "Round Table Discussion," Carson Pirie Scott & Co., November 21, 1950, folder: Race Relations, Job Opportunities—Chicago, Visits to and Meetings with Business and Community Leaders, box: American Section 1950, Race Relations Dept. (Job Opportunities Program to Visiting Lectureship), AFSC Archives.

64. Report of the Division Fund, folder: Job Opportunities Program—Report to the Division Fund, Chicago R.O. 1951, box: AFSC Chicago Regional Office 1951–1952, AFSC Archives.

65. Correspondence to Louis Pemberton, April 2, 1951, box 166, folder 1699, CUL Records, UIC; Report of Industrial Department, January–December 1952, box 167, folder 1713, CUL Records, UIC; and correspondence to Charles Stone, September 18, 1952, box 166, folder 1702, CUL Records, UIC.

66. Thomas Colgan, Carson Pirie Scott Training Conference, January 29, 1951, folder: Job Opportunities—Chicago Branch, Workshops and Conferences, 1951,

box: AFSC Chicago Regional Office 1951–1952, AFSC Archives; Ernst, "Quaker, Negroes, and Jobs."

67. Ernst, "Quaker, Negroes, and Jobs"; John Yoshino, Carson Pirie Scott & Co., Joan Chapman, Administrative Assistant in Personnel Department, October 17, 1955, folder: Job Opportunities Program, Visits to Firms (Stores) 1955, box: AFSC Chicago Regional Office 1954–1955, AFSC Archives; Ivis Nashir, Carson Pirie Scott & Co., Joan Chapman, Staff Assistant to Head of Personnel, October 27, 1955, folder: Job Opportunities Program, Visits to Firms (Stores) 1955, box: AFSC Chicago Regional Office 1954–1955, AFSC Archives; John Yoshino, Carson Pirie Scott & Co., Joan Chapman, Personnel Department, April 12, 1955, folder: Job Opportunities Program, Visits to Firms (Stores) 1955, box: AFSC Chicago Regional Office 1954–1955, AFSC Archives.

68. Ernst, "Quaker, Negroes, and Jobs."

69. Robert S. Browne, correspondence to Julius A. Thomas, Director of the Department of Industrial Relations, National Urban League, March 3, 1952, box 166, folder 1701, CUL Records, UIC.

70. Thomas Colgan, correspondence to W. J. (Bill) Moulder, Fellowship House of Knoxville (TN), October 17, 1952, folder: Job Opportunities—Out of State Visits and Correspondence 1952, box: AFSC Chicago Regional Office 1951–1952, AFSC Archives.

71. Colgan, correspondence to Moulder, October 17, 1952.

72. H. J. Nutting, Minority Groups, February 16, 1951, box 18008, folder 2, Marshall Field and Company Archives, CHM.

73. Richard S. Dowdy Jr., correspondence to Fred Chusid, Employment Representative, Commission on Human Relations, April 8, 1953, box 18008, folder 2, Marshall Field and Company Archives, CHM.

74. Dowdy, correspondence to Chusid, March 23, 1953, box 18008, folder 2, Marshall Field and Company Archives, CHM.

75. Commission on Human Relations, Investigation Report, April 29, 1953, box 18008, folder 2, Marshall Field and Company Archives, CHM.

76. Yvonne Priest, JOP in Chicago, Employer Contacts, November 1953, folder: Job Opportunities—Chicago, Contacts with Commercial firms, industrial firms, insurance, etc. 1953, box: AFSC Chicago Regional Office 1953, AFSC Archives; Areas of Concentration from May 1952 to June 1953, folder: Job Opportunities—Chicago, General Reports on JOP Program 1953, box: AFSC Chicago Regional Office 1953, AFSC Archives.

77. Present Status of Negro Employes, July 23, 1954, box 18008, folder 2, Marshall Field and Company Archives, CHM.

78. Present Status of Negro Employes, November 14, 1955, box 18008, folder 2, Marshall Field and Company Archives, CHM.

79. Annual Report of Negro Employes, January 23, 1961, box 18008, folder 2, Marshall Field and Company Archives, CHM.

80. John Yoshino, Marshall Field and Company, Lloyd Richman, May 18, 1955, folder: Job Opportunities Program, Visits to Firms (Stores) 1955, box: AFSC Chicago Regional Office 1954–1955, AFSC Archives; John Yoshino, City Club, 19 South

LaSalle Street, Speaker Edwin C. Berry, "The Revitalized Program of the Urban League," July 3, 1956 (dictated on April 30, 1956), folder: Job Opportunities—Chicago, Contacts with Committees, Commissions, Clubs, etc. 1956, box: AFSC Chicago Regional Office 1956, AFSC Archives.

81. Employe Statistics, October 27, 1969, box 18018, folder 18-0-0-5-4, Marshall Field and Company Archives, CHM.

82. Nancy Finke, correspondence to George A. Sivage, President of Marshall Field and Company, December 14, 1968, box 18008, folder 2, Marshall Field and Company Archives, CHM.

83. Ad Hoc Committee for Consumers Who Care, correspondence to George A. Sivage, President of Marshall Field and Company, December 16, 1969, box 18008, folder 2, Marshall Field and Company Archives, CHM; Mrs. Chester A. Higgins, correspondence to George A. Sivage, November 27, 1969, box 18008, folder 2, Marshall Field and Company Archives, CHM; George A. Sivage, correspondence to Mrs. Chester A. Higgins, December 3, 1969, box 18008, folder 2, Marshall Field and Company Archives, CHM; Mrs. Chester A. Higgins, correspondence to George A. Sivage, December 7, 1969, box 18008, folder 2, Marshall Field and Company Archives, CHM; George A. Sivage, correspondence to Mrs. Chester A. Higgins, December 9, 1969, box 18008, folder 2, Marshall Field and Company Archives, CHM.

84. Sugrue, *Sweet Land of Liberty*, 133.

85. These states were California, Colorado, Connecticut, Illinois, Indiana, Iowa, Kansas, Massachusetts, Michigan, Minnesota, Nebraska, New Jersey, New York, Ohio, Pennsylvania, Rhode Island, Washington, and Wisconsin.

86. These fourteen states were California, Colorado, Connecticut, Indiana, Kansas, Massachusetts, Michigan, Minnesota, New Jersey, New York, Ohio, Pennsylvania, Washington, and Wisconsin. Murray, *States' Laws on Race and Color*, 8.

87. Cohen, *Consumers' Republic*, 185.

88. "KY Legislature Kills Bill Forbidding J.C. in Department Stores," *Baltimore Afro-American*, March 16, 1946.

89. "Negro Rights Bills Introduced in KY," *New York Amsterdam News*, February 14, 1948. See also "KY Solon Introduces 4 Bills on Race Rights," *Los Angeles Sentinel*, February 19, 1948.

90. Hardin, *Fifty Years of Segregation*, 87.

91. Gregory and Lipsyte, *Nigger: An Autobiography*, 49.

92. Gregory and Lipsyte, 49.

93. "AFRO Protest Brings Removal of Obnoxious Child's Book," *Baltimore Afro-American*, January 10, 1948. Other instances include boycotting the American Tobacco Company "for its marketing of 'Nigger Hair tobacco,'" "the Whitman Candy Company for its 'Pickaninny Chocolate' product line," and Shell Oil Company for an advertisement that featured an African American gorging on watermelon in the 1940s. These demonstrations, and others like them, forced major corporations to publicly apologize to black consumers and remove offensive advertisements and products. See Weems, *Desegregating the Dollar*, 60.

94. Sugrue, *Sweet Land of Liberty*, 137.

95. Julia Sandy-Bailey, "The Consumers' Protection Committee: Women's Activism in Postwar Harlem," in Laughlin and Castledine, *Breaking the Wave*, 117.

96. "Shoppers Hit 'Disservices' of W. 125th," *New York Amsterdam News*, November 1, 1947.

97. Earl Brown, "Declares Gouging Stores 'OK'd' by Honest Merchants," *New York Amsterdam News*, December 20, 1947.

98. Earl Brown, "Exposes Gouging Silent Partners," *New York Amsterdam News*, January 10, 1948; and Brown, "Grants Prepared to Meet War Demands," *New York Amsterdam News*, October 16, 1943.

99. Sugrue, *Sweet Land of Liberty*, 142.

100. Tóibín, *Brooklyn*, 115, 117.

Chapter Five

1. The "Lost Law" of 1872 explicitly stated that "any restaurant keeper or proprietor, any hotel keeper or proprietor, or proprietors or keepers of ice-cream saloons or places where soda-water is kept for sale, or keepers of barber shops and bathing houses, refusing to sell or wait upon any respectable, well-behaved persons, without regard to race, color, or previous condition of servitude, or any restaurant, hotel, ice-cream saloon or soda fountain, barber shop, or bathing-house keepers, or proprietors, who refused under any pretext to serve any well-behaved, respectable person, in the same room, and at the same prices as other well-behaved and respectable persons are served, shall be deemed guilty of a misdemeanor, and upon conviction in a court having jurisdiction, shall be fined one hundred dollars, and shall forfeit his or her license as keep or owner or a restaurant, hotel, ice-cream saloon, or soda fountain, as the case may be, and it shall not be lawful for the Assessor [Register] or any officer of the District of Columbia to issue a license to any person or persons, or to their agent or agents, who shall have forfeited their license under the provisions of this act, until a period of year shall have elapsed after such forfeiture." Because of the law's description of person(s), activists intentionally positioned persons who fit the definitions of respectable and well behaved on the movement's front lines. William Stone Albert and Benjamin G. Lovejoy, *The Compiled Statutes in Force in the District of Columbia: Including the acts of the second session of the Fiftieth Congress, 1887–89*, 183.

2. In the spring of 1943, Pauli Murray led Howard University students in a sit-in movement against Thompson Restaurant in Washington, D.C.

3. A sit-in was a central tactic of the movement to integrate public accommodations in the South. It was borrowed from the labor movement, where it was used successfully to improve work conditions in the automobile and steel industries. Similarly, at lunch counters, protesters occupied seats on the principle "sit until served." In 1960, sit-in movements succeeded in opening lunch counters at department stores, including Davison-Paxon in Atlanta, Hochschild-Kohn in Baltimore, Thalhimers and Miller & Rhoads in Richmond, Burdine's in Memphis, Gus Blass and Pfeiffer's in Little Rock, and Goldsmith's in Memphis. See Whitaker, *Service and Style*, 231; and Green, *The Secret City*, 298.

4. Korstad and Lichtenstein, "Opportunities Found and Lost," 811.

5. Glickman, *Buying Power*, 264.

6. See Cohen, *Consumer's Republic*.

7. Susannah Walker, "Black Dollar Power: Assessing African American Consumerism since 1945," in Kusmer and Trotter, *African American Urban History since World War II*. See also Weems, *Desegregating the Dollar*.

8. In 1960, the ten largest American cities (in order of population size, from largest to smallest) were New York, Chicago, Los Angeles, Philadelphia, Detroit, Baltimore, Houston, Cleveland, Washington, D.C., and St. Louis. Sternlieb, "Future of Retailing in the Downtown Core," 103.

9. Dawson, *Behind the Mule*, 77.

10. In 1950, 24,437 southern black women labored as waitresses compared with 6,560 in the Northeast, 8,958 in North Central, and 2,184 in the West. Similarly, in 1960, 30,532 African American waitresses were employed in the South, while 9,589 labored in the Northeast, 10,919 in North Central, and 3,083 in the West. Cobble, *Dishing It Out*, 24, 210.

11. In addition to the race segregation, some southern department stores had gender-segregated facilities. For example, as late as 1970 in Richmond, despite the ratification of the Civil Rights Act of 1964, Thalhimers's Men's Soup Bar remained closed to women and Miller & Rhoads's tearoom had "a corner for men only and women had to wait in line for a seat." These facilities were finally integrated after the Richmond Chapter of the National Organization for Women challenged the legality of these spaces. See Ellen Robertson, "Mary Holt Woolfolk Carlton, a Social Worker Who Advocated for Women's Issues, Dies at 98," *Times Dispatch*, July 25, 2013.

12. As I discussed in earlier chapters, modern refers to class identities produced by consumer capitalism rather than industrial capitalism.

13. Cohen, *Consumer's Republic*, 383.

14. Longstreth, "The Mixed Blessings of Success."

15. Mary K. Zajac, "Final Sale," *Baltimore Style Magazine*, May/June 2006.

16. "Man to Man" Advertisement, *Washington Post*, February 19, 1951.

17. District of Columbia Statutes and Codes, 1890, quoted in Jones, "Before Montgomery and Greensboro."

18. Annie Stein to Mrs. Walker Smith, November 24, 1951, Coordinating Committee for the Enforcement of the D.C. Anti-Discrimination Laws (hereafter cited as CCEAD) Records (MS 404), Historical Society of Washington, D.C. (hereafter cited as HSW).

19. Caplan, *Farther Along*, 119; Meeting Minutes, March 13, 1951, CCEAD Records (MS 404), HSW.

20. "Citizens Continue Protest against Color Bar in Washington Restaurants," *Afro-American*, March 17, 1951.

21. Meeting Minutes, April 18, 1951, CCEAD Records (MS 404), HSW.

22. Stein to Cynthia Anderson, July 12, 1951, CCEAD Records (MS 404), HSW.

23. CCEAD Press Release, January 19, 1952, CCEAD Records (MS 404), HSW.

24. Jones, *Labor of Love, Labor of Sorrow*, 224–25.

25. Caplan, *Farther Along*, 109, 119.

26. Alice Trigg to Stein, n.d., CCEAD Records (MS 404), HSW.

27. Jones, "Before Montgomery and Greensboro," 150.

28. Schalk, "Negroes, Restaurants, and Washington, D.C."

29. Quoted in Jones, "Before Montgomery and Greensboro," 151.

30. Progress Report, July 1951. Protesters were so adamant about keeping African Americans from shopping at Hecht's that on one occasion when an African American woman and her child were entering the store, Alice Trigg "acidly" said to her, "You have no race pride." A few moments later, the woman came out of the store and said to Alice, "I wasn't buying anything I was ducking someone." Trigg to Stein, [Friday; n.d.], CCEAD Records (MS 404), HSW.

31. Trigg to Stein, [Friday; n.d.], CCEAD Records (MS 404), HSW.

32. For more on Howard students in the 1930s, see Holloway, *Confronting the Veil*.

33. Stein to Armour J. Blackburn, Dean of Student Activities at Howard University, n.d., CCEAD Records (MS 404), HSW.

34. Trigg to Stein, n.d., CCEAD Records (MS 404), HSW; "Hecht's Picket Line Stepped Up," *Afro-American*, September 1, 1951.

35. Caplan, *Farther Along*, 121.

36. Fradin and Fradin, *Fight On!*, 148.

37. Between 1940 and 1950, Washington, D.C.'s African American population increased from 187,266 to 280,803. By 1960, the city's black community had expanded to 411,737. It would continue to grow until 1980. D.C.'s white population experienced a different trajectory: between 1940 and 1950, it increased from 474,326 to 517,865; but thereafter, it sharply declined, as whites relocated to suburban counties in Maryland and Virginia. Gibson and Jung, "Historical Census Statistics on Population Totals by Race."

38. Caplan, *Farther Along*, 121; Alice A. Dunnigan, "Bias Ends Quietly at D.C. Department Store," *Atlanta Daily World*, February 1, 1952.

39. Schalk, "Negroes, Restaurants, and Washington, D.C."

40. "Hecht Store Fires Two Who Talked to 'Strikers,'" *Afro-American*, July 7, 1951; Stein to Mr. G.B. Pettengill, Department of State, July 14, 1951, CCEAD Records (MS 404), HSW.

41. Stein to Mr. G.B. Pettengill, July 14, 1951; Stein to Mme. Vijaya Lakshmi Pandit, Ambassador of India to the United States, July 25, 1951, CCEAD Records (MS 404), HSW.

42. Green, *Secret City*, 314–15.

43. "Negro Boycott Set for Capital Stores," *New York Times*, March 17, 1958.

44. "Drive Aims to Increase Negro Jobs," *Washington Post and Times Herald*, March 7, 1958.

45. Robert G. Spivack, "Watch on the Potomac," *Chicago Daily Defender*, April 1, 1958; "Negro Clergy Urge 1-Day Buying Ban," *Washington Post and Times Herald*, March 24, 1958.

46. Paul Sampson, "Shopping Ban Aired at Meeting," *Washington Post and Times Herald*, March 20, 1958.

47. "Shopping Ban Sponsors Firm," *Washington Post and Times Herald*, March 22, 1958.

48. "Negroes in Boycott of 5 Capital Stores," *New York Times*, March 28, 1958.

49. Lester Tanzer, "Negroes Boycott 5 Big Washington Stores for Day; Sales Job Goal May Have Receded," *Wall Street Journal*, March 28, 1952.

50. "Pastor Predicts Negro Clerks," *Washington Post and Times Herald*, March 29, 1958.

51. Lester Tanzer, "Negroes Boycott 5 Big Washington Stores for Day; Sales Job Goal May Have Receded," *Wall Street Journal*, March 28, 1952.

52. Edward Peeks, "Buy Where You Can Work," *Afro-American*, January 13, 1962; Edward Peeks, "Clerics with CORE in Store Boycott," *Afro-American*, February 3, 1962.

53. Solomon, *Washington Century*, 124.

54. Edward Peeks, "Group Demands Charge," *Afro-American*, May 13, 1961; Solomon, *Washington Century*, 124.

55. "CORE Pickets Hecht's in Dispute," *Washington Post and Times Herald*, February 23, 1964.

56. "CORE, Hecht's Reach Accord," *Washington Post, Times Herald*, March 8, 1964.

57. In 1950 the total number of nonwhite sales workers in the retail industry in Washington, D.C., was 1,314; in 1960, the number increased to 1,914; and by 1970, the number was 4,027. U.S. Bureau of the Census, *Census of Population, 1950*; U.S. Bureau of the Census, *Census of Population, 1960*; U.S. Bureau of the Census, *Census of Population, 1970*.

58. Doretha Davis, oral history interview, May 19, 2008, interview U-0359, Southern Oral History Program Collection, Southern Historical Collection Manuscript Department, Wilson Library, University of North Carolina at Chapel Hill. See also Roy Covington, "Negroes' Protests Close Local Diners," *Charlotte Observer*, February 10, 1960; "Special Report on Sitdowns, NAACP Staff Activity in the Sitdowns," Branch Department File, Pamphlets, and Manuals, 1959–1962, 1969, and undated, National Association for the Advancement of Colored People Papers, Microfilm Part 29 1966–1972, Series B, Reel 14, LOC.

59. Davidson M. Douglas, "The Quest for Freedom in the Post-*Brown* South: Desegregation and White Self-Interest," in Delgado and Stefancic, *Critical White Studies*, 120.

60. For much of its existence, W. T. Grant strived to be and fulfilled the definition of a department store. It sold "low-priced, basic merchandise such as soft goods, draperies, and small wares" and, by the 1960s, carried furniture and appliances. However, some stores resembled "variety stores" and "discount stores," while "others were perceived as junior department stores." Michman and Greco, *Retailing Triumphs and Blunders*, 63–64.

61. W. T. Grant Company maintained two lunch counters: one for whites and one for African Americans. These lunch counters differed in waitstaff, offerings, and location. The white lunch counter was serviced by an all-white waitstaff,

served a delectable variety of foods, and was located on the store's upper level. Also, the cooks were situated behind the lunch counter, which ensured that the store's white patrons were always served a hot meal. The black lunch counter, on the other hand, was serviced by an all-black waitstaff, served a limited array of foods (e.g., hot dogs, hamburgers, French fries, and salad), and was located on the lower level of W. T. Grant. African American patrons often complained about the counter's limited menu. According to Davis, "They would come down there and say, 'Why can't I have a vegetable and a meat?' . . . We didn't have it because we weren't set up for hot food like that. We had a cook, two cooks, but that was all upstairs." Davis, interview.

62. Charlotte's white and black populations grew steadily in the postwar era. Between 1940 and 1950, this southern city's total population increased by 32.8 percent; and between 1950 and 1960, it increased once again by 50.4 percent. Blacks and whites in Charlotte occupied separate existences. They resided in separate neighborhoods, worked in separate fields, attended separate schools and churches, and frequented separate public accommodations and amusements. U.S. Bureau of the Census, *U.S. Census of Population: 1950, Vol. II, Characteristics of the Population, Part 33, North Carolina* (Washington, D.C.: U.S. Government Printing Office, 1952); and U.S. Bureau of the Census, *U.S. Census of Population: 1960, Vol. I, Characteristics of the Population, Part 35, North Carolina* (Washington, D.C.: U.S. Government Printing Office, 1963).

63. Only a few accommodations remained segregated: the city's only junior college, city-owned swimming pools, restaurants, and theaters (in fact, African Americans were barred entirely from theaters).

64. Since the 1940s, black Charlotteans have demonstrated against race discrimination only a handful of times. Douglas specifies, "In the 1940s, a group of black protesters, led by a reporter from the *Pittsburgh Courier*, picketed the Charlotte Post Office to challenge the postal service's discriminatory employment practices. Similarly in 1953, several black men sat down at the Dogwood Room at the Charlotte airport and demanded service; as a result, the restaurant began operating on a nondiscriminatory basis." Douglas, "Quest for Freedom in the Post-*Brown* South," 120.

65. Oppenheimer, *Sit-In Movement of 1960*, 118.

66. Roy Covington, "Students Seek Aid of Negro Adults," *Charlotte Observer*, March 14, 1960.

67. Douglas, "Quest for Freedom in the Post-*Brown* South," 120. Robert Matthews, "And the Voice of the Students Shall Be Heard through the Land," *Baltimore Afro-American*, May 14, 1960.

68. Roy Covington, "Negroes Continue Protest at Diners," *Charlotte Observer*, February 10, 1960.

69. "Negroes Expect Integrated Cafeteria," *Charlotte Observer*, March 8, 1960; Dena Shenk, "Views of Aging African American Women: Memories within the Historical Context," *Journal of Aging and Identity* 5, no. 2 (2000): 109–25.

70. Oppenheimer, *Sit-In Movement of 1960*, 120.

71. The historian Susan Porter Benson argues that for white workers, department store counters were social barriers and the foundation for worker solidarity. As a social barrier, the counter delineated a space for saleswomen to comfortably work and customers to shop. But more than this, counters separated the social classes: "On the selling side [were] women of the working classes; middle class women with a choice shunned the low status and difficult conditions of store work. On the buying side were women of the middle and upper classes." Counters also served as the basis for working-class consciousness. Benson notes that saleswomen huddled and congregated behind the counter. Here they shared stock work and paperwork, grievances, celebrations, and gossip. This bond was reinforced by employees' leisure activities during and after work hours. Saleswomen integrated the rituals of women's culture into their work culture: showers and parties to commemorate engagements, marriages, and births. Not all department stores, however, had sales staff that were this close and intensely friendly, but it is significant that even when managers noted that a department was quarrelsome and divided, they almost always marveled that it still united in self-defense against outside threats. Benson, "'The Clerking Sisterhood' Rationalization"; and Susan Porter Benson, "The Work Culture of Sales Clerks in American Department Stores, 1890–1940," in Norton and Alexander, *Major Problems in American Women's History*, 306.

72. Davis, interview.

73. Carson, *In Struggle*, 13.

74. Davis, interview.

75. Davis, interview.

76. *New York Times Upfront*, January 18, 2010.

77. Scholars often focus on the integration of lunch counters for black customers, but the integration of counters also meant that African American workers now had a place of respite. Geneva Tisdale recalled, before the Greensboro movement, the color line was intact when she started in that the kitchen staff was black and the waitresses were all white, while workers and customers of color were relegated to "a snack bar out in the middle of floor" and white workers and customers ate at the lunch counter. The racial order of Woolworth's, however, did not bother Geneva until the student movement started: "And when it got started, then I got to thinking about it. It wasn't no more right that, you known, that we could [not] be served, because we ourselves worked there. We fixed all of the food that went down, and then we couldn't sit ourselves." One can only imagine her elation—and likely some fear given the violent response of whites to the protest movement—when her supervisor "called all three of her girls out that was working behind the counter which was black—myself, Susie Morrison [Kemball] at that time, and a girl named Anita Jones . . . and talked to us." The supervisor instructed, "The day we open up . . . I want you girls, you come in to work, but bring you some dress clothes. I'm going to give you a signal when I want to go upstairs and dress as a customer. Come and walk around in the store like you're shopping . . . then come over to the counter." (Tisdale fondly recalled wearing her Sunday dress and ordering an egg salad

sandwich and a soda.) As store management and the women expected, local news reporters came and took their picture, not knowing that the first to sit at the counter were, in fact, Woolworth workers of color. See oral history interview with Geneva Tisdale by Jim Schlosser, 1998, Greensboro Voices/Greensboro Civil Rights Oral History Collection, University of North Carolina at Greensboro.

78. Davis, interview.

79. Davis, interview.

80. Davis, interview.

81. Ora Lomax, interview by Leslee Key, February 7, 2009, Voices of Freedom Oral History Project, Virginia Commonwealth University Library Special Collections, Richmond, VA.

82. Lomax, interview.

83. Haynes, *Red Lines, Black Spaces*, 97.

84. Lomax, interview.

85. "Claims Negro Balks Clerks: Shoe Store's Manager Says Whites Accept His 4 Salesmen," *New York Amsterdam News*, September 27, 1933, 1.

86. Strang, Churchill, and Collins, "Blacks in Sales," 208. See also Gordon Bloom, F. Marion Fletcher, and Charles R. Perry, *Negro Employment in Retail Trade: A Study of Racial Policies in the Department Store, Drugstore, and Supermarket Industries*, Philadelphia: Industrial Research Unit, Wharton School of Finance and Commerce, University of Pennsylvania, 1972.

87. Three of the more publicized incidents were a bomb threat at JCSU on February 10, 1960, if any students protested; the arrest of three students at a demonstration at Belk's department store on February 23; and the arrest of a student at a Belk's demonstration on February 27. The February 23 arrests came as students blocked both the main entrance and an emergency exit to Belk's basement cafeteria, all the while chanting in low voices, "Freedom, freedom, everybody likes freedom." Students, who merely bumped a few white customers, were charged with assault. The February 27 incident involved accusations of police assault and harassment. According to protesters, who later complained to the city council on March 1, the police had knocked down a girl, and threatened and called the arrested student "nigger." Covington, "Negroes Continue Protest at Diners"; Roy Covington, "Three Students Are Arrested during Demonstrations Here," *Charlotte Observer*, February 24, 1960.

88. Waynick, Brooks, and Pitts, 52–53; Coffin, *Brookshire & Belk*, 42.

89. Minutes of the Mayor's Community Relations Committee, February 12, 1963, and March 12, 1963, quoted in Leach, "Progress under Pressure," 201.

90. Henry Spencer, "The New South: A New Southern Climate," *Sacramento Observer*, November 25, 1971.

91. U.S. Bureau of the Census, *Census of Population, 1950*; U.S. Bureau of the Census, *Census of Population, 1960*; U.S. Bureau of the Census, *Census of Population, 1970*.

92. Margaret Price, "Reports from Three States in Sit-Ins," *Chicago Daily Defender*, June 23, 1960; "Atlanta Negroes Suspend Sit-Ins," *New York Times*, October 23, 1960.

93. John D. Pomfret, "Negroes Building Boycott Network," *New York Times*, November 25, 1962.

94. Sugrue, *Sweet Land of Liberty*, 257.

95. "Sit-In Strategy Will Move to Other Areas," *New York Amsterdam News*, July 30, 1960.

96. Countryman, *Up South*, 83.

97. Countryman, 106, 107; Sullivan, *Build Brother Build*, 75. Sullivan claimed the campaign had no real leadership. This lack of structure enabled the creation of an impressively broad ecumenical coalition of clergy free from any in-fighting or internal divisions.

98. Countryman, *Up South*, 106.

99. Sugrue, *Sweet Land of Liberty*, 128.

100. Carson, *Student Voice*, 89. Rich's, however, continued to violate the rights of its African American workers and, thus, was the subject of protest time and again. Most notably, on April 3, 1973, 350 employees led by Hosea Williams, civil rights leader and former aide to King, walked out of Rich's claiming discrimination in hiring, pay, and promotion practices. The strike lasted for seven weeks and ended when the strikers accepted mediation by the Community Relations Commission. Around this time, Rich's appointed Jesse Hill, a leader in the 1960 sit-in movement against the store, as the first African American member of its board of directors; and several years later, in August 1980, the store hired its first black store manager. See Clemmons, *Rich's: A Southern Institution*, 215–16.

101. Enrico Beltramini, "Operation Breadbasket in Chicago: Between Civil Rights and Capitalism," in Ezra, *Economic Civil Rights Movement*, 125, 126.

102. "SCLC Operation Expands in NYC," *Afro-American*, June 20, 1970, 2.

103. "Kaufmann's to Integrate Work Force," *Pittsburgh Courier*, March 19, 1966; "Selective Buying Drive Hovers over Kaufmann's," *Pittsburgh Courier*, March 5, 1966; "Store Was Given an Ultimatum," *Pittsburgh Courier*, May 26, 1966; "Expect Department Store Jobs for Negroes to Be Wide Open," *Pittsburgh Courier*, May 14, 1966.

104. "UNPC Tired of Firms Dawdling: Hit Gimbels' and Hornes' with Boycott for Easter," *Pittsburgh Courier*, April 9, 1966.

105. "Picket Gimbels, Horne: Claim Boycotting Starting to Hurt 2 Department Stores," *Pittsburgh Courier*, April 16, 1966 (italics added).

106. "UNPC Tired of Firms Dawdling: Hit Gimbels' and Hornes' with Boycott for Easter."

107. "Picket Gimbels, Horne: Claim Boycotting Starting to Hurt 2 Department Stores"; "Proposal after Proposal Made as Horne, Gimbels Lines Swell," *Pittsburgh Courier*, April 23, 1966.

108. "Proposal after Proposal Made as Horne, Gimbels Lines Swell."

109. "UNPC Vows to Keep Vigil after Settling Boycotts," *Pittsburgh Courier*, May 7, 1966.

110. Ford, "SNCC Women, Denim, and the Politics of Dress," 626.

111. Cohen, *Consumer's Republic*, 189.

Chapter Six

1. Gilbert and the staff of the Washington Post, *Ten Blocks from the White House*, 71. See also Claude Koprowski, "D.C. Retail Sales Dip Following April Riots," *Washington Post and Times Herald*, July 12, 1968.

2. Eugene L. Meyer, "Sears Files $2 Million Suit against D.C. for Riot Costs," *Washington Post*, June 17, 1970.

3. Isenberg, *Downtown America*, 230.

4. National Capital Planning Commission, *Civil Disturbances in Washington, D.C.*, 5; Lisicky, *Woodward & Lothrop*, 100. See also Tager, *Boston Riots*.

5. Lisicky, *Woodward & Lothrop*, 100. See also National Capital Planning Commission, *Civil Disturbances in Washington, D.C.*

6. Mary McGrory, "Has Everyone Had Enough?," *Boston Globe*, April 8, 1968. Insurgents also left alone businesses that marked themselves as pro-black by scrawling "Soul Brothers and Sisters Work Here, Don't Put Us Out of Work" or simply "Soul Brother" on doors and windows.

7. Meyer, "Sears Files $2 Million Suit against D.C. for Riot Costs."

8. "Easter Shopping Business off Sharply in Riot Areas," *Los Angeles Times*, April 13, 1968.

9. Koprowski, "D.C. Retail Sales Dip Following April Riots."

10. "Most Rioting Subsides: Orderly Protests Being Scheduled; New Pittsburgh, Baltimore Violence," *Wall Street Journal*, April 8, 1968.

11. Isenberg, *Downtown America*, 205.

12. Isenberg, 231.

13. Edwin Hoffman, quoted in Lisicky, *Woodward & Lothrop*, 100.

14. On American suburbanization, see George Sternleib, "The Future of Retailing in the Downtown Core," 103; Steve Macek, *Urban Nightmares*, 7; Jackson, *Crabgrass Frontier*, 4, 283. On urban decline, see Nicolaides and Wiese, *Suburb Reader*, 322; and Wiese, *Places of Their Own*, 143. See also Kruse and Sugrue, *New Suburban History*.

15. Lisicky, *Woodward & Lothrop*, 100.

16. Sternleib, "Future of Retailing in the Downtown CORE," 103.

17. Carol Kleiman, "Minorities Isolated from Job Hot Spots," *Chicago Tribune*, July 28, 1991.

18. The relocation of American department stores began as early as the 1920s, when higher-end stores such as Saks Fifth Avenue, I. Magnin, Marshall Field's, and Strawbridge & Clothier, as well as a few less prominent department stores, established locations outside center cities to meet the needs of an increasingly mobile population. But it was the emergence of shopping centers in the 1940s and 1950s that drastically altered the landscape of American retailing.

19. Bluestone, Hanna, Kuhn, and Moore, *Retail Revolution*, 18.

20. Susan Strasser, "Woolworth to Wal-Mart: Mass Merchandising and the Changing Culture of Consumption," in Lichtenstein, *Wal-Mart: The Face of Twenty-First-Century Capitalism*, 31–56, 50–52.

21. Lichtenstein, *Retail Revolution*.

22. S. S. Kresge Company Annual Report 1962, box: S. S. Kresge Company Annual Reports 1948–1976, folder: S. S. Kresge Company Annual Report 1962, Sears, Roebuck, and Company Archives (hereafter cited as Sears Archives), Hoffman Estates, IL.

23. S. S. Kresge Company Annual Report 1962, Sears Archives.

24. Turner, *Kmart's Ten Deadly Sins*, 188; S. S. Kresge Company Annual Report 1962, Sears Archives.

25. In 1981, the retailer hired Cheryl Tiegs as spokeswoman for her own line of clothing and footwear. Four years later, after observing the popularity and profitability of the Cheryl Tiegs clothing collection, Kmart signed actress Jaclyn Smith to do the same. Almost immediately, Kmart's clothing sales and profits increased enormously. In 1986, "apparel's share of total Kmart sales climbed to 24 percent, up 20 percent. The gain in profits was even fatter." On the heels of the Jaclyn Smith success, Kmart appointed Martha Stewart as the corporation's first home entertaining and lifestyle consultant in August 1987. Ten years later, Stewart launched Martha Stewart Living Everyday at Kmart. This product line remained on store shelves until Stewart's contract with Kmart ended in 2009. Kmart also recruited golfer Fuzzy Zoeller and racecar driver Mario Andretti to promote sporting goods and automotive products, respectively, in the 1980s. In 1997, Kmart released Zoeller after he "joked" that Tiger Woods—who had just become the first person of color to win the Masters Golf Tournament—would request fried chicken and collard greens for the banquet at the 1998 tournament. See Bob Ortega, *In Sam We Trust: The Untold Story of Sam Walton and How Wal-Mart Is Devouring the World*, 156; Kmart Corporation Annual Report 1988, box: Kmart Corporation Annual Reports 1977–1992, Sears Archives; Jennifer Steinhauer, "Martha Stewart's at Kmart, Changing the Sheets," *New York Times*, February 20, 1997; Richard Sandomir, "Zoeller Learns Race Remarks Carry a Price," *New York Times*, April 24, 1997; and Gary Alan Fine and Patricia Ann Turner, *Whispers on the Color Line*, 242n10.

26. Turner, *Kmart's Ten Deadly Sins*, 44.

27. Ownby, *American Dreams in Mississippi*, 163.

28. Ownby, 163.

29. Bluestone et al., *Retail Revolution*, 22; Thomas Jessen Adams, "Making the New Shop Floors: Wal-Mart, Labor Control, and the History of the Postwar Discount Retail Industry in America," in Lichtenstein, *Wal-Mart: The Face of Twenty-First-Century Capitalism*, 215.

30. Adams, "Making the New Shop Floors," 215–16, 218–19. The Fair Labor Standard Act of 1938 mandated that retail establishments making more than $1 million a year must pay their workers a minimum wage; those making less than $1 million a year were exempt and could provide lower wages.

31. Adams, 225–29.

32. Davis, "Dead-End Jobs and the African American Occupational Structure," 100–103.

33. Barmash, *Macy's for Sale*, 66, 74, 76, 90, 103.

34. Weil, *Sears, Roebuck, U.S.A.*, 259.

35. Davis, "Dead-End Jobs and the African American Occupational Structure," 108.

36. In the 1980s, specialty stores, such as the Gap, the Limited, Waldenbooks, Home Depot, and Best Buy, capitalized on what department stores abandoned—a knowledgeable, experienced sales force—to become new industry leaders. They "invest[ed] substantial funds in hiring and training their sales people" and in designing store environments to meet the wants of individual market segments. For example, "many of the specialty stores located on Rodeo Drive in California create an atmosphere of excitement through innovative displays and merchandising, while at the same time employing salespeople who understand the importance of relationship marketing. There is a focus on customer satisfaction and the way the customer is treated." Ronald D. Michman and Edward M. Mazze, *Specialty Retailers: Marketing Triumphs and Blunders* (Westport, CT: Greenwood Publishing Group, 2001), 3, 11.

37. Spector and McCarthy, *Nordstrom Way*, 10.

38. Howard, *From Main Street to Mall*, 154.

39. New Haven, Connecticut, was famous as "the model city" of urban renewal projects in the mid-twentieth century.

40. Weil, *Sears, Roebuck, U.S.A.*, 231.

41. "North Lawndale," in *Local Community Fact Book*, 73; and Klineberg, *Heat Wave*, 92.

42. Klineberg, *Heat Wave*, 93.

43. Community No. 29—North Lawndale Description of Area (Draft), box 1, folder 5: December 1954, 1954 Undated Items, Greater Lawndale Conservation Committee Papers (hereafter GLCC Papers), CHM.

44. Turk, "From the West Side to the 'Softer Side.'"

45. See Meier and Rudwick, *Black Detroit and the Rise of the UAW*.

46. Grossman, *Land of Hope*, 199.

47. Unknown author, Introduction, April 12, 1955, box 1 1950–June 1955, folder 7 April–June 1955, GLCC Papers, CHM.

48. GLCC News Notes, July 1957, box 4 April–November 1957, folder 2 June–July 1957, GLCC Papers, CHM.

49. Turk, "From the West Side to the 'Softer Side.'"

50. Announcement, February 1958, box 5 December 1957–February 1958, folder 7 February 1–31, 1958, GLCC Papers, CHM.

51. See Auslander, *Taste and Power*; and Abelson, *When Ladies Go A-Thieving*.

52. "Christmas Shopping Tour for Underprivileged Children in the Greater Lawndale Area," November 13, 1963, box 21, GLCC Papers, CHM.

53. *Lawndale Journal*, February 1963, box 20 October 1962–February 1963, folder 6 February 1963, GLCC Papers, CHM.

54. "Display Ad 20—No Title," *Chicago Defender*, November 16, 1963.

55. "Display Ad 22—No Title," *Chicago Defender*, January 8, 1966.

56. "Consumer Education Series to Begin June 8," *Lawndale Journal*, 1962, box 18 January–May 1962, folder 7 May 16–31, 1962, GLCC Papers, CHM.

57. Orleck, *Storming Caesars Palace*, 86.

58. See Sugrue, *Sweet Land of Liberty*; and Holt, *Children of Fire*.

59. Semi Annual Report on the Jobs for Youth Program at the Sears YMCA to the Weiboldt Foundation (1964), box 3B: folders 79–105, folder: Sears Roebuck and Company, July–December 1964, Greater Lawndale Conservation Committee, UIC Archives.

60. "25 Lawndale Women Graduate Tomorrow," *Chicago Tribune*, March 21, 1968.

61. "Sears Clerical JOBS Project Boom to 33 Young Women," *Chicago Defender*, July 1, 1967.

62. "25 Lawndale Women Graduate Tomorrow."

63. "Sears Clerical JOBS Project Boom to 33 Young Women."

64. "Helping Keep Students in School," *Tower News*, June 7, 1974, Sears Archives.

65. Charles R. Perry, "The Negro in the Department Store Industry," in Bloom, Fletcher, and Perry, *Negro Employment in Retail Trade*, 109.

66. Perry, 112.

67. Seligman, *Block by Block*, 220.

68. Seligman, 216.

69. "Jesse Jackson Oral History on Chicago in 1966," in Hampton and Fayer, *Voices of Freedom*, 308–9; and Seligman, *Block by Block*, 217–18.

70. Seligman, *Block by Block*, 220.

71. On these local campaigns, see "CORE Maps Drive over Jobs at Sears," *New York Times*, September 5, 1961; "Picketing in New Orleans," *New York Times*, December 17, 1961; "CORE Gets KY Store to Hire Negro Sales Clerks," *Chicago Daily Defender*, February 28, 1962; "CORE Maps Nationwide Step-Up in Job Drive," *Pittsburgh Courier*, July 14, 1962; "Dismiss Charges in KY," *Chicago Daily Defender*, August 5, 1963; "Equal Hiring, Equal Pay: Latest Drive for Rights," *Chicago Daily Defender*, February 18, 1963; "Massive 'Black Monday Protest' Set Ag," *New Pittsburgh Courier*, November 15, 1969; and Ralph Koger, "Sears Boycott Ends, HRC Plays Key Role," *New Pittsburgh Courier*, March 28, 1970.

72. Kornbluh, "To Fulfill Their 'Rightly Need.'"

73. Quoted in Turk, *Equality on Trial*, 88.

74. The historian Lane Windham argues that, at Woodward and Lothrop in Washington, D.C., workers tackled race and gender discrimination via unionism. They "used their contract[s] to address issues that were shaped by gender" such as their relegation to lower-ranked jobs where they earned considerably less than their male counterparts. Unionism proved to be an effective tool, especially in comparison to the EEOC's legal approach. Through the union, "workers won the right to move into any job outside their department; the company had to promote its own workers who were interested in better-paying jobs before it hired from the outside. Thus women now had a clear and legally backed path into higher-commissioned jobs." Still, workers struggled to implement lasting changes due to employer behaviors, department store consolidations, federal labor laws, globalization, and technology. See Lane Windham, *Knocking on Labor's Door*, 143.

75. Sears, Roebuck & Co., Fayetteville, N.C.-Subj.; Charlie J. Lawson, Lillian Campbell-Victims, December 5, 1966, File Number 170-54-21, National Archives and Record Administration, College Park, MD (hereafter cited as NARA-CP); and

Sears, Roebuck & Co., Laurinburg, N.C.-Subj.; Charlie J. Lawson, Lillian Campbell -Victims, December 5, 1966, File Number 170-54M-19, NARA-CP.

76. Weil, *Sears, Roebuck, U.S.A.*, 224.

77. Annual Report, 1973, Sears Archives. See also "EEOC v. Sears, Roebuck & Co" and "EEOC v. Sears, Roebuck & Co. (Appellate Opinion)," in Weisberg, *Application of Feminist Legal Theory to Women's Lives*, 571–93.

78. "Making the Race Fair," *Parent News*, October–November 1973, Sears Archives. President Lyndon B. Johnson made a similar analogy in his speech announcing affirmative action at Howard University in June 1965.

79. Annual Report, 1973, Sears Archives.

80. Frances Grice, "What's Happening Now: Sears Seeks Due Process to Deny Others Civil Rights," 1979, Part V, box 377, folder: Sears, Roebuck & Company v. U.S., Mar-Oct 1979, NAACP Records, LOC.

81. Donald R. Katz, *The Big Store: Inside the Crisis and Revolution at Sears*, 138–39.

82. Weil, *Sears, Roebuck, U.S.A.*, 224, 225.

83. Annual Report, 1979, Sears Archives.

84. "Affirmative Action Plan Applauded," *Tower News*, April 2, 1976, Sears Archives.

85. Weil, *Sears, Roebuck, U.S.A.*, 225–26; Annual Report, 1976, Sears Archives.

86. Annual Report, 1979, Sears Archives.

87. Weil, *Sears, Roebuck, U.S.A.*, 226.

88. Zuckerman, "Beyond Dispute," 182.

89. Annual Report, 1975, Sears Archives.

90. "Sears Helped Them Past the Roadblocks of Big Business," *Sears Today*, November–December 1986, Sears Archives.

91. Perry, "Negro in the Department Store Industry," 107.

92. Blacks were 30.6 percent of the Memphis Standard Metropolitan Statistical Area (SMSA). Civilian Labor Force, yet they were only 26.3 percent of Sears's total Memphis employment.

93. Charge of Discrimination, 1973 and 1974, folder: Sears, Roebuck, & Co. Adv. EEOC (R-Memphis), box 137, RG 403, NARA-CP.

94. NOW, an American feminist organization, was founded in 1966. It was formed to pressure the EEOC to carry out the sex discrimination mandate of Title VII of the 1964 Civil Rights Act and became intricately involved with the EEOC. In fact, in 1970, Aileen Hernandez, the EEOC's first female commissioner, left the federal agency and became NOW's second president.

95. Zuckerman, "Beyond Dispute," 91.

96. Quoted in Milkman, "Women's History and the Sears Case," 377.

97. Quoted in Roy Wilkins, The Roy Wilkins Column, Release for March 17–18, 1979, Part V, box 377, folder: Sears, Roebuck & Company v. U.S., Mar-Oct 1979, NAACP Records, LOC.

98. Nathaniel Wright Jr., "Black Empowerment: Background on Why Sears Should Be Supported," Parts 1 and 2, 1979, Part V, box 377, folder: Sears, Roebuck & Company v. U.S., Mar-Oct 1979, NAACP Records, LOC.

99. Vernon Jordan, "The Government and Affirmative Action," February 14, 1979, box 156, folder 1709, CUL Records, UIC Archives.

100. Clarence D. Coleman, Memorandum re: Statement by the Black Leadership Forum on the Sears Suit, February 16, 1979, box 156, folder 1709, CUL Records, UIC Archives. See also James W. Compton, Chicago Urban League's Position on the Sears Suit, March 27, 1979, CUL Records, UIC Archives.

101. Jerry Szatan, Income Specialist of the CUL, Interdepartmental Correspondence on Professor James E. Jones Jr.'s Analysis of Sears Suit, February 26, 1979, box 156, folder 1709, CUL Records, UIC Archives.

102. Jesse Jackson, "An Appeal and a Challenge to Sears to Withdraw the Suit: Sears vs. the U.S. Government," unknown publication; and Statement by the Executive Committee of the NAACP National Board of Directors on the Implications of the Suit by Sears, Roebuck and Co. against 10 federal agencies, issued on March 8, 1979, Part V, box 377, folder: Sears, Roebuck & Company v. U.S., Mar-Oct 1979, NAACP Records, LOC.

103. James W. Compton, Interdepartmental Correspondence on PUSH Meeting, February 26, 1979, box 156, folder 1713, CUL Records, UIC Archives.

104. Jesse Jackson, The Call to National Leadership, February 1979, box 156, folder 1709, CUL Records, UIC Archives.

105. Quoted in Milkman, "Women's History and the Sears Case," 376.

106. "EEOC to Appeal Sears Case," *Chicago Tribune*, April 11, 1986.

107. Venus Green, "Flawed Remedies," 46.

108. Vertis Laval, Charge of Discrimination, June 20, 1975, folder: EEOC v. Sears, Roebuck File, box 137, RG 403, NARA-CP.

109. Determination: Vertis Laval, May 26, 1977, folder: EEOC v. Sears, Roebuck File, box 137, RG 403, NARA-CP.

110. Shirley Mims, Charge of Discrimination, March 21, 1972, folder: EEOC v. Sears, Roebuck File, box 137, RG 403, NARA-CP.

111. Determination: Shirley Mims, May 16, 1977, folder: EEOC v. Sears, Roebuck File, box 137, RG 403, NARA-CP.

112. Carolyn J. Triplett, Charge of Discrimination, April 4, 1975, folder: EEOC v. Sears, Roebuck File, box 137, RG 403, NARA-CP.

113. Determination: Carolyn J. Triplett, April 10, 1977, folder: EEOC v. Sears, Roebuck File, box 137, RG 403, NARA-CP.

114. "EEOC Sues Sears, Roebuck, and Company: Suit Allege Discrimination against Women, Blacks, and Hispanics," *U.S. Equal Employment Opportunity Commission News*, October 22, 1979, folder: Sears, Roebuck & Co. adv. EEOC (R-Montgomery), box: EEOC/Sears Litigation, Record ID: 403-03-0072, NARA-CP.

115. David B. Parker, "EEOC Discovers Its Investigation of Sears Is So Flawed, It Should Settle and Not Sue," *Employment Relations Report*, August 1, 1979, Equal Employment Opportunity Commission v. Sears, Roebuck, Co., Civil Action No. 79-507-N, United States District Court for the Middle District of Alabama, November 13, 1979, folder: Sears, Roebuck & Co. adv. EEOC (R-Montgomery) (2), box: EEOC/Sears Litigation, Record ID: 403-03-0072, NARA-CP; Defendant's Request for Production of Documents, December 3, 1979, Equal Employment Opportunity Commission v. Sears, Roebuck, Co., Civil Action No. 79-507-N, United States District

Court for the Middle District of Alabama, f: Sears, Roebuck & Co. adv. EEOC (R-Montgomery), box: EEOC/Sears Litigation, Record ID: 403-03-0072, NARA-CP.

116. Memorandum of Points and Authorities in Support of Defendant's Motion to Dismiss, November 13, 1979, Equal Employment Opportunity Commission v. Sears, Roebuck, Co., Civil Action No. 79-507-N, United States District Court for the Middle District of Alabama, folder: Sears, Roebuck & Co. adv. EEOC (R-Montgomery), box: EEOC/Sears Litigation, Record ID: 403-03-0072, NARA-CP.

117. Memorandum Opinion, May 22, 1980, Equal Employment Opportunity Commission v. Sears, Roebuck, Co., Civil Action No. 79-507-N, United States District Court for the Middle District of Alabama, November 13, 1979, folder: Sears, Roebuck & Co. adv. EEOC (R-Montgomery) (2), box: EEOC/Sears Litigation, Record ID: 403-03-0072, NARA-CP.

118. Affidavit in Support of Defendant's Motion to Dismiss Plaintiff's Complaint, November 9, 1979, Equal Employment Opportunity Commission v. Sears, Roebuck, Co., Civil Action No. 79 Civ. 2708, United States District Court for the Southern District of New York, folder: EEOC NY Vol. 1, box 3: EEOC/Sears Litigation, NARA-CP.

119. Affidavit in Support of Defendant's Motion to Dismiss Plaintiff's Complaint, November 9, 1979.

120. Affidavit in Support of Defendant's Motion to Dismiss Plaintiff's Complaint, November 9, 1979.

121. Reply Memorandum of Points and Authorities to Plaintiff's Memorandum of Points and Authorities in Opposition to Defendant's Motion to Dismiss, January 21, 1980, Equal Employment Opportunity Commission v. Sears, Roebuck, Co., Civil Action No. 79-507-N, United States District Court for the Middle District of Alabama, folder: Sears adv. EEOC (Race—Montgomery - 3), box: EEOC/Sears Litigation, Record ID: 403-03-0072, NARA-CP.

122. Defendant's Reply to Plaintiff's Opposition to Motion for Summary Judgment, July 24, 1980, Equal Employment Opportunity Commission v. Sears, Roebuck, and Co., Civil Action No. C79-1957A, United States District Court for the Southern District of Georgia, Atlanta Division, folder: Sears adv. EEOC (R-ATL), box 12: EEOC/Sears Litigation, NARA-CP.

123. Memorandum of Points and Authorities in Support of Defendant's Motion to Dismiss, November 13, 1979, Equal Employment Opportunity Commission v. Sears, Roebuck, Co., Civil Action No. 79-507-N, United States District Court for the Middle District of Alabama, folder: Sears, Roebuck & Co. adv. EEOC (R-Montgomery), box: EEOC/Sears Litigation, Record ID: 403-03-0072, NARA-CP.

124. Affidavit of Earle Dewey Kitchen in Support of Motion to Dismiss, Equal Employment Opportunity Commission v. Sears, Roebuck, Co., Civil Action No. 79-507-N, United States District Court for the Middle District of Alabama, folder: Sears, Roebuck & Co. adv. EEOC (R-Montgomery), box: EEOC/Sears Litigation, Record ID: 403-03-0072, NARA-CP.

125. "The EEOC, Sears, and the Courts," *Chicago Tribune*, June 9, 1981.

126. Chris Agrella, "Bias Suit against Sears Is Dismissed in Alabama," *Chicago Tribune*, May 23, 1980.

127. Williams, *State of Black America 1981*, 289; Arnold H. Lubash, "US Judge Dismisses One Federal Bias Suit Brought against Sears," *New York Times*, June 19, 1980.

128. "Second Job-Bias Suit against Sears Roebuck Is Dismissed by Court," *Wall Street Journal*, June 19, 1980.

129. Merrill Brown, "U.S. Settles Its Racial Bias Suits against Sears," *Washington Post*, June 5, 1981.

130. "The EEOC Settled Four Race Bias Suits against Sears," *Los Angeles Times*, June 5, 1981.

131. Brown, "U.S. Settles Its Racial Bias Suits against Sears."

132. Merrill Brown, "U.S., Sears Settle Several Bias Cases," *Boston Globe*, June 5, 1981.

133. Brown, "U.S., Sears Settle Several Bias Cases."

134. See Wiese, *Places of Their Own*; and Pattillo-McCoy, *Black Picket Fences*.

135. Dawson, *Black Visions*, xii.

136. Katz, *The Big Store*, 362.

137. Carroll v. Sears, Roebuck, & Co., 514 F.Supp. 788 (1981), United States District Court, W. D. Louisiana, Shreveport Division, April 20, 1981; Carroll v. Sears, Roebuck, & Co., 708 F.2d 183 (1983), United States Court of Appeals, Fifth Circuit, June 30, 1983.

138. Carroll v. Sears, Roebuck, & Co., 708 F.2d 183 (1983), United States Court of Appeals, Fifth Circuit, June 30, 1983.

139. Weil, *Sears, Roebuck, U.S.A.*, 252–53; and Bluestone et al., *Retail Revolution*, 16.

140. Lichtenstein, "Wal-Mart and the New World Order," 25.

141. Ortega, *In Sam We Trust*, 130.

142. Lichtenstein, "Wal-Mart and the New World Order," 26, 27.

Epilogue

1. Jacqueline Dorsey Parker, interview by the author, June 24, 2015.

2. On dead malls, see Steven Kurutz, "An Ode to Shopping Malls," *New York Times*, July 26, 2017.

3. Pattillo-McCoy, *Black Picket Fences*, 202.

4. Landry, *New Black Middle Class*, 90.

5. United States Department of Labor, Bureau of Labor Statistics, Labor Force Statistics from the Current Population Survey, 1995.

6. United States Department of Labor, Bureau of Labor Statistics, Labor Force Statistics from the Current Population Survey, 2014.

7. United States Department of Labor, Bureau of Labor Statistics, Labor Force Statistics from the Current Population Survey, 2017.

8. Brian K. Landsberg, "Public Accommodations and the Civil Rights Act of 1964: A Surprising Success?," *Hamline University's School of Law's Journal of Public Law and Policy* 36, no. 1 (2015): 18.

9. Landsberg, 18–19.

10. Randall Kennedy, "The Civil Rights Act's Unsung Victory: And How It Changed the South," *Harper's Magazine*, June 2014.

11. Baynard Rustin, quoted in Landsberg, "Public Accommodations and the Civil Rights Act of 1964," 19.

12. Quoted in Landsberg, 21.

13. Quoted in Landsberg, 21. See also Randall Kennedy, "Struggle for Racial Equality in Public Accommodations," in Grofman, *Legacies of the 1964 Civil Rights Act.*

14. Benson, *Counter Cultures,* 293. Across the board, labor conditions have declined for workers in most, if not all, industries and worsened with globalization, technological advancements, and a probusiness, antiworker milieu. Factories and other businesses closed, jobs were eliminated and outsourced, wages were slashed just as health care and other benefit costs skyrocketed, while corporations reneged on their pension obligations. Reflectively, unions declined in size, density, and influence; strikes—expressions of worker dissent—virtually disappeared.

15. Benson, 290.

16. Samantha Christmann, "Anchors Away: Department Store Struggles Hurt Local Malls," *Buffalo News,* February 9, 2018 (updated February 11, 2018).

17. Ruetschlin and Asante-Muhammad, "The Retail Race Divide."

18. United States Department of Labor, Bureau of Labor Statistics, Labor Force Statistics from the Current Population Survey, 2017.

19. Ruetschlin and Asante-Muhammad, "The Retail Race Divide."

20. Ruetschlin and Asante-Muhammad.

21. Steven Greenhouse, "Lawsuit Claims Race Bias at Wet Seal Retail Chain," *New York Times,* July 12, 2012; Tiffany Hsu, "Wet Seal to Pay $7.5 Million to Settle Race Discrimination Suit," *Los Angeles Times,* May 9, 2013; and Steven Greenhouse, "Abercrombie & Fitch Bias Case Is Settled," *New York Times,* November 17, 2004.

22. "Abercrombie & Fitch Bias Case Is Settled," *New York Times,* November 17, 2004.

23. Derek Thompson, "The Silent Crisis of Retail Employment," *Atlantic,* April 18, 2017.

24. Green, Gipp, and Wild, *Everybody's Brother.*

25. Walter LaFeber, *Michael Jordan and the New Global Capitalism,* 54.

26. Parker, "Shopping While Black."

27. Notable Shopping While Black incidents include the following: in 1993, African American municipal judge Claude Coleman was falsely accused of credit card fraud while shopping at Bloomingdale's department store in Short Hill, New Jersey; in 1995 employees of an Eddie Bauer in suburban Washington, D.C., falsely accused three young black men of shoplifting and forced one of the men to disrobe; in 1998, the Children's Place in Lynn, Massachusetts, instructed its employees that to prevent theft they should follow black customers, not provide them with shopping bags, not invite African Americans to open credit cards, and withhold information about sales and promotions; and, in 2000, after his eleven-year-old daughter was accused of shoplifting, Frederick Finley was killed by Lord & Taylor security guards at a mall in suburban Detroit.

28. Clare O'Connor, "New York AG to Barneys, Macy's: Turn Over 'Shop and Frisk' Racial Profiling Policies by Friday," *Forbes,* October 29, 2013, accessed

November 8, 2013, http://www.forbes.com/sites/clareoconnor/2013/10/29/new-york
-ag-to-barneys-macys-turn-over-shop-and-frisk-racial-profiling-policies-by-friday/.

29. Curtis Skinner, "Boycott Threatened after Racial Profiling Claims at Macy's, Barneys," Reuters, November 4, 2013, accessed November 8, 2013, http://www.reuters .com/assets/print?aid=USBRE9A313Q20131104.

30. J. David Goodman, "Macy's and Barneys among Stores to Post Shoppers' 'Bill of Rights,'" *New York Times*, December 10, 2013.

31. Kenneth Lovett, "Macy's Agrees to Pay $650G to Settle State Probe into Racial Profiling at Its Herald Square Store," *New York Daily News*, August 20, 2014.

32. Lovett, "Macy's Agrees to Pay $650G."

33. Selim Algar, "Barneys Settles Racial Profiling Suit," *New York Post*, October 3, 2014.

34. Jennifer Peltz, "'Treme' Actor Settles Profiling Suit vs. Macy's," Associated Press, July 18, 2014.

35. Algar, "Barneys Settles Racial Profiling Suit."

36. Loewen, *Sundown Towns*, 237.

37. Pamela Wood, "State Civil Rights Commission, NAACP Raise Concerns about Towson Mall's New Teen Policy," *Baltimore Sun*, September 2, 2016.

38. Rabuck, "Racist Curfew in Madison."

39. Selections of the West Towne Mall's "Youth Escort Policy," quoted in Rabuck, "Racist Curfew in Madison."

40. Rabuck, "Racist Curfew in Madison."

41. Quoted in Parker, "Shopping While Black," 1474.

42. Ruetschlin and Asante-Muhammad, "Retail Race Divide."

Bibliography

Archives

American Friends Service Committee Archives
    American Friends Service Committee Records
Chicago History Museum
    Carson Pirie Scott Records
    Claude A. Barnett Papers
    Greater Lawndale Conservation Committee Papers
    Marshall Field and Company Archives
    Sidney Lens Papers
Chicago Public Library / Vivian G. Harsh Research Collection of Afro-American
      History and Literature
    Illinois Writers Project / Negro in Illinois
Hagley Museum
    Strawbridge & Clothier Collection
Historical Society of Washington, D.C.
    Coordinating Committee for the Enforcement of the D.C. Anti-Discrimination
      Laws
Richard Jones, personal papers, in the possession of Richard L. Jones III
Library of Congress
    National Association for the Advancement of Colored People Records
    National Urban League Records
Macy's Archives
    Macy's Records
Maryland Historical Society
    Hochschild Kohn Collection
National Archives and Record Administration, College Park, MD
    Equal Employment Opportunity Commission Records
National Park Service / Maggie L. Walker National Historic Site
    Maggie Lena Walker Family Papers Archives Collection
Sears, Roebuck, and Company Archives, Hoffman Estates, IL
    Kmart Company Records
    S. S. Krege Company Records
Tamiment Library and Robert F. Wagner Labor Archives
    Department Store and Office Workers' Organizing Collection
    Retail Wholesale and Department Store Union, Local 1-S, Department Store
      Workers Union Records

University of Illinois at Chicago Special Collections
Chicago Urban League Records
Gary Urban League Records
Greater Lawndale Conservation Committee
United Service Employees Union Records
Valentine Richmond History Center
Independent Order of St. Luke Collection
Virginia Historical Society
Miller & Rhoads Collection
Thalhimer Brothers, Inc.

Oral Histories

William Atkinson, Tamiment Library
Doretha Davis, Southern Oral History Program Collection, University of North Carolina at Chapel Hill
Delia Griffin, G. Fox & Company Oral History Project, Connecticut History Society
Ora Lomax, Virginia Commonwealth University Library Special Collections
C. Virgil Martin, Chicago History Museum
Marcella Loring Michelson, Tamiment Library
Jacqueline Dorsey Parker, interview with the Author
Edith Parker, interview with the Author
John Sondheim, Jewish Museum of Maryland
Geneva Tisdale, Greensboro Voices/Greensboro Civil Rights Oral History Collection, University of North Carolina at Greensboro

Dissertations

Davis, Katrinell Monya. "Dead-End Jobs and the African American Occupational Structure: The Workplace Experiences of High School Educated African American Women, 1970–2000." PhD diss., University of California, Berkeley, 2008.
Hunter, Gary Jerome. "'Don't Buy Where You Can't Work': Black Urban Boycott Movements during the Depression, 1929–1941." PhD diss., University of Michigan, 1979.
Leach, Damarita Etta Brown. "Progress under Pressure: Changes in Charlotte Race Relations, 1955–1965." Master's thesis, University of North Carolina at Chapel Hill, 1976.
Nelson, H. Viscount, Jr. "Race and Class Consciousness of Philadelphia Negroes with Special Emphasis on the Years between 1927 and 1940." PhD diss., University of Pennsylvania, 1969.
Reekie, Gail. "Sydney's Big Stores: Gender and Mass Marketing." PhD diss., University of Sydney, 1987.
Zuckerman, Emily B. "Beyond Dispute: *EEOC v. Sears* and the Politics of Gender, Class, and Affirmative Action, 1968–1986." PhD diss., Rutgers University, 2008.

Unpublished Manuscripts

Turk, Katherine. "From the West Side to the 'Softer Side': Women's Community, Class, and Consumerism in Sears Roebuck's Chicago, 1952–1973." Unpublished manuscript, 2007.

Newspapers/News Sources/Magazines

Associated Press
Atlanta Daily World
Atlanta World
Atlantic
Baltimore Afro-American
Baltimore Style Magazine
Baltimore Sun
Boston Globe
Buffalo News
Charlotte Observer
Chicago Daily Defender
Chicago Daily Tribune
Chicago Defender
Chicago Enquirer
Chicago Tribune
Chicago Whip
CNBC
Colored American Magazine
Crisis Magazine
Dry Goods Chronicle and Fancy Goods Review
Forbes
Harper's magazine
Herald American
Jet magazine
Kiplinger magazine

Los Angeles Sentinel
Los Angeles Times
Meriden Morning Records
Messenger
New Pittsburgh Courier
New York Age
New York Amsterdam News
New York Amsterdam Star-News
New York Daily News
New York Post
New York Times
New York Times Upfront
Opportunity
Philadelphia Tribune
Pittsburgh Courier
Reuters
Richmond News-Leader
Sacramento Observer
Saturday Evening Post
Times Dispatch
USA Today
Wall Street Journal
Washington Post
Washington Post and Times Herald
Women's Wear Daily

Journals

Afro-Americans in New York Life and History
American Communist History
Black Women, Gender, and Families
Catholic World
Cinema Journal
Feminist Studies
French Historical Studies

Hamline University's School of Law's Journal of Public Law and Policy
Hartford Courant, Northeast Magazine
Historical Archaeology
Journal of Aging and Identity
Journal of American History
Journal of the American Institute of Planners

Journal of Policy History

Journal of Retailing

Journal of Social History

Journal of Social Issues

Journal of Southern History

Journal of Urban History

Labor History

Law and History Review

New Labor Form

New Republic

OAH Magazine of History

Pennsylvania Magazine of History and
   Biography

Perspectives in Vernacular Architecture

Phylon

Politics and Society

Review of Black Political Economy

Science & Society

Signs

Southern Jewish Historical Society

Washington History

Yale Law Journal

Court Cases

Carroll v. Sears, Roebuck, & Co., 514 F.Supp. 788 (1981), United States District
   Court, W. D. Louisiana, Shreveport Division, April 20, 1981.

Carroll v. Sears, Roebuck, & Co., 708 F.2d 183 (1983), United States Court of
   Appeals, Fifth Circuit, June 30, 1983.

New Negro Alliance v. Sanitary Grocery Co., 303 U.S. 552 (1938).

Government Records

Albert, William Stone, and Benjamin G. Lovejoy. District of Columbia, *The
   Compiled Statutes in Force in the District of Columbia: Including the acts of the
   second session of the Fiftieth Congress, 1887–89* (Washington, D.C.: Government
   Printing Office, 1894).

Chicago Commission on Race Relations. *The Negro in Chicago: A Study of Race
   Relations and a Race Riot.* Chicago: University of Chicago Press, 1922.

District of Columbia Statutes and Codes, 1890.

Gibson, Campbell, and Kay Jung. "Historical Census Statistics on Population
   Totals by Race, 1790 to 1990, and by Hispanic Origin, 1970 to 1990, for Large
   Cities and Other Urban Places in the United States." U.S. Census Bureau,
   Population Division Working Paper No. 76, 2005.

National Capital Planning Commission. *Civil Disturbances in Washington, D.C.,
   April 4–8, 1968, A Preliminary Damage Report.* Washington, D.C., May 1968.

Report of the Eighth Annual Convention of the National Negro Business League,
   Topeka, Kansas, August 14–16, 1907.

Report of the Ninth Annual Convention of the National Negro Business League,
   Baltimore, Maryland, August 19–21, 1908.

Report of the Fourteenth Annual Convention of the National Negro Business League,
   Philadelphia, Pennsylvania, August 20–23, 1913.

U.S. Bureau of the Census. *Census of Population, 1950.* Washington, D.C.: U.S.
   Government Printing Office, 1950.

———. *Census of Population, 1960.* Washington, D.C.: U.S. Government Printing
   Office, 1961.

―――. *Census of Population, 1970.* Washington, D.C.: U.S. Government Printing Office, 1972.

―――. *Changing Characteristics of the Negro Population* by Daniel O. Price (1960 Census Monograph). Washington, D.C.: U.S. Government Printing Office, 1969.

―――. *Negroes in the United States, 1900.* Washington, D.C.: Government Printing Office, 1904.

―――. *Negroes in the United States, 1910.* Washington, D.C.: Government Printing Office, 1915.

―――. *Negro Population in the United States, 1790–1915.* New York: Arno Press and the New York Times, 1968.

U.S. Department of Commerce and U.S. Bureau of the Census. *The Social and Economic Status of the Black Population in the United States: An Historical View, 1790–1978.* Washington, D.C.: Government Printing Office, 1979.

U.S. Department of Labor. *Negro Women in Industry.* Washington, D.C.: Government Printing Office, 1922.

U.S. Department of Labor, Bureau of Labor Statistics. Labor Force Statistics from the Current Population Survey, 1995.

―――. Labor Force Statistics from the Current Population Survey, 2014.

―――. Labor Force Statistics from the Current Population Survey, 2017.

Film

Badger, Clarence G., dir. *It* (1927). Image Entertainment, 2004.

Articles, Books, and Other Secondary Sources

Abelson, Elaine. *When Ladies Go A-Thieving: Middle-Class Shoplifters in the Victorian Department Store.* New York: Oxford University Press, 1989.

Adams, Maurianne, and John Bracey, ed. *Strangers and Neighbors: Relations between Blacks and Jews in the United States.* Amherst: University of Massachusetts Press, 1999.

Arnesen, Eric. "Whiteness and the Historians' Imagination." *International Labor and Working-Class History* 60 (October 2001): 3–32.

Auslander, Leora. *Taste and Power: Furnishing Modern France.* Berkeley: University of California Press, 1996.

Austin, Allan W. *Quaker Brotherhood: Interracial Activism and the American Friends Service Committee, 1917–1950.* Urbana: University of Illinois Press, 2012.

Barmash, Isadore. *Macy's for Sale.* New York: Weidenfeld & Nicolson, 1989; reprinted Washington, D.C.: Beard Books.

Belisle, Donica. *Retail Nation: Department Stores and the Making of Modern Canada.* Vancouver, BC: UBC Press, 2011.

Benson, John, and Gareth Shaw, eds. *The Evolution of Retail Systems, c.1800–1914.* London: Leicester University Press, 1992.

Benson, Susan Porter. "'The Clerking Sisterhood' Rationalization and the Work Culture of Saleswomen in American Department Stores, 1890–1960." *Radical America* 12 (March–April 1978): 41–55.

——. *Counter Cultures: Saleswomen, Managers, and Customers in American Department Stores, 1890–1940.* Urbana: University of Illinois Press, 1986.

Biondi, Martha. *To Stand and Fight: The Struggle for Civil Rights in Postwar New York.* Cambridge, MA: Harvard University Press, 2006.

Bjelopera, Jerome P. *City of Clerks: Office and Sales Workers in Philadelphia, 1870–1920.* Urbana: University of Illinois Press, 2005.

——. "White Collars and Blackface: Race and Leisure among Clerical and Sales Workers in Early Twentieth-Century Philadelphia." *Pennsylvania Magazine of History and Biography* 126 (July 2002): 471–90.

Black Women in Connecticut: Achievement against Odds. Hartford: Connecticut Historical Society, 1984.

Bloom, Gordon, F. Marion Fletcher, and Charles R. Perry. *Negro Employment in Retail Trade: A Study of Racial Policies in the Department Store, Drugstore, and Supermarket Industries.* Philadelphia: Industrial Research Unit, Wharton School of Finance and Commerce, University of Pennsylvania, 1972.

Bluestone, Barry, Patricia Hanna, Sarah Kuhn, and Laura Moore. *The Retail Revolution: Market Transformation, Investment, and Labor in the Modern Department Store.* Boston: Auburn House Publishing, 1981.

Brandt, Nat. *Harlem at War: The Black Experience in WWII.* Syracuse, NY: Syracuse University Press, 1996.

Brodkin, Karen. *How Jews Became White Folks and What That Says about Race in America.* New Brunswick, NJ: Rutgers University Press, 1999.

Brown, Elsa Barkley. "Constructing a Life and a Community: A Partial Story of Maggie Lena Walker." *OAH Magazine of History* 7, no. 4 (Summer 1993).

——. "Womanist Consciousness: Maggie Lena Walker and the Independent Order of Saint Luke." *Signs* 14, no. 3 (Spring 1989): 610–33.

Butler, Elizabeth Beardsley. *Saleswomen in Mercantile Stores.* New York: Charities Publications Committee, 1912.

Caplan, Marvin. *Farther Along: A Civil Rights Memoir.* Baton Rouge: Louisiana State University Press, 1999.

Carson, Clayborne. *In Struggle: SNCC and the Black Awakening of the 1960s.* Cambridge, MA: Harvard University Press, 1981.

——, ed. *The Student Voice, 1960–1965: Periodical of the Student Nonviolent Coordinating Committee.* Westport, CT: Meckler, 1990.

Chatelain, Marcia. *South Side Girls: Growing Up in the Great Migration.* Durham, NC: Duke University Press, 2015.

Cherry, Frances, and Catherine Borshuk. "Social Action Research and the Commission on Community Interrelations." *Journal of Social Issues* 54, no. 1 (1998): 119–42.

Clemmons, Jeff. *Rich's: A Southern Institution.* Charleston, SC: History Press, 2012.

Cobble, Dorothy Sue. *Dishing It Out: Waitresses and Their Unions in the Twentieth Century.* Urbana: University of Illinois Press, 1991.

Coffin, Alex. *Brookshire & Belk: Businessmen in City Hall.* Charlotte: University of North Carolina, 1994.

Cohen, Lizabeth. *A Consumers' Republic: The Politics of Mass Consumption in Postwar America.* New York: Alfred A. Knopf, 2003.

———. *Making a New Deal: Industrial Workers in Chicago, 1919–1939.* Cambridge: Cambridge University Press, 1990.

"A Common Type of Dry Goods Shopper." *Dry Goods Chronicle and Fancy Goods Review* 4 (July 9, 1887): 1.

Cooper, Patricia. "The Limits of Persuasion: Race Reformers and the Department Store Campaign in Philadelphia, 1945–1948." *Pennsylvania Magazine of History and Biography* 126 (January 2002): 97–126.

Countryman, Matthew J. *Up South: Civil Rights and Black Power in Philadelphia.* Philadelphia: University of Pennsylvania Press, 2005.

Crossick, Geoffrey, and Serge Jaumain, eds. *Cathedrals of Consumption: The European Department Store, 1850–1939.* Aldershot, England: Ashgate Publishing, 1999.

Crossland, William A. *Industrial Conditions among Negroes in St. Louis.* St. Louis, MO: Press of Mendle Print, 1914.

Crowder, Ralph L. "'Don't Buy Where You Can't Work': An Investigation of the Political Forces and Social Conflict within the Harlem Boycott of 1934." *Afro-Americans in New York Life and History* 15, no. 2 (July 1991): 7–44.

Dalfiume, Richard M. "The 'Forgotten Years' of the Negro Revolution." *Journal of American History* 55 (June 1968): 90–106.

Dawson, Michael C. *Behind the Mule: Race and Class in African-American Politics.* Princeton, NJ: Princeton University Press, 1994.

———. *Black Visions: The Roots of Contemporary African American Ideologies.* Chicago: University of Chicago Press, 2001.

Decter, Avi Y., and Melissa Martens, eds. *Enterprising Emporiums: The Jewish Department Stores of Downtown Baltimore.* Baltimore: Jewish Museum of Maryland, 2001.

Delgado, Richard, and Jean Stefancic, eds. *Critical White Studies: Looking behind the Mirror.* Philadelphia: Temple University Press, 1997.

Delton, Jennifer. *Racial Integration in Corporate America, 1940–1990.* New York: Cambridge University Press, 2009.

DeVault, Ileen. *Sons and Daughters of Labor: Class and Clerical Work in Turn-of-the-Century Pittsburgh.* Ithaca, NY: Cornell University Press, 1990.

Devinatz, Victor G. "A Reevaluation of the Trade Union League, 1929–1934." *Science & Society* 71, no. 1 (January 2007): 33–58.

Donovan, Frances. *The Saleslady.* Chicago: University of Chicago Press, 1929.

Drake, St. Clair. *Churches and Voluntary Associations in the Chicago Negro Community.* Chicago: U.S. Works Projects Administration, 1940.

Drake, St. Clair, and Horace Cayton. *Black Metropolis: A Study of Negro Life in a Northern City.* 1945; Chicago: University of Chicago Press, 1993.

DuRocher, Kristina. *Raising Racist: The Socialization of White Children in the Jim Crow South.* Lexington: University Press of Kentucky, 2011.

Edwards, Paul K. *The Southern Urban Negro as a Consumer*. New York: Prentice-Hall, 1932.

"Evaluation of Services to Customers." *Journal of Retailing* 5 (October 1929): 25–26.

Ezra, Michael, ed. *The Economic Civil Rights Movement: African Americans and the Struggle for Economic Power*. New York: Routledge, 2013.

Farrar, Hayward. *The Baltimore Afro-American, 1892–1950*. Westport, CT: Greenwood Press, 1998.

Fauset, Jessie Redmon. *Plum Bun: A Novel without a Moral*. 1928; Boston: Beacon Press, 1990.

Fine, Gary Alan, and Patricia Ann Turner. *Whispers on the Color Line: Rumor and Race in America*. Berkeley: University of California Press, 2001.

Ford, Tanisha. "SNCC Women, Denim, and the Politics of Dress." *Journal of Southern History* 79, no. 3 (August 2013): 625–58.

Fradin, Dennis Brindell, and Judith Bloom Fradin. *Fight On! Mary Church Terrell's Battle for Integration*. New York: Clarion Books, 2003.

Frank, Dana. "Where Are the Workers in Consumer-Worker Alliances? Class Dynamics and the History of Consumer-Labor Campaigns." *Politics and Society* 31 (September 2003): 363–79.

Frazier, E. Franklin. *Black Bourgeoisie: The Rise of a New Middle Class in the United States*. 1957; New York: Collier Books, 1962.

Gilbert, Ben W., and the Staff of the Washington Post. *Ten Blocks from the White House: Anatomy of the Washington Riots of 1968*. New York: Frederick A. Praeger, 1968.

Glickman, Lawrence. *Buying Power: A History of Consumer Activism in America*. Chicago: University of Chicago Press, 2009.

Goldfield, David R. *Black, White, and Southern: Race Relations and Southern Culture, 1940 to the Present*. Baton Rouge: Louisiana State University Press, 1990.

Goluboff, Risa L. *The Lost Promise of Civil Rights*. Cambridge, MA: Harvard University Press, 2007.

Green, Adam. *Selling the Race: Culture, Community, and Black Chicago, 1940–1955*. Chicago: University of Chicago Press, 2006.

Green, CeeLo, Big Gipp, and David Wild. *Everybody's Brother*. New York: Grand Central Publishing, 2013.

Green, Constance McLaughlin. *The Secret City: A History of Race Relations in the Nation's Capital*. Princeton, NJ: Princeton University Press, 1969.

Green, Venus. "Flawed Remedies: EEOC, AT&T, and Sears Outcomes Reconsidered." *Black Women, Gender, and Families* 16, no. 1 (Spring 2012): 43–70.

———. *Race on the Line: Gender, Labor, and Technology in the Bell System, 1880–1980*. Durham, NC: Duke University Press, 2001.

Greenberg, Cheryl Lynn. *Or Does It Explode? Black Harlem in the Great Depression*. New York: Oxford University Press, 1991.

———. "The Politics of Disorder: Reexamining Harlem's Riots of 1935 and 1943." *Journal of Urban History* 18 (August 1992): 395–441.

Greene, Lorenzo J., and Carter G. Woodson. *The Negro Wage Earner.* Washington, D.C.: Association for the Study of Negro Life and History, 1930.

Gregory, Dick, and Robert Lipsyte. *Nigger: An Autobiography.* New York: Washington Square Press, 1964.

Grofman, Bernard, ed. *Legacies of the 1964 Civil Rights Act.* Charlottesville: University of Virginia Press, 2000.

Grossman, James. *Land of Hope: Chicago, Black Southerners, and the Great Migration.* Chicago: University of Chicago Press, 1989.

Gubar, Susan. *White Skin, Black Face in American Culture.* Oxford: Oxford University Press, 1997.

Hale, Grace Elizabeth. *Making Whiteness: The Culture of Segregation in the South, 1890–1940.* New York: Pantheon, 1998.

Hampton, Henry, and Steve Fayer. *Voices of Freedom: An Oral History of the Civil Rights Movement from the 1950s through the 1980s.* New York: Bantam Books, 1990.

Hardin, John A. *Fifty Years of Segregation: Black Higher Education in Kentucky, 1904–1954.* Lexington: University Press of Kentucky, 1997.

Harding, John, and Russell Hogrefe. "Attitudes of White Department Store Employees toward Negro Co-Workers." *Journal of Social Issues* 8, no. 1 (1952): 18–28.

Harris, Cheryl I. "Whiteness as Property." *Harvard Law Review* 106 (June 1993): 1707–91.

Haynes, Bruce D. *Red Lines, Black Spaces: The Politics of Race and Space in a Black Middle-Class Suburb.* New Haven, CT: Yale University Press, 2001.

Hedgeman, Anna Arnold. *The Trumpet Sounds: A Memoir of Negro Leadership.* New York: Holt, Rinehart, and Winston, 1964.

Hepp, John Henry. *The Middle-Class City: Transforming Space and Time in Philadelphia, 1876–1926.* Philadelphia: University of Pennsylvania Press, 2005.

Hine, Darlene Clark. *Hine Sight: Black Women and the Reconstruction of American History.* Brooklyn: Carlson Publishing, 1994.

Hobbs, Allyson. *A Chosen Exile.* Cambridge, MA: Harvard University Press, 2014.

Holloway, Jonathan Scott. *Confronting the Veil: Abram Harris Jr., E. Franklin Frazier, and Ralph Bunche, 1919–1941.* Chapel Hill: University of North Carolina Press, 2002.

Holloway, Joseph E. *Africanisms in American Culture.* Bloomington: Indiana University Press, 1990.

Holt, Thomas C. *Children of Fire: A History of African Americans.* New York: Hill and Wang, 2010.

Honey, Michael K. *Southern Labor and Black Civil Rights: Organizing Memphis Workers.* Urbana: University of Illinois Press, 1993.

Horton, James Oliver. *Free People of Color inside the Black Community.* Washington, D.C.: Smithsonian Institution Press, 1993.

Howard, Vicki. *From Main Street to Mall: The Rise and Fall of the American Department Store.* Philadelphia: University of Pennsylvania, 2015.

Hunter, Tera. *To 'Joy My Freedom: Southern Black Women's Lives and Labors after the Civil War.* Cambridge, MA: Harvard University Press, 1997.

Isenberg, Alison. *Downtown America: A History of the Place and the People Who Made It.* Chicago: University of Chicago Press, 2004.

Jackson, John P., Jr. *Social Scientists for Social Justice: Making the Case against Segregation.* New York: New York University Press, 2001.

Jackson, Kenneth T. *Crabgrass Frontier: The Suburbanization of the United States.* New York: Oxford University Press, 1985.

Jones, Beverly W. "Before Montgomery and Greensboro: The Desegregation Movement in the District of Columbia, 1950–1953." *Phylon* 43, no. 2 (1982): 144–54.

Jones, Jacqueline. *Labor of Love, Labor of Sorrow: Black Women, Work, and the Family from Slavery to Present.* New York: Basic Books, 2010.

Katz, Donald R. *The Big Store: Inside the Crisis and Revolution at Sears.* New York: Penguin Books, 1988.

Kelley, Blair L. M. *Right to Ride: Streetcar Boycotts and African American Citizenship in the Era of Plessy v. Ferguson.* Chapel Hill: University of North Carolina Press, 2010.

Kelley, Robin D. G. *Race Rebels: Culture, Politics, and the Black Working Class.* New York: Free Press, 1996.

Klineberg, Eric. *Heat Wave: A Social Autopsy of Disaster in Chicago.* Chicago: University of Chicago Press, 2002.

Kornbluh, Felicia. "To Fulfill Their 'Rightly Need': Consumerism and the National Welfare Rights Movement." *Radical History Review* 69 (1997): 76–113.

Korstad, Robert. "Civil Rights Unionism and the Black Freedom Struggle." *American Communist History* 7, no. 2 (2008): 255–58.

———. *Civil Rights Unionism: Tobacco Workers and the Struggle for Democracy in the Mid-Twentieth-Century South.* Durham: University of North Carolina Press, 2003.

Korstad, Robert, and Nelson Lichtenstein. "Opportunities Found and Lost: Labor, Radicals, and the Early Civil Rights Movement." *Journal of American History* 75, no. 3 (December 1988): 786–811.

Kranz, Rachel. *African-American Business Leaders and Entrepreneurs.* New York: Facts on File, 2004.

Kreydatus, Beth. "'You Are a Part of All of Us': Black Department Store Employees in Jim Crow Richmond." *Journal of Historical Research in Marketing* 2, no. 1 (2010): 108–29.

Kruse, Kevin M., and Thomas J. Sugrue, eds. *The New Suburban History.* Chicago: University of Chicago Press, 2006.

Kusmer, Kenneth L., and Joe W. Trotter, eds. *African American Urban History since World War II.* Chicago: University of Chicago Press, 2009.

Lacy, Karyn R. *Blue-Chip Black: Race, Class, and Status in the New Black Middle Class.* Berkeley: University of California Press, 2007.

LaFeber, Walter. *Michael Jordan and the New Global Capitalism.* New Edition. New York: W. W. Norton, 2002.

Lancaster, Bill. *The Department Store: A Social History*. London: Leicester University Press, 1995.

Landry, Bart. *The New Black Middle Class*. Berkeley: University of California Press, 1987.

Larsen, Nella. *Passing*. 1929; New York: Modern Library, 2000.

Laughlin, Kathleen A., and Jacqueline L. Castledine, eds. *Breaking the Wave: Women, Their Organizations, and Feminism, 1945–1985*. New York: Routledge, 2011.

Leach, William. *Land of Desire: Merchants, Power, and the Rise of a New American Culture*. New York: Vintage Books, 1993.

———. "Transformations in a Culture of Consumption: Women and Department Stores, 1890–1925." *Journal of American History* 71, no. 2 (September 1984): 319–42.

Lee, Sophia Z. "Hotspots in a Cold War: The NAACP's Postwar Workplace Constitutionalism, 1948–1964." *Law and History Review* 26, no. 2 (Summer 2008): 326–77.

Lichtenstein, Nelson. *The Retail Revolution: How Wal-Mart Created a Brave New World of Business*. New York: Metropolitan Books, 2009.

———. *State of the Union: A Century of American Labor*. Princeton, NJ: Princeton University Press, 2002.

———, ed. *Wal-Mart: The Face of Twenty-First-Century Capitalism*. New York: New Press, 2006.

———. "Wal-Mart and the New World Order: A Template for Twenty-First-Century Capitalism?" *New Labor Form* 14, no. 1 (Spring 2005): 20–30.

Lisicky, Michael J. *Woodward & Lothrop: A Store Worthy of the Nation's Capital*. Charleston, SC: History Press, 2013.

Local Community Fact Book, Chicago Metropolitan Area, 1960. Prepared by Chicago Community Inventory, University of Chicago, 1963.

Loewen, James W. *Sundown Towns: A Hidden Dimension of American Racism*. New York: Touchstone, 2006.

Longstreth, Richard. "The Mixed Blessings of Success: The Hecht Company and Department Store Branch Development after World War II." *Perspectives in Vernacular Architecture*, vol. 6, Shaping Communities (1997): 244–62.

Lott, Eric. *Love and Theft: Blackface Minstrelsy and the American Working Class*. New York: Oxford University Press, 1995.

Macek, Steve. *Urban Nightmares: The Media, the Right, and the Moral Panic over the City*. Minneapolis: University of Minnesota Press, 2006.

Mack, Kenneth. "Rethinking Civil Rights Lawyering and Politics in the Era before Brown." *Yale Law Journal* 115 (2005): 256–354.

MacLean, Nancy. *Freedom Is Not Enough: The Opening of the American Workplace*. Cambridge, MA: Harvard University Press, 2006.

Margo, Robert A. "Schooling and the Great Migration." Working Paper No. 2697, National Bureau of Economic Research, Cambridge, MA, September 1988.

McBride, Theresa. "A Woman's World: Department Stores and the Evolution of Women's Employment, 1870–1920." *French Historical Studies* 10 (1977): 664–83.

McKay, Claude. *Harlem: Negro Metropolis.* New York: E.P. Dutton, 1940.

Meier, August, and Elliot M. Rudwick. *Along the Color Line: Explorations in the Black Experience.* Urbana: University of Illinois Press, 1976.

———. *Black Detroit and the Rise of the UAW.* New York: Oxford University Press, 1979.

Meyerowitz, Joanne. *Women Adrift: Independent Wage Earners in Chicago, 1880–1930.* Chicago: University of Chicago Press, 1991.

Michman, Ronald D., and Alan James Greco. *Retailing Triumphs and Blunders: Victims of Competition in the New Age of Marketing Management.* Westport, CT: Greenwood, 1995.

Michman, Ronald D., and Edward M. Mazze. *Specialty Retailers: Marketing Triumphs and Blunders.* Westport, CT: Greenwood, 2001.

Milkman, Ruth. "Women's History and the Sears Case." *Feminist Studies* 12, no. 2 (Summer 1986): 375–400.

Miller, Michael Barry. *The Bon Marché: Bourgeois Culture and the Department Store, 1869–1920.* Princeton, NJ: Princeton University Press, 1981.

Mills, C. Wright. *White Collar: The American Middle Classes.* Cambridge: Oxford University Press, 1951.

Mitchell, Michele. *Righteous Propagation: African Americans and the Politics of Racial Destiny after Reconstruction.* Chapel Hill: University of North Carolina Press, 2004.

Mjagkjj, Nina. "A Peculiar Alliance: Julius Rosenwald, the YMCA, and African-Americans, 1910–1933." *American Jewish Archives* 44, no. 2 (Fall–Winter 1992): 585–605.

Moreno, Paul. *From Direct Action to Affirmative Action: Fair Employment Law and Policy in America, 1933–1972.* Baton Rouge: Louisiana State University Press, 1997.

———. "Racial Proportionalism and the Origins of Employment Discrimination Policy." *Journal of Policy History* 8 (October 1996): 410–39.

Mullins, Paul R., "Race and the Genteel Consumer: Class and African American Consumption, 1850–1930." *Historical Archaeology* 33, no. 1 (1999): 22–38.

Muraskin, William. "The Harlem Boycott of 1934: Black Nationalism and the Rise of Labor-Union Consciousness." *Labor History* 13, no. 3 (1972): 361–73.

Murray, Pauli, ed. *States' Laws on Race and Color.* Cincinnati, OH: Woman's Division of Christian Service, 1951; reprinted, Athens: University of Georgia Press, 1997.

New Negro Alliance Year Book 1939. Washington, D.C.: Alliance, 1939.

Nicolaides, Becky M., and Andrew Wiese, eds. *The Suburb Reader.* New York: Routledge, 2006.

Norton, Mary Beth, and Ruth M. Alexander, eds. *Major Problems in American Women's History.* Lexington, MA: D.C. Heath, 1996.

O'Brien, Patricia. "The Kleptomania Diagnosis: Bourgeois Women and Theft in Late Nineteenth-Century France." *Journal of Social History* 17 (Fall 1983): 65–77.

Ohrbach, Nathan. *Getting Ahead in Retailing.* New York: McGraw-Hill, 1935.

Olesker, Michael. *Journeys to the Heart of Baltimore*. Baltimore: Johns Hopkins University Press, 2001.

Opler, Daniel. *For All White-Collar Workers: The Possibilities of Radicalism in New York City's Department Store Unions, 1934–1953*. Columbus: Ohio State University Press, 2007.

Oppenheimer, Martin. *The Sit-In Movement of 1960*. Brooklyn: Carlson Publishing, 1989.

Orgeron, Marsha. "Making *It* in Hollywood: Clara Bow, Fandom, and Consumer Culture." *Cinema Journal* 42, no. 4 (2003): 76–97.

Orleck, Annelise. *Storming Caesars Palace: How Black Mothers Fought Their Own War on Poverty*. Boston: Beacon Press, 2005.

Ormsby, Stella. "The Other Side of the Profile." *New Republic* 72 (August 17, 1932): 21.

Ortega, Bob. *In Sam We Trust: The Untold Story of Sam Walton and How Wal-Mart Is Devouring the World*. New York: Times Books, 1998.

Ottley, Roi. *New World A-Coming: Inside Black America*. Boston: Houghton Mifflin, 1943.

Ownby, Ted. *American Dreams in Mississippi: Consumers, Poverty, and Culture, 1830–1998*. Chapel Hill: University of North Carolina Press, 1999.

Pacifico, Michele F. "'Don't Buy Where You Can't Work': The New Negro Alliance of Washington." *Washington History* 6, no. 1 (Spring/Summer 1994): 66–88.

Parent-Lardeur, Françoise. *Les demoiselles de magasin*. Paris: New Editions Ouvrières, 1970.

Parker, Traci. "Shopping While Black." In *The SAGE Encyclopedia of Economics and Society*, 1473–75. SAGE Publications, 2015.

Pasdermadjian, Hrant. *The Department Store: Its Origins, Evolution, and Economics*. London: Newman Books, 1954.

Patten, Simon. *The Consumption of Wealth*. 1899.

Pattillo-McCoy, Mary. *Black Picket Fences: Privilege and Peril among the Black Middle Class*. Chicago: University of Chicago Press, 1999.

Phillips, Kimberley. *AlabamaNorth: African American Migrants, Community, and Working-Class Activism, 1915–1945*. Urbana: University of Illinois Press, 1999.

Pitrone, Jean Maddern. *F.W. Woolworth and the American Five and Dime: A Social History*. Jefferson, NC: McFarland Publishers, 2003.

Powell, Raphael P. *Human Side of a People and the Right Name: The Great Book of New Education*. New York: Philemon, 1937.

Rabuck, Kim. "A Racist Curfew in Madison." SocialistWorker, August 3, 2017. Accessed August 22, 2017. http://socialistworker.org/2017/08/03/a-racist -curfew-in-madison.

Rappaport, Erika. *Shopping for Pleasure: Women in the Making of London's West End*. Princeton, NJ: Princeton University Press, 2000.

Reed, Christopher Robert. *The Rise of Chicago's Black Metropolis, 1910–1929*. Urbana: University of Illinois Press, 2011.

Reed, Touré F. *Not Alms but Opportunity: The Urban League & the Politics of Racial Uplift, 1910–1950*. Chapel Hill: University of North Carolina Press, 2008.

Renoy, George. *Les Grands Magasins*. Bruxelles: Rossel, 1986.

Rich, Wilbur C., ed. *African American Perspectives on Political Science.* Philadelphia: Temple University Press, 2007.

Richings, G. F. *Evidence of Progress among Colored People.* Philadelphia: Geo. S. Ferguson, 1902.

Roediger, David. *Wages of Whiteness: Race and the Making of the American Working Class.* New York: Verso, 1991.

Rogin, Michael. *Blackface, White Noise: Jewish Immigrants in the Hollywood Melting Pot.* Berkeley: University of California Press, 1998.

Ruetschlin, Catherine, and Dedrick Asante-Muhammad. "The Retail Race Divide: How the Retail Industry Is Perpetuating Racial Inequality in the 21st Century." *Demos*, June 2, 2015. Accessed April 1, 2018. http://www.demos.org /publication/retail-race-divide-how-retail-industry-perpetuating-racial -inequality-21st-century.

Saenger, Gerhart. "How Can We Fight Discrimination?" *Survey* 86 (December 1950): 545–48.

Saenger, Gerhart, and Emily Gilbert. "Customer Reactions to the Integration of Negro Sales Personnel." *International Journal of Opinion and Attitude Research* 4 (Spring 1950): 57–76.

Sandoval-Strausz, A. K. *Hotel: An American History.* New Haven, CT: Yale University Press, 2007.

Schalk, Adolph. "Negroes, Restaurants, and Washington, D.C.," *Catholic World* 174 (January 1952): 279–83.

Self, Robert O. *American Babylon: Race and the Struggle for Postwar Oakland.* Princeton, NJ: Princeton University Press, 2003.

Seligman, Amanda I. *Block by Block: Neighborhoods and Public Policy on Chicago's West Side.* Chicago: University of Chicago Press, 2005.

Semmes, Clovis E. *The Regal Theater and Black Culture.* New York: Palgrave Macmillan, 2006.

Shenk, Dena. "Views of Aging African American Women: Memories within the Historical Context." *Journal of Aging and Identity* (2000): 109–25.

Sitkoff, Harvard. *A New Deal for Blacks: The Emergence of Civil Rights as a National Issue.* New York: Oxford University Press, 1978.

Skotnes, Andor. *A New Deal for All? Race and Class Struggles in Depression-Era Baltimore.* Durham, NC: Duke University Press, 2013.

Smith, C. Fraser. *Here Lies Jim Crow: Civil Rights in Maryland.* Baltimore: Johns Hopkins University Press, 2008.

Snyder, Brad. *Beyond the Shadow of the Senators: The Untold Story of the Homestead Grays and the Integration of Baseball.* New York: McGraw Hill, 2004.

Solomon, Burt. *The Washington Century: Three Families and the Shaping of the Nation's Capital.* New York: HarperCollins Publishers, 2004.

Spector, Robert, and Patrick D. McCarthy. *The Nordstrom Way: The Inside Story of America's #1 Customer Service Company.* New York: Wiley, 2000.

Stange, Maren. *Bronzeville: Black Chicago in Pictures, 1941–1943.* New York: New Press, 2004.

Stern, Elizabeth. *I Am a Woman—and a Jew.* New York: Arno Press, 1969.

Sternleib, George. "The Future of Retailing in the Downtown Core." *Journal of the American Institute of Planners* 29, no. 2 (1963): 102–12.

Strang, William A., Gilbert A. Churchill, and Robert H. Collins. "Blacks in Sales: Why Are There So Few?" *Review of Black Political Economy* 6, no. 2 (1976): 200–212.

Strickland, Arvah E. *The History of the Chicago Urban League.* Urbana: University of Illinois Press, 1966.

Sugrue, Thomas J. *Origins of the Urban Crisis: Race and Inequality in Postwar Detroit.* Princeton, NJ: Princeton University Press, 1996.

———. *Sweet Land of Liberty: The Forgotten Struggle for Civil Rights in the North.* New York: Random House Trade Paperbacks, 2009.

Sullivan, Leon. *Build Brother Build.* Philadelphia: Macrae Smith, 1969.

Sykes, Gertude. "Dress Regulations in New York Metropolitan Stores." *Journal of Retailing* (January 1929): 28–29.

Tager, Jack. *Boston Riots: Three Centuries of Social Violence.* Boston: Northeastern University Press, 2001.

Tóibín, Colm. *Brooklyn.* New York: Scribner, 2009.

Trade Union Unity League. *The Trade Union Unity League (American Section of the R.I.L.U.): Its Program, Structure, Methods, and History.* New York: Trade Union Unity League, 1930s. Accessed March 21, 2012. http://www.archive.org/stream /TheTradeUnionUnityLeagueamericanSectionOfTheR.i.l.u.ItsProgram/TUUL1 _djvu.txt.

Trotter, Joe William, Jr. *Black Milwaukee: The Making of an Industrial Proletariat, 1915–45.* Urbana: University of Illinois Press, 1985.

Turk, Katherine. *Equality on Trial.* Philadelphia: University of Pennsylvania, 2016.

Turner, Marcia Layton. *Kmart's Ten Deadly Sins: How Incompetence Tainted an American Icon.* Hoboken, NJ: John Wiley & Sons, 2003.

Veblen, Thorstein. *The Theory of the Leisure Class: An Economic Study of Institutions.* 1899.

Von Eschen, Penny M. *Race against Empire: Black Americans and Anticolonialism, 1937–1957.* Ithaca, NY: Cornell University Press, 1997.

Walton, Whitney. *France at the Crystal Palace: Bourgeois Taste and Artisan Manufacture in the Nineteenth Century.* Berkeley: University of California Press, 1992.

Waynick, Capus M., John C. Brooks, and Elsie W. Pitts, eds. *North Carolina and the Negro.* Raleigh: North Carolina Mayors' Co-operating Committee, 1964.

Webb, Clive. "Jewish Merchants and Black Customers in the Age of Jim Crow." *Southern Jewish Historical Society* 2 (1998): 55–80.

Weems, Robert. *Desegregating the Dollar: African American Consumerism in the Twentieth Century.* New York: New York University Press, 1998.

Weil, Gordon L. *Sears, Roebuck, U.S.A.: The Great American Catalog Store and How It Grew.* New York: Stein & Day, 1977.

Weisberg, D. Kelly, ed. *Application of Feminist Legal Theory to Women's Lives: Sex, Violence, Work, and Reproduction.* Philadelphia: Temple University Press, 1996.

Whitaker, Jan. *Service and Style: How the American Department Store Fashioned the Middle Class*. New York: St. Martin's, 2006.

Who's Who in Colored America, 1930–1932. Brooklyn, NY, 1933.

Who's Who in Colored America, 1938–1949. Brooklyn, NY, 1940.

Wiese, Andrew. *Places of Their Own: African American Suburbanization in the Twentieth Century*. Chicago: University of Chicago Press, 2004.

Williams, James D., ed. *The State of Black America, 1981*. National Urban League, 1981.

Williamson, Joel. *The Crucible of Race: Black-White Relations in the American South since Emancipation*. New York: Oxford University Press, 1993.

———. *New People: Miscegenation and Mulattoes in the United States*. New York: Free Press, 1980.

Wiltse, Jeff. *Contested Waters: A Social History of Swimming Pools in America*. Chapel Hill: University of North Carolina Press, 2007.

Windham, Lane. *Knocking on Labor's Door: Union Organizing in the 1970s and the Roots of a New Economic Divide*. Chapel Hill: University of North Carolina Press, 2017.

Wolcott, Victoria W. *Race, Riots, and Roller Coasters: The Struggle over Segregated Recreation in America*. Philadelphia: University of Pennsylvania Press, 2012.

Wolfinger, James. *Philadelphia Divided: Race and Politics in the City of Brotherly Love*. Chapel Hill: University of North Carolina Press, 2007.

Woods, Jeff. *Black Struggle, Red Scare: Segregation and Anti-Communism in the South, 1948–1968*. Baton Rouge: Louisiana State University Press, 2004.

Wright, Gavin. *Sharing the Prize: The Economics of the Civil Rights Revolution in the American South*. Cambridge, MA: Belknap Press of Harvard University Press, 2013.

Wright, John A. *Discovering African American St. Louis: A Guide to Historic Sites*. 2nd ed. St. Louis: Missouri Historical Society Press, 2002.

Wright, Richard R., Jr. *The Negro in Pennsylvania: A Study in Economic History*. New York: Arno Press, 1969.

Index

Note: Figures are indicated by page numbers in *italics*.

civil rights unionism, 83–84

Clark, Leslie, 77

Clearing House on Open Occupancy, 180

Cleveland, 84

CLFP. *See* Citizen's League for Fair Play (CLFP)

Clinique, 172

Clinton, Hillary, 231

clothing, 12–13, 42, 133, 232, 254n7, 276n25

club, department store as, 19–20

Cohen, Lizabeth, 12, 49, 59, 66, 241n14

Coleman, Claude, 283n26

Colgan, Thomas, 133–36

collection agencies, 45

Collins, Jas H., 241n3

"Colored Minstrel Boys, Oh, What Music" (toy), 43–44

colorism, 67–69. *See also* "passing"

Committee on Appeal for Human Rights, 178

Committee on Equal Employment Opportunity (CEEO), 162

Committee on Fair Employment Practices in Department Stores (CEPDS), 125–31

Committee on Friendly Relations, 173–74

Communist Party, 70, 83, 91

Community Action Program, 198

Community Relations Committee, 261n27

Congress of Industrial Organizations (CIO), 72, 83, 99, 101, 108, 112, 123

Congress of Racial Equality (CORE), 7; Chicago desegregation efforts of, 79–80; and Committee on Fair Employment Practices in Department Stores, 125, 130–31; employment movement of, 176; Hecht's and, 164–65; poll on receptiveness to African American salespeople, 76; public accommodations and, 119–20; racist products and, 144–45; Sears and, 203; Wanamaker's and, 127

Conshankin, Bishop, 57–58. *See also* Hamid, Sufi Abdul

Consolidated Housewives League, 79, 145

conspicuous consumption, 240n39, 241n13

Consumers' Protective Committee, 145

Consumers' Unit No 1, 145

consumption: acceleration of, 114–15; African American department store, 41–53; and African American sales personnel, 118–19; as civic responsibility, 117; and civil rights movement, 7–8, 10; conspicuous, 240n39, 241n13; and discount retail, 186–87; in Great Depression, 54; as liberation, 12; middle class, 5–6; new modes of, 187–92; patriotic, 95; as resistance, 11–12; and World War II, 95

Coordinating Committee for the Enforcement of D.C. Anti-Discrimination Laws (CCEAD), 148, 154–55, 158–59, 161

CORE. *See* Congress of Racial Equality (CORE)

Cosmopolitan Social and Tennis Club, 65

Country Delight Dairy, 178

Covington, Bettie J., 203–4

credit, 44–45, 246n96

Crossland, William A., 40

CUL. *See* Chicago Urban League (CUL)

Cumberbatch, James, 92

curfews, 235

customer service, 37, 39, 42–43, 123, 152, 230

Davidson, Eugene, 62

Davis, Benjamin, Jr., 89

Davis, Benjamin J., 101

Davis, Doretha, 167, 169–71, 271n61

Davison-Paxon, 267n3

Dawson, Michael, 150

"dead malls," 225–26

Dean, Mary, 99

hotels, 3–4
"House Palatial, The," 19–20
Housewives League, 84
Houston, Charles, 62
Howard, Vicki, 60, 193
Howard University, 62, 79, 267n2
Hutzler Brothers, 46, 81
Hyde, Helen, 98–99
Hyde Park Cooperative Society, 76

I. Magnin, 275n18
Imes, William Lloyd, 65, 70
immigrants: as department store
    employees, 21–23, 26; as waitresses,
    151
Immigration Act of 1924, 22
income, 230; of African American work-
    ers, 31–32, 91–92, 101, 108–10, 112,
    138, 244n54, 259n86; of discount
    store employees, 189–90
Independent Order of St. Luke, 37
intimate apparel, 42
It (film), 15–16, 24, 52–53
"it girl," 15–16
Ives-Quinn Bill, 97, 122
Ivey's, 165, 174

Jackson, A. P., 111–12
Jackson, E. Franklin, 162
Jackson, Jesse, 210
J.C. Penney, 3, 191, 237n5
JCSU. *See* Johnson C. Smith University
    (JCSU)
jeans, 181
Jenkins, Issie L., 215–16
Jews, 21–22, 75, 80, 97, 103, 194. *See
    also* American Jewish Congress
Jim Crow, 4–5, 86, 96, 119. *See also*
    segregation
J. L. Hudson, 229
job applications, 77
Jobs for Youth program, 198–99
Johnson, Eric, 154
Johnson, Fannie, 30
Johnson, Henry, 179–80

Johnson, Howard Cooper, 127–28
Johnson, John H., 65
Johnson, Leon, 92
Johnson, Lyndon B., 150, 187
Johnson, Mary, 32, 74
Johnson, Mattie, 34–35, *35*
Johnson C. Smith University (JCSU),
    165, 174, 273n87
Jones, Anita, 272n77
Jones, Beverly, 157
Jones, Charles, 170
Jones, Richard Lee "Dick," 39, 103–4,
    108
Jordan, Michael, 232
Jordan, Vernon, 209
Jordan Marsh Company, 75–76
Journal of Retailing, 20
Julius Garfinckel & Company, 163
Julius Gutman, 22, 81

Kaufman, Harry, 60
Kaufman Clothing Company, 34
Kaufmann, Arthur, 129–30
Kaufmann's, 178–79
Kaufman's, 60–63, 123–24
Keller, Eloise, 106
Kelley, Robin D. G., 11
Kemball, Susie, 272n77
Kemp, Ira, 65, 68
Kennedy, John F., 149–50
Kennedy, Randall, 228
Kentucky, 143
Kessler-Harris, Alice, 211–12
King, Martin Luther, Jr., 175, 177–78,
    183–84, 274n100
King, Mildred C., 141
Kitchen, Earl Dewey, 218
Klein, Samuel, 87, 255n12
Klein's, 255n19
Klein's Department Store, 27, 85–91
Kmart, 3, 8, 189–91, 276n25
Koch's, 66, 69, 250n42
Korstad, Robert, 6, 83
Kovenetsky, Sam, 98
Kreydatus, Beth, 33

Labitue, James, 92
labor-oriented civil rights movement, 6–8. *See also* National Association for the Advancement of Colored People (NAACP); unions
LaFeber, Walter, 232
La Guardia, Fiorello H., 92
Lamb, Franklin, 95
Landburgh's, 163–64, 185
language, 102
Laval, Vertis, 213
La Vogues, 172
laws: anti-discrimination, 142–43, 154–55; fair employment, 118
Lawson, Belford V., 61–62
Lawson, Charles J., 203
Leach, William, 16, 24, 246n96
League for Industrial Democracy (LID), 60
League of the Struggle for Negro Rights, 86
Lee, Bill, 42
Lens, Sidney, 109–10
Lerner, 172
Leventhal's, 61
Lewis, Harold, 62–63
Lewis, Jesse W., 62
liberalism, racial, 120–42
Liberia, 104
Lichtenstein, Nelson, 6
LID. *See* League for Industrial Democracy (LID)
Liggett Drug, 165, 168
Limited, 277n36
"linked fate," 151
Lit Brothers, 51, 126, 129
Little, Malcolm, 82
Little Black Sambo (film), 102
Lloyd v. Tanner, 186
Local 1-S. *See* United Retail, Wholesale, and Department Store Employees Union (URWDSEU)
Loescher, Frank, 125, 127–28
Loeser's & Company, 71
Loewen, James W., 234

Lomax, Ora P., 172–73
Lord & Taylor, 29, 237n5
Loring Michelson, Marcella, 91, 98
"Lost Law," 148, 267n1
Lott, Eric, 24
Love, Arthur, 92
lunch counters, 79–80, 146–52, 158–62, 165–70, *166–67,* 272nn71,77. *See also* Hecht's

Macy's, *17, 94;* African American employees at, 27; closure of stores by, 3, 229; discount retail and, 191; elevator operators at, 92, 244n54; employee newsletters at, 33; luxury at, 238n6; racism of customers at, 29–30; racist products sold at, 144; segregation at, 26, 28; Shopping While Black incidents at, 233–34; in Tóibín's *Brooklyn* novel, 146; unions and, 93–97, 100–2; United Retail, Wholesale, and Department Store Employees Union and, 75, 90; urban renewal and, 193; white reactions to African American employees at, 78
Macy's Executive Training Squad, 99
MAG. *See* Mandatory Achievement of Goals (MAG)
mail, shopping by, 49–50
Malcolm X, 82
mall closings, 225–26
mall curfews, 235
Mammy, 29
Mandatory Achievement of Goals (MAG) (Sears affirmative action program), 205–7
Mandel's, 139
Manley, Effa, 249n36
Marchand, Roland, 24
March on Washington for Jobs and Freedom, 6
Marshall Field's, *18,* 40, 43, 46–47, 139–42, 191, 238n6, 275n18
Martin, C. Virgil, 133–35
May's, 40, 81, 172, 178

McCoy, James, 179
McFetridge, William L., 110
McGill, Nathan K., 106
McGregor, James, 6–7
McGuire, R. Grayson, Jr., 62
McKay, Claude, 67
McLaughlin, Robert E., 162
McLean, Nancy, 8
McLellan's, 165
Mehling, J. W., 80
Meier, August, 56
merit-hiring campaigns, 73–78, 114, 162
Metropolitan Department Store, 37
Michael Kors, 229
Michelson, Clarina, 86–88
middle class, 5–6; civil rights movement and, 11–14; conspicuous consumption by, 240n39; department store and, 9–10; segregation and, 240n35; white identity, 19–26; worker-consumer alliances and, 152, 182
Miller, Jack, 97–98, 101
Miller, Jackson H., 33
Miller & Rhoads, 27–28, 30, 54, 172, 267n3, 268n11
Mims, Shirley, 213–14
Minority Enterprise Small Business Investment Company, 207
minstrel shows, 24–25, 43
Mitchell, John, Jr., 240n35
"monkey business," 255n12
Montgomery Bus Boycott, 8, 53
Montgomery Ward, 49, 81, 225, 237n5
Moore, Fred, 65, 68
Morgan State College, 81
Morrison, Susie, 272n77
Mosley, Virgie, 111, 259n86
"mugging night sticks," 101–2, 144
Murphy, Carl, 51
Murphy, John J., 51
Murphy, Sarah, 74
Murray, Pauli, 79, 267n2
music, 240n32

NAACP. *See* National Association for the Advancement of Colored People (NAACP)
National Association for the Advancement of Colored People (NAACP), 149, 178; consumer activism of, 145–46; department store movement and, 7; and "Don't Buy Where You Can't Work" movement, 62; labor activism of, 70, 72–73, 83, 123, 125, 161–62, 180; public accommodations and, 119–20; and racist product sales, 102, 144–45; Sears and, 207–8, 210
National Association of College Women, 76
National Industrial Recovery Act (NIRA), 85, 87
National Labor Relations Board (NLRB), 112–13
National Organization for Women (NOW), 208
National Recovery Administration, 87
National Urban League (NUL), 7, 66, 72–75, 83, 118, 120–23, 209–10, 261n19
National Welfare Rights Organization (NWRO), 203
Nazism, 75, 80
Negro American Labor Council, 176
Negro Industrial Clerical Alliance, 70
Negro Labor Victory Committee, 100
Negro Liberator (newspaper), 89
"Negro Market," 55, 105–6
Neiman Marcus, 192, 207, 237n5
New Deal, 10, 56, 59
Newman's, 173
New Negro Alliance (NNA), 60–62
New Negro Alliance v. Sanitary Grocery Co., 7, 61, 70
newsletters, employee, 25–26, 28, 30, 33, 93–94
New York, 63–71, 67, 81–82, 85–103, 255n12
New York Age (newspaper), 65–66, 68
New York Urban League (NYUL), 63–64, 70, 99–100, 117, 122

Rabuck, Kim, 235
Race Relations Committee (American Friends Service Committee), 124–25, 261n27
racial liberalism, 120–42
racial profiling, 232–33, 283n26
racist merchandise, 144–45
racist narratives, 24–26
Ralph Lauren, 229
Raylass Department Store, 172
Redmond, Cheryl, 200–201
Reed, Touré F., 120–21
Regents of the University of California v. Bakke, 208
Reid, Arthur, 65, 68
respectability, 34, 56–57, 66–69, 118, 120
restrictive covenants, 194
Retail, Wholesale, and Department Store Union (RWDSU), 84, 101
"retail apocalypse," 2–3
returns, 42
Rich's, 175, 178, 193, 274n100
riots, 81–82, 183–84, *184,* 185, 202
Robinson, Jackie, 102, 157
Robinson, Rachel, 157
Roediger, David, 24
Rogin, Michael, 24
Roosevelt, Franklin D., 59, 96
Roper, Elmo, 130
Rosenbaum's, 123
Rosenberg, Rosalind, 211
Rosenwald, Julius, 35, 194
Rosenwald Fund, 121
Ross, Alice, 154
Ross, Delano, 138
Rudwick, Elliot, 56
RWDSU. *See* Retail, Wholesale, and Department Store Union (RWDSU)

Saenger, Gerhart, 118–19, 263n56
St. Louis, 79–80
Saint Luke Emporium, 37, *38,* 47–48
Saks Fifth Avenue, 13, 99–100, 192, 237n5, 275n18

Sambo, 29, 102
Samuel Carroll et al v. Sears, Roebuck, and Company, 221–22
Sandy W. Trice & Company Department Store, 37, 47
Satter, Mark, 197
Schomber, Arthur A., 65
Schwartz, Harry, 155
Scott, F. H., 134
Scott, Hazel, 157
Scott, John L., 178
Scott, Robert, 33
Scott Hudgens v. National Labor Relations Board, 186
Scruggs, Vandervoort and Barney, 80
Sears, Richard Warren, 35–36, 49; troubles of, 222–23
Sears, Roebuck & Co., *199;* destruction of Washington, D.C., location, in rioting, 183–84, *184;* and "Don't Buy Where You Can't Work" campaign, 58; Equal Employment Opportunity Commission and, 8, 202–22; hiring of African Americans by, humanitarian motivations for, 35–36; in "orchids and onions" campaign, 81; and rise of discount retail, 191; sit-ins at, 165; store closings, 3; urban renewal and, 193–202
Second Great Migration, 194, 239n29
segregation: in baseball, 102; class and, 240n35; in department stores, 17–18, 28, 41–42, 46–47, 268n11; in employee newsletters, 28; and *Plessy v. Ferguson,* 11; in postwar era, 120–42; of staff, 28–29; transportation, 11, 240n34; and working-class whites, 24
Selective Patronage, 152, 176
self-service retailing, 73–74, 95–96
Seligman, Amanda I., 202
Sengstacke, John, 113, 134–35
services: offered by department stores, 20
Seymour's, 174
Sharpton, Al, 233